Feeling Singular

Feeling Singular

Queer Masculinities in the Early United States

BEN BASCOM

OXFORD
UNIVERSITY PRESS

Oxford University Press is a department of the University of Oxford.
It furthers the University's objective of excellence in research, scholarship,
and education by publishing worldwide. Oxford is a registered trade mark of
Oxford University Press in the UK and in certain other countries.

Published in the United States of America by Oxford University Press
198 Madison Avenue, New York, NY 10016, United States of America.

© Oxford University Press 2024

All rights reserved. No part of this publication may be reproduced, stored in a retrieval system, or transmitted, in any form or by any means, without the prior permission in writing of Oxford University Press, or as expressly permitted by law, by license or under terms agreed with the appropriate reprographics rights organization. Inquiries concerning reproduction outside the scope of the above should be sent to the Rights Department, Oxford University Press, at the address above.

You must not circulate this work in any other form
and you must impose this same condition on any acquirer

Library of Congress Cataloging-in-Publication Data
Names: Bascom, Ben (Benjamin D.), author.
Title: Feeling singular : queer masculinities in the early United States / Ben Bascom.
Other titles: Queer masculinities in the early United States
Description: New York, NY : Oxford University Press, [2024] | Originally presented as
author's thesis (doctoral)—University of Illinois at Urbana-Champaign, 2017. |
Includes bibliographical references and index.
Identifiers: LCCN 2023048033 (print) | LCCN 2023048034 (ebook) |
ISBN 9780197687505 (hardback) | ISBN 9780197687512 (epub)
Subjects: LCSH: Eccentrics and eccentricities—United States—Biography. |
Eccentrics and eccentricities—United States—History. | Men—United States—Case studies. |
Masculinity—United States—History. | Individuality.
Classification: LCC CT9990 .B35 2024 (print) | LCC CT9990 (ebook) |
DDC 973.09/9—dc23/eng/20240110
LC record available at https://lccn.loc.gov/2023048033
LC ebook record available at https://lccn.loc.gov/2023048034

DOI: 10.1093/9780197687536.001.0001

Printed by Integrated Books International, United States of America

Contents

Acknowledgments   vii

Introduction: Feeling Singular in the Early United States   1

1. Memorializing the Republic of Failure   25

2. Civic Virtue and State Power: The Politics of the Particular in
   the Racialized Republic   68

3. Federalism in Drag: Timothy Dexter's *Pickle* and Other
   Perverse Properties   107

4. Perambulations in Print: Norms and Normativity in
   the Itinerant Republic   149

5. The Queer Hermit: William "Amos" Wilson and the
   Antisocial Republic   193

Coda: Masculinity's Monumental Hair Problem   232

Works Cited   239
Index   255

Acknowledgments

Thank you. All of you. The following names and their attachments to this book project helped *Feeling Singular* find its way in the world, and they deserve more praise than can be gestured at through these elongated sentences. The major ideas explored herein began under the watchful guidance of Trish Loughran, getting their ballast in a graduate seminar when she introduced nearly eighteen of us to poor John Fitch. Since that moment in 2010, she has advised me to be more careful and deliberate in my approach to scholarship. Her generous encouragement and the reading of multiple drafts of this book project demonstrate the mark of a caring mentor who has dedicated more than a decade of her career to see another scholar flourish. Justine Murison also models what it means to mentor, meeting students where they are at and helping them discover where they can grow; her constant, undeviating support has been an essential framework. While in the dissertation process, Siobhan Somerville guided me through readings in queer studies, and Stephanie Foote offered crucial critical interventions. These four scholars all made for a powerhouse dissertation committee. Since my first day as a graduate student, Gordon Hutner has been an essential steadying force in my career, and during the long winter of 2020–2021 he provided a vital push for me to revise this book's introduction and first chapter, and he even took steps to introduce me to an Oxford University Press editor. Other people from the University of Illinois at Urbana-Champaign were influential in my scholarly trajectory, like Dale Bauer, Leon Chai, Christopher Freeburg, Jamie Jones, Curtis Perry, and Michael Rothberg. My undergraduate educations at Brigham Young University-Provo and Snow College were similarly excellent, made so by the rigor and sustenance of my professors. I learned how to write and think through Snow College's Erick Faatz, Melanie Jenkins, and Gary Parnell; while at BYU, Nancy Christiansen, Ed Cutler, Rick Duerden, Trent Hickman, Kimberly Johnson, Kristin Matthews, Brian Russell Roberts, and Matthew Wickman directed me on the path to become a researcher and an educator. I am especially grateful for the hundreds of conversations—over email and in office hours—with Kristin and Matthew, as they both remain for me lodestars. And lastly, my undergraduate Writing Center and English

viii ACKNOWLEDGMENTS

major friends—Kjerstin Evans Ballard, Rachel Birkner, the late Kaila Brown, Katherine Fisher, Dallin Lewis, Katie McNey, and Jeremy Walker—have remained close to my heart even as our geographies keep us distant.

The dearest academic friends who have shown the love and support needed while writing this book include Silas Moon Cassinelli, Heather Chacon, Katy Didden, Silas Hansen, Emily Johnson, Scott Larson, Don James McLaughlin, John Musser, Patricia Sunia, and Katie Walkiewicz. They have all shared the important spaces that make writing possible, from library rooms to coffee shops to dance floors. While a graduate student my conversations with Lauren Applebaum, Stephanie Seawell Fortado, Chris Hedlin, Amy Huang, Miriam Kienle, Alicia Kozma, Jennifer Lozano, Heather McLeer, Xuxa Rodriguez, Sarah Sahn, Michael Shetina, Débora Tiénou, and Wendy Truran sustained me during the many years of coursework and exam preparations. Beyond the intimacies of university degrees, other academics have helped with the long process of writing this book, from reading drafts to commenting on conference papers, so gratitude to Sari Altschuler, Stephen Best, Jamie Bolker, Daniel Couch, Peter Coviello, Lindsay DiCuirci, Katy Didden, Elizabeth Maddock Dillon, Duncan Faherty, Elizabeth Freeman, Kadin Henningsen, Jared Hickman, Joyce Huff, Shelby Johnson, Frank Kelderman, Carl Robert Keyes, Melanie Kiechle, Greta LaFleur, Scott Larson, Christopher Looby, Mark Alan Mattes, Don James McLaughlin, Rob McLoone, Alex Moskowitz, Meredith Neuman, Sandy Petrulionis, Jillian Sayre, Ana Schwartz, Danielle Skeehan, Sam Somers, Jordan Alexander Stein, Patricia Sunia, Priscilla Wald, Katie Walkiewicz and Kari J. Winter. I am particularly fortunate to benefit from Jordan's writerly vision and expansive attention, in addition to an anonymous reader for OUP.

My colleagues at Ball State University have been immensely supportive, from the monthly writing group with Katy Didden, Molly Ferguson, Emily Rutter, Sreyoshi Sarkar, and Vanessa Rapatz to the wisdom of colleagues such as Adam Beach, Pat Collier, Cathy Day, Joyce Huff, Sean Lovelace, Debbie Mix, Rai Peterson, Mary Loy Vercellotti, and Sarah Vitale. Scholars at other institutions have been generous with their time and care, and so I need to specifically thank Hester Blum, Marcy J. Dinius, Melissa Homestead, Christy Pottrof, and Jonathan Senchyne. This book received an important jumpstart through Sean X. Goudie and Priscilla Wald's 2018 First Book Institute at Penn State's Center for American Literary Studies. While there, I learned from the directors regarding how to pursue publication and then received feedback from Jordan Carroll, Juliana Chow, Amy Greenberg, Mary Kuhn,

Christopher Perreira, Katie Walkiewicz, Sunny Xiang, and Xine Yao. In the wonderful Worcester winter of 2019, I was an NEH fellow at the American Antiquarian Society where I met Alex Beringer, Sonia Hazard, Elspeth Martini, Don James McLaughlin and his husband Benjamin, the late Neal Salisbury, and Justin Tackett. The staff and librarians at the AAS are the definition of welcoming: Dan Boudreau, Ashley Cataldo, Babette Gehnrich, Vincent L. Golden, Lauren B. Hewes, Amanda Kondek, Elizabeth Pope, Sally Talbot, Amy Tims, Laura Wasowicz, and Nan Wolverton helped me locate materials and directed me toward dozens of capacious directions. They enable solitary research to become a community-building, collaborative endeavor. An early career research fellowship at the Peabody-Essex Museum allowed me to explore a rich array of Newburyport material history, and I am deeply grateful for the support of stellar librarians Kathy Flynn, Jen Hornsby, and Catie Robertson. Jen deserves a special note of thanks for her labor to secure images for this book. At the end of this project, I was fortunate to research at The Library Company of Philadelphia, and thanks should be given to A. Wynn Eakins, Emily Guthrie, Sharon Hildebrand, Max Moeller, Christine Nelson, Erika Piola, Arielle Rambo, Em Ricciardi, and Sarah Weatherwax, with an extra appreciation to Emily Smith who obtained dozens of images for me as she concluded her employment with the library.

It has been a smooth-sailing dream to work with Hannah Doyle at Oxford, who has shown profound editorial care and provided unmatched excitement for this book. The production editor, Rachel Ruisard, has been deeply attentive, and working with Ganga Balaji's team has been terrific. Near the end of the editing, I benefited from the indexing and editorial expertise of John Beauregard. Portions of Chapter 2 appear in slightly different form in "Queer Anachronism: Jeffrey Brace and the Racialized Republic," originally published in *Arizona Quarterly*, Volume 75, Number 1 (Spring 2019), and portions of Chapter 5 were adapted from the article, "Feeling Solitary in the Seductive Republic: Narrative Deviance in Elizabeth 'Harriot' Wilson and William 'Amos' Wilson," originally published in *Early American Literature*, Volume 59, Number 1 (Spring 2024) and used by permission of the University of North Carolina Press. I am deeply grateful for the editors of these journals (Lynda Zwinger, Marion Rust, Katy Chiles, and Cassie Smith) and the generous readers who helped me refine my thinking.

My family is large and unwieldy, and in an ample sense, they are all the ones I long to share meals with, and so many have already been mentioned above. Though permit a few words of gratitude for Jeff and his dear Casey

X ACKNOWLEDGMENTS

and the Indianapolis orbit they have helped me find. I always feel at home in Muncie's queer arms, and C. S. Hendershot is the epitome of someone who makes and builds such inviting spaces, who shows the world how to show up. My sisters Rachel, Miria, MaryNell, Laura, Heidi, and Holly, and my parents Marilyn Jeanette and Sterling LaVell, were encouraging along the way. Early in my time working on this book, David Hays was the perfect soul to bounce around with—both materially and metaphysically—and his approach to scholarship and life continues to be an inspiration. So again, thank you. All of you.

Introduction

Feeling Singular in the Early United States

And some have greatness thrust upon them.

—Malvolio in *Twelfth Night*

Anybody can make history. Only a great man can write it.

—Oscar Wilde[1]

Fantasy is the place where the subject encounters herself already
negotiating the social.

—Lauren Berlant[2]

In the sprawling life narrative that he wrote to a Pennsylvania parson, John
Fitch pauses his account to call himself "one of the most singular men perhaps that has been born this age" (22). The grandiose aside aspires to merit
a pause, though perhaps only receives a sigh for its unearned audacity, its
chutzpah from a nondescript name that may conjure for the reader no
person *that* singular. Aligning himself with controversial eighteenth-century
deists, Fitch laments at the end of his manuscript narrative that his minister
friend does not have "the same thurst for honor and popularity" that could
mark his life as being more significant than a mere man of God (140). The
aside implies his sense of feeling "singular"—of being special or marked for
importance—but also registers his failure to become the household name he
had imagined for himself. Although Fitch's phrasing might be read as mis-
placed humor, it becomes clear through reading his digressive and associa-
tive manuscript that he felt a great deal about himself, so much so that he

---

[1] Oscar Wilde, *The Artist*, 359.
[2] Lauren Berlant, *Desire/Love*, 75.

Feeling Singular. Ben Bascom, Oxford University Press. © Oxford University Press 2024.
DOI: 10.1093/9780197687536.003.0001

2   INTRODUCTION

would continually risk offending the sensibilities of his humbler interlocutor to declare the man more important than Jesus, more venerable than Socrates.

What did it mean to *feel* singular in the early United States? How did individuals manufacture feelings of uniqueness in an early national context that has been understood historically to value uniformity?[3] This book answers these questions through exploring the life narratives of early U.S. figures who aspired to become important, memorable citizens through print publication but failed to attain that status. In the early republic, concern over merit, worth, and value coalesced around what critics have called "mushroom gentleman," an epithet used to describe a self-made individual who rose to prominence without the conventional forms of social control, like inheritance and family.[4] I argue that the desire to be remembered—and the fantasy that anyone can shape their life into something memorable through writing and book form—is central to the story we tell about the emergence of individualism. This book thinks about the marketing of individualism as a strategy for cultural relevance, and it narrates how the desires to be remembered as significant in the early United States often worked in tandem to the forces that pushed one beyond the confines of cultural relevance. As such, *Feeling Singular* offers a counterhistory to the rise of liberal individualism, turning aside the icons of republican belonging (Franklin, Washington, and the authors who helped fabricate them into cultural touchstones), to examine instead the underside to such paradigms of public success and achievement.

That underside becomes markedly visible with another contemporary of John Fitch, an itinerant peddler and poet named Jonathan Plummer who composed a similarly garrulous account of himself. Like Fitch, Plummer sought to write himself into the annuls of his age, desiring to be carried into the hearts and minds of others; but unlike Fitch, Plummer actually produced his narrative into print during his life, hawking his book from his peddler's basket with personal fanfare. Even still, his efforts manifest the weirdness and oddity that accompanied such desires to be recognized as a renowned

---

[3] See William Huntting Howell's *Against Self-Reliance: The Arts of Dependence in the Early United States*, which argues for the cultural value of imitation and mimicry in the early United States, and Daniel Diez Couch's *American Fragments: The Political Aesthetic of Unfinished Forms in the Early Republic*, which offers readings of the unfinished form of the literary fragment as a politically resonant way to think about society's margins.

[4] See Alan Taylor, "From Fathers to Friends of the People: Political Personas in the Early Republic," *New Perspectives on the Early Republic: Essays form the Journal of the Early Republic, 1981-1991*, eds. Michael A. Morrison and Ralph D. Gray (U of Illinois P, 1994), 140.

public individual, such as when he comments on the typographical limits of his life narrative in the prefatory address:

> You must allow us to use we and us in some places in the room of I, &c.—If you deny us this liberty, we fear it will be a damage to our printers—They have a pretty large stock of types; but we fear they will not be able to muster, without trouble, capital I's enough to print all this work. (v; see Fig. I.1)

Attempting to downplay his use of the first-person pronoun, Plummer narrates his direct address to the reader as a product of the conditions of printing. Writing in the opening of his strange life narrative that he "is perhaps the first poet who ever undertook to publish an undisguised, and authentic, account of his life and adventures," Plummer sets himself up as a

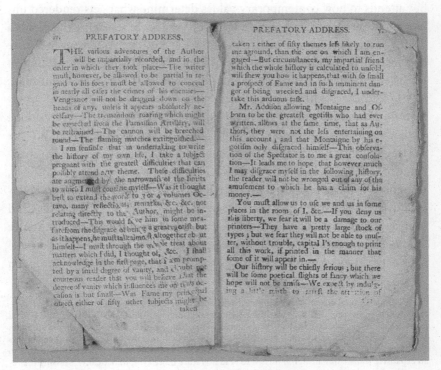

Figure I.1 Page iv and v of the extremely rare first installment of Jonathan Plummer's *Sketch of the History of the Life and Adventures of Jonathan Plummer* (1796), demonstrating the elongated s and the author's humorous self-awareness of printing type. Courtesy of the Phillips Library.

4 INTRODUCTION

singular, unique individual, further explaining: "A writer so singular, on a subject, so uncommon, must naturally produce something new" (9). That newness ends up pushing Plummer out of the boundaries of the normal, placing him beyond the orbit of conventionality and into the dustbin of local eccentricity. In this manner, he asserts that he is "singular" in the same breath that exhales him from cultural relevance, and he remains a curiosity, something to gaze upon in fascination from the distance of time. *Feeling Singular* endeavors to think about the Jonathan Plummers and the John Fitches of the early United States and what their queered masculinities have to say about the norms that otherwise ground the canon and literary personalities of early U.S. literature.

The variables that make particular textual lives rise into prominence and significance shift and change with the seasons of time. *Feeling Singular* navigates the terrain of contemporaneous irrelevance and insignificance but attends to how contemporary values determine what gets rendered important, what merits attention. Indeed, the very act of salvaging the past is a deeply fraught endeavor that frames how the study of American literature has sustained and transformed itself, from F. O. Matthiessen's reading of the ostensibly democratic 1850s under the banner of *American Renaissance* (1941) and Perry Miller's invention of a spiritualized New England settlement in *Errand into the Wilderness* (1956) to the New Americanist critique of that work through historicizing its object in transnational frames.[5] The starting point of *Feeling Singular* is that the United States is a mess of incoherence that tends to be misread as self-evidently coherent, or as a stable, recognizable formation governed by a logic of inclusion.[6] The literary manufacture of tropes and types that constitute "the American" as a singular and solitary subject has continually baffled observers and critics, and the desire for a backformation that stabilizes the past (in order to cohere the present) runs deep. The desire for a singular synthesis is in many ways the problem

[5] The transnational turn in American studies emerged from scholarship responding to a Cold War–era popular consensus that buttressed American exceptionalism narratives regarding the United States' relation to globality. That work, particularly the edited collection *Cultures of United States Imperialism* by Amy Kaplan and Donald E. Pease, responded directly to the previous generation's (Matthiessen and Miller) seemingly unqualified celebration of America. Importantly, this turn to an expansive transnationalism has turned to read literature more symptomatically, assessing the repressed cultural work of state power. *Feeling Singular* endeavors to highlight the ramifications of that state power in hyperlocal scenes, showing how such vectors of power work through material and imaginative means on individual (and individualized) bodies.

[6] For work on the incoherence of belonging in the early republic, see Trish Loughran, *The Republic in Print*, which troubles the narrative of collective coherence that tends to ground print-based models of U.S. nation formation.

INTRODUCTION 5

of the field, which toggles between a "republican consensus" to a model of emerging liberalism to narrate the early years of the nation.[7] In this book, I pivot around such discussions to analyze what the singular, unassimilable figure has to say about the stories we tell about belonging.

Before the nineteenth-century valorization of self-reliance, men who appeared too unduly attached to their own singularity were perceived as outsiders. Bringing such figures into the center of early national culture, this book queers the disinterested norms of republican public culture—and then imagines these men as queer rejoinders to the forming nation-state.[8] My use of the term *queer* here suggests the always unformed status of coherent subjectivity, and how all such coherence relies on vectors of power and legibility. I assemble an archive of understudied life writings by men who sought to make themselves into important citizens but failed to attain the representative status of a Franklin or a Washington. These figures include John Fitch (1743–1798), a struggling working-class mechanic; Jeffrey Brace (1742–1827), a formerly enslaved Black Revolutionary War veteran; Timothy Dexter (1747–1806), a self-declared "Lord" who secured a fortune through a risky venture in bedpans and whalebone corsets; Jonathan Plummer (1761–1819), an itinerant peddler and preacher; and William "Amos" Wilson (1762–1821), a reclusive stonecutter who came to be known as "the Pennsylvania Hermit." Despite leaving behind copious manuscripts and printed autobiographies, they dwindled instead into cultural insignificance, failing to achieve what scholars have called the hallmarks of "republican masculinity."[9]

This book is organized by categories of tenuous belonging: a failed inventor, a tragic outsider, a flamboyant pretender, a farcical exhorter, and a disaffected exile propel this foray into disintegrating narratives. In the first chapter, a poor white mechanic gets relegated to the outskirts of the republican project by the elite men he aspired to attract; in the second chapter, a

---

[7] For more on the republican synthesis, see books by Bernard Bailyn, J. G. A. Pocock, and Gordon Wood. For work on liberalism and the early United States, see James T. Kloppenberg's *The Virtues of Liberalism* (Oxford UP, 1998) and *Toward Democracy: The Struggle for Self-Rule in European and American Thought* (Oxford UP, 2016). For work that theorizes liberalism, see Michael Sandel's *Liberalism and the Limits of Justice* (Cambridge UP, 1982).

[8] Queer critiques of the subject—or what became called "the antisocial thesis"—inform my sense of queer as a rejoinder to the formation of coherence. I'm also influenced by Davina Cooper's *Feeling Like a State: Desire, Denial and the Recasting of Authority*, who invites readers to think of "[t]he conceptual usefulness of the state" as being "temporally and spatially specific" (175).

[9] For more on republican masculinity, see, for instance, Sarah Chinn's *Spectacular Men: Race, Gender, and Nation on the Early American Stage* (2017), Richard Godbeer's *The Overflowing of Friendship: Love Between Men and the Creation of the American Republic* (2009), and Catherine O'Donnell Kaplan's *Men of Letters in the Early Republic: Cultivating Forums of Citizenship* (2008).

6 INTRODUCTION

formerly enslaved African farmer who, after fighting for his liberty in the Revolutionary War, settled in Vermont and encountered a series of racist incursions on his property rights. Both of these men bring together questions of aspirations for success and their eventual elision from the realms of republican self-possession. I then turn to two figures who encapsulate what might be called farcical failure, who escape social dismissal along lines of class and race to reinvent their rejection as a fantasy space of inclusion. The last chapter departs from the first four by meditating on what it means to refuse the silence of dejection through embracing the politics and aesthetics of disaffection; that is, I turn toward a solitary hermit who chose to live alone after his sister was executed for infanticide but left behind a written testament that he believed would suture the broken intimate and social ties that would otherwise tether him to the future.

Throughout the readings, manifestations of weirdness coalesce and consolidate in various ways. The figures I read thwart the impulse to travel linearly—from point A to point B—as they do not fit neatly within accepted timelines; rather, they provide a scattershot path of roads not taken in the cultural mythologies that ground American literary studies. In many ways, this orientation toward the underdog, the forgotten, is a hallmark of microhistory, which methodology scholars have drawn upon to let a part tell something about a whole.[10] But instead of circling back continually to a whole, these lives *queer* the whole from which they were never really a part; indeed, they sit *apart* in ways that the very effort to bring them into a larger formation illuminates the vexed nature of such projects of liberal inclusion under the banner of a nascent nationalism. I mark this as *queer* in the sense of how they all deviate—and thereby descry—a variety of norms that have in some manner stabilized the field of early U.S. literary studies, functioning as a barometer of republican belonging, operating as shorthand for imagined significance.

I.1. From Founders to Foundlings: State Affects and Republican Significance

Accounts of the era here under investigation have predominantly been about the creation of large structures of belonging—that boogeyman of a budding

---

[10] See Carlo Ginzburg's *The Cheese and the Worms*. Gratitude to Jordan Alexander Stein for this reference and his felicitous turn of phrase in the next section, "From Founders to Foundlings."

INTRODUCTION 7

nation and its supposedly coherent ideological content—in ways that end up recentering the figures who are credited with orchestrating such seismic events. This tautological configuration focuses on those figures of presumed importance *because* of the cultural logics that make legible the achievements associated with their names. Such significance is marked by the title that enfolds and eponymously names them: as "Founding Fathers," they resituate the sense of dominance and normativity that scholars and historians have constructed to define the period.[11] George Washington and Benjamin Franklin, in the decades following the 1790s, became models that young men were encouraged to imitate. What this project does, however, is examine the writings of non-normative, outsider, and marginalized individuals during this time period, figures who felt they could access the masculinist privileges and influences reserved for the so-called Founder figures. In their fraught aspiration to become important, recognized, and remembered, the figures I look at articulate the very norms and protocols of belonging that subjected them to the world of footnotes, curiosities, or bizarre exceptions preserved in libraries and archives, referenced as counterpoints to supposedly worthier subjects. In this manner, they could be said to preemptively resist the cultural amnesia that consigned them to obscurity, leaving behind an assortment of textual ephemera—either through aborted books or precariously preserved manuscripts—to pay witness to their ostensible elision from the modes of cultural dominance that render them discordant. Feeling shortchanged from the cultural positions that opened before others while only tantalizing them, the key figures here sought to produce a record of their lives to be read not only then but by others on future dates. Using their works—and the people that encountered them—as my material, I assemble a counter-canon of texts and contexts that underscores the significance of unproductive modes of failure and the bad aesthetics of falling far from cultural forms. The figures that ground this study into material history, then, make use of error, accident, and wrongness in ways that actually form a critique of the cultural field marking them as unworthy of the very attention they sought (and, perhaps ironically, now in this monograph receive). Where only certain forms of narrative success were celebrated, the individuals I examine offer failures that criticize the values that subjugated them.[12]

---

[11] See, for instance, Andrew M. Schocket's *Fighting Over the Founders: How We Remember the American Revolution* (2015), for a compelling account of the implications of this field construction.

[12] My use of failure differentiates from Jack Halberstam's work in *The Queer Art of Failure*, who notes that "[t]he desire to be taken seriously is precisely what compels people to follow the tried and

8   INTRODUCTION

The central figures in this study ignored prohibitions against distilling private, intimate details into the genres of public writing. The established figures who produced what is recognized as the era's norms left life writings for entirely different purposes. Benjamin Rush wanted to have his personal life narrative limited to his family (writing in his introduction about this very dynamic) and the Federalist Alexander Graydon used his *Memoirs* to try to "smother that obtrusive thing called *self*," imagining that private personality had no place in public discourse. These figures remained culturally significant figures partly *because* they gestured toward this reluctance to have their private and intimate lives publicized. The figures I look at, however, sought to write their lives into a cultural fabric that actively resisted them. They were demarcated as knots to be untied from the privilege of citizenship, aberrations to be eventually forgotten under the weight of the looming shadow of a mode of republican masculinity that would (temporarily) foreclose the alternatives that their lives raised. Rather than achieving contemporaneous cultural import, then, the figures I look at wrote—or had another write—their own life narratives to stake rhetorical claims to positions of cultural prominence in their society. They all draw upon theories of the publicness and availability of print to disseminate and circulate representations of their private lives into the world.[13] To them, print gave them an imagined readership, though in doing so it also pronounced their rejection from public spaces. Desiring to be harbingers of prospective change, these figures wanted a world that had ignored them to be transformed into a world that would listen and respond to their claims against it. Through their writings, they desire to escape the cultural powers that ended up limiting their cultural longevity. The Black Revolutionary War veteran and formerly enslaved farmer Jeffrey Brace perhaps most readily manifests this dynamic. Brace asserts that the republic is corrupt—that it is inherently *not* a republic—when his and others' subjection remain legalized under chattel slavery. But in outlining how he feels compelled to produce his life into a textual form, he also comes to articulate by name those who have wronged him and his family, naming and declaring private concerns within written public genres such as when "Mrs. Powell"

true paths of knowledge production around which I would like to map a few detours" (6). In the early national context, the paths to failure were far more numerous and multiple than the chance opportunity for success.

[13] This effort to produce a text that circulates like discourse—that places the figures who wish to disseminate their stories as magnets for attention—follows Greg Urban's point in *Metaphysical Community* that "discourse tends to shape itself in such a way as to maximize its circulation" (250).

INTRODUCTION 9

forced indentures on his daughter: "But that good christian woman, never attempted to learn her to read, neither did she ever give her the bed. I could get no redress" (177–178). For Brace, the politicizing of his private and intimate life into a public form does not produce calls for justice but rather brings public outrage against him, with that very public heaping *more* injustice on him.[14]

Republicanism relies on a dismantling of privacy, such that the private sphere is perpetually held apart from the public to secure subjects from exposed private interests.[15] This can be seen in the iconic gesture of George Washington leaving public life after the Treaty of Paris to attend to his Virginia farm. The canonical account *forgets* that he returned to public life because he was having difficulty shipping his enslaved-labor-produced goods across state lines. In other words, his seemingly disinterested political acts to support the new Constitution were undergirded by what he saw as the need to secure a federal relation that would triangulate market-related competition between states so that he could privately amass wealth. This insertion of a repressed private motivation manifesting in the public sphere as a public "good" signals what Elizabeth Maddock Dillon explains as the foundational component of affect and interpersonality within the public sphere's supposedly disinterested reason. "[T]he public sphere has never operated as a disinterested realm of reasoned debate," Dillon argues, countering a tradition in the historiography that emphasizes a type of gentlemanly restraint (*The Gender of Freedom* 6). Following Dillon's insights into how privacy may be considered "as *coproduced* together with public identity in the print public sphere" (19), I am interested in delving deeper into the private feelings that secure the production of particular masculine norms, such as Washington's performative deflection for attention (despite his very clear interpersonal investments). "It is not merely affect that must be understood to matter in the public sphere (as opposed to reason)," Dillon continues: "rather, affect and

---

[14] For the figures I study, having a life positioned as singular becomes the rationale for their entrance into the print public sphere, though the very texts that index their uniqueness bear testament to the exclusions and restrictions that they face. We might see this at specific work within Black Atlantic texts that particularize racial identification. The category of "African" enabled an occasion to put forward a liberal subjectivity that had claim not for general representability but instead asserted the importance of a particular difference. Phillis Wheatley, Olaudah Equiano, and James Forten self-published their own likenesses in such a manner that did not abstract themselves into generality but instead emphasized their uniqueness. In Chapter 2, I focus on how racial particularity became the ballast of a crucial critique of the abstracting function of white republican masculinity itself.

[15] See Justine Murison, *Faith in Exposure: Privacy and Secularism in the Nineteenth-Century United States.*

10 INTRODUCTION

desire must be understood less as the effusions of certain kinds of subjects than as constituting all subjects. In other words, the desire for recognition shapes individuals in their most private dimensions" (9).[16] This grounding of personal desire—which gets abstracted in republican but frontloaded in liberal models of the early United States—shows how there is always some horizon of desire that motivates, even if, as I show in the last chapter, that desire is to *not* have desire.

The figures I examine wished to be recognized as important citizens, ably available to shape the cultural life around them. I attend to the material texts they produced in relation to the aspirations that sustained them in their moment of production. Indeed, these material texts evince the insistence *not* to be merely designated as cultural detritus. They emphasize a singular identity that reorients the world around them. In this sense, I use the artifact of a manuscript, a failed book, or an obscure printing to document a series of ill-fated desires to achieve larger cultural shifts or to be the center of cultural productions. This focus on the material text renders visible a network of social attachments that aspire to republican norms.[17] These figures, and the texts they produce, are might-have-beens seeking to recenter cultural agency around themselves as persons of importance, reproducing themselves askance to the cultural norms that demarcated them as outsiders to the promise of republican significance. By *republican significance* I am indicating how an individual could become abstracted into a politics of collective good, set up as a representative model for others to follow a path to similar renown. Franklin excelled at producing these effects through staging others in

---

[16] The notion that "the desire for recognition" shapes the inner lives of individuals offers a way to see how affect connects the subject's interior to the exterior. Lauren Berlant describes "Fantasy" as "the place where the subject encounters herself already negotiating the social" (*Desire/Love* 75). The interaction between fantasy and affect co-produce the epiphenomenon of gender.

[17] Throughout this introduction, I have set up the republican norms that, through their failure to be secured as normative, actually produce the archival and cultural conventions that mark the exclusion of others. Republicanism operates through abstracting the particularities that seemingly make one unable to stand in as a representative figure. The norms that produce white, property-owning maleness as the precondition to representability are unstable and constantly require the force of state power to secure their normalizing function. One significant exception to the rule—that comes to stabilize that rule—is the biography of Deborah Sampson, whose life story shows the unstable category of maleness that otherwise seeks to stabilize the representational apparatus of the republic. Indeed, Sampson's masculinity—as portrayed by Herman Mann in *The Female Review*—elucidates a certain anxiety about its formation, at one moment noting a love affair with a woman: "Their blushes and palpitations were, doubtless, reciprocal; but, I judge, of a different nature" (203–204). Sampson traveled throughout the early republic on a speaking tour before their memoirs were written, and displayed before audiences their clothed body in an effort to make exceptional their story. The curious reality of a body presented as female while telling a story of what was considered a "masquerade" delves into a truth about the norms that structure republicanism.

INTRODUCTION   11

relation to himself. In the letters that open the second installment of his life narrative, he includes a letter by Abel James that calls the work of his textual life "useful and entertaining not only to a few, but to millions." *Republican significance* makes certain individuals feel they have access to establishing norms that become the site of others' subjection, forming the ideals that they are measured against. In this way, *republican significance* injects a liberal model of belonging as the centerpiece to republican representation. As a term, *republican significance* constellates together the drive and effects of individuals who believe they are worthy of being representative, that their affective attachments to a "common good" rhetoric stabilizes and domesticates state power. There is always some singular element that escapes the desired-for republican abstraction.[18]

The move to offer one's individual and particular self to the public as a collective good motivates the authors I read, feeling themselves as singular as a Franklin or as important as a Washington but somehow without the means to achieve the iconic status they believed they deserved. Each text I look at, then, documents a failure to set in motion the proposed changes and alterations their authors sought to accomplish. In this way, *Feeling Singular* plumbs the representation and performance of fraught, ill-fated desires as they fall short from their intended object. These figures are rendered excessive, perverse, and uncouth, stable only insofar as they restabilize the emerging norms that their failures or shortcomings buttress. In this way, they are actually central to the story propelled by a Founders- and canon-centric account of the early United States. Their stories constitute the underbelly of republican significance, offering tales of failure and incoherence that set in motion the drive in the first place to locate harmony and cultural generality through plotting the well-rehearsed lives of the culturally significant. Part of republican significance is that only certain lives become mined for interpersonal, intimate truths—namely, the lives of white men known as the Founders. Not all lives are measured equally, of course, and the differently situated bodies that come

---

[18] Elizabeth Maddock Dillon sketches out the difference between liberalism and republicanism in a way that further highlights this effort of the individual to be received into the realm of republican significance:

> republican politics place the good of the *polis* above all other concerns. Civic virtue, the ultimate aim of the republican citizen, is achieved only by leaving personal (private) interests behind and pursuing the public good in a disinterested fashion. The liberal, on the other hand, locates the highest 'good' in personal freedom rather than in freedom *from* personal concerns and thus sees the protection of private interests (such as private property) as a primary aim of the public sphere and state. (142)

12   INTRODUCTION

to occupy the U.S. republican populace rely on a series of cracks and power imbalances that render only particular personalities worthy of attention and repetition. "Human dependence and servitude," writes Theodor Adorno ironically, "could scarcely be more faithfully described than by the American interviewee who was of the opinion that the dilemmas of the contemporary epoch would end if people would simply follow the lead of prominent personalities" (106). This following of "prominent personalities" describes the experience of American elites seeking to propel their cultural legacies and longevities, aspiring to mobilize the stability of culture as a coherent structure that can reproduce its own norms.

I.2. Queering Masculinity

In distinct but related ways, each of the figures I look at represents a deviation from early American norms, being too prone to transgress public/private boundaries and too attached to social prohibitions. Masculinity names the cultural aesthetics that emerge from these dynamics.[19] While each aspired to public legibility and prestige, all failed to secure for themselves the disinterested public influence that became a hallmark of republican masculinity, and each dwindled, inevitably, into cultural neglect. Rather than a triumphal recovery narrative that illuminates neglected recesses of cultural memory, as if the locating of forgotten texts held value in and of itself, this project explores how, within the obscure, historically ignored material here under examination, the seeds of neglect are embedded in the narratives themselves. Specifically, the turn toward being forgotten, I argue, is rooted in the way these figures express private desires through public media. Unlike Franklin, who carefully constructed and chose the errata that he pretends to correct, these would-be republican heroes cannot foresee how their mistakes and deviance would fit within larger cultural imaginaries. For example, John Fitch wrote a deeply personal multivolume manuscript about his failure to obtain

---

[19] Jack Halberstam in *Female Masculinity* explains that "Masculinity in this society inevitably conjures up notions of power and legitimacy and privilege; it often symbolically refers to the power of the state and to uneven distributions of wealth. Masculinity seems to extend outward into patriarchy and inward into the family; masculinity represents the power of inheritance, the consequences of the traffic in women, and the promise of social privilege" (2). This notion of fixity and performed legitimacy gets nicely complicated in Judith Kegan Gardiner's definition of *masculinity* as "a nostalgic formation, always missing, lost, or about to be lost, its ideal form located in a past that advances with each generation in order to recede just beyond its grasp. Its myth is that effacing new forms can restore a natural, original male grounding" (10).

INTRODUCTION 13

public support for his steamboat invention, a book which cost him the very social recognition he desired. Furthermore, Jonathan Plummer declared that if he were denied the reading audience he felt destined to have for his personal life narrative, that he would carry a printing press into the next world to fulfill that wish. These eccentrics felt the need to share their written lives and textual bodies with completely uninterested, sometimes hostile reading publics in such a manner that often increased the likelihood that they would in fact *not* be read.

Throughout, I argue that *masculinity*, as a cultural form, propelled these figures to insert garrulous textual productions of themselves into uninterested public spheres.[20] Their inability to win the attention they courted clarifies how republican masculinity valued performances of disinterestedness and dispassion, not the roughshod, Jacksonian masculinity flourishing in the beginning decades of the nineteenth century.[21] Instead, the masculinities coded as perverse and excessive in the early United States that these figures express eventually culminate in the mid-nineteenth-century figure Walt Whitman—who manufactured his own queer relation to his book *Leaves of Grass*, returning again and again to the scene of composition, showing a significant shift in the publics of nineteenth-century American masculinity.[22] The trajectory of this transformation (from collective to individual, from Federalist to Democratic-Republican) becomes even more vivid when these narratives are taken together insofar as their authors all document their self-perceived exclusions from positions of cultural significance and notoriety, positions that Whitman came to embody even *through*

[20] This focus on masculinity builds from feminist interrogations of gender relations, particularly Robyn Wiegman's effort to show "how feminism's critical interrogations of gender have productively disassembled the normative cultural discourse that weds masculinity to men and thinks about women only in the register of the feminine. Such 'unmaking' . . . of the category of men importantly remakes masculinity as pertinent to if not constitutive of female subjectivity, thereby rendering complex feminism's ability to negotiate the distinctions and interconnections between sex, sexuality, and gender" ("Unmaking" 33). My work similarly illustrates the construction of the category of republican men, only through examining the failures and excesses of masculinity that remain repressed within the early national literary archive.

[21] Recent works on masculinity in the early republic by Thomas Foster, Toby Ditz, and Mary Beth Norton have discussed the multiplicity of masculinities in this time period. Instead of reifying a singular, hegemonic masculinity tied to aristocratic values, Toby Ditz argues that "several models of masculinity competed with one another throughout the colonial era and would continue to do so after the revolution" (256). This model of "contending masculinities rather than a single dominant standard" offers a chance to observe how norms of masculine identity constellate around the symbolic power of certain individuals, such as the reception of Franklin as the paragon republican citizen (266).

[22] Thanks to Trish Loughran for this insight about how Whitman's relationship to masculinity and material texts significantly differs from the major figures in this study.

14 · INTRODUCTION

his non-normative attachment to his compulsively revised and enlarged *Leaves of Grass*.[23]

Before the messy masculinity of a figure like Walt Whitman *became* hegemonic, it operated as a queering of a set of norms that today we take for granted. Jack Halberstam writes of masculinity as a floating cultural form that attaches to various bodies and persons, uncoupled from sexual and gender identity. For Halberstam, masculinity is a form of attachment to a series of norms in the public sphere that validate certain behaviors. Following that work, I focus on how masculinity in the early republic normalizes one's attachment to desiring significance and recognition within public spheres. Halberstam's work asserts the fluidity of masculine gendered expression in a way that challenges the normative stasis of a dichotomously gendered world. That world, of course, is produced and reproduced through power relations that repeat over time and create the inertia of habit or stabilize into a symbol like Franklin.[24] I intentionally mark the masculinity of the figures I study to denaturalize their relations to the gendered public sphere: specifically, I argue that their failure to produce themselves as culturally significant touchstones in the early republic tells something about the masculinist public sphere. Through exploring the myth of masculine independence in the United States even as it emerged within a context that, at first, did not validate such masculinist forms of self-sufficiency, I show how what is conventionally understood

[23] We might think of how Simone de Beauvoir describes the construction of masculine autonomy, when she notes: "He knows that his will emanates only from him, but he can nevertheless attempt to impose it upon others" (65). This is, of course, the myth and fantasy that structures conceptions of masculinity, offering a Romantic notion of independence that falls far from reality. Writing in the rise and wake of European fascism—and its attendant critique of violent abstraction and salvaging of individualism—Beauvoir notes the desire for "being a sovereign and unique subject amidst a universe of objects" (7). The fantasy of overpowering influence informs how masculinity idealizes hierarchy, power imbalance, and subjection. Where in the eighteenth-century the fantasy of masculine subjection was part of its mythos of power, the nineteenth-century emergence of possessive individualism altered how such forms of identity looked.

[24] For more work on the symbols and icons that coalesce around early U.S. political celebrities, see Ed White and Michael Drexler's compelling *The Traumatic Colonel: The Founding Fathers, Slavery, and the Phantasmatic Aaron Burr*, specifically Chapter 1, titled "The Semiotics of the Founders," which argues for an ideological coherence between monarchical and republican personalities in the period. Drexler and White's book provides a methodology that deeply influences my own. In their work, they determine not to treat "the Founders as actual agents who need to be more aggressively historicized with empirical data . . . [but instead as] phantasmatic phenomena best explored from a broadly literary perspective—as a broad characterological drama whose plot often remains obscure" (6). Through locating the imaginative and figurative aspects of cultural figures like the founders, they are able to sketch out the ideologies that inhere to, and reproduce from, their representation. Where they are interested in categorizing the ideological content of "Founder Chic," I highlight the alternative, queer, and ephemeral possibilities grounded in the narratives of those relegated beyond Franklinian achievement.

INTRODUCTION 15

today as hegemonic masculinity was initially a mode of deviance that placed men outside the normative parameters of masculinity.

Scholarship on masculinity in the early national United States tends to be grounded in economic terms, making ambition legible insofar as it manifests through market economies. In this perspective, wealth and market value define the manliness of men. Dana Nelson has discerned how masculinity and early national republicanism emerged as sites of disciplinary potential to produce what she calls "a professional manhood" (14). Masculinity in this configuration offers a heuristic to assess the value of certain bodies and lives, differentiating success from failure. "After the passage of the Constitution," she writes, "the nation began forming and reforming institutional devices for policing men who failed in their national self-discipline" (13). For Nelson, "professional manhood" ties directly into the abstracting potential of republican belonging in that it highlights "national manhood's investment in management logic on behalf of its own gender, racial, and class advantage" (15). In this model, masculinity operates as a filtering device that rewards those who conform to its logics of success and legibility, bringing self-identifying men together under the onus of managing those who fall short of the ideals they set forth. Financial success, it follows, still required some form of normative domestic kinship to make that success fully legible. For instance, John Fitch and Jonathan Plummer achieved some success in their capitalist markets, but their failure to sustain or reproduce the normative domestic form ultimately foregrounds their eventual unraveling outside the logics of capitalist success.[25] In this way, Nelson's model of "professional manhood" sets the stakes for the figure of the bachelor or the recalcitrant husband, particularly in the way they fall beyond normative management. Following Nelson's model of masculinity, Andrew Lyndon Knighton explains how the "exemplary models of manhood that, flourishing beyond the limits of normative productivity, unraveled the surety of the linkage between 'man' and 'management'" (20). Seeking to "dignify the unproductive ambivalences of the nineteenth century" (23), Knighton locates idleness (an attribute that the figures studied here actually lack) as a particularly provocative way into examining problematic masculinities. Knighton, however, emphasizes economic dynamics

---

[25] John Gilbert McCurdy's work on the figure of the bachelor and his changing fortunes in the early United States shows how he was "either the embodiment of personal freedom or another symptom of a society bereft of family values" (4). Fitch's abandonment of family responsibilities (which I discuss in Chapter 1) and Plummer's bachelorhood (which I discuss in Chapter 4) signal the domesticating relationship between capitalism and heteronormativity.

16   INTRODUCTION

as the primary determinant of masculine success. In turning to the marginal men in my archive, then, I am drawn to those whose excessive labors and public declamations—whose constant strivings for work, success, notoriety, and achievement—actually demarcate their failure to be proper men not *because* they failed economically but despite such dynamics. In the end, there seems to be something *to* these men that vouchsafes their separation from the norms toward which they aspire.

The gesture of making private details public has often been regarded as an appeal to sympathetic connection across a broad and undifferentiated public. Sherry Turkle, for one, has written extensively on the psychological and sociological effects that this contemporary condition for seeking connection across media forms has on those who rely on such connection, finding them enmeshed in a system of deferred desire and unrequited longing.[26] Being alone and unrecognized, it would seem, remains an unfavored and undesirable experience in American culture, with loners pathologized and the disconnected demarcated as depressed. In the early U.S. republic, the fear of being disconnected from a public—and the worry of being without influence and thereby bereft of social privilege—similarly drove many key figures to obsess about how they would be remembered and recalled by future generations. Though many, such as Thomas Jefferson, preferred to remain silent in print about private matters, more precariously placed individuals relied on making public their private lives and desires to garner attention and notice. Garry Wills writes that "Washington embodied the classical ideal of restraint" (130) through "constantly testing public opinion and tailoring his actions to suit it" (103). Where Washington and Jefferson seemingly mastered the ability to perform and project a proper self for public consumption, those without an assured public were far less fortunate. This book focuses on moments where private life becomes inserted into genres of public discourse in ways that trouble and contest ideologies regarding the seemingly careful separation of such masculinist spheres. Indeed, the private realm comes to be observed as a sphere that hinders one's capability to be public. The private remains hidden and unmentioned, but when made mentionable it alters the contour of the public, limiting the ability for the figures

---

[26] See *Alone Together: Why We Expect More from Technology and Less from Each Other* (2011). "My own study of the networked life," Turkle concludes, "has left me thinking about intimacy—about being with people in person, hearing their voices and seeing their faces, trying to know their hearts. And it has left me thinking about solitude—the kind that refreshes and restores. Loneliness is failed solitude. To experience solitude you must be able to summon yourself by yourself; otherwise, you will only know how to be lonely" (288).

INTRODUCTION 17

I examine to achieve the desires they articulate for themselves. In this way, we might think of liberalism as a queering of republicanism's sacrosanct private realm—and in this story, masculinity becomes the vexed category that incurs that rupture.

I.3. Feeling Singular, Becoming Eccentric, and Other Enlightenment Book Disorders

This book is an experiment: how does one discuss the cultural archive generally tasked with solidifying and "founding" the early United States without centralizing the project of nation-building, federal-republic constituting, or otherwise state power normalizing? In a recent C-SPAN talk, historian Joseph Ellis scoffed at the idea that one could study the founding of the United States, with its specific locale and time period, *without* focusing on the so-called Founding Fathers themselves. In many ways, this book attempts to counter such a perspective. Following in the wake of what tends to be considered the emergence of the U.S. nation-state, I instead highlight slippages from that supposed ideal and focus on the incompatibilities and incomprehensibilities of republican belonging—and how, indeed, the cultural logics of the early United States necessitated illogics and inconsistencies.[27] In doing so, I focus on how one can seek to narrate failure when the cultural materials at one's disposal have been marshalled historically to foreground fame, illustrate illustriousness, and pinpoint the prerogatives of propertied white men who, as Duncan Faherty observes, are assigned primary agency within national mythologies, as "Framers of the Constitution. Architects of Democracy. Founding Fathers. Builders of a Nation" (2). Throughout this book, I gesture at what might be considered failed blueprints and alternative models, writings by those who, before Melville's Bartleby, simply "would prefer not to" or even preferred an otherwise as they resided in the shadows and crevices of our inherited narratives of national founding.

Using insights gleaned from queer theory, I examine a unique cultural formation that arranged precarious individuals around ill-fated hopes for

---

[27] Carrie Hyde in her compelling return to the legally and legislatively unformed status of "citizenship" before the Civil War in *Civic Longing: The Speculative Origins of U.S. Citizenship* (2018) guides my thinking: "Citizenship's terminological prolixity and legal under-conceptualization," she writes, "in the early republic was, understandably, a source of confusion" (5). Focusing on such incoherence, Hyde demonstrates how fiction and literary works found purpose to theorize the lack of clarity that state-sponsored texts and institutions neglected to shore up.

18   INTRODUCTION

cultural inclusion. I think of their hopes for inclusion as an aspiration that *queers* the cultural value of desiring republican significance and influence in a world that ends up marking such hopes as evidence of perversity or eccentricity. In this sense, I think of *queer* as both a verb—something subjects *do* to a larger normalizing formation—and as a mode of being in response to exclusionary structures. Scholars such as José Esteban Muñoz and Rei Terada have thought about the philosophical impact of queerness, with the latter describing "queer consciousness" as a mode "that has sensed most keenly the moments when fact is ambiguously social or natural, and has had motive and energy to examine and reexamine even those pervasive conditions that seem most natural" (9). Plummer, accused of being a "hermaphrodite," offers the figuration of a queer individual through his articulation of nonnormative sexual object-choice, and Jeffrey Brace and William Wilson's experience with state power show how their narratives queer the norms that placed them outside the positions of interest and legibility that they desired. While Franklin emerges as an icon of public validation, the cultural recognition reserved for the figures I examine emphasize their failures. Through these unique case studies, I build from work on early national life narratives by Ann Fabian, Susan Clair Imbarrato, and Karen Weyler to show how such autobiographical writings contest-though-reproduce social norms, offering alternative or foreshortened ways of imagining belonging in the republic. In thinking about histories of failure in early America, then, I account for the years preceding Scott Sandage's formative work on nineteenth-century failure, telling the "story of America's unsung losers: men who failed in a nation that worships success" (3).[28]

Shining a light on the mirror of the U.S. nation-state, *Feeling Singular* reflects queer differences.[29] How do unique, singular individuals become larger-than-life characters that structure recognizable cultural formations? What are the figural mechanisms that do that, and how do subjects get interpolated into a system that asks for their identification? As I will reference

---

[28] The proliferation of the antithesis of success is poignantly noted in Sandage's emphatic one-liner: "Failure stories are everywhere, if we can bear to hear them" (9). See Scott Sandage, *Born Losers: A History of Failure in America* (Cambridge: Harvard UP, 2005).

[29] The metaphor of mirrors signals the interrelation between narcissism and the Lacanian mirror stage, which in many ways overlaps with how the United States conceptualizes its attachment to masculine independence. For more insights on mirrors, see Margaret J. M. Ezell's essay "Looking Glass Histories," who states: "For the twentieth and twenty-first centuries, the mirror has been a critical element in psychoanalytic discourse of identity and its formation. It is essential in psychoanalytic discourse of identity and its formation. It is essential in the narration of the dramas of the individual but also of the universal psyche" (321).

INTRODUCTION   19

in the Coda, the behemoth of Benjamin Franklin haunts this book, as he crystallizes the dominant norms against which all other life writers in this period are measured. In establishing the cultural representation of Franklin as a norm that subjugates the figures I examine, I am influenced by Judith Butler's work on the capacity of norms to contain their difference. Writing in *Undoing Gender* that "any opposition to the norm is already contained within the norm, and is crucial to its own functioning" (51), Butler emphasizes that "the norm cannot be reduced to any of its instances" while also maintaining that "neither can the norm be fully extricated from its instantiations" (52). The unique aspect of Franklin is that his narrative story, visual likeness, and his cultural influence are repeated so often in the early republic that he becomes both an iterative trope and a particular figure. In this sense, he offers to queer approaches of the early republic a particularly resonant example of the production of a norm that can be (and is) queered by the alternatives that his ascension into cultural significance seeks to eliminate.

Where Franklin was asked by multiple people to write his life story—particularly if he could shape the story of his life into a model for others to follow—this book examines the writings and texts of and about individuals who hoped to have such a cultural affect but come to occupy the outsides of an emerging literary canon. For instance, when John Fitch wrote his life narrative, he imagined that its publication would so rattle the republic that he pleaded with the Philadelphia librarian who acquired it to wait until "the warmth of the present age [that is] so much in favour of the first officers of the Government" cools (207–208). Relatedly, soon after the memoir of Jeffrey Brace was published in his small Vermont community, he and his family were warned out of town by the selectmen. In both of these circumstances, the material text of the book—the manuscript or the hurriedly printed typescript—becomes a site that foregrounds exclusion. The material object of the text points toward a history of thwarted influence. Because each figure cannot abstract something about themselves that would allow them less friction upon their entrance into reading publics, the materialities of their written selves reflect that particularity.

Queer theory provides a language to demystify the abstraction that Franklin's shadow produces, illustrating how norms are always in flux and never actually normal. Indeed, norms are conventions of repetition that become naturalized as expected and expectable. In an essay that critiques how queer studies tend to disavow historicist methods, Valerie Traub imagines "a queer historicism dedicated to showing how categories, however mythic,

20   INTRODUCTION

phantasmic, and incoherent, came to be" (81). There is a particular history to the figure of the "white male" that required the foreclosure of inchoate and incoherent alternatives that trafficked side by side their more prominent ideals. Where Traub argues that queer studies avoid the opportunities of textual materiality, I use such textual opportunities to theorize the formations of the norms of republican belonging, specifically thinking about the desires that the figures I examine sought to endow the material texts they had produced. I draw upon material text methodologies in this book for a number of reasons, but two may be noted here: the materials themselves invite such attention, because they are mostly singular, unique productions that did not circulate as the authors had hoped; second, the effort to think about the materiality of failed books and thwarted manuscripts is in intimate dialogue with the subjectivities that produced them.

As opposed to *becoming singular*—which suggests a teleology of progress—*feeling singular* gets at the messy, inchoate ways subjects attempt to manufacture themselves into coherence without a pattern to follow. Singularity is perpetually in tension with republican models of belonging. Indeed, the unabstractable *singularity* of individuals becomes the mode through which eccentricity emerges, a capacity central to subjectivity itself. The root of the word *eccentric* derives from words that mean circle or center, stemming originally from an astronomical term to describe an off-kilter orbit. In its first *OED* definition, the adjective is "used of circles of which one is within the other" though they do not have a common center. In the astronomical sense, the word signifies an orbit that does not have the understood center of the universe as its main fulcrum point. I am drawn to this etymology for how it describes eccentric lives as lives out of orbit, mismatched and unconventional, deviating from a norm. The eccentric, then, helps found and form the seemingly stable norms that constitute it as such.

To be regarded as important—to feel singular and be recognized as significant—seems today like a self-evident virtue. But to lay claim on the public to know one's interiority requires specific invitations. Any publicity is good publicity, the commonplace goes, suggesting that being in the public eye is more important than what one is known for. This did not work, however, for Jonathan Plummer's eccentric patron, the self-titled "Lord" Timothy Dexter, who inserted himself in newspapers throughout New England and earned the ire of others who begrudgingly called him "the celebrated monied man of Newbury Port." In the early republic, publicity required a careful balance of self-effacement and the virtuosity of public performance,

INTRODUCTION 21

cordoning intimate and private foibles far from the risk of public exposure. "[C]lassical virtue," historian Gordon Wood claims, "had gradually become domesticated" as "politeness and civility spread" in the years following the Revolution and coinciding with the building of the republic (13). The men I examine, however, become known for being too garrulous and impolite about their own self-conceived greatness, without the virtues of selflessness and submissiveness that Wood grounds as ideologically dominant within the years of the early republic.

"The *Vulgar* thus through *Imitation* err;" writes Alexander Pope in *An Essay on Criticism*: "As oft the *Learn'd* by being *Singular*" (25). Cautioning against singularity as a penchant toward error, Pope conflates it with imitation. Being singular signifies a moving away from rote conventionalities and instead an embracing of difference and peculiarity. In the *OED*'s definition of this version of "singular," it specifies "Differing *from* others in opinion; standing alone; peculiar in this respect" (def. 12). A more common definition in the *OED* defines it as "Different from or not complying with that which is customary, usual, or general; strange, odd, peculiar" (def. 13). The focus on departing from a norm, and being rendered visible as "strong, odd, peculiar," grounds the cultural work of writing about one's self in ways that define how all subjects push toward expressions of attention and significance. *Feeling Singular*'s title draws upon this notion of standing askance to norms, and of "not complying," to highlight the norms then formulating around identity. But in addition to this focus on the peculiar, I am also engaged with questions concerning how the *unique* sets a collective into legible formation.

When one *feels singular*, they emanate a difference that places them outside relations with others. Singularity offers a way into thinking about the radical contingency and chaotic energy that precedes categories. Following Eve Kosofsky Sedgwick's first Axiom in *Epistemology of the Closet*, this book attends to her observation, "*People are different from each other*" and, subsequently, her astonishment at "how few respectable conceptual tools we have for dealing with this self-evident fact" (22). Instead of a turn to founding larger categories of identification, I am interested in parsing the radical individuality that gets produced through the construction of singular subjectivities. There is a logic of attention that accumulates around identity that perpetuates a logic of exclusion, made evident in a zero-sum barrier that attempts to calcify abstractions as self-evident categories. Individuality—and singularity—become explained through a larger identity concept that makes

22   INTRODUCTION

it legible. I am interested in resisting a zero-sum logic of attention to the weird particularities of the figures I examine, holding at a distance the subsumption into a *type* and instead focusing on the strangeness of particularity. *Feeling Singular* offers to hold open the messy categories that accrued around individual subjects before they solidified into stabilized tropes, such as white maleness. The construction of that abstraction, of course, was piecemeal and contains its own particular history, and the stories contained in this book offer glimpses into that abstraction's repressed enabling conditions.

What's at stake in a reparative reading of figures who desired and yet failed to achieve their conception of cultural significance in the early United States? Sedgwick, in her later career intellectual work, moved away from the suspicious readings of the closet to offer a way of reading that avoids the trap of exposure. In *Touching Feeling* (2003), she begins her well-cited chapter on reparative reading by reframing a conversation that subtly questions a commonsensical understanding of how state power deals maliciously with society's marginalized outsiders, specifically pointing out how the unmasking of malevolent motivation does not inevitably challenge those conditions. Instead of honing distance through critical suspicion, she endorses an entanglement with parody—taking the piss out of any "strong theory" (134). Sedgwick concludes the chapter by sitting with textual objects in a "queer-identified practice of camp" (149) that allows for "the sappy, aestheticizing, defensive, anti-intellectual, or reactionary" formations that would otherwise be considered complicit with the assumptions of a dominant culture (150).[30] Campy reading practices, then, inform my approach to the proliferating subjectivities in the early United States, following what Susan Sontag has called "the sensibility of failed seriousness, of the theatricalization of experience" (10). Such campy reading practices inform how I read the self-declared "Lord" Timothy Dexter in Chapter 3, where I intentionally juxtapose time periods to produce an anachronistic formulation to erode our sense of the staid stability of Federalism.

[30] What are the motivating factors that mark suspicious readings *as such* and how do they influence the shape of the aesthetics of belonging in the early United States? The suspicious mode of cultural studies has many manifestations, and perhaps they are best formulated by thinking through the way power and influence in the U.S. context tends to create its own outside that agitates for inside status. Stories of the founding of the United States remain attached to the fantasy of disavowed self-interest. "An essential strand of American political interpretation and judgment," writes Frederick M. Dolan in his *Allegories of America*, "relies on the strategy whose dialectic and dilemmas I isolated at the outset of this chapter: unmasking the particularity of desire beneath the professions of dispassionate reason" (47).

The ur-trope in U.S. culture is the synecdoche: a part for the whole, where the singular part becomes eventually to represent the whole. The "We the People" in the Constitution's "Preamble" offers a synecdoche that consolidates power, abstracting messy particularities into "the People" that implies "a more perfect Union" comes through a transformation, where the part stands in for the whole. How does such a new form occur, and what representational apparatus enables the individual, singular subject to manifest as representative? This line of thinking is influenced by Lauren Berlant's interests "to track the becoming general of singular things" in their 2011 assessment of their previous work, writing about "how the singular becomes delaminated from its location in someone's story or some locale's irreducibly local history and circulated as evidence of something shared" (*Cruel Optimism* 12).[31] The telescoping of the singular into something general, of course, works through excluding certain figures from access to such generality. In this book, I examine the lives of individuals who could not be representative, but in doing so, I highlight the mechanisms that make representation imaginable.

In Jean-Luc Nancy's essay "Being Singular Plural," he reads the phrase "people are strange" [les gens sont bizarre] as "one of our most constant and rudimentary ontological attestations" (6). In thinking about becoming singular and feeling eccentric, Nancy's theorization provides a useful moment for my argument. In his essay, he plumbs the etymology of "bizarre" and connects it to "a sense of valor, commanding presence, and elegance" (10). That history of an elevated "bizarre" that initially signaled a sense of merit and worth shifts in the contemporary parlance of "bizarre" as exceptionally strange, outrageous. In thinking of synecdoche, and its connection to the formation of larger collectives, we might see how this work of designating the extreme is part of what comes to constitute an isolated subjectivity. "A single being is a contradiction in terms," writes Nancy, theorizing the basis of "Being Singular Plural" (12). "To want to say 'we' is not at all sentimental," Nancy writes; "not at all familial or 'communitarian.' It is existence reclaiming its due or its condition: coexistence" (42). In thinking of synecdoche, as a part for a whole (or a whole for a part), the configuration of

---

[31] I use they/them pronouns for Lauren Berlant here and throughout per their request and identification. For more on the use of they/them pronouns, see Greta LaFleur, " 'What's in a Name?': They/Them," *Journal of the Early Republic* 43.1 (Spring 2023): 109–119.

24 INTRODUCTION

American singularities attempts to stabilize the object of America. " 'People,' writes Nancy, "are silhouettes that are both imprecise and singularized, faint outlines of voices, patterns of comportment, sketches of affects" (7). From across a portrait of "People," this book theorizes an ideology of singularity that attends to the flickering accounts of identities that flash from the past when we rub our hands against the canon.

1
Memorializing the Republic of Failure

Often I have seen [John Fitch] stalking about like a troubled spectre, with downcast eyes and lowering countenance, his coarse, soiled linen, peeping through the elbows of a tattered garment.

—Thomas P. Cope[1]

Everybody wants to leave something behind them, some impression, some mark upon the world. And then you think, you've left a mark on the world if you just get through it and a few people remember your name. Then you've left a mark. . . . If you shoot an arrow and it goes real high, hooray for you.

—Dorian Corey[2]

The day will come when some more powerful man will get fame and riches for my invention; but nobody will believe that *poor John Fitch* can do anything worthy of attention!

—John Fitch[3]

An early twentieth-century postcard of the Old Town Cemetery of Bardstown, Kentucky, points out the burial spot of John Fitch, the ill-famed inventor of an eighteenth-century steamboat who died in that town in 1798. Leafless, spindly trees stretch toward an overcast sky with a single dark stake—made of wood or metal—marking the grave, pointing up slightly off center from the ground below one of four prominent tree trunks (see Fig. 1.1). At the bottom of the card, in red-orange text, are the words "Post Marking the grave in Old Town Cemetery of John Fitch, the unhonored inventor of the first Steam Boat, Bardstown, Ky." There's nothing exceptional about the composition of the image: it resembles an ordinary late winter or early spring

---

[1] *Hazard's Register*, Vol. 7. Qtd. in Thompson Westcott, *Life of John Fitch*, 338.
[2] Jennie Livingston, *Paris Is Burning*.
[3] Qtd. in Watson 447.

Feeling Singular. Ben Bascom, Oxford University Press. © Oxford University Press 2024.
DOI: 10.1093/9780197687536.003.0002

Figure 1.1 Postcard of John Fitch's burial site in Bardstown, Kentucky. Courtesy of David Lyle Hays.

scene of a nondescript graveyard with sparse memorials in various states of disarray. But the text offers a curious rhetorical maneuver that *honors* the "unhonored," making a memento to the supposedly unremembered even as that very gesture comes to mark the production of (lost) memory. John Fitch isn't forgotten, though, and he's not even "unhonored"; instead, he is honored with the narrative of being forgotten and then remembered again (and indeed again and again), and in that gesture attempting to redeem forgotten failures.

Monuments and memorials embed around them this dialectic of failure, where they indicate an anxiety of remembering that seeks to overcompensate for loss. The "Post" that marks Fitch's grave resembles in miniature the future Washington Monument planned to tower over Federal City, offering a tiny obelisk to point out the insignificant weight of an unremembered (though by that gesture acknowledged and thereby remembered) life. The cultural shadow cast today by the Washington Monument in the Capital obscures its own piecemeal and faltering construction, with drying avenues of funding and political controversies delaying its erection.[4] The excesses in size inflate

---

[4] Begun as a private venture, with a decade of fundraising prior to beginning construction, the project halted in 1854, soon after the Know-Nothings had confiscated a granite stone gift from the

MEMORIALIZING THE REPUBLIC OF FAILURE   27

to epic proportions the desire to make certain that some future remembers, and in the case of Washington, for better or worse, this and other monuments proliferate his fame. Indeed, the first issue of *The Washington National Monument* (1871), a periodical pamphlet dedicated to finishing the decades-stalled project, calls such monuments "the rear-guards of civilization—the last witnesses of the fall of governments and of the overthrow of nations—standing on the outposts of time, solemnly protesting against the advance of the destroyer" ("An Appeal" 6).

Important here is the connecting of memorials to the trappings of an impending failed "civilization," as memorials stave off anxieties about a seemingly fated future destruction.[5] Washington's monument galvanizes the desire to remember and mark as significant particular lives over others, emblazoning the famed Cincinnatus who becomes celebrated for iconic deflection. Debates over where to place the body of the deceased commander embroiled concerns regarding the security of the body: if it were left in a private resting place, early nationalists feared some so-called foreign power would one day purchase the land; contrarily, if the body were interred where William Thornton, the designer of the Capital, had intended—on perpetual display in a catacomb under the figurative seat of government—such grandiose entombment seemed at variance with republican governance.[6] The places where bodies decay—and what figments of bodies are made to outlive that decay through the apparatuses of memorials and the fantasies of cultural longevity—resonates with long-lasting ideological significance.

In juxtaposing Fitch's small marker with Washington's colossal monument, I want to consider how memorials index a type of cultural failure. In a popular image of Washington's actual burial site, a lone man stands before

pope, and was picked back up two decades later, being finished in 1884 with a steam-driven elevator shuttling individuals through the interior of the then tallest building in the world.

[5] This half-formed monument was often described as being in a state of faux-ruins, as Mark Twain and Charles Dudley Warner in *The Gilded Age* imply in their description of "a factory chimney with the top broken off" surrounded by "[t]he skeleton of a decaying scaffolding" (*The Gilded Age*, 1883, 172).

[6] William Thornton wanted to revive the deceased body of George Washington as soon as he learned of his passing, suggesting in his 1820 typewritten script "Sleep" that he had "proposed to attempt his restoration, in the following manner. First to thaw him in cold water, then to lay him in blankets, & by degrees & by friction to give him warmth, and to put into activity the minute blood vessels, at the same time to open a passage to the Lungs by the Trachaea, and to inflate them with air, to produce an artificial respiration, and to transfuse blood into him from a lamb" (*Papers of William Thornton*, Vol. 1, Ed. C. M. Harris [Charlottesville: U of Virginia P, 1995], 528).

28 FEELING SINGULAR

a wooden fence, hat removed in a gesture of contemplation (see Fig. 1.2). The picture evokes an intimate and simple mourning scene, one where an individual is brought before the representation of open light—perhaps even the touch of something ethereal if not divine—that the picture stages. Washington's ghost is never far from his embodied mourners, the picture implies.[7] Contrarily, despite his best efforts, the specter of John Fitch doesn't haunt the study of early national America. As I note in the Introduction, the cranks and eccentrics who thought themselves on the equal playing field of prominence in early national culture—and described themselves so, despite the profound material disparities of their positions—offer a way to reconceptualize the formations of national belonging that predominate studies of this period's autobiographical writings. Rather than seeing these figures as themselves exceptional, I explore their sometimes prolific, often overwrought writings to register the type of recognition that would be bestowed on their more monumentalized compatriots.

As a brief foray into John Fitch's biography, we can plot how he was born in the 1740s, married and then abandoned his wife and family in the 1760s, bartered silversmith services for the Continental Army during the American War of Independence, mapped out the Northwest Territory in the 1780s, and then, while living near Philadelphia, one day grew so tired walking that when a man passed him with a robust set of horses he wondered how to throttle steam power to drive a carriage on land. Or at least that's how he narrated the moment "a thought struck" him to create a steam-powered transportation device (113). "[F]ealing my country so much indebted to me," Fitch reflects after the final failure of his steamboat company, "I shall breath [sic] my last for the purpose of makeing [sic] my country asshaimed [sic] of their base treatment to me" (114–115). He represented that last experience several times in his writings to record what he felt was a fateful confluence of inventive genius and embodied exhaustion, an event that led him to construct what historians consider the first functional river-ferrying steamboat. Further troubles embroiled Fitch and his designs to climb above his mechanic status, however, when his married business partner became involved with a widow, and they asked him to feign being her husband to ward off the

---

[7] Grief as a site of belonging—and specifically its patriotic implications—has been very usefully analyzed in Max Cavitch's *American Elegy: The Poetry of Mourning from the Puritans to Whitman* (2006), particularly his chapter "Elegy and the Subject of National Mourning." See also Dana Luciano's *Arranging Grief: Sacred Time and the Body in Nineteenth-Century America* for an exploration of the biopolitical implications around cultures of mourning.

Figure 1.2 Image of man reflecting on the nondescript burial location of George Washington. "Tomb of Washington" by George Lehman from a drawing by J. R. Smith. Courtesy of the American Antiquarian Society.

Figure 1.3a Four manuscript books that John Fitch used to write his life narrative. Courtesy of The Library Company of Philadelphia.

controversy of multiple pregnancies. Considering such a pretense an affront to his fraught masculinity, Fitch cut all ties with his fledgling business and the few investors he had remaining. But before he left the relative comforts of the eastern seaboard for Kentucky, he deposited his life's writings—consisting in several manuscript books—in a Philadelphia library, believing that one day others would want to read and, in his mind, redeem his failed struggles (see Figs. 1.3a, b, c).

Yet Fitch seems to want more than for others to read of his struggles: he wanted to couch himself as a singular individual who merits

Figure 1.3b The four manuscript books Fitch used to compose his life narrative. Courtesy of The Library Company of Philadelphia.

attention. Fantasies of greatness infect the cultural imaginary of white American men, who are written into illusions of singular selfhoods.[8] We might think of what R. W. B. Lewis asserts in *The American Adam: Innocence, Tragedy, and Tradition in the Nineteenth Century* (1955) regarding the emergence of "the image of a radically new personality . . . an individual emancipated from history, happily bereft of ancestry, untouched and undefiled

---

[8] Consider Ethan Allen, who gets imagined as single-handedly shaping the ideological contour of early Vermont. Such figures have produced figments of their psychic lives untethered to the apparatus of the external formations that produce and manage them, and somehow this fantasy of influence formulates the very ideological content of white-male masculinity. See, for instance, Michael A. Bellesiles's *Revolutionary Outlaws: Ethan Allen and the Struggle for Independence on the Early American Frontier* (1993), which asserts that Allen "personified the greatest American myth, maintaining the façade of rugged individualism which covers the reality of essential family and communal networks" (262). In addition to portraying an Allen who "refused to bend before any adversity and transferred his determination to others," Bellesiles complicates that sense of "living proof of the liberal creed of gaining one's own salvation through action" through asserting that that very myth has no bearing in material history (263). Yet even still, the entire book seeks to locate the individual reality of Ethan Allen through puncturing what he subsequently calls the myth of "Anarchistic individualism" (263). This is all to say, that the figure called Ethan Allen still operates to condense and distill very specific ideological content regarding the construction (and qualification) of individuality.

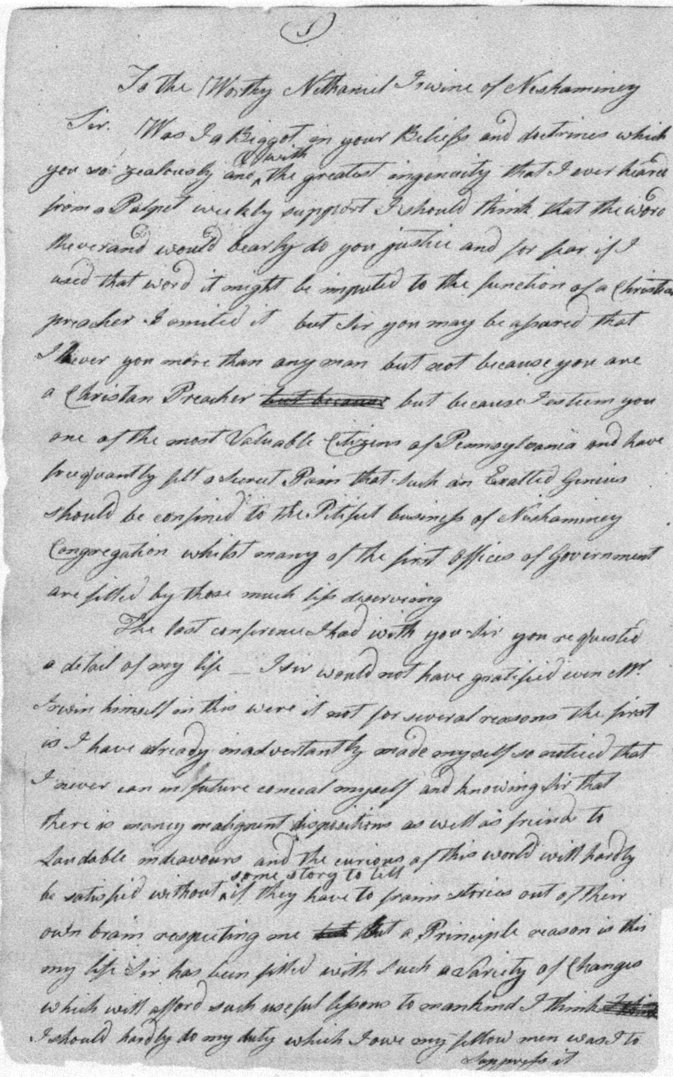
(1)

To the Worthy Nathaniel Irwine of Neshaminey

Sir. Was I a Biggot in your Beliefs and doctrines which you so zealously and with the greatest ingenuity that I ever heard from a Pulpit weekly support I should think that the word Reverand would hardly do you justice and for fear if I used that word it might be imputed to the function of a Christian preacher I omited it but Sir you may be assured that I Revere you more than any man but not because you are a Christian Preacher ~~but because~~ but because I esteem you one of the most Valuable Citizens of Pennsylvania and have frequently felt a Secret Pain that such an Exalted Genius should be confined to the Pitiful business of Neshaminey Congregation whilst many of the first Offices of Government are filled by those much less deserving

The last conference I had with you Sir you requested a detail of my life — I Sir would not have gratified even Mr. Irwin himself in this were it not for several reasons the first is I have already inadvertantly made myself so noticed that I never can in future conceal myself and knowing Sir that there is many malignant dispositions as well as friends to Laudable indeavours and the curious of this world will hardly be satisfied without some story to tell if they have to frame stories out of their own brain respecting me ~~but~~ But a Principle reason is this my life Sir has been filled with such a Variety of Changes which will afford such useful lessons to mankind I think ~~that~~ I should hardly do my duty which I owe my fellow men was I to Suppress it

Figure 1.3c Opening page of John Fitch's life narrative, written as a letter to the Reverend Nathaniel Irwin. Courtesy of The Library Company of Philadelphia.

by the usual inheritances of family and race; an individual standing alone, self-reliant and self-propelling" (5). Although this unhistoricized, androcentric figure functions as a buttress to Cold War–era configuring of American exceptionalism, it gives us pause to consider the content that drives the figures of masculine solitude underlying many midcentury studies of American literature. Interested in examining myth, Lewis fashions a coherent ideology that he attaches to representations of the solitary male in American culture. To be sure, Fitch similarly *imagined* himself stepping beyond his moment, thinking that he was less being shaped by history and more an agent in that process. In a sympathetic newspaper account, he is ranked among Philadelphia's "number of ingenious men," which, according to the author, is larger "than any other part of the known world—a Franklin, as a philosopher, politician and electrician—a Godfrey and a Rittenhouse, as astronomers—a West, as the greatest painter of the age—a Wheeler, the constructor of cannon, out of wrought iron—a Fitch and a Voight, for propelling a boat through the water, with great celerity, by the force of steam—."[9] Placed in relation to these more recognized names, Fitch seems validated in his aspiring to cultural prestige. But from such imagined great heights, his actual fall through losing his steamboat company—and his closest friends—foregrounds the atomized insignificance of an individual against the backdrop of what seems a more connected and privileged social network.

Indeed, Fitch is a spectacular failure. But what does it mean to fail spectacularly? How does the *privilege* to fail embed within it particular gender, race, and class implications? Failure, as a concept, becomes legible through a narrative of aborted fulfillment, illuminating a horizon of aspiration that recedes as events unfold in unforeseen downward directions. Fitch is a spectacular failure partly because a later generation instrumentalized his loss of economic ability.[10] One such 1830s magazine article blamed Fitch's failure to secure his steamboat rights on "those whose station in life placed it in their power to assist him, [but] looked coldly on"; another lamented how "efforts of genius and enterprise, if unaccompanied by wealth, too often suffer and languish, and frequently are abandoned and lost to the world."[11] Articulating power differences based on wealth and social power, these newspapers construct barriers that Fitch stumbled against. Queer theorist Jack Halberstam

---

[9] "The Gazetteer," *Independent Gazetteer*, 1789.

[10] Although those contemporaneously in power spurned Fitch, later in the nineteenth century he was resuscitated as a victim to the emerging federal government, becoming a figure for Democratic-Republicans to articulate their view of problematic power differentials embedded within federalism. Specifically, Fitch was recovered *as* a man whose masculinity troubled the supposedly disinterested republican masculinity.

[11] See "Steam Boats," *Magazine of Useful and Entertaining Knowledge* (Feb. 1831): 118 and "The First Steamboat," *Atkinson's Saturday Evening Post* (May 21, 1831): 1.

34   FEELING SINGULAR

imbues failure with the affirmation of resistance, arguing that we should "recognize failure as a way of refusing to acquiesce to dominant logics of power," yet for Fitch such subversive potential seems unavailable (88).[12] Fitch did not wish to resist so much as to be retained within the very norms he is seen to transgress, and the later generation that recovered him deployed his failure as a way to secure the rights of white men at the expense of women and people of color. Yet the memory of Fitch functions to lubricate the very power differentials that secured his absence from the echelons of republican significance and that rendered him an object of misremembered achievement, marked as "unhonored" and "unacknowledged" in subsequent accounts, like the twentieth-century postcard.

This chapter shows how John Fitch negotiates the fraught personalities and powers that excluded him in the years following the creation of the United States, and how that exclusion offers insights on the cultural reach of republican masculinity. Angry at "[t]he uncandid dealings of our Nation" (199), Fitch believes, I argue, that he should be the center of republican significance, even though he finds himself in positions of unrepublican subservience. Those feelings focus on his surprise, and indeed frustration, that he is subject to a series of power relations and differentials inherent to republican belonging—just as women and people of color are, however differently situated—that belies not only his identity (a white man) but his desire to attain to a position of influence in the expanding U.S. republic. I begin by examining his personal writings, situating them in relation to his desire to be read and received as significant. From there, I turn to how Fitch complicates the stories scholars tell about republican belonging in the early nation, rethinking histories of individualism and singularity within a collectivizing republic that attempted to privilege group identification over individual identity, and how that dynamic facilitated the specific formulation of U.S. empire in the early decades of expansion.[13] Desiring to be made into a model citizen even as he falls from the protections of respectability,

---

[12] Halberstam queries whether "failing, losing, forgetting, unmaking, undoing, unbecoming, [and] not knowing may in fact offer more creative, more cooperative, more surprising ways of being in the world" (2–3). This queer approach to failure—where one sees the ironic *rewards* it offers through providing a moment to quit and critique the system that ensures there be winners *and* losers—seems impossible for a person like Fitch, whose failure does not provide him subversive potential. In fact, his failure is utilized to substantiate a system that deprives women and people of color of the very privileges he feels he was denied.

[13] Prior to the nineteenth-century validation of self-reliant American masculinity, the figure of the undomesticated and un-attached male troubled republican efforts to produce national collectivity and cohesion. See Louis Masur, " 'Age of the First Person Singular': The Vocabulary of the Self in New England, 1780–1850," *Journal of American Studies* 25.2 (Aug. 1991): 189–211.

Fitch manifests his inability to perform the very early national norms that contest his claims to influential citizenship. In concluding this way, I emphasize how Fitch believes that he failed to garner republican accolades and cultural significance due to his inability to separate his private and intimate life from his efforts to produce a public persona centered on being the sole inventor of the steamboat.

1.1. Textual Bodies That Matter

Despite his protestations, John Fitch isn't really so exceptional, insofar as dozens of his contemporaries had designed and constructed steamboat models.[14] Where critics have focused on the steamboat as the symbol of Fitch's failure, his failed ascendancy to the cultural form of the book offers a more pronounced implication of that failure. Shortly after his business ventures failed, he wrote a four-volume rambling quasi-autobiography that he wished to be produced into a widely circulated book. Fitch aspires to write a book that would then circulate among his contemporaries; in many ways, the saga of steamboat production seems to have been the vehicle for him to narrate his sense of justification for putting his life into book form. Joyce Appleby, Stephen Carl Arch, and Laura Rigal have laid out the history of his steamboat invention and the legal account of his failure to win a federal patent, with Appleby calling Fitch a proto-capitalist figure who simply could not sustain financial support from his creditors, thus pushing back the development of the steam engine by two decades. Arch calls Fitch a proto-Romantic, having emerged into a sense of selfhood before a cultural apparatus existed to validate his insistence on singularity, and Rigal positions Fitch within the architecture of the federal processional, writing specifically of him as a casualty to Constitutional consolidation and explaining that he "desire[d] to produce himself and to be produced as a public property, an embodiment of republican legitimacy, and a monument to freedom, like the exemplary figures of state upon whom his life and steamboat depended" (59). Where I differentiate myself from these critics, however, is the context for understanding Fitch's failures. Even though his steamboat was a profound loss to him, it was his desire to be made into a significant figure through any means necessary that haunted him as he undertook the writing of his life.

[14] A few of these inventors include Nathan Read (1759–1849) from Salem, MA; Jacob Perkins (1766–1849) from Newburyport, MA; and James Rumsey (1743–1792) from Virginia.

36 FEELING SINGULAR

While the steamboat is certainly a crucial moment in his life—one that prepared him for a series of events that he narrates, providing the very occasion for his writings—Fitch in his final written asides, and what the editor of his published works (printed in 1976) Frank D. Prager denotes as his postscripts, represents interpersonal failures as determining him to require a future recovery. In his way, and through the writing of his book, he captures the sense that there is something internal to *himself* that seemingly destines him to experience the disappointment that marks his life.

Fitch's writings are rife with a deep irony. He begins his life narrative with a direct address to his friend, "the Worthy Nathaniel Irwine of Neshaminey"—who had "requested a detail of my life"—but includes a coded slight on the profession of this Presbyterian preacher (19). "I Rever [sic] you more than any man but not because you are a Christian preacher," Fitch writes, mixing a compliment with a critique: "but because I esteem you one of the most valuable citizens of Pennsylvania and have freequantly [sic] felt a secreet [sic] pain that such an exalted genius should be confined to the Pitiful business of Neshaminey Congregation whilst many of the first Offices of Government are filled with those much less deserveing" (19). Signaling a troubled form of respect that acknowledges the apparent importance of the preacher's social position while lamenting that it is not greater, Fitch here confesses "a secreet pain" that the minister's religious attachment limits his social position. Wanting his friend to be more important than he can at present be *because* of his profession, Fitch aspires to a model of political significance that demotes religion and valorizes the nation-state's "Offices of Government." This conflicted valorization of secular modes of belonging emerges as a guiding trope in Fitch's writing, where he praises the possibilities that religious affection and iconography offer even as he attempts to move beyond them. He frames his life narrative in response to this minister, appealing to religious affection and attachment to imagine himself exceeding the constraints and obligations of those very forms of religious deference.

Describing himself as "an unnoticed Indigent Citizen" (157), Fitch compiled an account of his steamboat misadventures and the subsequent barriers he encountered on what he hoped would be his inevitable journey toward cultural significance. Beginning, as is conventional, with personal records that detail his genealogy, Fitch claims for himself "a very respectable family if not what is called Noble" (19–20). He thus sets himself up as a proper republican subject, one who values transparency and envisions himself a renowned inventor, destined for future recognition if not immediate accolades.

MEMORIALIZING THE REPUBLIC OF FAILURE   37

Where figures like Washington, John Adams, and Thomas Jefferson declined to write their memoirs for public consumption, Fitch desired to put his textual life forward for a public reckoning. Those Founders agonized about including personal anecdotes in their writing. For instance, Jefferson in the *Memoirs* that he undertook in 1821 notes that he "begin[s] to make some memoranda, and state some recollections of dates and facts concerning myself, for my own more ready reference, and for the information of my family" (1). At one point, after spending the majority of his text outlining his political work, he notes: "I am already tired of talking about myself," without ever having delved very deeply into his personal life beyond dates and his infamous frustrations at the Continental Congress's edits of the Declaration of Independence (41).

Contrary to that taciturnity, Fitch observes in the opening to his minister friend (to whom he addresses his life narrative): "I have already inadvertantly [sic] made myself so noticed that I never can in future conceal myself" (19). Where Jefferson basks in his solitary hermitage, taciturn about himself, Fitch proclaims himself as far too "noticed" to ever be away from public inspection. As such, he feels it incumbent on himself to correct what he conceives as lies that "inadvertantly" thrust him onto a public stage. By contrast, Fitch emphasizes his interpersonal life throughout his writings, seemingly never tiring of including more personal details and intimate anecdotes, in asides and sighs that render visible the contour of his interior life. Where Jefferson and Adams declined to delve into personal intrigue and intimate scandal in their public writings, Fitch seems to relish it, keeping his writing "under seal for 30 years" once he was finished because he believed that the "warmth of the present age is so much in favour of the first officers of the Government whom I have so strenuously called in question . . . that I much fear that they [his writings] would be destroyed without ever giveing [sic] the world an opportunity of knowing in what manner I have been treated by them" (207–208).[15] Though Fitch recognizes his writings do not necessarily *fit* his moment, he believes that there will be a day when they will have won him the fleeting cultural significance that he had spent so many years chasing, and that his desire for such renown places his papers in archival precarity.

---

[15] Adams and Jefferson were not above disclosing the private foibles and faults of one another, however, during the heated political campaigns and transitions of the late 1790s. Yet even here, they stacked accusations and critique against one another *through* the mediation of others, with Jefferson's campaign accusing Adams of having a "hideous hermaphroditical character" and Adams's campaign replying in return that Jefferson was "a mean-spirited, low-lived fellow, the son of a half-breed Indian squaw, sired by a Virginia mulatto father."

Crafting a textual life, held in four manuscript books and preserved in the Library Company of Philadelphia, Fitch hungered after significance in the republic. He wanted to have his name remembered. He first began the manuscripts that have been assembled into his life writings in January 1790, writing "John Fitch His Book" at the top of the page and dedicating the contents of the book to "my children and future generations" (see Fig. 1.4).

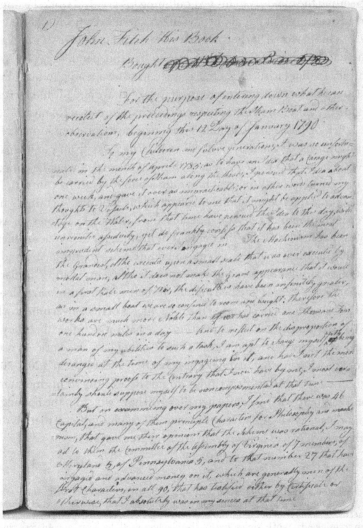

Figure 1.4 Opening page of John Fitch's first attempt to write down his side of the steamboat saga story. Courtesy of The Library Company of Philadelphia.

He seemed to feel that his writings would have a significance beyond himself, that they would be valuable for future consumption. "Men of forturne [sic]," Fitch writes, "generally think that they have a right to treat those in indigent Circumstances with imperiousness, and contempt, but should the indigent Citizen speak to them as his Equals, or with a dignified Tone, the contrast would be so great it would hardly be reconcilable" (191). The figure of the "indigent Citizen" who claims equality offers an aesthetic of revolutionary republican independence, asserting a mode of (white male) equality even as it articulates an irreconcilable formulation of class disparity.

Attending to these manuscript books, one can readily imagine Fitch reading and rereading his life narrative, as we see the punctuation in his hand yet in different colored ink. Words, paragraphs, and sentences are crossed out and altered; and page numbers added with directions to jump ahead or go back for further elaboration on a point that, in his hurried hand, quickly turned into an unfinished tangent (see Fig. 1.5).[16] The more recognizable figure who rose to prominence as a class-ascending eighteenth-century American with the form of a book, Benjamin Franklin, offered his written self as an abstractable equation for others desirous of such republican significance. But instead of authoring his own life for print, like Franklin (who knew that at least the majority of the manuscript would be circulated if not printed), Fitch understood his future textual reception would require others' aid. He asked future editors to clarify his prose so that he could be understood by future readers. From the material manuscript, we know he deliberated over words and phrases, making emendations, writing to the librarian who held his manuscripts: "as I am no grammarian I wish the whole of my works revised, but not altered in substance" (207—see also Fig. 1.6). Wanting his book to be edited "but not altered in substance," he imagined his textual body would be cleaned up in the proper prose of his period, which he understood as a prerequisite to becoming important to future readers. Being "no grammarian" should have been one of the least of his concerns, as

---

[16] His changes and alterations also illuminate an emerging sense of selfhood, where in one instance he describes helping his local community in Connecticut build a church and "being conscious altho' I was weak that I could do more than one half of the individuals did" (33). Having originally written "people" (which is crossed out in his hand) instead of "individuals," Fitch here signals a conscious shift to think about individuality as opposed to the collective "people." Separating himself from the other "individuals," Fitch continually makes such rhetorical gestures to emphasize his singular personality in contrast to a larger collective.

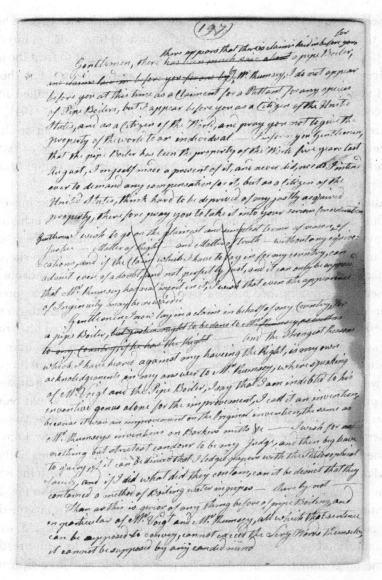

Figure 1.5 Page from volume 3 of John Fitch's life narrative to show his own revising and editing work. Courtesy of The Library Company of Philadelphia.

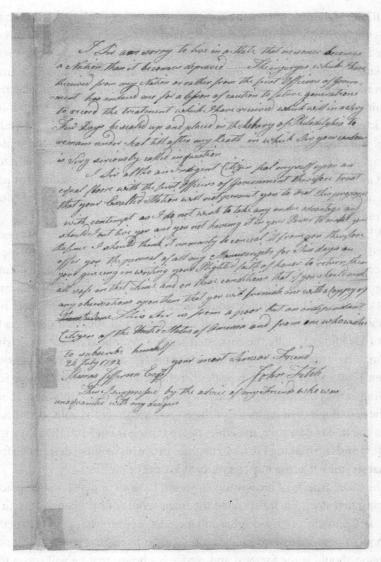

Figure 1.6 Image of the letter Fitch wrote to the librarian regarding how to protect his life narrative. Courtesy of The Library Company of Philadelphia.

42   FEELING SINGULAR

I will later elaborate, but it still expresses a sense of a social convention that he knowingly cannot rightly perform.[17] Matthew Garrett emphasizes this disparate relationship to textuality between Franklin and Fitch, writing that for the latter figure failure was "inscribed from the start, and the most dramatic *formal* contrast between the two memoirs is Franklin's ability to effectively manipulate the flow of his narrative, while Fitch never exceeds the paradigmatic failure of his youth" (75). Garrett focuses on the aesthetics of authorship, showing Franklin's success at crafting a narrative and Fitch's sense of being *crafted* by others' narratives. In this sense, Fitch's fraught desire to be read *as* a person like Franklin is located at the level of his manuscript pages that never circulate within his public as he had desired (contrary, of course, to Franklin's own textual Atlantic crossings).

What I want to make clear here is that Fitch desires to have his textual corpus made into a form that he knows he cannot achieve yet he still aspires to accomplish. Fitch felt certain that his narrative would be read by "future generations" within the conventions and forms of republican belonging (144). Believing his writings would certify his eventual significance, Fitch also wanted his writings to settle all the fictions and apparent untruths told about his life, especially the contested saga of steamboat invention. Writing the materials that have become known as his *Life* and *Steamboat History* between 1790 and 1792, Fitch repeatedly returned to the corpus of these texts, delving at the conclusion into the story of his falling out with Voigt. Though in the actual material manuscript these sections are not visibly cordoned off from the major narrative, the effect of separating them from the majority of the text ends up making Fitch's struggle to prove his original design of a functional steamboat as the most significant feature of his life.

The other aspects of his writing, however, have an underexamined place in shaping that story. Fitch deposited the manuscripts of his life narrative in the Library Company of Philadelphia and included a cover letter with instructions on how to proceed toward publication: "This is to request you that whenever a person should come forward and pledge his honor that he will revise them over and do them justice and spare no man however high in office but convey

---

[17] The norms of book history value retaining the very writing problems that Fitch wished to have eliminated. For instance, Frank D. Prager's 1976 edited and condensed volume of Fitch's four book manuscripts retains the mechanic's curious spellings and inserts periods instead of the dashes Fitch utilized. Ironically, then, Fitch's idiosyncratic prose has been preserved in print—instead of altered for clarity—as a way to testify to the historical authenticity of the text.

MEMORIALIZING THE REPUBLIC OF FAILURE 43

my ideas of them and give security for publishing one thousand coppies [sic]" (208). Desiring to have his written words emerge as a counterpoint to "the Commissioners of Congress" and other contemporary political leaders who he felt had spurned him, Fitch explains that he wished his writings would "be published in [the Commissioners'] lifetime that they may say all they can against but in such manner that it will not be in their power to destroy these works" (209).

Wishing to place his writings in what he assumes would be a hotly contested debate (believing that they would draw great ire, and potentially lead to their destruction), Fitch seeks to include himself, in textual form, into the public discourses from which he had been roundly rejected. After finishing his life narrative, he wrote a letter to a friend in 1794 that agonized over his sense of being publicly spurned: "however unpopular it may be at this time to do one justice, I am persuaded the time will come when it will not be thought disagreeable to be called my friend."[18] Imagining his life writings operating as a type of prosthetic of his self—a phantom speaking from the silent grave—Fitch places himself within the realm of cultural longevity associated with the writing of lives into books. Aspiring to the significance of one's life turned into a book, Fitch affirms his singularity even as he gestures at his dependence on "a person" who would "pledge his honor" to do right by his works. But unfortunately for Fitch, his textual life never emerged into the form he hoped it would, settling instead into the cultural register of an early national failure, printed not in its entirety and not corrected for the grammar mistakes that embarrassed him.

Previous scholarship has mainly read Fitch as a failure. Ric N. Caric suggests that Fitch "stretched the eighteenth century's culture of masculine performance up to and beyond its limits" (537–538).[19] For Caric, Fitch exemplifies the "failure of early modern culture" to accommodate new forms of agency (542). Positing Fitch as askew to his time, Caric portrays him as a transitional figure, one who presages coming modes of liberal identity that

[18] Library of Congress, Fitch Papers, Fitch to Thornton, Sept. 20, 1794. Qtd. in Andrea Sutcliffe, *Steam: The Untold Story of America's First Great Invention* (New York: Palgrave, 2004), 153.

[19] The title of Caric's essay, "To the Convivial Grave and Back: John Fitch as a Case Study in Cultural Failure, 1785–1792," demarcates Fitch as a failure from the start. Even the famed nineteenth-century historian Henry Adams in *The United States in 1800* describes Fitch in the language of failure: "No one denied that [Fitch's] boat was rapidly, steadily, and regularly moved against wind and tide, with as much certainty and convenience as could be expected in a first experiment," he writes, with his signature universalized nineteenth-century perspective; "yet Fitch's company failed. He could raise no more money; the public refused to use his boat or to help him build a better; they did not want it, would not believe in it, and broke his heart by their contempt. Fitch struggled against failure" (47).

44 FEELING SINGULAR

do not fit within republican discourse.[20] Historian Scott Sandage explains that during the Jacksonian era—the period that first resuscitated the memory of Fitch—"failure was so common that its refuse landed in myriad libraries, museums, and public archives," suggesting that this "paper trail" offers "the hidden history of pessimism in a culture of optimism" (9). Fitch's manuscript collection—particularly its printing in the very form that Fitch disproved of—is a monument to failure, eluding the aspiration and hopes its author entertained because it never broadly circulated within the timeframe he imagined.

1.2. The Body of John Fitch

In a way, then, the failure for Fitch to circulate his life narrative exemplifies the material barriers he experienced to win success with his steamboat. Near the end of his life narrative, Fitch laments how his interlocutor, "the Worthy Nathaniel Irwine of Neshaminey," lacks "the same thurst [sic] for honor and popularity" that would enable his audience to "do much greater things than ever George Fox or the greatest heroes of the World ever did" (140). Fitch wished to write himself into the forms of republican belonging, positioning himself as a model for others to follow. "[W]hen I take a view of my Past life," he writes in the opening manuscript of his life, "as singular as it is[,] I am sure if Deity is just . . . that I stand in no need of a midiator [sic] or of applying to his particular friends to interceed [sic] for me" (133). Refusing the logics of representation and mediation (even though he asks for such mediation in formalizing into print his manuscript books), Fitch declares himself to be unique, worthy even of having his own life narrative written and eventually printed. Contrary to Franklin, for whom "[t]he logic of his career," as Michael Warner notes, was "the logic of representation" (*The Letters* 96), Fitch affirms himself as the source of his own irreplaceable significance.[21]

---

[20] The context of Fitch's failure may be understood in relation to how Stephen Mihm describes "[s]elf-fashioning and self-advancement" as "a viable way of life for a growing number of white men" in the period after the Constitution (24). For Mihm, capitalism offered for some an advancement that positioned certain individuals into the mythos of republican belonging. But "in the increasingly freewheeling culture of capitalism in the new nation," Fitch fell victim to desiring validation from the federal structure that actually ensured his failure (61).

[21] Considering all the academic and scholarly ink that has been spilt endeavoring to determine if Franklin was serious or facetious when he clarified his thirteenth virtue ("HUMILITY: Imitate Jesus and Socrates"), I would like to think of Fitch as one who desired to showcase his own "singular" self. Where Franklin postures and produces a façade, Fitch imagines he can just be his own messy

Asserting that one stands out, or is a self-declared representative, in the early republic pushed one away from a set of relations that would otherwise secure the self within the confines of republican significance. The period sought to inculcate a sense of collective belonging that valorized the repression of individuality. William Huntting Howell explains that within American republicanism, "he who becomes more like all of the other republicans in working for harmonious improvement of the whole becomes properly himself; the subject grounded in the essentially republican ideals of imitation, iteration, and personal effacement works together with other like-minded subjects to create a new nation-state" (9). Deferral of interests and the abstraction of desire were the expected outcomes for the type of public service Fitch imagined for himself, though in his writings he expresses a sense of singularity and uniqueness that complicates such conceptions. Instead of effacing himself, then, Fitch felt himself singular, believing that he had a creative genius that the public should acknowledge and appreciate.

Upon learning of his death, Fitch's few remaining friends proposed disinterring his remains and removing them to Philadelphia's Laurel Hill Cemetery, where a monument to testify to the mechanic's desire to be remembered could be erected:

> His darling wish (he said) was to be buried
> On the margin of the Ohio;
> Where the song of the boatman might penetrate
> The stillness of his resting-place,
> And where the sound of the steam-engine
> Might send its echoes abroad.
> *Nihil mihi optatius accidere poterat.* (Westcott 371)

The text from this failed monument—a never-materialized witness to Fitch's failure to arrive at his fraught desire—suggests a melancholic affect that sympathetically represents the struggles of a poor mechanic against a larger collective. That configuration of Fitch is a quintessentially Jacksonian presentation of masculinity. Counterpoised to Franklin's youthful and self-written epitaph—"The Body of / B. Franklin . . . Like the Cover of an Old Book / . . .

---

self. In this sense, Fitch sets himself up as the masculine model that he wishes to reproduce. For more on Franklin's use of imitating, see William Huntting Howell, *Against Self-Reliance: The Arts of Dependence in the Early United States*, 21–28.

46 FEELING SINGULAR

Lies here, . . . / But the Work shall not be wholly lost: / For it will, as he believ'd, appear once more, / In a new & more perfect Edition"—Fitch seems far more anxious about his future's attenuated reception. Although, ironically, Franklin's wish was materialized through the printing and reprinting of his manuscripts into a book, Fitch could not even achieve his "darling wish" to have his remains settle near the Ohio River, much less to have his name proliferated as a famed inventor during his time. That the monument is never materialized demonstrates the production of Fitch as a recovered failure, unable to be rescued from the obscurity of a Kentucky burial for a contemplated memorial in Philadelphia.[22] Even the Latin—which roughly translates into "there is nothing more desirable to have happened to me"—places in the past tense a wish that remains unfulfilled.

Within the textual remnants of his life, Fitch portrays himself with an excessive sense of self-importance bordering on bathos. This becomes clearly evident in his somewhat humorous description of his birth, though the tone of this account remains ambiguously serious. Writing of "the fatal time of bringing me into existance [sic]," Fitch explains, "all nature seemed to schrink [sic] at the convulsed elliments [sic] which seemed to forebode the destiny of the innocent infant then makeing [sic] its way into existance [sic]" (21). Using grandiose language of "fatal time" and "destiny," Fitch positions himself as significant, whose birth caused "convulsed elliments" marking his entrance into the world that he believed did not want him.[23] From the moment of his birth, Fitch suggests, he was destined to have to struggle through life. Wishing to win the sympathy of his reading audience, Fitch conveys the sense of a grand opening to his life tinged with a fateful struggle that loomed before him with an uncertain promise: that is to say, Fitch really wants to seem important even if he has to manufacture a sense of foreboding that accompanied his birth. His fatalistic representation

---

[22] Interestingly, Fitch's body was disinterred in 1927 and reburied in the center of town in Bardstown, Kentucky, with a large plaque demarcating his burial. On that plaque, erected in compliance to a 1926 act of Congress, Fitch is remembered as a "SOLDIER AND INVENTOR." This rendering of Fitch as a patriotic subject who "REAPED NEITHER PROFIT NOR GLORY FROM HIS INVENTIONS" demonstrates the ways the recovery of seemingly forgotten or neglected white men in the early republic rely on resituating anachronistic norms regarding an individual's own sense of patriotism, as Fitch would certainly take issue at his portrayal as a right-feeling subject of the U.S. nation-state.

[23] Considering Fitch's fraught relation to the concept of gender, the absent figure of his mother in the act of birth—which he seems either to deny or to index euphemistically through the phrase "convulsed elliments" during his birth—seems significant. He would have known very little of his mother prior to her own death when he was four. His father remarried, and in his life narrative Fitch expresses far more affection for his stepmother than his father, the latter being a prominent object of his resentment.

MEMORIALIZING THE REPUBLIC OF FAILURE   47

of his life's opening seems tied to his sense of cultural significance. Fitch builds from this fantastical beginning to explain that "the singularity of my make[,] shape[,] disposition[,] and fortune in this world" had been determined by being "born on the very line and not in any township whatever" (22). Once again appealing to a larger construction of meaning that confers him with significance, Fitch puts the imaginary lines on which he was born as typologically meaningful. Although Fitch claims the ability to narrate the moment of his birth, he notes that many things about his birth he could not "recollect . . . at present" (21). Representing the "convulsed" world that foretold his birth, while also gesturing at the limits to his presumed memory, Fitch creates himself as an exceptional individual from the outset of his life narrative.[24]

Fitch's presumed exceptionality highlights an important shift in the emergence of history understood as being tethered to individual effort. Fitch projects a sense of history that is produced through the intentional work of individuals, fashioning himself into a would-be shaper of history. Imagining individuals (as opposed to "Providence") as shapers of history, Fitch believes his narrative can shape the course of history, writing on the seal to his book manuscripts that "should Mr. [Thomas] Jefferson ever be aiming toward the presidents [sic] chair" that he wishes "by all means to obtain leave to breake the seals and extract what affects the Commissioners of Congress and then seal them again." (208). "Nay Sir," he continues:

> I wish it done to all the scounderals [sic] that is stepping forward for more favours from their country. I mean Lewis Clymer Fitzsimmons McKain Rush &c &c and if Robertson had been more worth notice I should have mentioned his name. I wish them to be published in their lifetime that they may say all they can against but in such a manner that it will not be in their power to destroy these works. And I think when the governour and managers know that this is my desire that there will be no scruples of breakeing the seals. (208–209)

---

[24] Fitch's supposed remembering of the scene of his birth has a precedent in eighteenth-century literary culture, from the opening of Laurence Sterne's *The Life and Opinions of Tristram Shandy* to "It" narratives that personified inanimate objects with entire biographies. One could imagine, in fact, Fitch trying to write himself with these novelistic genres in mind, though I have uncovered no evidence that Fitch read fiction. Fitch writes fondly of reading "Salmons Geography" as an eleven-year-old after purchasing the book from the money he earned through cultivating "protatoes" [sic] (26).

48 FEELING SINGULAR

Asserting the potency and eventual efficacy of his desire, Fitch imagines that his textual corpus could topple the great names of the republic. Additionally, he worries about the specious precarity of his own manuscripts, which could just as easily be answered by Benjamin Rush or Thomas Fitzsimmons by tossing the entirety into a fire. The language of "this is my desire" objectifies the motivating object of his attachment and turns desire itself into a protective possession, one that he believes will safeguard the manuscripts from destruction. In this way, the expression of his desire—and its textual representation—stages Fitch as inside the cultural forms he wishes to court: he feels he has access to recognition and cultural significance, able to participate within such realms of possibility. As such, Fitch's attempts to make legible his desires highlight the particularity of his efforts to emerge into significance, placing himself on the stage of the period's history-makers. Indeed, Arch argues that Fitch invents "himself as distinct, original, and singular" in ways that illustrate a view of history as "radical and revolutionary... mov[ing] by leaps and bounds, by discontinuous alterations" (170).

1.3. Feeling Singular and the Dawn of Dependence

The independent self is a myth, of course—a fiction within language that buttresses very specific ideological content.[25] Gilles Deleuze and Félix Guattari write that "the self is only a threshold, a door, a becoming between two multiplicities" (*A Thousand Plateaus* 275). If the self is a type of fiction, a faux construction of coherence, its emergence as a historical category tethered to subjectivity does specific cultural work. The rise of the United States as a governing apparatus promoted the consumption of specific biographies—or the writings of singular lives—that offered the figment of narrative coherence through the grammatical fiction "self-made." Ethan Allen, Daniel Boone, and Israel Putnam, among others, coalesce around their imagined resources of the self that could extricate them from challenging circumstances—or, more often than not, lead them full-on into problems out of which they can then produce their own apparent skill of extraction. The haphazard biography

---

[25] G. Thomas Couser in his study of autobiography writes insightfully on the significance of the first-person pronoun in creating an ideology of selfhood: "In English the pronoun that signifies the self is triply singular: in number, in capitalization, and in being the sole single-letter pronoun. Typographically identical with the Roman numeral *I* and phonemically identical with the word *eye*, it puns on the notion of a single point of view" (13).

MEMORIALIZING THE REPUBLIC OF FAILURE 49

industry that emerged in the decades after the Constitution's ratification fed a desire within readers to become affectively oriented to the production of the United States, appealing to what Noah Webster describes as his desire "to call home the minds of youth and fix them upon the interests of their country, and... assist in forming attachments to it" (*A Collection of Essays and Fugitive Writings* 23).[26] Stories of "those illustrious heroes and statesmen, who have wrought a revolution" should be rehearsed, Webster affirms, early and often, to inspire affective attachments to the state. But simultaneously, this effort to produce and consume individualizing accounts ends up valorizing names over relations, events over contexts, affirming the figuration of a self as a coherent and contained object even as a "nation" gets imagined as sovereign and specific.[27]

In many ways, then, Fitch is very much a product of this historical moment on the eastern seaboard of North America, where individuality began to shift toward valorizing uniqueness as a public good. Fitch desired to cohere into a discernible self, which he put forward in his book manuscript, tethering his desires to be a rights-bearing subject with the figment of his imagined intellectual property. Although Fitch's insistence on individualism resonates with contemporary cultural myths regarding American masculine independence and self-reliance, his particular mode of emphasizing himself as an agent actually places him outside emerging norms in the early United States. As Koenraad W. Swart and Barry Alan Shain have argued, individualistic tendencies were believed to provide a "disintegrating force in society," disrupting the ideals of balance, disinterestedness, and selfless service (Swart 82).[28] Shain asserts that early national "Americans awarded the public's needs preeminence over the immediate ones of discrete individuals" (3). In these narrative fantasies about how "the common or public good enjoyed preeminence over the immediate interests of individuals" (3), we might see how

[26] See also Scott E. Casper's magisterial *Constructing American Lives: Biography and Culture in Nineteenth-Century America* for a thoroughgoing review of the production of biography and the ideological content behind their circulations. Casper explains that such accounts of "[l]ives of American worthies invariably espoused republican simplicity and devotion to the nation" (37).

[27] An important example of this might be Israel Putnam's narrative, which was first made accessible in print through David Humphreys's *An Essay on the Life of the Honorable Major General Israel Putnam* (1788). In this account—and the subsequent versions—the embellished story of Putnam's hunting of a wolf that had killed many of his Connecticut village's sheep, offers an example of the headlong masculinity then emerging as a norm.

[28] Swart explains that the mid-nineteenth century saw the emergence of "individualism" as a cultural value. The term was coined, he notes, "to designate the disintegration of society, which many conservatives believed had resulted from the French Revolution and the doctrine of the individual rights of man" (78).

50 FEELING SINGULAR

an ideology of selflessness obscures the inclusion of certain individuals, like Fitch, who messily announce their insistence to participate. In this sense, one's personal merit, as defined by the new republican governing structure, required an orientation toward solidifying the conceived public's interest.[29] Fitch's "personal merit," as defined by these republican models of cultural value, was always being contested, despite how he asserts in his personal writings that his steamboat would be of utmost importance to the fledging nation, lamenting the "strange Ideas I had . . . of serving my country, without the least suspicion that my only reward would be nothing but contempt and opprobrious names" (151). Fitch, as an individual, emerges in later accounts as being noticeable only as an insignificant, even trivial subject, marked by personal failure and spurned by the very ones who worked to construct the ideals that both attracted and excluded him. Indeed, republican ideology asserts that there should be no ostensible reward for public service other than the production of publicness itself. Hoping to attract the notice and attention of government leaders, Fitch instead experienced the shame of being blocked and barred, marked as being outside the very governing system from which he sought recognition of his singularity.

Fitch cobbled together state-sanctioned patent rights through journeying from state to state while the Articles of Confederation loosely organized the former colonies together. He lost the financial backing that he had worked so tirelessly to obtain when the Constitution consolidated patents and intellectual property rights under federal jurisdiction.[30] In many ways, Fitch misrecognizes the actual functions of state power, believing that his state patents from the governors and presidents of several mid-Atlantic states

---

[29] Welsh minister and nonconformist Richard Price tapped into an emerging cultural mythos when he wrote in his *Observations on the Importance of the American Revolution* (1785) that the Americans set "personal merit" over and above older, courtly models of validation, contributing to an up-from-your bootstraps mentality in relation to American men and commerce (70). Although individuals in both North America and Europe praised how "the articles of confederation . . . order[ed] that no titles of nobility shall be granted by the united States" (Price 71), the cultures of inheritance, class difference, and social deference continued to shape and structure the lives of individuals like Fitch, particularly those who desired to produce themselves as agents of possible social restructuring and development.

[30] Doron S. Ben-Atar in *Trade Secrets: Intellectual Piracy and the Origins of American Industrial Power* (2002) analyzes the relationship between state rights under the Articles and the Constitution's representation of a federal system. He notes: "State governments awarded monopolies, granted bounties, exempted from taxation, and handed out cash gifts to attract skilled artisans to settle in their midst. . . . While states increasingly erected a system to grant and regulate patents, the shortcomings of the system were readily apparent. . . . Inventors and introducers who wanted to ensure continued exclusivity over machinery had to file for patents in each and every state" (132). Ben-Atar also explains that "[i]n the early national republican imagination, patents remain associated with the antirepublican idea of monopoly" (192).

MEMORIALIZING THE REPUBLIC OF FAILURE 51

could function as a supreme law. Before a national market existed, and years before federalism centralized the patenting process under the Constitution, he courted the patronage from specific individuals he believed were in power. He affirms the sovereignty of state(s) power even as he demands their recognition of his presumed rights. "I have expended my time and money to a very large amount," he writes in a 1788 newspaper letter about his frustration with the ratification of the Constitution, noting that he put "full faith of the law . . . , and with as much confidence as a man would build a house on a lot he had bought from the public." [31] As he decries: "When *my* right is destroyed, the right of such purchases may well tremble—a fatal precedent would it be!"[32] Deploying the language of rights to assert what he sees as a federal apparatus disintegrating his claims to property, Fitch came even to claim that his supposed loss of rights parallels the loss of rights incurred when, in recent Pennsylvania memory, "a large number of men [of color] who were in actual possession of freedom, and mixed into the common mass of freemen, would have been selected out and made slaves." This important slippage of rights-based rhetoric—tied to a subject's relation to state power—and the abstraction of race as a category that presupposes only certain bodies have access to full citizenship, emerges here in Fitch's contestation over his supposed lost intellectual property rights. Problematically, he conflates his loss of patent rights to the loss of liberty borne by re-enslaved freemen.

Literary historians of the early United States have asserted, through their use of the vexed terminology "early republic," that dispassion and self-lessness cohered in, and uniformly assisted the livelihood of white men. Drawing upon scholars of the republican synthesis, like Bernard Bailyn, Gordon Wood, and J. G. A. Pocock, these literary historians articulate an

[31] Fitch registers the economic straits of the years following the Revolution, particularly the transition from the Articles of Confederation to the Constitution. Although most historians emphasize the dysfunction of the Articles under which Fitch and other entrepreneurs and mechanics operated—with Herbert Aptheker asserting that his historian colleagues have described "the period of the Confederation [as] . . . an era of unmitigated failure" (17)—in Fitch's case the Articles actually provided a workable model for him to feel his way toward cultural achievement, allowing him to build individual relationships with state authorities, such as Patrick Henry, who validated his claims to inventive originality. Henry, the then-governor of Virginia, offered Fitch a certificate "conditioned for executeing [sic] his Steam Boat" (158). For more on how historians see the Articles of Confederation as tantamount to a failure to be fixed through the coming Constitution, see Kathleen DuVal, *Independence Lost: Lives on the Edge of the American Revolution* (2015), who writes: "The failings of the Articles of Confederation are well known, yet it is important to remember that they were in operation for over a decade" (294–295). This sense of the well-known and uncontested status of the failed Articles effaces Fitch's story, as Fitch actually succeeded at his steamboat ventures *until* the Constitution solidified the conceptual structure of national federalism.

[32] See John Fitch, "Mr. Oswald," *Independent Gazetteer* (Sept. 11, 1788), 3.

52 FEELING SINGULAR

early national U.S. politics that fostered an ideological environment of self-less, gentlemanly disinterestedness.[33] The very terminology of "early" and "republic" presupposes not only an eventual *fall* into individualistic competition but that a coherent collective at one moment viably emerged.[34] Similarly seeking to locate a way to discuss consensus and collective identification, Edward Cahill argues that the "definitive republican conflict between the interests of the individual and those of the collective" became resolved through representing "the federal union as an object of pleasurable perception" (149). Uniting individuals through their relation to admiring the beauty and potentiality of collectivity, Cahill argues that the conflicts of, and resistances toward, federalism became resolved through the aesthetics of contemplation and abstraction. Considering the eventual celebration of Fitch in the mid-nineteenth century, one can see why the figure of a disgruntled white man would rally other poor, un-propertied white men to lobby for a transformation to republican belonging, though of course such change fell along racial and gender lines that continued to subject women and people of color to the outsides. Following what Elizabeth Maddock Dillon has provocatively called "the fiction of liberalism," we might re-envision the mishmash and uneven narrative of individualism in a period that traditionally has been read as valorizing collective identification, and perhaps then observe how the fantasy of republican coherence seeks to efface its own negative consequences (15).[35]

Within this context, it may seem easy to place Fitch outside the orbit of an early national U.S. culture that is an ostensible republic, especially

[33] An important corrective to the myth of a classless and virtuously republican early national United States is Billy Smith's edited volume *Down and Out in Early America*, which makes several pointed critiques at Gordon Wood's assertion of a halcyon early American equality: "American historians are not immune to such myths," Simon Newman writes in his contribution: " 'Poverty and economic deprivation,' contends Gordon Wood in his magisterial study of the American Revolution, 'were not present' in the colonies that became the United States. The historians whose research Wood ignored pointed out the absurdity of his remark, but one can only wonder what the poor of revolutionary and early national America would have made of a historian who claimed that they did not exist and that their experience of insufficient food, fuel, clothing, and shelter was impossible" (41–42). See also Newman's *Embodied History: The Lives of the Poor in Early Philadelphia*.

[34] The languages of republicanism and liberalism have long structured studies of early American literature, informing the type of power structures that critics seek to illustrate. For Bruce Burgett, "liberalism responds to the question of self-government by grounding political authority in the representative and legislative apparatuses of the nation-state . . . [whereas r]epublicanism . . . grounds political authority in public-sphere institutions located outside of the state apparatus" (20–21).

[35] In *The Gender of Freedom*, Elizabeth Maddock Dillon describes "the public sphere as governed by desire—by the desire of subjects to emerge into the space of subjectivity or social recognition" (6). Contrary to the Habermasian public constituted through rational critical debate, Dillon argues that the very possibility for such a public relied on the subjugation of differently situated individuals who had no access to the privileges of such a forum.

MEMORIALIZING THE REPUBLIC OF FAILURE 53

to the extent that he calls himself "one of the most singular men perhaps that has been born this age" (22).[36] He already asserts a sense of self-hood that locates him outside the parameters of a uniform collectivity that would consolidate around a republic. Rather than play the appropriate game of selfless institution-building and disinterested economic advancement, he calls things in the capitalist terms of advancement that make him *seem* unfit within the historiography of the U.S. "early" republic. He is the symptom of the putative republic's very failure to ever be what it espoused. According to Arch, Fitch offers what may seem like nascent manifestations of liberalized subjectivity in the new nation, attached to conceptions of individuality that are in conflict with the period's valorizations of selfless collectivity. This way of thinking of the entangled and competing forms of governing ideologies usefully orients the shifting worlds of John Fitch, where he becomes too liberally inflected in declaring his inventive genius in a period that tried to enhance the value of collective identification. Whereas Fitch aspires for recognition from various states in his several patents—hoping to have his individual rights validated through multiple sites of identification—he performs himself in the public in such a way that he appears unrestrained, even excessive. Instead of seeming beholden to the conventions and forms of republican representation, Fitch instead actively promotes his own economic interests by calling them the public good.

1.4. Courting Empire

Such accounts of the relationship between individuality and public good inform the ideological foundations of U.S. empire. The feigned abjection of

---

[36] Teresa Goddu situates the shifting ideologies of the early republic through a reading of individuality and republican virtue. Reflecting on how the individual fits within a republican market ideology, Goddu explains that "[t]he self-regulating individual operating in the market would naturally stimulate a harmony of interests beneficial to all. Self-interest would lead to the public good; individual freedom would generate prosperity. If the market had a moral base in the individual, then, it would operate by the law of virtue." (41). The individual, for Goddu, gets read as both the harbinger and placeholder of republican virtue, grounding the pursuit of self-interest as the lynchpin that propels the nation's collective (and here positivist) forward motion. For Goddu, early national individuality works insofar as that individual inhabits a series of norms and expectations to produce an ideal republican. Following Goddu's sense of the tension between general and particular formations, the delicate balance between individual desire and collective good foregrounds the complicated series of attachments that kept certain unruly individuals in check (namely, Fitch) while allowing others to hide their private interests under the banner of public good.

54 FEELING SINGULAR

self-interest (in the name of aspiring toward some abstract "good") belies and abstracts how Fitch invoked the rhetoric of republicanism to obscure how his steamboat would help the expansion of settler colonialism in what is now Kentucky. Scholars in Native, ethnic, and critical race studies, such as Frederick Hoxie, Theda Perdue, and Ronald Takaki, have pointed out the way the rhetoric of U.S. republicanism was merely a lexicon for imperial expansion: that is to say, there was never some halcyon moment of disinterested virtue that governed the early United States, but instead the intensification of incursions on sovereign territory and the expansion of chattel slavery through the rhetoric of virtue.[37] As Andy Doolen succinctly observes, "viewing the American past through the lens of republicanism produces a series of omissions around the subject of empire" (*Fugitive Empire* 187). But there's also a way of considering how early Americans fashioned the rhetoric of republicanism as their own projection to cover the motivating impulse they sought to obscure.

In this way, the establishment's resounding rejection of Fitch is more about him and less about his idea. When we think of Fitch's steamboat as a mechanical contraption that he and his contemporaries imagined could tether together disparate economies under the guise of an expanding network of propertied white men, we see how his blockage from directly benefiting from this economy stymied *his* participation in U.S. economic imperialism. The republican method of reorganizing an empire under the guise of capitalist individualism continued steaming on into the nineteenth century. In a strange letter draft, written to Congress in 1785 though also addressed to "our infant Empire," Fitch declares his dissatisfaction with how his contemporaries have "such a strange infatuation . . . that it seems they would rather lay out their money in Baloons [sic] and Fireworks, and be a pest to society, than to lay it out in something that would be of use to themselves and Country" (4.25). Here he asserts that he is the properly disinterested subject who can remain above the flash of fireworks and the hot air of balloons. Claiming that even if his company

---

[37] Ed White considers how the historians who are republican synthesizers emphasized a specifically urban worldview that inflected how they imagined the myth of consolidation: "Because the original synthesis pledged its methodological allegiance to the Founding Federalists and their project of ordering and organizing the masses, even the most finely nuanced extension of the synthesizing project will carry with it a commitment to the federalist view of the unruly back populations. Republicanism remains the purview of the urban intellectual, the theorist, and the writer, who give signification for those who messily live it" (*The Backcountry and the City* 13).

MEMORIALIZING THE REPUBLIC OF FAILURE 55

should miscary in our Boat, we make something worth our money, and introduce a most Useful Art into our Nation, and bring one of the first powers in nature *into the service of our Empire*, without sending our money too, or being beholden to foreign nation [emphasis added]

Fitch's optimism for his steamboat, which he poignantly named "The Perseverance," led him to lambast a society that did not value the work he sees himself as poised to accomplish. Here Fitch postures himself as selflessly offering "a most Useful Art" that he envisions will participate in the economic advancement of "our Empire" through his own efforts. His problem, I will argue, is that his desires to escape his failure illustrate his self-advancement through the production of an object that would "bring one of the first powers in nature into the service of our Empire"—in other words, he is thinking of empire in ways that he, as a poor mechanic, is not supposed to have access, articulating expansive imperial opportunities that the ostensible republic would disavow (even as it begins to consolidate around others).

The arbiters of cultural significance in the early United States certainly showed interest in finding a figure like Fitch who could stabilize their project of expansion. This can be seen in the figure of Daniel Boone, and his excursions into Kentucky, which offer an important context for thinking of Fitch's aspirations to facilitate U.S. expansion, especially in the context of the first printed book (by John Filson) that presented Boone as a figure to normalize American expansion. Although Boone becomes read as a forerunner—literally, a pioneer—in the shifting boundaries of U.S. territory in the late eighteenth century (in ways to which Fitch aspired after), the cultural production of Boone as such a hero belatedly emerges in the nineteenth century.[38] Critics like Richard Slotkin have described Boone's leap "into the American imagination" through the work of others who produced stories about him (66). As I highlight in the introduction to *Feeling Singular*, such figures cannot *write* themselves into the position to which they desire to be assigned, but instead they must perform a faux passivity qualifying them for a national inscription into the structures of republicanism. In Boone's case, he first obtained textual celebrity through John Filson's *The Discovery, Settlement and Present State of Kentucke* (1784), which included a narrative of

---

[38] Historian Honor Sachs explains how "we traditionally think about imperial or national politics as emerging from state officials and city centers," though through examining "those settlers, traders, hunters, and missionaries who operated on the frontiers, backcountries, or borders of territories" we might see a fuller history of "the course of empires and nation-states than governing officials" (9).

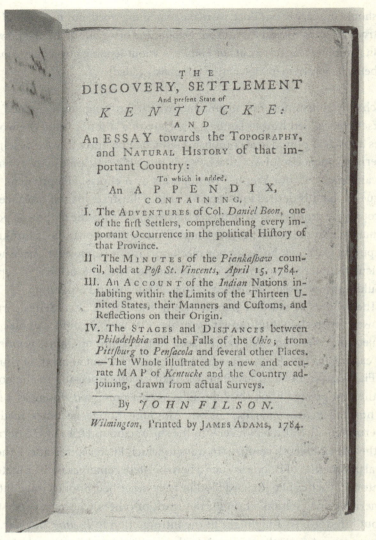

Figure 1.7 Title page of John Filson's *The Discovery, Settlement and Present State of Kentucke*, first published in Wilmington in 1784. Courtesy of the American Antiquarian Society.

the pioneer's life (see Fig. 1.7). Filson accompanied his book with the most-up-to-date map of the area, offering a lexicon of on-the-ground information for settlers both along the Ohio River and into the hills of Kentucky, and then included distances between various cities to the middle of Kentucky (see

MEMORIALIZING THE REPUBLIC OF FAILURE 57

Figure 1.8 Foldout map from John Filson's book on Kentucky. "This map of Kentucke: drawn from actual observations, is inscribed with the most perfect respect, to the honorable congress of the United States of America, and to His Excell'cy George Washington, late commander in chief of their army" (Philadelphia: H.D. Pursell, 1784). Courtesy of the Library of Congress.

Fig. 1.8). To build the book's ethos, the names of Daniel Boone, Levi Todd, and James Harrod are on the bottom of the subscribers' page, noting that they "recommend [the accompanying book and map] to the public, as exceeding good performances, containing as accurate a description of our country as we think can possibly be given; much preferable to any in our knowledge extant; and think it will be of great utility to the publick" (3). This gesture to state the "utility" for "the publick" positions the expansion of white settlers

58   FEELING SINGULAR

into rhetorically charted territory as productive to constituting the public good, which explicitly refutes the decision of 1763 that had acknowledged the sovereignty of Indigenous nations west of the Appalachian Mountains. Contrary to these prior designations, Filson asserts that "a proper description, and map of [Kentucky], were objects highly interesting to the United States" (5). That interest comes from the speculating capacity to make rich through the selling of claimed land, which embroiled the area in a sea of subsequent lawsuits, as Americans at the conclusion of the 1783 treaty began aspiring for small fortunes through "speculating in land" (Faragher 3).

The significance of the very name *Kentucky*, which some consider to be a Haudenosaunee word for "land of tomorrow," overlaps with Filson's project of preparing the area to become demarcated as part of the United States. While the territory was not a state of the union until 1792, the slippage of the word "*State*" in the title comes to gesture toward how the U.S. nation-state builds its imperial network through the stabilizing of spaces *into* states, in the material sense of that word. The book's title implies that this area is a stabilized *state*, ready for the incorporation within the federal apparatus to recognize its independence *within* the union. Filson describes the specific relationship then securing Kentucky to the United States as through its relation to Virginia. This depiction is colonial in nature, as Filson describes the area "[a]s yet united to the State of Virginia" whereby these displaced citizens of the Old Dominion "are governed by her wholesome laws, which are virtuously executed, and with excellent decorum" (29). With the area called Kentucke operating under a colonial relation to Virginia, Filson's prolepsis—marking Kentucky as a "state" prior to its official designation as such—obscures the violence that presages such incorporation. Kentucky is made to appear an inevitable state of the United States, and the temporary law of Virginia merely the stepping stone for an eventual incorporation into the union.[39]

The fact that Filson wished to write a book about Kentucky in the 1780s speaks to the emerging fascination this land fostered in the cultural imaginary of the nascent United States. An unmarried schoolteacher, Filson seemed to have a desire for both new experiences and to benefit financially

---

[39] My thinking along these terms of the settler colonial construction of the inevitability of statehood has benefited from the keen thinking of Kathryn Walkiewicz, whose book on Indigenous and Black activisms concerning the question of statehood versus territory has enabled me to recognize these specific dynamics. See *Reading Territory: Indigenous and Black Freedom, Removal, and the Nineteenth-Century State* (2023).

from them. Many scholars note that the book was a type of literary invest-ment in land speculation, much like Gilbert Imlay's later 1793 book (which subsequently offered a republication of Filson's). Filson's book was ini-tially published in Wilmington, translated into French and published in Paris in 1785, and New York in 1793, with later editions appearing out of Philadelphia. Similar to Fitch's own class-ascendancy aspirations, Filson ded-icated his book to George Washington, who declined the honor to subscribe for a second edition. Historians James A. Ramage and Andrea S. Watkins describe the importance of the text in motivating settlers to infiltrate the land called Kentucke, writing that Filson "sought to encourage settlement to cap-italize on his investment" (203). They offer the unsubstantiated claim that many of the settlers—mostly from the neighboring states of North Carolina and Virginia but, like Filson, also Pennsylvania—"had a copy of Filson's book and a copy of his map" (203). Although this cultural fantasy tells us perhaps more about our imaginations of the period than the period itself, especially because Filson wasn't able to secure a second issue of the book while living, the image of settlers arriving to the west of the Appalachia, with book in hand, dramatically enacts the process of settler colonial incursion as an Enlightenment project. The book, as a totem, offers a template for how to interact with the land, and it maps out the resources that could be used for exploitation.[40] In the last section of the Appendix, Filson includes de-tailed mileage information that could allow settlers to track their travel from Philadelphia to the Falls of Ohio (826 miles), from Philadelphia to Pittsburgh (320 miles), and from Pittsburg to the "Mexican Gulph" (1,935 miles). These distances track daily travel in making knowable the route for individuals to imagine their own travel. Most importantly, these tables render knowable the space outside the North American continental seaboard, and the mileage links the familiar urban to the less familiar rural. Similar to Jefferson's *Notes on the State of Virginia*—the first version of which was completed in 1781, enlarging it two years after that—Filson's *The Discovery* presents itself as a legitimizing force to impel future inhabitants of the space to make use of the land as they desire, and it connects the space and resources to Enlightenment world-mappings.

---

[40] Filson is recorded to have had brought with him a copy of a religious and moral book, *Admonitions from the Dead*, which suggests his enthusiasm for a very specific type of reading, one that would belie the myth of the rough-and-tumble settler. Indeed, such letters as "On the Vanity and Danger of accumulating Wealth" portray the need to regulate one's desires, avoiding the forces that would unhinge them.

60 FEELING SINGULAR

This wish to make of Kentucky a desirable economic venture becomes pronounced in the last section of the opening piece, where the author outlines the "Trade of Kentucke" (38). The section opens with a classic eighteenth-century aphorism regarding the construction of civilization as a product of commerce, noting: "A CONVENIENT situation for commerce is the grand hinge upon which the population, riches and happiness of every country greatly depends. I believe many conceive the situation of Kentucke to be unfavourable in this respect" (38). Filson has to work against this presumption, that the space is "unfavourable" to the increase in population that white settlement avows. Working against natural historians like Buffon and others who would question the viability of reproductive life outside the confines of white sociality, Filson here stresses a euphemism between the ease at which commerce is situated and its reproductive capacity for population. In an illustration he drew of himself in the frontispiece of a favorite book, he appears with a high, shiny forehead, cavernous eyes, and a skeletal nose, resembling perhaps the future literary schoolmaster of Sleepy Hollow, Ichabod Crane (see Fig. 1.9 for a reproduction). As a bachelor, Filson appears to be an odd, queer figure calling for such desires for reproductive settlement, made even stranger by a farewell poem that he, according to book historian Rueben T. Durrett, wrote about his refusal for domestic formations and desire for death:

> Adieu ye limpid streams and cooling shades,
> Adieu ye groves, ye meadows, fields and meads,
> Adieu to all this scene and yon green bowers,
> Adieu to sweets and all this field of flowers; (77)

Eighteen lines begin with "Adieu," following the structure of heroic couplets, advancing a repetitive sense of goodbye that stumbles to a close. The white encroachment on land in Kentucky invites a type of goodbye, where individuals are tasked with the implicit obligation to justify their decision to turn from their social belonging and make contested claims to lands. In this unremarkable poem, the speaker jumps to his death to "forget the pains of love" (78). Repetitively severing ties with sociality, the poem offers a dissatisfying presentation of dissatisfaction, perhaps not dissimilar with Rei Terada's sense of queerness as the rupture that suggests "the given world could and should be otherwise" (8). The poem, then, becomes a strange monument to the failed production of lasting attachments, with the subject determining instead to cast himself "in yonder gulf" to "end my pain" (78).

Figure 1.9 Self-portrait that, according to book historian Rueben T. Durrett, John Filson purportedly drew of himself in the front cover of the book *Admonitions from the Dead in Epistles to the Living* (1754), which he carried with him on his journeys to the Ohio River Valley. Image from Reuben T. Durrett's *John Filson, the First Historian of Kentucky* (Louisville, KY: 1884), 132. Courtesy of the American Antiquarian Society.

62   FEELING SINGULAR

Even as Filson walks off the stage, he figuratively prepared the way for what became a veritable culture industry around Daniel Boone. Filson includes Boone's "adventures," which he calls "curious and interesting, and therefore have published them from his own mouth" (6). Of course, the narrative draws more upon Filson's own voice, and indeed the Boone who emerges appears as a conventionalized figure of abstraction. It is almost like the accident of Filson including Boone's narrative—as opposed to one of many others—prepares for the cultural obsession with the figure. "Curiosity is natural to the soul of man," Filson-as-Boone begins, "and interesting objects have a powerful influence on our affections" (49). This opening abstraction claims that the motivating factor impelling Boone to leave sociality is the pull of curiosity, which, he argues, emerges from "the permission or disposal of Providence, from selfish or social views, yet in time the mysterious will of Heaven is unfolded, and we behold our conduct, from whatsoever motives excited, operating to answer the important designs of heaven" (49). Contending that his own personal feelings come to substantiate a higher cause—that of deifying his desires into a prosthetic function of "the important designs of heaven"— he implies that the settlement of Kentucky also operates toward this higher aim. This is how both Filson, Fitch, and Boone come to facilitate the function of U.S. empire, through catering to a republican language of deference even as they are seeking personal advancement.

For Filson, Boone serves a very specific purpose in substantiating his "history," which is to vouchsafe his land speculations in Kentucky. With the accompanying introduction of Daniel Boone as a singular subject, through the inclusion of his first narrative (written by Filson, though rendered as a transcription in the narrative's framing), the narrative offers a way to think about the construction of white male masculinity that produces settlement outside the established parameters of the eastern seaboard. To this end, this text also endorses the fantasy of refusing what gets considered the worldliness of self-advancement, as Boone, after having escaped initial Indian captivity, explains to his brother:

> You see now how little nature requires to be satisfied. Felicity, the companion of content, is rather found in our own breasts than in the enjoyment of external things; And I firmly believe it requires but little philosophy to make a man happy in whatsoever state he is. This consists in a full resignation to the will of Providence; and a resigned soul finds pleasure in a path strewed with briars and thorns. (53–54)

MEMORIALIZING THE REPUBLIC OF FAILURE   63

This passage draws upon classic eighteenth-century fantasies of redemptive stoicism—that contentment is the antidote for a society that corrupts. Boone represses the very desire of economic expansion that he comes to signify for later generations. Whereas Filson ends in unmarked death, Boone—as the subsequent product of his extrapolated narrative—emerges as a singular commodity of American consumption, one that fashions the ideology of republican empire that informs and justifies expansion to itself.

Filson's book itself functions as a charade, operating more as an advertisement for Kentucky settlement than an unbiased "Essay" or a disinterested articulation of, as its title page declares, "the Topography, and Natural History of that important Country" (1). There is a disjuncture in the book's declared intentions and the operations of the actual content. The late nineteenth-century book historian and antiquarian Rueben T. Durrett describes Filson's book as "a quaint leather-bound octavo of one hundred and eighteen pages," arguing that the "title-page [is] . . . quite out of proportion to the matter which followed. It reminded one of a huge portico in front of a small house, or a great door leading into a diminutive apartment" (28–29). For Durrett, the book's prefatory material outshines its material content, functioning as a cumbersome entryway to the packaged ideology of Kentucky settlement, producing the fantasy of a large entry way even as the content appears meager. The book recalls to the mind a massive porch that invites, but in inviting tries to obscure the "diminutive apartment" that is the interior. The book manufactures its own constructed worth through an excessive "APPENDIX" that overwhelms the rest of the book, making that digestive supplement far outweigh the rest of the book, as if Filson may have begun with one idea but the project ballooned to encompass more and more.[41]

---

[41] Filson determines to "close the appendix" with a conclusion that philosophizes regarding the "four natural qualities necessary to promote the happiness of a country," which he elaborates as "good soil, air, water and trade" (107). He asserts that Kentucky has all but the latter, only because it is "situated in the central part of the extensive American empire," and that it will become "an asylum in the wilderness for the distressed of mankind" (107, 108). His bloviating regarding "The land of promise, flowing with milk and honey," which he waxes toward in this conclusion, counters the earlier rhetoric of more dispassionate descriptions (109). This portrayal firmly ensconces him as a booster of Kentucky and undercuts the tales he tells regarding being an unbiased reporter of the natural affairs of the area. But most importantly, he clearly arrives to the substantiation of the book form, which John Fitch himself haltingly aspires to achieve.

64 FEELING SINGULAR

1.5. Feeling Steamed

John Fitch tried his best to leap into the cultural imagination, though instead of being abstracted into a category or a type—as critics like Slotkin and
Henry Nash Smith say happened to Boone—he remains a historical counterpoint to the individuals who became colonizing figures of the field of early
American studies. It is evident that Fitch believed that, in addition to the
movement of the goods and productions of U.S. economies, his steamboat
would facilitate the white settlement of newly claimed spaces beyond the
seaboard. Fitch's desire to offer a mechanical contraption that would further
open the continent's interior to the waterways of trade met with resistance
partly because the leading contender for a patent already had connections
with the new federal government. Curiously, Filson's book on Kentucky pass-
ingly notes the need for a boat "propelled by the force of mechanical powers"
(45). Filson considered "the navigation of the Mississippi, either by these
lakes, or New Orleans" as paramount to the ascendancy of the U.S. nation-
state, and he explained how "This plan is now in agitation in Virginia, and
recommended to government by two gentlemen of first rate abilities, Mr.
Charles Rumsey and Doct. James McMacken" (44–45). Though he gets the
name wrong, he is clearly demonstrating how James Rumsey, a year before Fitch advertised his invention, had shown George Washington a boat
"constructed to work against stream" that "may be of the greatest usefulness
in our inland navigation."[42] While in retirement from public office after the
Revolutionary War, Washington had sought to locate a way to increase the
access of traffic from Chesapeake Bay to the interior for the transportation
of goods (mostly to benefit his own commercial prospects), which led him
to see potential in Rumsey's idea.[43] Even though Fitch saw himself offering
something of "infinite advantage" to the constituted union, Washington instead validated Rumsey's contribution, describing it as something "of the
greatest usefulness."[44]

---

[42] George Washington, Certificate to James Rumsey, September 7, 1784, *The Writings of George Washington from the Original Manuscript Sources, 1745 – 1799*, Vol. 27 (Washington, D.C.: U.S. Government Printing Office, 1931–1944), 468.

[43] For more on this, and George Washington's relationship to such endeavors, see Edward J. Larson in *The Return of George Washington, 1783–1789* (2014). Although Washington chose to invest in canals as a way to suture the states together and encourage more commerce, Larson notes how Washington's concern over stable markets and ease of transportation motivated his desire to support the production of transportation technologies that would connect the frontier to the coastal economic centers.

[44] While there is no evidence that Fitch read Filson's book, it proves striking that several years before Fitch's embodied exhaustion led him to imagine steam transportation Filson was propounding such prospects.

MEMORIALIZING THE REPUBLIC OF FAILURE 65

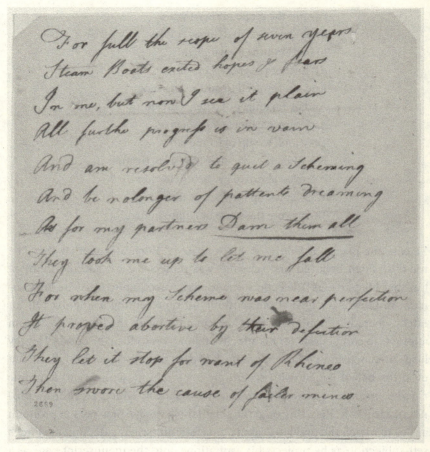

Figure 1.10 Poem by John Fitch found in the Peter Force Papers, Series VIIID, Item 47.2, in the folder marked "Correspondence & Related Material," undated. Courtesy of the Library of Congress.

Before his death, Fitch enshrined the image of the failed mechanic-inventor within an unpublished manuscript poem (see Fig. 1.10). Eventually collected by his legal executor and deposited in the Library of Congress amid remnants of his letters and manuscript life papers, this poem narrates his reason for giving up on his steamboat hopes as stemming from his "partners" who "let me fall." Although the poem is bad, in the way an eighteenth-century mechanic untrained within the conventions of the period's literary aesthetics might write, its badness offers an interesting way to frame Fitch's desires to use various forms of self-expression to narrate the source of his failure as an interpersonal rupture:

66 FEELING SINGULAR

> For full the scope of seven years
> Steam boats excited hopes & fears
> In me, but now I see it plain
> All further progress is in vain
> And am resolved to quit a scheming
> And be no longer of patents dreaming
> As for my partners _Dam them all_
> They took me up to let me fall
> For when me scheme was near perfection
> It proved abortive by their defection
> They let it stop for want of Rhineo
> Then swore the cause of failure mineo.[45]

Placing the blame of failure on his "partners," Fitch affirms that they "let me fall." Fitch believed his "scheme" was perfect for his specific moment but that his partners' "defection" made the project "abortive." The enjambment in lines 2–3 suggests the centrality of representing a singular self for Fitch, where his "hopes and fears" carry on to break the line. Fitch's poem attempts to compensate for his affective failure to produce the cultural legacy he desired, writing a ballad to memorialize his feelings about his failure. But even the ballad is bad, with seemingly uncertain masculine and feminine rhymes, most pronouncedly the last two syllables, which awkwardly pronounce "mineo." Inserting onto the singular possessive first-person pronoun an "o" to match the previous rhyme, this feminine rhyme documents Fitch's self-subjection as he projects his aspirations onto the manuscript page as a testament to his inefficacy.

One problem with reading Fitch's life and writings is that we know the end at the beginning. We know in picking up the published book that contains his life narrative that the various manuscript volumes never accomplished what Fitch had written them out to do. Jefferson became president; Fulton, remembered as the steamboat creator. And yet the scene of failure entices and stimulates this chapter's reading, offering the allure of fulfilled expectation

---

[45] This poem can be found in Andrea Sutcliffe, _Steam: The Untold Story of America's First Great Invention_ (New York: Palgrave, 2004), 129–130. Courtesy of the Library of Congress.

MEMORIALIZING THE REPUBLIC OF FAILURE   67

in combination with the affective orientation of failed hope and crushed optimism—a devastation that ends in suicide.

To conclude, then, I turn to Peter Brooks's psychoanalytically inflected reading of narrative and expectation. "Narratives both tell of desire—typically present some story of desire—and arouse and make use of desire as dynamic of signification," Brooks writes, emphasizing the galvanizing force of *desire* in the repetition of the word (37). "Desire is always there at the start of a narrative," Brooks continues, "often in a state of initial arousal, often having reached a state of intensity such that movement must be created, action undertaken, change begun" (38). In picking up the manuscript of Fitch's life, we may have the desire to come to understand the stakes and contexts of its production, knowing full well that the desiring subject who produced it failed to arrive at a sense of fulfillment, that desire remains petrified in the manuscript as nascent book. We may wonder *why* his desire never came to fruition and what in the material and textual artifacts themselves foretell this. For Brooks, desire inheres in the very form of narrative structure, and in a curious turn he uses the metaphor of the steam engine to convey an "emerging conception of human desire" in the late eighteenth century (41). Brooks asserts: "Life in the text of the modern is a nearly thermodynamic process; plot is, most aptly, a steam engine" (44). Asserting that the steam engine is the most appropriate metaphor for modern human desire, Brooks offers a way to read Fitch and his failed manuscripts as the paramount problem of desire, associated materially in Fitch with the very metaphor that comes to stabilize modern subjectivity: steam power. The ephemerality of fulfilled desire—its structure of motivation and its ineluctable nature—and the gaseous vapors of hot steam eluded Fitch, again and again, even has he tried to materialize a steamboat that, for him, signified not just the weight of his overwhelming desire but the cumbersome republican metaphors with which he and other tangential, not-quite-incorporated citizens, grappled.

2

Civic Virtue and State Power

The Politics of the Particular in the Racialized Republic

> Racism operates by the determination of degrees of deviance in relation to the White-Man face, which endeavors to integrate nonconforming traits into increasingly eccentric and backward waves. . . . From the viewpoint of racism, there is no exterior, there are no people on the outside. There are only people who should be like us and whose crime it is not to be. . . . Racism never detects the particles of the other; it propagates waves of sameness until those who resist identification have been wiped out (or those who only allow themselves to be identified at a given degree of divergence). Its cruelty is equaled only by its incompetence and naïveté.
> —Gilles Deleuze and Féliz Guattari, *A Thousand Plateaus*[1]

In the fourth item that George Washington enumerates as "essential to the well being" of the former colonies—declared but not elaborated in the Circular Letter that floridly announced his (first) transition from public commander to retired gentleman in 1783—he invites "the people of the United States . . . to forget their local prejudices and policies, to make those mutual concessions which are requisite to the general prosperity, and in some instances, to sacrifice their individual advantages to the interest of the community" (17).[2] The abstractions embedded within "mutual concessions" and "sacrifice" that make available "general prosperity" and "Community" imply cultural assumptions that buttress free trade and (white) social relations. Indeed, sacrifice as a public good applies unevenly across the propertied and the unpropertied, the elite and the lowly. Where the signers of the

---

[1] Gilles Deleuze and Féliz Guattari, *A Thousand Plateaus*, 178.

[2] This Circular Letter has resonances with the iconic 1796 Farewell Address, which was crafted multiple times, at least in 1792 when Washington had Madison dictate his notes, often under the assistance of Alexander Hamilton.

Feeling Singular. Ben Bascom, Oxford University Press. © Oxford University Press 2024.
DOI: 10.1093/9780197687536.003.0003

CIVIC VIRTUE AND STATE POWER 69

Declaration of Independence "mutually pledge[d] to each other our lives, our fortunes & our sacred honour," the enslaved lives that facilitated and constituted those "fortunes" stand on the outside of the republican project. Applauded as the ideal republican citizen, Washington's famous gesture to excuse himself from power and direct influence—retiring as general of the Continental Army—placed him as a model for republican disinterestedness, one who selflessly defers to an imagined common good. But that iconic act, where he leaves public life to attend to his Virginia farm, *forgets* that he returned to public life to support the 1787 Constitution partly because he was having difficulty importing his enslaved-labor-produced goods across newly independent state lines.[3] This Circular Letter, then, performs dissimulation, offering a genuflecting legerdemain that presents Washington as a figure that forms the charade of benevolent state power.

Perhaps this anecdote of Washington is simply to suggest the obvious: that the facilitators of state power often have ulterior motives. Appeals to virtue lubricate the social machinations that would otherwise expose the ambitions and self-investments that drive the motivations of figures like Washington— and many, many others, from John Fitch to John Filson as explored in the previous chapter—to make themselves *appear* disinterested, virtuous actors on the wobbly stage of the public good. State power in the United States has often operated through this production of abstraction, assuaging its spectating citizens to discipline their potential impulse to disrupt the show through their overly zealous desire to participate. Christopher Castiglia describes this process whereby "[c]itizens become administrators . . . of themselves" as the internalization of the state's investment in certain models of citizenship (6). Within this production of state power, then, race became a category of particularity that models "local prejudices," intervening and disrupting Washington's fantasy of complete white supremacist abstraction. Racialized particularity within the ideological formulation of republican masculinity was deployed as a "local prejudice" to justify the ongoing slavery, plotting populations along a stadialist position askance to civilization.[4]

[3] See Edward J. Larson, *The Return of George Washington, 1783–1789* for more on this specific postwar issue and Washington's frustrations with the difficulty to conduct interstate commerce.

[4] Zakiyyah Iman Jackson's *Becoming Human: Matter and Meaning in an Antiblack World* (2020) interrogates the ways Enlightenment discourses of humanity did not focus on exclusion so much as "the violent imposition and appropriation—inclusion and recognition—of black(ened) humanity in the interest of plasticizing that very humanity" (3). In this way, inclusion within the paradigm of republican masculinity also encodes a type of violence. The civilizational mission of Enlightenment colonization—and its connection to stadialist conceptions of whiteness—might be referenced in

70 FEELING SINGULAR

Whiteness constituted what Washington and other elites understood as the bedrock—and thereby necessarily unmentioned—category that stabilized and enabled a collective imaginary.[5] That is to say, a civilizational regime of whiteness collated the disparate appeals to sacrifice that gave Washington his position within the pantheon of civil servant. A servant, after all, is a racialized and classed category appropriated by the propertied through their "humble and obedient servant" letter signoffs. What I will focus on in this chapter is how the category of racial difference—specifically, the body of the Black non-European—comes to signify the intractable "local" that cannot be abstracted into the "general."[6] In this formulation, the early Republic's rhetoric of "general prosperity" sought to instill a formation of whiteness that conditioned what and who could be considered as part of the "general" within the General's imaginary. Race manifests, as Ruth Wilson Gilmore argues, through power differentials that attempt to hierarchize livability and relations to property; the way whiteness is abstracted as a generalizable property, then, helped construct the figment of a common good that disproportionately makes requests of particular bodies.[7]

In the previous chapter, I examined how John Fitch fell flat from his aspirations to be an inventor, pointing toward the way failure as a cultural narrative relies on an imagined opportunity. In this chapter, I move from a class-specific analysis to one that compounds race as a category in the state's interpellation of fraught subjectivity. John Fitch's and Washington's appeals to the common good highlight how the effectiveness of one's genuflection

---

an anecdote of Washington requesting from William Stephens Smith, a former aid-de-camp, to return his book of Oliver Goldsmith's *History of the Earth and Animated Nature* from Newburgh to Mount Vernon (see Kevin J. Hayes, *George Washington: A Life in Books*, 195). In the second volume of Goldsmith's book, he lays out a hierarchy of humanity that configures "not above six distinct varieties in the human species" (212–213), arguing later that "whiteness is the colour to which mankind naturally tends" (240).

[5] Robert G. Parkinson in *Thirteen Clocks: How Race United the Colonies and Made the Declaration of Independence* makes this very point, noting specifically "how the American Revolution and the founding of the United States contributed to the institutionalization of modern racism" (12).

[6] The first seal of the United States includes shield iconography held by figures of "Justice" and "Liberty," and depicts six flags that represent Dutch, English, French, German, Irish, and Scottish ancestry, offering a formulation of the future nativist nation that would exclude Catholic Europe. This racialized state aesthetics ensure that those not from the six categories of nativity are positioned within a blockage point that interrupts the ability to appear as disinterested. In this formulation, non-whiteness becomes the particular factor that makes the singular incapable of becoming representative, jamming the metonymic properties that make a part a synonym for a whole.

[7] Ruth Wilson Gilmore defines racism as "the state-sanctioned and/or legal production and exploitation of group-differentiated vulnerabilities to premature death, in distinct yet densely interconnected political geographies" (261).

CIVIC VIRTUE AND STATE POWER 71

is determined by proximity to power and influence. In this chapter, I read the transcribed memoir of a formerly enslaved African who secured his liberty after participating—as an enslaved soldier—in the Revolutionary War. The aspiration of Boyrereau Brinch, later known as Jeffrey Brace, to settle in Vermont and raise a family, after that state moved to recognize others like him as rights-bearing subjects, guides the unfolding argument in this chapter. The unfinished project of republican masculinity, which would position the transcribed memoir of Brinch/Brace as an outcast from the category of belonging, is challenged by the authorial voice in *The Blind African Slave*, which offers a neglected testimony to the Atlantic slave trade and the struggle to secure a livelihood for persons of color after legal emancipation. Yet in the ostensible free state of Vermont, Brace was rendered an outcast, warned out of communities due to his skin color, and separated from the domestic sphere that he longed to reproduce. And more to the point, the publication of his book led to the intensification of the state's antagonism against him, suggesting the way his desire to belong confronted the civilizational regime of the republic.

2.1. Bearings

In his early nineteenth-century memoir, Jeffrey Brace (1742–1827) reports on his transportation from Africa to the Americas: "We had suffered for food, to a degree, of which even a faint description would be considered as fabulous, therefore I forebear to disclose it" (111). Pausing to withhold description, Brace avers that readers would consider his story unbelievable—part fable, part exaggerated history—should they know the details in full. Instead, the story requires him to deliberate his points, as it offers a biting critique of the Enlightenment's investment in exploitative labor and joins discourse on natural rights with the failure of Christianity to be "benevolent." "I was taken from the ship," he recalls:

> starved, whipped and tortured in the most shameful manner, obliged to work unceasingly, in order I suppose that the clement, benevolent and charitable whiteman, should be satisfied that the heathen spirit, of an African boy of noble birth, should be sufficiently subdued, rendered tame, docile and submissive; and all for my good that I should thereby become a tame, profitable and honest slave. The natural man must be obliterated, that

72 FEELING SINGULAR

> even the thought of liberty must never be suffered to contaminate itself in a
> negro's mind; and the odious thing, equality, should be taught by European
> discipline never to raise its head. (111–112)

In taking aim against the twin pillars of America's revolution—liberty and market capitalism—Brace illuminates their interconnection as a product of European Enlightenment that subjects Africa as a resource to be pillaged. Paralleling "tame, docile and submissive" with "tame, profitable and honest," Brace shows how a system of religious subjection exploits his labor even as the American Revolution was being written into "fabulous" histories of independence.

Brace experienced his own mode of independence after fighting in the Revolutionary War, settling in Vermont soon after his manumission in the 1780s. In the ostensibly free state of Vermont, Brace sought to farm sugar from maple trees. In this manner, his narrative offers a materialist response to the economic conditions of the enslaved-labor sugar trade, implying maple sugar as an alternative to supporting the slave-produced commodity, one that follows the 1805 *Farmer's Almanack*'s injunction to "Make your own sugar, and send not to the Indies for it. Feast not on the toil, pain and misery of the wretched" (qtd. Kittredge 121). But instead of succeeding in the maple sugar market, his children were taken away from him and placed in indentured servitude, and his wife was subjected to a white neighbor's abuse while tapping their maple trees. Brace's memoir *The Blind African Slave* (1810)—an understudied anti-slavery narrative—articulates a model of republican belonging that anachronistically conflates founding U.S. documents to rhetorically stage his freedom. One way to read this is that Brace identifies with the very norms that exclude him. But that identification, I argue, becomes more complicated when considered as an aspirational and *queer* figuring of a possible (though foreshortened) futurity. Through tracing the cultural reception (or lack thereof) of this curious memoir, the following pages imagine how Jeffrey Brace spoke back to the early republican government (specifically, the figures who set that formation in motion) and then gestures toward the possible alternatives his life story offers to frame early nineteenth-century African American life narratives and the politics of belonging.

Similar to other nineteenth-century Black anti-slavery writers, Brace contests the exclusive definitions of citizenship that a figure like Thomas Jefferson propelled. Worried about the "[d]eep rooted prejudices entertained by the whites" (118) and the "ten thousand recollections, by the blacks, of

CIVIC VIRTUE AND STATE POWER 73

the injuries they have sustained" (119), Jefferson proposes in his *Notes on the State of Virginia* (1785) that emancipated Blacks "should be colonized to such place as the circumstances of the time should render most proper, . . . to declare them a free and independant [sic] people, and extend to them our alliance and protection, till they shall have acquired strength" (118).[8] Jefferson's well-rehearsed fears surrounding racial integration in the United States—that Africans could never be incorporated into the (white) American republic because of their remembered histories of being counted as property—indexes a relatively quotidian example of the racist ideologies promulgated by the individuals popularly known as the Founders. Espousing a separation between the formerly enslaved and the newly independent (white) republican, Jefferson and others imagined a social world that could be transformed according to their own desires. But that ideology of white restriction was never a static and uncontested force of cultural oppression but rather an invasive, perpetuating influence that did not go unanswered by the individuals relegated by its influence: namely, Black settlers in North America. For example, Brace claimed for himself the very rights that Jefferson would safeguard as a property of whiteness in such a way that highlights the potentialities for historical otherwises and might-have-beens. Brace includes himself within the confines of the properly patriotic republican—narrating his skirmishes as a soldier and his efforts to procure familial stability—in such a way that critiques the whiteness of the U.S. republican project and places himself within the parameters of early national citizenship.

After "my services in the American war . . . emancipated me" (169), Jeffrey Brace explains in his memoir, "it still seemed to me as it ever had done that I was fortunes [sic] football and must depend upon her gentle kicks" (170). Despite emancipation, with its promise of equality and belonging, Brace's transcribed memoir points out the lingering investments of slavery after settling in Vermont, the first state that offered immediate emancipation to all men over the age of twenty-one in its 1777 Constitution.[9] While in Vermont,

[8] Jefferson was an early proponent of what would become the American Colonization Society (1817), which sought to remove emancipated Black slaves from North America to Africa (at first Sierra Leone and then later what would become Liberia). This insistence on the "unnatural" presence of Blacks in America and the "natural" presence of whites is a crucial ideological rationale for the settler colonial dynamics of early national U.S. culture. In becoming an independent nation, this effort to forget the histories of Black enslavement through literally removing those formerly enslaved shows the concerted effort to make claims for whiteness as the de facto form of belonging in America.
[9] For more on the history of African American settlers in Vermont, see Elise A. Guyette, *Discovering Black Vermont: African American Farmers in Hinesburgh, 1790–1890* (2010) and Harvey Amani Whitfield, *The Problem of Slavery in Early Vermont* (2014). These books, particularly

74 FEELING SINGULAR

Brace determined to raise a family and secure for himself and his children the rights of citizenship. That aspiration, however, was circumscribed at every turn, leading him to produce his life narrative, *The Blind African Slave*, with the help of a white amanuensis, which responds and testifies to those attenuated and foreshortened liberties. Through his life narrative, Brace attaches himself to the promise of republican belonging in the early United States, hoping to circulate within print and be influential to an undifferentiated reading public. Although Brace represents himself in proximity to the conventional parameters of republican living—from properly raising a family to virtuously performing in the public sphere—he comes to manifest the racial limits of the U.S. republican project.[10] In this way, Brace aspires to a series of norms that actively refuse him, and in that aspiration he insists on the legibility and viability of his desires.

In *The True Patriot: or, An Oration, on the Beauties and Beatitudes of a Republic* (1802), Mason Locke Weems, popular book agent and author, lays out his reasons for preferring a republican mode of governance. Asserting it as the best government for producing a uniformity of citizens, Weems declares: "Yes, wisest of politicians! Let us as little children *love one another*, and our republic shall soon become as a temple of GOD, built of living stones, each possessing the place assigned him by the Supreme Architect; and steadily exerting all his strength and lustre to render it a fit abode of peace and happiness for ever" (6). Explaining "that republics take the best care of peoples [sic] lives and wives, children and chattels" (47), Weems implies that the "lustre" of the early U.S. republic relies on normalizing its white, male citizens' relations to domestic formations and property. This iteration of "lustre" moves from definitions of "sheen" or "polish" to emphasize instead a

---

Whitfield's, rightly point out the problem with indexing Vermont's ostensibly anti-slavery legislature when considering the other modes of labor restriction and coercion very much present.

[10] For work on the racializing logics of belonging in revolutionary America and the early U.S. republic, see Elise Lemire, *"Miscegenation": Making Race in America* (2002); Eliga H. Gould, "The Laws of War and Peace: Legitimating Slavery in the Age of the American Revolution," *State and Citizen: British America and the Early United States*, eds. Peter Thompson and Peter S. Onuf (2013), 52–76; Corey Capers, "Black Voices, White Print: Racial Practice, Print Publicity, and Order in the Early American Republic," *Early African American Print Culture*, eds. Lara Langer Cohen and Jordan Alexander Stein (2012); and Sharon M. Harris, *Executing Race: Early American Women's Narratives of Race, Society, and the Law* (2005), 63–67. For work on how these racial logics work out in the early decades of the nineteenth century, see Alexander Saxton, *The Rise and Fall of the White Republic* (1990); Sandra M. Gustafson, "Prophesying the Multiracial Republic," *Imagining Deliberative Democracy in the Early Republic* (2011), 125–151; and Douglas Bradburn, "White Citizen, Black Denizen: The Racial Ranks of American Citizenship," *Citizenship Revolution: Politics and the Creation of the American Union, 1774–1804* (2009), 235–271.

masculine energy, one that ensures a "splendour or brilliancy of fame, deeds, birth," as one nineteenth-century dictionary defined figurative connotations of the term.[11] Claiming to "have proved that Republics contribute most to *Peace* and *Plenty*," Weems expounds upon how the republican form of governance makes possible the reproduction of its white domestic forms on the American continent: "The poor Indian Squaw, often suffering the hunger and fatigue of the hunting life, seldom affords more than two children; while a healthy New Jersey wife cherished up in the warm arms of *Peace* and *Plenty*, thinks nothing of giving a dozen fine rosy boys and girls to her delighted husband, and to her indebted country" (47). For Weems, the white, American domestic form justifies republican governance through the "lustre" of reproduction, securing itself as the destined reproductive order of belonging in the new nation.[12] The "country" itself becomes "indebted" to the work of white women, who reproduce republican citizens, as opposed to the nonwhite bodies who are prohibited from such reproduction.[13] Weems propels a racialized logic of national futurity that denigrates and marginalizes nonwhite domestic formations.

Jeffrey Brace never received his invitation to participate in the nation's reproductive futurity despite his efforts to produce a family. Indeed, his assertion "[t]o raise and educate my children" once in Vermont contests the racial logics that would actively refuse such African settlement in North America (172). Desiring to make his children "useful and honest citizens in this life," Brace refuses to be the "sentimentalized 'poor negro'" (89), which John Saillant describes as the dominant cultural form for representing Black people in this period. Saillant argues that such portrayals of Black suffering provided a "counterdiscourse to republican ideology, rubbing against one of its sorest points: the persistence of an enslaved, oppressed class in a republic founded by a liberty-loving people" (90). Brace rejects this portrayal of Black abjection, offering a glimpse into the life of a Black individual who aspires to

---

[11] In his *Memoir*, Thomas Jefferson articulates his desire to produce a system that would eradicate "ever fibre . . . of ancient or future aristocracy" (40), yet in his correspondence with John Adams, he lauds the "natural aristocracy among men. The grounds of this are virtue and talents. . . . The natural aristocracy I consider as the most precious gift of nature for the instruction, the trusts, and government of society."

[12] Scholars of queer Indigenous studies, such as Mark Rifkin and Scott Morgensen, show how whiteness links to domestic reproduction and the fantasy of national futurity, consolidating the new nation's efforts to naturalize settler colonialism and naturalize white claims to land, or what Rifkin calls "the ongoing enmeshment of discourses of sexuality in the project of fortifying the United States against incursion by *uncivilized* formations that jeopardize the 'common sense' of national life" (5).

[13] Nicole Eustace in *1812: War and the Passions of Patriotism* (2012) argues for a capacious sense of citizenship that considers reproduction as a mode to participate in national belonging.

76 FEELING SINGULAR

liberal subjecthood, explaining: "after my emancipation . . . , I not speaking very good English for my own amusement and instruction, imployed [sic] all my leisure hours in reading the Bible" (191).[14] Learning to read, Brace attempts to become both a republican empowered through self-development as well as a citizen who pursues his desires. Settling in Vermont, and wishing to reproduce the republican domestic family, Brace draws upon the emerging logics of Enlightenment self-making, utilizing market capitalism (through sugar production) to assert his rights. In doing so, Brace articulates a Black mode of belonging that resists the emerging colonization ideologies that claimed non-white bodies could not settle in the United States. Although such dynamics of a continued exclusion from citizenship after emancipation are in a sense unsurprising, what I would like to highlight here is Brace's expressed outrage. In this sense, I seek to render visible the *feelings* of Brace as he witnesses his exclusion from republican citizenship, specifically how he manifests a refusal to be left out of the republican formations that reject him. Expressing indignation for what he imagines as his trampled rights, Brace describes at one moment feeling "hunted down at last" when he had appealed to Vermont's selectmen to recognize his rights (184). Indeed, Brace comes to portray himself as being enveloped within a system that refuses to acknowledge him, describing himself as "fortunes [sic] football," receiving the "kicks" that signal his seeming passivity.

Such a fatalistic response to the white powers of Vermont shaped his children, "whose feelings were alive to every approbrium that was cast upon their father; they would often threaten to avenge my wrongs, but this I always discouraged" (186). The generational divide here illustrates the tension between immediate redress for the republic's attachment to slavery (and white supremacy) and a competing desire to work within the republic's emerging systems and structures. Brace believes in a change that can occur through appeals to the republican structures of belonging, that those structures *can* and *will* be reoriented. Brace describes his children having "feelings . . . alive to every approbrium," but he seeks to inculcate within them a mode of propriety to articulate that felt frustration in specific ways: "the best way for us . . . to get redress was to return good for evil, and thereby shame and mortify the ostentatious destroyers of our rights" (186). Resisting the sentimentalizing of his struggle, Brace shows himself as a father who—albeit stoically—produces

---

[14] For more on Black literacy in antebellum America, see Christopher Hager, *Word by Word: Emancipation and the Act of Writing* (2013).

CIVIC VIRTUE AND STATE POWER   77

a republican family, informing his children how to "redress" their "destroyers of . . . rights" through casting "shame." In this sense, Brace positions himself as a true republican, able "to return good for evil" through dispassionate influence, acknowledging a propriety of feeling and expression that solves his social problems instead of what he represents as the rashness of his children's responses.

Brace's feelings about his subjection, and his insistence to claim republican belonging, offer an under-read counternarrative to more familiar early U.S. writings about the incorporation of Africans into the political public sphere.[15] Benjamin Rush and Thomas Jefferson offer useful context to consider the white ideologies that positioned Africans as incapable of republican belonging. Both imagine a field of political possibility that refuses either to let Africans be Black (Rush) or to let Africans be American (Jefferson). Both Rush and Jefferson are drawn to the question of what to do about slavery and with Black bodies in the new republic, particularly because of the way slavery suggests a racial exception to a nation putatively founded on liberty and independence. Charting out their visions of what we might call the affective arrangements of Black futurity helps us see the forces of exclusion that sought to delegitimize Brace's life, his feelings toward his family, and his claims to republican belonging. The two differing perspectives of Rush and Jefferson suggest some of the ideological gulfs that divided Brace from his desires to belong within the emerging republic, and place his strivings for recognition within the context of early republicanism. Rush's and Jefferson's disparate ways of imagining Black belonging in the new nation showcase some of the constraints on Jeffrey Brace's expressions of feeling, aspirations to domestic formation, and desires for republican belonging. Race, for both Rush and Jefferson, provides the very ground of belonging and unbelonging in the republic, a vexed site of social orientation and republican futurity. Central to both is the use of racism as a practice of power that attempts to effect biopolitical dominance over the legible modes of republican belonging in the early United States.[16] Jeffrey Brace emerges within this production of

[15] While prominent Black men in Philadelphia, such as Richard Allen, Absalom Jones, and James Forten, offered important critiques of the racist attenuations of Black agency in the public sphere after the rise of the Democratic-Republican Party, Brace not only lived in the outskirts of Vermont during his life but continues to be marginalized within studies of Black public life in the early republic.

[16] Jefferson's desire to remove Black individuals from America through colonization to Africa and Rush's fascination with eliminating racial difference to extend the rights of republican citizenship bear important relation to Foucault's account of how race works in the rise of biopolitics in the modern world. In *Society Must Be Defended*, Foucault argues that biopower maintains its "power of death" (254) through racism; that is to say, "racism is bound up with the workings of a State that is

78 FEELING SINGULAR

the republican ideal as a Black figure who refuses to allow himself to be subject to the disappearing act of republican biopower, insisting on the legibility of his passion and indignation within the republic and asserting his desires for Black family formations. His frustrated claims of belonging confront the ideologies that Rush and Jefferson promote, offering a counter to their racialized model of republican belonging. Indeed, Brace insists on a form of Black affective attachment that pushes against the respective projects of Rush and Jefferson, highlighting one man's specific claims to domestic belonging to the U.S. republic *through* written memory and the passions and feelings that such a contested project constellates.

In a way, Brace fits perfectly into Jefferson's yeoman republic, settling Vermont and clearing the land for crops of corn and wheat, and beginning a new venture into maple sugar production. In a 1790 letter to Benjamin Vaughan, Jefferson described how "late difficulties in the sugar trade have excited attention to our sugar trees, and it seems fully believed by judicious persons, that we can not only supply our own demand, but make for exportation" (qtd. McEwan 76). Fantasizing the possibilities for producing sugar from trees, Jefferson continues: "What a blessing to substitute a sugar which requires only the labour of children, for that which is said renders the slavery of blacks necessary." This curious use of the passive voice—"for that which is said"—turns the agency of sugar production into a passive rumor of slavery, one that can seemingly be contested. The uncertainty embedded into the phrase makes slave-produced sugar an apparent rumor "said" by a nameless and unspecified agent. Always interested in deferring responsibility when thinking of the enslavement of others, Jefferson here becomes excited about the prospect of a home-grown industry that would eliminate dependence on British-controlled sugar. Jefferson's excitement about the possibilities of in-land produced sugar became pronounced after he visited Bennington, Vermont, in 1791 to recuperate from his Philadelphia headaches with fellow Virginian James Madison. Later that year, in August, Benjamin Rush responded to Jefferson's request for him to write on the production of sugar through the maple tree. In the letter printed in 1792, Rush concludes with an exulting sense that producing sugar through trees may be "the happy means

---

obliged to use race, the elimination of races and the purification of the race, to exercise its sovereign power" (258). In this sense, one important vector of the instantiation of the United States' assumption of power is through the (continued) subjection of (Black) bodies.

of rendering the commerce of slavery of our African brethren in the sugar Islands as unnecessary, as it has always been inhuman and unjust" (14).

As historian Alan Taylor notes, the production of sugar through maple trees was "the ideal commodity for new settlers because its production required little labor and less capital" (*William Cooper's Town* 120). Brace settled in Poultney, Vermont, a few years before Jefferson's visit to Bennington, fifty miles south, but while there his experience attempting to tap trees for sugar modeled the dynamics of slavery that Rush wished to move beyond. While there, "one Jery Goram, who wanted my land, & to whom I refused to sell it, pulled down my fence and let in cattle" (179). Moving beyond their neighborly differences, Brace explains

> [t]he next year Goram came to me, and wished to join with me in making Sugar, and offered to find Kettles, as I had none, also help me make troughs if I would find trees, and do a share of the work, which was agreed to, by me. At the close of the season, I had 8 lb. When we came to divide, he and his family had found means to get away the remainder; as we had two hundred trees tapped, I thought the compliment was small, and expostulated but to no effect. (180)

This labor dispute with a white man eventually set the stage for a property quarrel that placed Brace's wife at the center, which I will turn to later. Additionally, this scene also signals what is now understood as the economic failure for tree-produced sugar to predominate the sugar market, with sugar failing to constitute a commercial-worthy endeavor due to what Taylor calls the "short and volatile" season and the "small, ill-trained producers" who failed to meet a "standardized quality demanded by urban consumers" (133). The aspirational possibilities of New England maple sugar production confronted the limitations surrounding the early national U.S. market, leading to the failure for maple-produced sugar to become the prized commodity Jefferson and others imagined it would. Instead, maple sugar remained an entirely local phenomenon used by and within individual families.[17]

---

[17] Loyalist Hector St. John de Crevecoeur wrote in his posthumously collected *Sketches of Eighteenth-Century America* of this desire for maple sugar production, though he insists on the local scene of the family as the producer and consumer of such home-grown sugar and does not imagine it as a widespread phenomenon: "Thus without the assistance of the West Indies, by the help of my trees and of my bees, we yearly procure the sweetening we want; and it is not a small quantity, you know, that satisfies the wants of a tolerable American family" (99).

2.2. Queer State Anachronisms

Announced in Vermont's *Franklin County Advertiser* and published as *The Blind African Slave* in 1810, Brace's memoir says he was born Boyrereau Brinch in the "kingdom of Bow-woo" (11) and stolen into slavery "in the sixteenth year of his age" (26). Although there is no known counterpart to this named kingdom, the book begins with a section on the "Laws & Customs peculiar to this Country" that has led many critics to read the narrative as a made-up travel account that projects an image of Africa as "nature unshackled by artifice," fostering "the pure and unsullied love of artless simplicity" (20). Historian Dickson D. Bruce dismisses the book as a "purported autobiography" (98) and Martin Klein claims "the ne're-do-well abolitionist lawyer who took down the narrative of Jeffrey Brace, insert[ed] a great deal of [himself] in the narrative" (51). However, if we take Brace as a historical figure, whose life narrative was transcribed by the aforementioned lawyer, we might gain insight into the structural dilemmas facing Black settlers to Vermont. These dismissals imply that because Brace himself did not personally write the narrative that it must inevitably be more fiction than fact, more of white unconscious than Black memory. Instead of asking what the narrative illuminates, in all its complexity, critics have been more prone to label it as *inauthentic*, determining that they (generally white men) are the arbiters of what makes something "African American." Opposing these dismissals, historian and literary critic Kari J. Winter in "The Strange Career of Benjamin Franklin Prentiss, Antislavery Lawyer" explains that "Prentiss took an avid interest in Brace's life story and spent countless hours interviewing him, transcribing his story, researching his African origins, and preparing the manuscript for publication" (126). We might, of course, be suspicious of such social dynamics—with Prentiss introducing the book as "a regular narrative from [Brace's] own mouth about his captivity" (4)—but that suspicion itself could be productively analyzed. What fantasies are maintained when the problem of mediation discredits the cultural value of early nineteenth-century Black texts? What sentimentalizing of memory occurs when Brace's voice is not included in the cacophony of Black discourse on slavery in the early republic?

The refusal to read the book on its own terms repackages the very ideologies of exclusion that had sequestered Brace to Vermont's margins and outside the realm of republican citizenship. While I do not wish to test or

CIVIC VIRTUE AND STATE POWER   81

claim the historical veracity of all that is represented in the book, I find it telling that this account of Atlantic world slavery would de facto be regarded under principles of authentication that valorize certain modes and occasions of written expression while delegitimizing others. I follow Kari Winter in calling the narrative "[a] hybrid, collaborative text that reflects Prentiss's biases and interests as well as Brace's" (72). I am less interested, then, to locate an "efficacious black voice" (98), as Bruce assesses where the book falls short, than in closely reading what this cultural object offers in thinking about the dynamics of belonging and inclusion in the early republic. Through reading the book as a cultural history for imagining the reception of Black settlers in America (those designated as quintessential outsiders vis-à-vis Jefferson and Rush), the book offers a way to think about Black citizenship in the decades before the more recognizable forms it took through later nineteenth-century court and legislative action.

Importantly, the material text that comprises *The Blind African Slave* appears in hurriedly set type, replete with typos and other non-regularized typographical characteristics associated with a rushed printing in rural Vermont. Near the end of the tenth of the eleven chapters, capitalized 'I's and 'O's are made with italicized lettering, suggesting even more the possible broken or limited type used to set its pages (see Fig. 2.1). The book opens with an introduction that Prentiss addresses "TO THE PUBLIC" and then concludes with an "APOLOGY" that gestures at the difficult composition. "[T]he narrator not speaking plain English," Prentiss writes, "it was extremely difficult to get a regular chain of his ideas; also in relating, he would frequently recollect circumstances, which he had omitted in their proper places" (203). This reference to "proper places" implies a narrative convention that Brace is measured against. For Prentiss, Brace presents an unruly narrative that he must conform to certain narrative and textual conventions, making it "as amusing and correct as possible" (203–204). In this sense, Brace's verbal presentation of himself is shaped into a textual format that is measured by expectations of which Brace himself would more than likely be unaware. Additionally, Prentiss qualifies how he edited the narrative: "Carefully avoiding every circumstance which might tend to wound the feelings of any individual or society of men" (204). In this manner, Prentiss concludes the narrative with an "APOLOGY" that both announces his role as an editor (and censor) to Brace's narrative and gestures at his desire to make it compatible and palatable to particular republican social mores (see Fig. 2.2a–b).

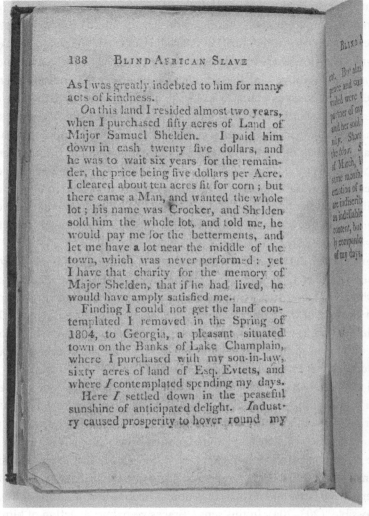

Figure 2.1 Image of page 188 from *The Blind African Slave*, where the use of random italics throughout the page suggests the rushed printing and missing type. Courtesy of the American Antiquarian Society.

In a way, the narrative is both too early and too late, arriving on a cultural scene that was materially and ideologically unprepared for its message. When Jeffrey Brace tells his life story to the poor and unemployed lawyer, which was subsequently printed before Vermont's local anti-slavery print networks

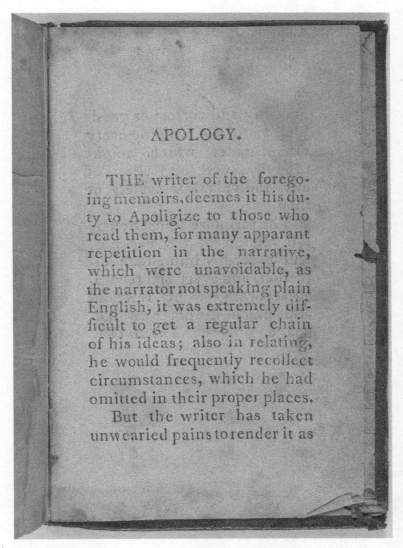

Figure 2.2a–b The last pages of *The Blind African Slave* with the author's "Apology" to the reader. Courtesy of the American Antiquarian Society.

formed, he hoped it would foment great changes in his world. Published two years after the U.S. government ended its legal dealings with the transatlantic slave trade (1808), the book long preceded the emergence of Vermont's antislavery society, which formed in 1834, one year before the creation of the

84 FEELING SINGULAR

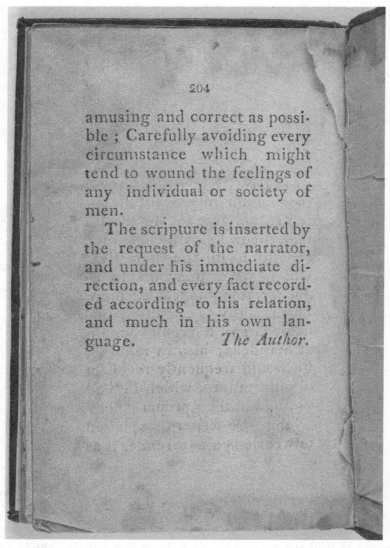

Figure2.2a–b Continued.

American Anti-Slavery Society.[18] The closer historical shift that may be usefully compared to this book is the organized movement to colonize western

---

[18] Joanna Brooks references the book's publication as a one-off that was destined to never make it in its moment due to the lack of book networks and infrastructure: "Books conceived and executed as acts of individual entrepreneurial authorship rarely succeeded in early African America. We see this for a number of single-printing black books published with no connection to organized social movements such as the 204-page *Blind African Slave; or, Memoirs of Boyrereau Brinch, Nicknamed Jeffrey Brace*, published in Saint Alban's [sic], Vermont (of all places), in 1810" (50). See "The Unfortunates: What the Life Spans of Early Black Books Tell Us About Book History," 40–52.

CIVIC VIRTUE AND STATE POWER   85

Africa through emancipated slaves, with the Vermont Colonization Society forming in 1819 (three years after the similarly oriented national society in 1816). Contrary to these efforts to remove free Black people from North America, Brace's narrative presents itself as a template for Black settlement in the United States, offering a voice of domestic assimilation that troubled the anti-slavery discourses that asserted Africans had no place in America. The book straddles what historian Richard S. Newman has described as the shift from early national anti-slavery, which focused on pursuing emancipation through established legal systems, to antebellum abolition, which "sought to pierce the American heart as a critical first step to obliterating slavery nationally" (7). Newman further explains that "the Revolutionary era's most influential thinkers and statesmen . . . [feared] that using the government to destroy slavery threatened America's grand experiment in republican nationhood" (33). Nevertheless, Brace offers a voice of African settlement that troubles emerging ideologies of recolonization by appealing to the very legal and legislative acts that came to vouchsafe his exclusion.

The book insists on the viability of non-white belonging in the early republic. The narrative opens with Prentiss staking claim to Black citizenship in the new nation. But even this takes the form of a misreading (or misquoting) of the United States' founding documents, where the Declaration of Independence is conflated with the Constitution:

> In *America*, that spirit of liberty, which stimulated us to shake off a foreign yoke and become an independent nation, has caused the New-England states to emancipate their slaves, and there is but one blot to tarnish the lustre of the *American* name, which is permitting slavery under a constitution, which declares that "all mankind are naturally and of a right ought to be free." (90)

Rhetorically equating the federal Constitution with the Declaration of Independence, this textual misremembering makes slavery an aberration that will inevitably be worked out as the "spirit of liberty" is expanded. [19]

---

[19] Contrary, in fact, to how James Madison, considered how "emancipation was to be achieved only with expatriation" (Saillant 80). In private correspondence to Robert Walsh in 1819, Madison recalls that during the Constitutional Convention, "A power to emancipate slaves was disclaimed; nor is anything recollected that denoted a view to control the distribution of those within the country" (24). Chief Justice Roger Taney's ruling in the 1857 *Dred Scott v. Sandford* case offers another mid-nineteenth-century interpretation of the Constitution vis-à-vis Black citizenship, arguing that "the right of property in a slave is distinctly and expressly affirmed in the Constitution. The right to traffic in it, like an ordinary article of merchandise and property, was guaranteed to the citizens of the United States, and in every state that might desire it, for twenty years. And the government in express

86 FEELING SINGULAR

Importantly, the text asserts that Brace has claims as a rights-bearing subject—that he falls under the Declaration's "we" even as it is mis-referenced as the Constitution—and hence his narrative performs his claim to citizenship. This way of remembering the nation's founding sentimentalizes the cultural position of racialized enslavement, plotting such a position as an aberration that would inevitably get worked out as the promise of revolutionary belonging pushes against the Constitution's prohibitions. In a way, it can be read as a moment of critical anachronism, where histories are conflated to justify the political ends of anti-slavery and Black incorporation into the republic.

Although it may be convenient to read this slip in referents as accidental, there is something to be gained through considering the conflation between the Declaration and the Constitution as intentional. In this sense, the conflation offers an alternative political formation that opens up the possibility for non-white citizenship. Indeed, the nineteenth-century abolitionist interpretation of the Constitution (that it actively refused Black citizenship) belies Brace's prospects to being a republican citizen. Brace's articulated desire produces a fantasy of possible attachment, specifically a fantasy that has material effects in his life, such that he becomes subject to even more invasive incursions against what he sees (and are legally vouchsafed) as his property rights. Christopher Lane points out the ineluctable difference between fantasy and desire in the introduction to his edited collection *The Psychoanalysis of Race*, writing: "if fantasy helps us 'realize' our desires and prejudices, it would seem a mistake to literalize fantasy by rendering it perceptually equivalent to desire, as if thought and act were identical" (4). What is the fantasy being rewritten through including Brace within the confines of republican citizenship, and through accepting the conflation of the Declaration with the Constitution? How does accepting his claims to belonging shift the presumed restrictions that would otherwise safeguard his exclusion? The anachronistic claim to Brace's belonging ties into a longer history of African American aesthetic resistance to the legalistic refusal of recognition. Ivy Wilson notes that "African American writers used aesthetics not only to produce feelings of sympathy from their readers . . . but also as a necessary corrective to the

---

terms is pledged to protect it in all future time if the slave escapes from his owner." Judge Taney goes even further than that, arguing that "the language used in the Declaration of Independence, show that neither the class of persons who had been imported as slaves nor their descendants, whether they had become free or not, were then acknowledged as part of the people nor intended to be included in the general words used in that memorable instrument." See Don E. Fehrenbacher, *The Dred Scott Case: Its Significance in American Law and Politics.*

CIVIC VIRTUE AND STATE POWER 87

diminishment of how they 'counted' in American society" (13). In this sense, reimagining the Declaration's presumed capaciousness as a corrective to the Constitution's exclusions illuminates how Wilson defines citizenship beyond that which "is produced procedurally within political systems" but instead to that which is "experienced affectively through the cultures of everyday life" (13). In this way, Brace's everydayness, and his claims to republican belonging through his family, illuminates a specific claim to citizenship and republican belonging.

Early in *The Blind African Slave*, Prentiss specifies that the book is "dependant [sic] upon [Brace's] own memory" (26). This reliance on memory occasions some uncertainty for Prentiss, who attempts to "demonstrate the strength of [Brace's] mind and the correctness of his memory" (26). The internal logics of the text already presuppose a reading strategy of exclusion—one that doubts before it believes, as I have indexed in its reception among twentieth-century scholars. Memory, within these hierarchical logics, becomes central to how Brace connects his present life struggling to survive in Vermont to a past that explains how and why he has arrived to New England seeking the vanishing hope of liberty and the fleeting promise of republican belonging. Brace's recorded memories enable him to feel toward the past to highlight slavery's hold on his life and intimate social attachments, where even though he had been emancipated for nearly thirty years the title of his life narrative still identifies him as a "slave." In this way, Brace's narrative speaks of slavery to highlight its continuity, as opposed to its cessation even after legislative acts that safeguarded his liberty. Memory becomes the site that allows Brace—a blind, formerly enslaved African settling in America— to stage modes of resistance that allow him to claim a form of citizenship.

Contrary to Brace's wish for his written life narrative to "be made an instrument for the redemption of my African brethren, from the galling chains of bondage; or for conveying the light of christianity to my native land" (194), the published memoir remained limited to the one edition and afterward fell into obscurity, never broadly circulating beyond the small Vermont town in which it was first printed. The newspaper press that published and circulated it ceased operations the very next week, with the printer Harry Whitney moving around various Vermont towns before filing for bankruptcy in 1817. Additionally, after the printing of the book, Brace and Prentiss were warned out of the town they resided in (Milton, Vermont) by the selectmen, a common practice in Vermont where authorities would inform new arrivals that they would receive no support should they require welfare (Winter

88 FEELING SINGULAR

62–63).[20] But the particularities of Brace being warned out *after* printing a memoir that named and critiqued established citizens for their racially charged violence against him show how his voice in the public sphere always brought him under heightened restrictions.

Even the title of the book—*The Blind African Slave*—highlights Brace's outsider position to the forms of republican belonging that he aspires to occupy. The emphasis on Brace as "The Blind African Slave" makes his memories less a glimpse into the past than the continued status of his life constrained and shaped by his past enslaved displacements and future disabilities (of blindness and loneliness). Not being blind during the time represented in his narrative, blindness instead works as a framing device that collapses disparate temporal moments into one body, associating the inability to see with Brace's constrained freedom and circumscribed liberty as a slave. Prentiss frames the narrative with a description of the book's contents, writing that it contains Brace's "adventures in the British navy, travels, sufferings, sales, abuses, education, service in the American war, emancipation, conversion to the christian religion, knowledge of the scriptures, &c. Interspersed with strictures on slavery, speculative observations on the qualities of human nature, with quotations from scripture" (1). While this catalogue of the contents of the narrative could usefully offer itself as advertising, telling potential readers how the narrative contained therein would fulfill sundry readerly inclinations and expectations, it also is a clear moment of Prentiss's editorial oversight and control. On the next page, the list is repeated but concludes differently, alerting us that the narrative concludes with meditations on Brace's "memory, and blindness" (4). Yet in the narrative, Brace only gestures at his blindness once, in the last chapter that describes his conversion. Thus, the book's very title—*The Blind African Slave*—conflates disparate moments in Brace's life that never technically overlapped.[21] (Brace was manumitted in 1783 and lost his eyesight between 1806 and 1810.) Even though blindness and slavery never historically overlapped for Brace's person, the title of the memoir connects them. While many contemporaneous memoirs emphasize *memoirs* in the title, beginning with that very word, the title to Jeffrey Brace's narrative instead doubly underscores his negative status—both

---

[20] For more on this practice, see Alden M. Rollins, *Vermont Warnings Out* (1995), 1.6. Additionally, Brace was unable to secure publication after being warned out of town and remained in poverty until he obtained a belated federal pension in 1821.

[21] I thank Duncan Faherty for providing me with this insight during the 2015 Futures of American Studies Institute at Dartmouth College.

CIVIC VIRTUE AND STATE POWER 89

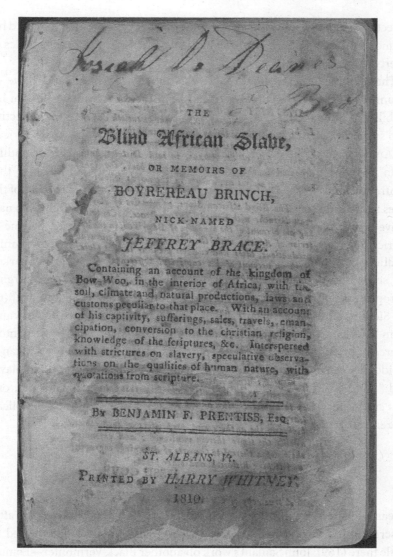

Figure 2.3 Title page of *The Blind African Slave*. Courtesy of Silver Special Collections, University of Vermont.

blind (eventually) and (once) unfree, though written onto the title page as manifesting both at the same time. The title's visual rhetoric emphasizes this conflation, with "Blind African Slave" on a single line and in a gothic-esque font, hearkening to a past even as it erases such temporal difference (see Fig. 2.3). This conflation of disparate times in Brace's life positions him as an

90 FEELING SINGULAR

object for sympathy. Blind, he requires the assistance of Prentiss to record his memoir; and a slave, he has an affecting tale to tell about the racial logics of liberty in the early republic.

Though Brace enters print through this conflation of "Blind" and "Slave"—a conflation that sentimentalizes the citizen Brace even as it gestures at his inability to fully inhabit that term in the U.S. context—the middle adjective also suggests a mediation that reframes his status in America. To be African in America, historian James Sidbury notes, was to reclaim "a degrading term" (6), one that also put forward a global, transnational identity "that confronted and engaged with the complicated questions that arose out of the roles that ethnic conflict played in the Atlantic slave trade" (68). Brace's narrative resists "the negative connotations" associated with the very name of "African" through specifying the cultural values of his African community (Sidbury 6). Sidbury asserts that the term *African* wasn't an ethnic marker, per se, but "instead a new diasporic identity that was founded on emerging European perceptions that residents of Africa shared a 'racial' essence" (6–7). Sidbury notes that certain authors self-identified as African to transform "a term so laden with connotations of primitivism and savagery into a source of pride" (7).[22] In this sense, Brace's self-description as an African—an identity category that he claims throughout his narrative, unlike "Slave" and "Blind"—shows his insistence on inhabiting a particular history, one that carries forward his former status as a slave into his claim to republican citizenship.

2.3. Vermont Contestations

"Hearing flattering accounts of the new state of Vermont," Brace notes after describing his involvement in the Revolutionary War, he determined to settle there (169). John Saillant's work on another Black Vermonter—Lemuel Haynes—provides useful context here, as Saillant argues that "Haynes's

---

[22] Placing this historical context in relation to the title of the memoir in addition to Saidiya Hartman's work in *Lose Your Mother*, where she notes: "It is only when you are stranded in a hostile country that you need a romance of origins; it is only when you lose your mother that she becomes a myth; it is only when you fear the dislocation of the new that the old ways become precious, imperiled, and what your great-great-grandchildren will one day wistfully describe as African" (98), helps frame the significance for how *The Blind African Slave* seeks to revise derogatory associations with the continent.

CIVIC VIRTUE AND STATE POWER 91

genius was to grasp the abolitionist elements within republicanism and the New Divinity and to argue that terminating slavery and welcoming blacks into commonwealth and congregation were essential to the politics and re-ligion of the American Revolution" (5). Brace similarly understood how the security of his emancipation overlapped with concerns regarding the expan-sion of republicanism, making Vermont, the first free state, particularly ap-pealing. While in Vermont, after experiencing racist aggression against him and his family by nearby white neighbors, he considered moving to Kentucky but worried "that being so near slavery again, they might haul me in; or that I should say something which would cause me to be prosecuted and punished as a seditious person" (187). Constantly made to feel out of place and threatened, Brace embodies the complicated and vexed status of the Black citizen in the early republic, especially one who also steps forward and makes himself visible and thus vulnerable in the public sphere. Living within the domestic fabric of the new nation, Brace's own personal domestic life is con-stantly threatened by his precarious status in the white republic. Other figures of the African diaspora in late eighteenth- and early nineteenth-century print narrate conversions to Christianity to resituate themselves toward positions of agency. After narrating his conversion to Christianity, which for Brace offers a mode of belonging similar to republican belonging, he describes his religious affections as offering him a forum to critique the cultural forces that denigrate him and his family. Importantly, he determines that "there was nothing intimated what color either God or man was" in the scriptures (193). Through his conversion, Brace "began to behold . . . [a] just God . . . who had supported and protected me through all trials and suffering while in the hands of my tyrants" (194). This turn of phrase offers an interesting moment of narrative ambiguity. Earlier he had described horrifying scenes, but after his conversion he feels that a "just God" has always "supported and protected me" even "while in the hands of my tyrants." This formulation of a Christian God who waits patiently for the *heathen*'s supplication is quite common in the print of similar diasporic African figures, from Phillis Wheatley's "On Being Brought from Africa to America" ("'Twas mercy brought me from my *Pagan* land") to Olaudah Equiano's continual reference to the "mercy of God" in bringing him into contact with Christianity. Similar to these famous figures of the Black Atlantic, Brace describes Christianity as a tool *against* the subjugating power of colonialism, as it becomes the ideological structure that leads him to feel "equally acceptable with all mankind" when surrounded by the oppressive institutions of slavery (193). Dealing with his exclusion from

92 FEELING SINGULAR

republican belonging, Christianity offers Brace a form of inclusion and attachment that troubles the republic's exclusionary practices.

Contrary to his expectations of ill-fated desire, Brace meets Susannah Dublin, a "native African female" (172), whom he marries.[23] Near the end of his narrative, Brace represents his wife as safeguarding their property rights in Vermont, reorienting conventional notions of masculine self-possession in the face of the racialized incursions against people of color during Vermont's settlement. In this moment, Brace explains how Susannah fends off their white neighbor, Jery Goram, "who wanted my land, & to whom I refused to sell it" (179). While Susannah is "tapping trees" for sugar, "Goram saw her at work and came down to drive her off, as he said he had the possession there, and would not suffer her to work upon the land" (180). Brace then describes a fight that ensues between the two:

> She then asked him whether [I] had not bought that land of Mr. Craw. Goram said if he had, it was his land, and he would occupy it, and she should not tap the trees, and then attempted to take the pail, which contained the spouts, from her. They both pulled and broke the pail; he got it away from her and dashed in into the brook, which broke it into pieces. He also flung away her tapping iron: at which she got away his ax and flung that into the brook after her things. Then he clinched and attempted to fling her in after them all; but she proving too stout for him, like to have wrestled him into the brook; at any rate she got him down, and rubbed him well in the face and neck, with good white March snow. (180–181)

The white snow "rubbed" on Goram's body contrasts with Brace's representation of domestic rupture while in Barbados. Brace, not present to defend his claims to property, relies on Susannah's strength to assert their mutual claim to republican belonging and American settlement. This scene contradicts the normative republican gender roles—where women ensure the reproduction of children as men safeguard their property—to instead show a Black woman wrestling with a white man and asserting her rights at belonging to contested land. "Prepare for making maple sugar," we read in the 1805 *The*

---

[23] This figuring of desire—that Jeffrey Brace articulates the racial specifics of his future spouse—deserves more attention than room permits, though perhaps a gesture toward Sharon Holland's insights "that there is no 'raceless' course of desire" because racism endeavors to limit and circumscribe the possibilities of attachment may inform this appeal to reproductive futurity (43). See Sharon Holland, *The Erotic Life of Racism* (2012).

Farmer's Almanack, "which is more pleasant and patriotic than that ground by the hand of slavery, and boiled down by the heat of misery." Here we have that pursued by a woman who literally fights to ensure that her family's rights are not denied.

In this scene of a Black woman wrestling a white man, we also see an act of refusal and an insistence on republican belonging. The town's selectmen became involved, but contrary to what may be expected, the law validated Susannah's rights to defend herself and her husband's property. Brace and his wife assert their viability to farm the land, and even receive the support of the selectmen who vouchsafe their rights. Where Jefferson's desire for colonization would render Black agency moot, here we have a scene of Black claims to settlement, and those claims being validated by the legal structures of the town's governance. Brace can stay on the property *because* of his wife's contestation with a man who tried to delegitimize her rights to work the land. This scene rewrites the iconic depiction of Frederick Douglass's later struggle to affirm his singular (and masculine) self in the face of the traumas that slavery produces. In Douglass's 1845 *Narrative of the Life of Frederick Douglass,* he writes of his fight with Covey "reviv[ing] a sense of my own manhood. I was a changed being after that fight. I was *nothing* before; I WAS A MAN NOW" (151). Susannah's fight reorients Douglass's now iconic fight: instead of a man claiming a masculine production of self-determination, we see a woman resisting and refusing. By the same token, Susannah's fight with Goram offers a substantially different gender formation than what we see in a figure like Harriet Jacobs, whose later slave narrative, *Incidents in the Life of a Slave Girl* (1861), depicts her hidden in a cramped garret for several years to escape the sexual violence of her master. In this scene of Susannah fighting off Goram, then, we might consider a different flashpoint for thinking about the literary history of gendered resistance against U.S. slavery, one that reorients gender roles and the expectations for such scenarios, depicting a woman emerging triumphant from a physical altercation in a way that revises Douglass's later portrayal of aggressive masculinity. In this sense, Jeffrey Brace and Susannah Dublin queer the republic through their insistence on belonging, particularly when that belonging becomes contested and challenged, rendered anachronistic to the conventional narratives of Black belonging.

But, of course, a story of racism affecting the life of an African family in the United States is an unsurprising circumstance within what Alexander Saxton has called "the White Republic." The interesting aspect, however, is the *way* Brace formulates his frustration at not being recognized as a rights-bearing

94 FEELING SINGULAR

subject, and his succinct articulation of the material barriers (a neighbor fighting with his wife) that prohibited him from full participation in the market economy. Throughout this chapter, I have framed Brace's critique within the liberal model of inclusion to which he aspires. Through the narrative about his life, Brace stages himself as being able to embody what Michael Warner calls "the full authority of representative legitimacy," or the consolidation of rights through print (96). But in doing so, he also holds onto the language of subjection that had labeled him property—that is, the *object* of the law. For Warner, print abstracts particularity and enables an individual to become subsumed into a larger generality; for Brace, however, print particularizes and singularizes him, highlighting his inability to conform to a political system that operates *through* his exclusion. Elizabeth Maddock Dillon follows this thread of the racial and gendered dynamics of liberalism to argue that the status of the liberal subject depends on state-sanctioned private property, making "whiteness and masculinity . . . qualif[ications] . . . for political participation" (21). In this sense, the very notions of liberty and self-possession to which Brace attaches actually hinge on his former status as property: his exclusion constitutes the very possibility of others' inclusion. Brace, as a newly propertied Vermont settler, cannot shake the status of having once *been* property, and so his claims to participate in market logics open him to further scales of subjection. Yet in his narrative, he asserts that his Blackness—specifically, his person as an African man—allows him to participate within the logics of white republican futurity.[24] As such, Brace reframes the parameters of republican belonging in the new nation, particularly as such positions fractured along the gendered lines of race. The *fabulous* aspect of Brace's narrative, then, is his assertion of a mode of recognition disallowed him but that he and his wife materially demand, with her tussling against the physical demands of a white man who threatened their livelihoods.

Despite how Brace feels the figurative foot of a gendered fate, his narrative demonstrates his desire to insert himself into the center of the U.S. republican

[24] The early republic's racial exclusions, as Maggie Montesinos Sale notes, motivated African American men to assert "a common masculinity, which they figured as innate and which they sought to demonstrate, despite the fact that they were largely excluded from the means through which normative masculinity was constructed" (48). In thinking about expansionist and colonization ideologies, I am influenced by Sale's provocative assessment that "the headlong expansion into the territories, sought by migrant, agricultural, slaveholding, and industrial interests alike, fundamentally transformed class relations in the United States, and gave new and primary saliency to the idea of 'whiteness'" (31). See *The Slumbering Volcano: American Slave Ship Revolts and the Production of Rebellious Masculinity* (1997).

CIVIC VIRTUE AND STATE POWER   95

project by settling in Vermont and producing a family. Brace engages with emerging republican and colonizationist ideologies, showing how both of these strands of early national discourse sought to assert the impossibility of non-white bodies to become republican citizens and settlers in the early United States. By placing Brace in conversation with republicanism, settlement, and belonging, I have shown how this neglected text reshapes the stakes of anti-slavery rhetoric in the nineteenth century. More to the point, Brace's narrated desires to belong as a normative republican in the early United States *queer* the emerging norms that would otherwise render his desires as unfit for public expression. In this sense, Brace claims access to the forms of republican belonging (marriage, family, and settlement) in ways that prove qualitatively different from the dominant norms of white republicanism, but through doing so he asserts what might now be read as a queer anachronism, placing both himself and his family as protected within the confines of republican citizenship, in such a way that imagines their futurity despite the ideological and material investments of white republicanism. Even though he aspires to norms that exclude him, that aspiration is not merely the desire for assimilation; instead, Brace's desire is radical, staged to unthread the very categories of belonging that foreground white republicanism, with its dependence on property exploitation. Locating his desire for republican belonging as part of a longer history of resisting the racializing exclusions of the early U.S. republic, Brace offers an important counterhistory to the strivings for liberty in the early republic.

2.4. Feeling Alone

The penultimate chapter of *The Blind African Slave* concludes with Brace reflecting on being "left without an earthly companion, to linger out the remainder of my days" (189). The affecting representation of the passing of his wife, and the language of mutual friendship and companionship, offers up the private and intimate realm for public consumption. Turning from this affecting expression of loneliness, the next chapter wanders back in time "to give an account of [Brace's] religious experiences" (190). He explains that during his "residence with the Widow Stiles" (from around 1768 to 1773), he was taught how "to read the Bible" and was even baptized but that "[d]uring my services in the American war, I paid little attention to her instructions" (190). This transition from a sad, lonely ending to a temporal jump that

96 FEELING SINGULAR

provides a backstory to Brace's emerging and fluctuating religiosity implicitly makes Christianity the solution to his sense of isolation. Yet he notes struggling to find "a church with whom I could commune" (199), moving from town to town in northwestern Vermont before settling in Georgia, Vermont, where his wife died.[25] With another promised happy ending denied, the textual figure of Brace finds in religion the solution to his "lonesome situation among the sons of men" (194).

But in Vermont, with no African-led churches that his counterparts in urban centers such as Boston or Philadelphia were able to attend, Brace uncomfortably situates himself within predominantly white spaces.[26] After narrating his conversion to Christianity, which for Brace offers a mode of attachment similar to republican belonging, he describes his religious affections as offering him a forum to critique the cultural forces that denigrate him and his family. Importantly, he determines that "there was nothing intimated what color either God or man was" in the scriptures (193). Through his conversion, Brace "began to behold . . . [a] just God . . . who had supported and protected me through all trials and suffering while in the hands of my tyrants" (194). This turn of phrase offers an interesting moment of narrative ambiguity. Earlier he had described horrifying scenes, but after his conversion he feels that a "just God" has always "supported and protected me" even "while in the hands of my tyrants." This formulation of a Christian God who waits patiently for the *heathen*'s supplication is quite common in the print of similar diasporic African figures, as referenced earlier by Phillis Wheatley and Olaudah Equiano. Similar to these famous figures of the Black Atlantic, Brace describes Christianity as a tool *against* the subjugating power of colonialism, as it becomes the ideological structure that leads him to feel "equally acceptable with all mankind" (193). Dealing with his exclusion from

---

[25] The white Baptist "Rev. Elder David Hulebert" (182) of Swanton, Vermont, baptized Brace in 1805. Hurlbert [sic] was one of the first Baptist pastors in the area, as the congregation in Georgia began without a pastor and shared a meetinghouse with the town's Congregationalists. See Henry Crocker, *History of the Baptists in Vermont* (Bellows Falls, VT: 1913), 358. Elise A. Guyette in *Discovering Black Vermont: African American Farmers in Hinesburgh, 1790–1890* (2010) observes that the largest concentrations of African Americans in Vermont between the 1790s and 1820s were in Vergennes, Windsor, and Burlington (22–23), though rarely was the percentage above 3 percent, and the majority of African Americans living within white households and not owning their own land.

[26] For more on the Black church in Vermont, see Harvey Amani Whitfield, "African Americans in Burlington, Vermont, 1880–1900," *Vermont History* 75.2 (Summer/Fall 2007): 101–123. For more on Black congregations in urban centers, see Richard S. Newman, *Freedom's Prophet: Bishop Richard Allen, the AME Church, and the Black Founding Fathers* (2008).

republican belonging, Christianity offers Brace a form of inclusion and attachment that troubles the republic's exclusionary practices.

Brace's life indexes the incongruent relationship between religious conversion and racialized belonging in the early republic, where religion offers a sense of belonging that the republican political formation would actively disallow. This is to say, Christianity, as Brace represents it, promises a mode of open belonging that allows a racialized subject to participate in the project of republican nation-building. Intellectual historian and literary critic Gauri Viswanathan argues that religious "conversion unsettles the boundaries by which selfhood, citizenship, nationhood, and community are defined," manifesting the "deconstructive activity central to modernity itself" (76). Where Viswanathan emphasizes the destabilizing potential of conversion—particularly for marginalized figures—most scholarship on early national conversion narratives has focused on a normative assimilationist logic, losing sight of the subversive potential to racialized conversions. Such a portrayal of the colonized subject desiring seemingly innocuous assimilation can be seen in the *Memoirs of Henry Obookiah, a Native of Owhyee* (1819), a narrative about a Hawaiian young man who arrives to New York in 1809 aboard a ship after his family is killed. Upon arrival, he is described as being "clothed in a rough sailor's suit, was of a clumsy form, and his countenance dull and heavy" (Dwight 20). Yet soon he begins "to shew himself dexterous as a mimick" (23) and develops a "talent at imitation" (27) that enables him to adapt to the new environment. He converts to Christianity and is embraced by his white neighbors in Connecticut.[27] Obookiah (traditionally Opukahaia) desires to "go back Owhyhee—tell folks in Owhyhee about Heaven—about Hell" (31) similar to Brace's hope "to be made an instrument" for what would later come to be recognized as colonialism's investment in native missionaries.[28] Whereas the extensive letter writing by Obookiah and his assistance from "the Board of Commissioners for Foreign Missions" testifies to his desire to be "a missionary to my poor countrymen—who are yet living in region and shadow of death" (50), Brace proposes to occupy the republican privileges in Vermont, refraining from participating in recolonizing efforts and instead asserting a settler colonial logic of belonging. To Jefferson and Rush, Brace

[27] Indeed, the "Federalist Pope," Timothy Dwight, took him in when he supposedly lamented just outside of Yale College, "No one gives me learning." For more on the apocryphal nature of this story—and for Obookiah's relationship to the emergence of the Foreign Mission School—see John Demos, *The Heathen School* (2014).

[28] See *The Life and Letters of Philip Quaque: The First African Anglican Missionary*, eds. Vincent Carretta and Ty M. Reese (2010), for another example of a native missionary going to Africa.

98 FEELING SINGULAR

is unfit for the republican project, whereas Obookiah makes actual plans to return to "Owhyhee."[29] On his deathbed, Obookiah "requested that his countrymen might be called" to impart his last testimony "in his native language," asserting "you are in a strange land—you have no father—no mother to take care of you when you are sick—but God will be your friend if you put your trust in him" (124). Historian John Demos explains that through Obookiah's narrated conversion, he moved "[f]rom the position of object . . . to that of subject, from proselytized to proselytizer, from recipient to giver" (26). But because the narrative concludes with Obookiah's insistence on resettling in his native land, and bringing Christianity there with all of its material trappings and ideological investments, we see his conversion used to validate Jefferson's own sense of the impossibility of non-white individuals becoming republican citizens in North America.

Although Brace's determination to settle Vermont, rather than recolonize his homeland, shows how far he pushes away from Jefferson's colonizationism, it also suggests his insistence on participating in publicness. For Brace, religion becomes a way to stake a claim to settling Vermont, empowering him to claim property—and, indeed, validating his wife's physical determination to retain property—whereas Obookiah is portrayed as wishing to return to his native land and reproduce the forms he would be disallowed in New England. Brace instead insists on the viability of his assumption to reproduce familial domestic forms in the early republic, even when the selectmen take his children away, and insists that his textual life narrative will circulate and produce the changes he desires to see. Indeed, the representation of Susannah fighting Goram and rubbing him "well in the face and neck, with good white March snow" demonstrates the couple's mutual insistence on resisting the marginalizing forces that effaced their efforts to settle and reproduce the image of the republican family (181).

Early nineteenth-century anti-slavery discourse sought to structure the trope of a connected national public, all parts equally implicated with the ongoing practice of slavery, without losing the sense of an all-powerful and all-seeing eye of God. But in configuring deity as such, it also opened a problem: if God is all-powerful—and if slavery is a national sin that implies the hypocrisy of white republicanism—how does one imagine the relationship between

---

[29] This particular desire is similarly illustrated in an anecdote about his time attending school in Andover, Massachusetts, where he "was seen one morning very early with a rule measuring the College buildings and fences. He was asked why he did it. He smiled, and said, 'So that I shall know how to build when I go back to Owhyee'" (36).

CIVIC VIRTUE AND STATE POWER   99

human agency and the sovereign divine? In *The Oracle and the Curse* (2013), Caleb Smith argues that such anti-slavery reformers "were, in their way, the agents of the progressively rationalizing, secularizing modernity described by Habermas and others, notably Max Weber" (12). The specific relationship between the eschatological discourse on slavery and the emerging sense of a racialized republican mode of belonging proved an important rhetorical strategy. Anti-slavery poems, sermons, and narratives, like Brace's, portrayed the suffering brought on by slavery and colonialism as both the affective material that could inspire a public to change its ways and the burden of evidence piling up before a just God who would on some future date execute vengeance. Brace's narrative might productively be counterposed to such a sermon. Given the year following the publication of Brace's book, George Richard's "Repent! Repent or Likewise Perish!" (1811)—who also went blind around the same time and subsequently killed himself after the death of his wife—provides such an occasion through its representation of a connected, extended republic that shares equally God's wrath for the continuance of slavery. Given in response to the widely reported 1811 theater fire in Richmond, Virginia, Richards used the occasion to connect slavery to the moral retribution of an angry God.[30] "Young men of Virginia!" the sermon exclaims, "Young men of Philadelphia! united as one, in sympathies of sufferance, and sorrow, we shall not divide between a band of brothers" (26). Using the occasion of a theater fire to bind together the citizens of the disparate states, accusing them equally of enabling slavery, Richards calls the fire and its destruction part of the "signs and tokens of approaching national judgment" (19). Emphasizing the particular trauma of the fire, Richards asserts: "No other hand can alleviate the torments inflicted by the wounds of the twenty sixth of December, excepting that God, who winged the burning arrows from his throne" (18). Desiring to convict his listeners (and eventual readers) of a shared, national sin that motivates the destroying "hand" of God, Richards then asserts that it is the combined weight of slavery and colonialism that has brought about such manifestations of wrath.[31] Importantly,

---

[30] Baltimore's *Federal Republican* devoted nearly the entirety of the second page of the January 9th issue to the "*Report of the Committee of Investigation*" for the "FIRE IN THE RICHMOND THEATRE." Various reports circulated all over the states, from Kentucky to New Hampshire and from New York to Massachusetts. In Vermont, reports of the fire led with titles such as "*Dreadful Calamity*" (*Washingtonian* 2.78 [Jan. 13, 1812], 2); "*Shocking Calamity!*" (*Vermont Republican* 4.3 [Jan. 13, 1812], 3); and "MOST DREADFUL CALAMITY" (*Green-Mountain Farmer* 3.30 [Jan. 13, 1812], 2).

[31] This sermon, it would seem, cost him greatly, as he subsequently "lost his pulpit, then his wife and his sight, and then finally his mind" (Bell 160).

100 FEELING SINGULAR

the sermon mobilizes the figuration of Black and Indigenous suffering as the source of the supposed divine onslaught against the nation, as manifested through such fires and other disasters.[32] In contemplating how the deaths of the theatergoers were the results of divine judgment, Richards asks if "eternal justice [has] no claims in behalf of twelve millions of Africans, who have been annually sacrificed, for almost a century past, to the demon of commercial avarice?" (25). Richards implies that the search for a rationale for the fire would lead back to larger claims of injustice, part of the "moral retribution . . . in favour of the Aboriginals of this country" (25). Asking if "the groans, the tears, the sighs, the mighty wrongs of more than one million, one hundred and ninety thousand slaves, [could remain] unregistered in the volume of omniscience?" (26), Richards imagines a social sphere that is interconnected, uniting church attenders in Philadelphia to the theatergoing public of Richmond, Virginia, *through* the wrongs that slavery and colonialism produce as a national sin, a sin that for Richards demands immediate attention.

For Richards, the failure to cease the enslaved suffering of Africans would bring about the "wrath of Almighty God" (14). Using the devastating fire as a sign of the end of times, the printed document that contained Richards's sermon concludes with tables that list the frequencies of fires, earthquakes, and plagues implicitly associated with the expansion of slavery (see Fig. 2.4a–c). Specifically, the rise in natural disasters charts the growth of chattel slavery in the South and the count of enslaved bodies in the North, making the association between the practice of slavery appear in tandem to the seeming increase in fires, earthquakes, and other such natural disasters. The layout of these categories and the numerical increases rhetorically support Richard's desire "to engrave one awful truth in deeper lines, upon the marble table of the human heart" (14): namely, that national unrighteousness, specifically in the form of maintaining and continuing slavery, caused the traumatic fire in Richmond. With the entire nation connected by guilt for the sin of slavery, Richards proceeds to detail those sins, describing the "fatal round, where morals, manners, sentiment, and taste, are all ingulphed [sic] within the vortex of surrounding vice" (30). Importantly, Richards presumes that it's not governmental intervention but the "wrath of Almighty God" that will destroy the world in pursuing the eradication of slavery.

---

[32] Although I have thought of Brace in terms of his effort to participate in settler colonialism, it bears mentioning that within his narrative there are no direct references to the Abenaki.

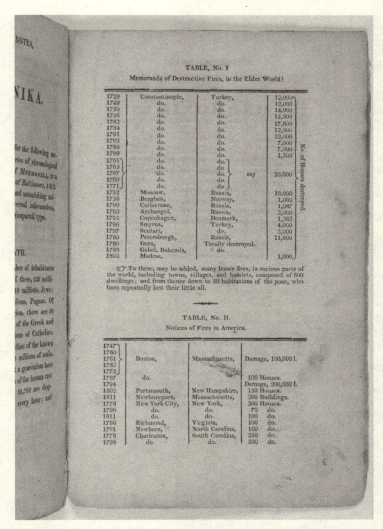

Figure 2.4a–c Several tables from the end of George Richard's published sermon *Repent! Repent! or Likewise Perish!* (Philadelphia: Lydia R. Bailey, 1812), depicting the parallel rise of natural disasters with the expansion of slavery in the United States and its territories in Tables I, II, and VIII in the sermon's appendix. Courtesy of the American Antiquarian Society.

102 FEELING SINGULAR

TABLE, No. II.

Notices of Fires in America.

1747 1760 1761 1763 1775	Boston,	Massachusetts,	Damage, 100,000 l.
1787	do.		100 Houses.
1794			Damage, 200,000 l.
1802	Portsmouth,	New Hampshire,	150 Houses.
1811	Newburyport,	Massachusetts,	300 Buildings.
1778	New York City,	New York,	300 Houses.
1796	do.	do.	70 do.
1811	do.	do.	100 do.
1786	Richmond,	Virginia,	100 do.
1791	Newbern,	North Carolina,	160 do.
1778	Charleston,	South Carolina,	250 do.
1796	do.	do.	300 do.

Nov 10/79 Eddy

TABLE, No. VIII

Census of Slaves, 1800 and 1810!

	1800.	1810.	Decreased.	Increased.
New Hampshire,	8	0	8	
Massachusetts,	0	0		
Connecticut,	951	310	641	
Vermont,	0	0		
Rhode Island,	308	108	200	
New York,	20,613	15,017	5,146	
New Jersey,	12,422	10,851	1,571	
Pennsylvania,	1,706	795	911	
Delaware,	6,153	4,177	1,976	
Maryland,	107,707	111,502		3,795
Virginia,	346,968	392,518		45,550
North Carolina,	133,296	168,824		35,528
South Carolina,	146,051	196,345		50,294
Georgia,	59,699	105,218		45,519
Kentucky,	40,343	80,501	nearly doubled.	40,221
Ohio,	0	0	(bled.	
Tennessee,	13,584	44,535	more than tre-	30,951
Mississippi Territory,	3,489	17,088	ditto.	14,599
Indiana Territory.	135	237		202
Orleans Territory.		34,660		
Louisiana Territory.		3,011	10,453	266,659
Michigan Territory,		24		
Illinois Territory,		128	Decrease in	Increase in
District of Columbia,		5,395	10 Years	10 Years.

1,191,304 Total No. of Slaves.

Figure 2.4a–c Continued.

CIVIC VIRTUE AND STATE POWER   103

These numerical tables at the conclusion of the printed sermon similarly index a certain secularizing of end-of-times rhetoric. Attaching numbers to such claims, the printed sermon seems vexed temporally, hearkening back to older sermonic traditions that typologically read natural disasters while simultaneously performing modern tabulations. Turning from the deaths of Virginia theatergoers to a meditation on the culpability of all white U.S. citizens and residents for the enslavement of Africans and sufferings of "Aboriginals," Richards figures a collective nation attached together through guilt. Speaking to the "Representatives of more than seven millions of people!" (21), Richards hopes to "arouze [sic] the inhabitants of the United States, and awaken individuals, to a solemn sense of this momentous truth, that 'except we repent, we shall all likewise perish'" (19). For Richards, the nation is united—though simultaneously threatened—through its combined guilt for continuing slavery and colonialism.[33] Richards specifically couches his end-of-times rhetoric within the context of threatened national failure, declaring "the hand that has raised you to the pinnacle, may rend the pillars of the federal temple from their base; and the just indignation of an injured and indignant people, may whelm you in the dust, beneath the ruins of the ruined capital of political glory" (23). With a grandiose sense of national connection, enveloped under "the federal temple," Richards would make the very possibility of republican belonging threatened through the continued subjection of Black and Indigenous individuals to the logics of slavery and colonialism. Additionally, he locates the problem within an abstract collective, not particularized into individuals but rather collapsed into a group.

Jeffrey Brace's memoir also makes slavery a national problem that should be addressed "to preserve the constitution of our general government" (9), as the author Prentiss writes in the opening frame. The book, as an individual commodity, contained within it an equation for individual change that contrasts with Richard's eschatological vision of impending divine judgment and action: "This simple narrative of an individual *African* cannot possibly compass all the objections to slavery," the introduction explains; "yet we hope that the extraordinary features and simplicity of the facts, with the novelty of the publication, will induce many to read and learn the abuses

---

[33] Up against a seeming mountain of change he wished to effect in his world, Richards "sunk under the ponderous load of grief! And the mind which used to soar to the celestial mansions of light, was lost, even to itself; a fixed insanity took place, which was the means of terminating the natural life of a brother, whose memory we have infinite reason for holding precious to our hearts" (Ballou 13). Richards, three years after giving this sermon, ended his life.

104 FEELING SINGULAR

of their fellow beings. If the miserable owner of human blood is not moved to acknowledge the iniquity of his possession, and thereby emancipate his slaves, he will at least alleviate their sufferings" (7). This rhetorical strategy, attributable to the white amanuensis-editor, frames the individualized act of reading as the site at which slavery can end. Instead of trafficking in the appeals to justice and divine judgment of early nineteenth-century anti-slavery discourse, the introduction lays out its seemingly simple terms for engaging with the world after reading the narrative. In a way, then, Brace's narrative is a secularization of the means to end slavery, attempting to convert individuals into anti-slavery proponents through the individualized change that reading can supposedly produce within a subject. Instead of divine judgment and the divinely induced liberation found in Richards, in Brace we see a liberal model of change effected through the individual.

Where Richards wants an eschatological conclusion to slavery—one that threatens to decimate the "federal temple"—Prentiss asserts that such anti-slavery work can be accomplished through a combination of individual realignments of feeling and the alteration of the legal codes that have justified and legalized slavery. But where to place Jeffrey Brace in this matrix of Richards's eschatological refusal and Prentiss's liberalism? Continually rebuffed, Brace turns his exclusion from early republican citizenship into an occasion to insist on his attachment to the very formations that exclude him, asserting that his narrative would inculcate "that freedom . . . which all mankind have an equal right to possess" (182). Brace returns from his sense of alienation with an insistence on being heard, on being received by the publics that had refused him—from the town of Milton that would kick him out to the fledgling United States that would refuse his and other non-white men as citizens for another fifty-five years. "And now after having passed through so many varying scenes of life," he explains to the lawyer who wrote down his story,

> and having lost my beloved companion, as before mentioned, and being left, as it were, alone in this world. I have concluded it my duty to myself, to all Africans, who can read, to the Church in short to all mankind, to thus publish these my Memoirs, that all may see how poor Africans have been, and perhaps now are abused by a christian and enlightened people. (200)

Brace's insistence on declaring himself as a recipient of the promise of republican belonging queers scholarly understandings of the early republic, turning his articulation of loneliness at the end of his book—and his desire

CIVIC VIRTUE AND STATE POWER 105

for a public of "all mankind" to receive his words—as a manifestation of what José Esteban Muñoz calls the coming of queerness that pushes the man buried as Jeffrey Brace, but born as Boyrereau Brinch, "beyond the quagmire of the present" (1). The present moment of composition, for Brace, is a scene of subjection that he pushes against, making his narrative "an insistence on potentiality or concrete possibility for another world" (1). But unlike Richards's end-of-times world, Brace asserts his quotidian desire to simply *be*, unencumbered by the constraints that have delimited him from republican belonging, to have his memory preserved, his family formation acknowledged, and his voice ringing across a print public. But that book, containing his queer, precarious hope, fell on ears that resented his claims to citizenship, leading the selectmen to lift up figurative and literal walls as they banished him.

The penultimate page of the book includes a woodcut of a nature scene, with grasses and short limbs surrounding a snapped tree trunk (see Fig. 2.5). The image fills the page, occupying a spot of emptiness with the Latin phrase "MIRICA SUNT / OPERA DEI," which translates into "wonderful are the works of God." This seemingly arbitrary image, perhaps used to fill the space, returns the emphasis on the aloneness of Brace that the penultimate chapter explores. It stands as a resolution to the interpersonal loss and dislocation that Brace has recounted throughout his book, especially the concluding turn to resolve how "[t]he partner of my life was called from me, and her soul wafted into a boundless eternity" (189). This image—the only of its kind in the book—parallels Brace's loss, showing a broken tree to signal his disconnections, figuring a woodcut to index Brace's own particular queered attachment.

This queer reading of Brace shows the challenge of sociality for persons of color confronting the limits of citizenship in the early republic. The unrequited desire for sociality frames queer theorist Michael Cobb's reading of loneliness in *Single: Arguments for the Uncoupled* (2012). Although speaking of the contemporary, he describes the state's vested interest in making individuals feel as if they either belong or don't belong. Cobb postulates: "People want to belong so they don't feel menaced by their isolation. I'm convinced that the nation-state might very well want us to feel such desperate desires for belonging. . . . The feeling of loneliness produces sensations of desperation that open one up to the cruel ideologies of totalitarianism—ideologies that produce compelling ideas, full of persuasive power, whose logics are much too consistent, much too able to misread the circumstances of the world, providing instead a paranoid 'sixth sense' " (19). The early republic's mobilization

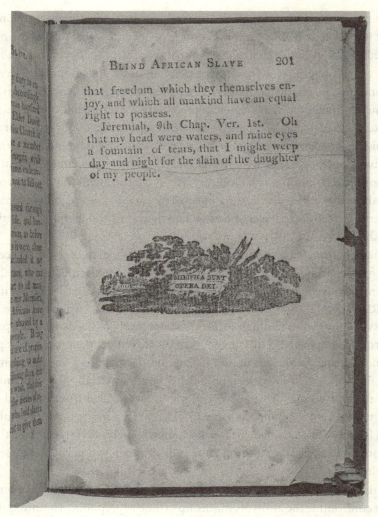

Figure 2.5 Last page of the final chapter in *The Blind African Slave* with a curious woodcut suggesting pastoral finality. Courtesy of the American Antiquarian Society.

of loneliness, and its production of unbelonging, operates differently across lines of racial difference, where Brace's desire to attain republican sociality actually queers those very formations. With Brace, we witness his intransigent refusal to settle into non-sociality, challenging the republican formations that rely on his subjection, and turning the representation of his "lonesome situation" toward the imagining of a new politics.

3

Federalism in Drag

Timothy Dexter's *Pickle* and Other Perverse Properties

> The agents of delusion are the great, the wise, rich and mighty men of the world.
>
> —Abraham Bishop, *Connecticut Republicanism*

> I have heard indeed that my predecessor [John Adams] sometimes decided things against his council by dashing & trampling his wig on the floor.
>
> —Thomas Jefferson to William Short, June 12, 1807

John Adams knew there was something dramatic about pulling a wig from atop one's head. Readers of Thomas Jefferson's *reading* of John Adams's "dashing & trampling his wig on the floor," as he notes in his letter to William Short referenced in the epigraph, have often signaled the hermit of Monticello's repulsion from expressive public displays that perform strong emotional declarations, making his observation of his predecessor's penchant for emotional explosions characteristic of his petty critiques. In his tome on early U.S. history, Henry Adams—the great-grandson of the former Adams—writes that "Wigs were Federalist symbols of dignity and power," making the tearing them off one's head an iconic moment of emotional intensity (435).[1] As historian Susan Branson notes, both Federalists and Democratic-Republicans in the early United States aspired to "control the

---

[1] Jefferson's antagonism toward what he called "the party, so falsely called federalists" stems from what he saw as an impulse to insert "authorities hereditary" into government positions. What's interesting here is that he seems to valorize a type of non-reproductive-based model of political inclusion, which might be read as whiteness, considering that before he took office he had already fathered Beverley Hemings with Sally Hemings. He would seemingly have a vested interest in ensuring that power and authority in the early republic not be tethered to his paternity. See Thomas Jefferson to David Howell, December 15, 1810, where he outlines his specific beliefs through supporting a Republican governor to Rhode Island.

Feeling Singular. Ben Bascom, Oxford University Press. © Oxford University Press 2024.
DOI: 10.1093/9780197687536.003.0004

108   FEELING SINGULAR

meaning of the nation's political symbols, ceremonies, and celebrations, and therefore define the nature of people's participation in American society" (3–4). The symbolics of the Federalist wig—torn from one's head in a moment of desperation—parallels the gesture of late twentieth- and early twenty-first-century drag cultures, best exemplified when Sasha Velour in the Grand Finale of RuPaul's *Drag Race* season 9 (2017) lifts her red wig from her bald head during the climax of Whitney Houston's "So Emotional."[2] This trans-historical reference—where the example of Sasha Velour in drag is *dragged* into the past to reread John Adams—informs the campy, queer methodology elaborated in the subsequent pages.

Early Federalist emotiveness, and the desire for pomp and pageantry to structure the site of political influence, may be understood as a particular form of drag, one that embraces a failed seriousness, literally and figuratively throwing back for the social certainties of monarchy.[3] Not only is there something drag-like to Federalist patriotism, but drag as a performative artform helps frame the complicated legacies of state power, political pageantry, and the early U.S. nation-state.[4] The idea of Federalist fashion became an important source of critique around the emerging political party system. The great-grandson Adams describes "the full paraphernalia of Federalism" as "wig and powder, cocked hat and small sword," making the accoutrements of such forms of masculinity an effort to dress up to play the part of Federalism (453). In jockeying for power, conflicts often centered on questioning and contesting Federalist masculinity. For instance, James Lyon, the son of Matthew Lyon, began several Republican newspapers and magazines that sought to cultivate specific readerships through attacking Federalists with

---

[2] In comparing Sasha Velour to John Adams, I am seeking to highlight the gendered aesthetics of last-straw gestures. I use the adjective "gendered" here to mark something that was often both un-mentioned and assumed. Gender, in this sense, becomes a strategy that allows the display and circulation of certain bodies-as-presented along particular genres. Gender and sexual identity, as Lauren Berlant notes, is a type of genre: "To call an identity like a sexual identity a genre is to think about it as something repeated, detailed, and stretched while retaining its intelligibility, its capacity to remain readable or audible across the field of all its variations. For femininity to be a genre *like* an aesthetic one means that it is a structure of conventional expectation that people rely on to provide certain kinds of affective intensities and assurances" (*The Female Complaint* 4).

[3] Drawing upon Elisa Tamarkin's point in *Anglophilia*, "We need to better examine how national-ism, as a form of feeling, an ideology, and a set of practices, works every bit as seriously at bringing some aspects of the outside in, as it does at keeping others out" (xxvi).

[4] In today's contemporary renaissance of drag, we are told its politics are always radical, but we might think about the moment in 2000 when Rudy Giuliani dressed up in drag and Donald Trump stuck his face between Giuliani's protruding breasts. This attempt at comedy does not only rely on misogynistic humor but also on a display of power in a splayed moment of vulnerability. Giuliani-as-woman being sexually harassed by a real estate mogul is, perhaps, a deeply American moment.

Figure 3.1 "Congressional Pugilists," Philadelphia, 1798. Courtesy of the American Antiquarian Society.

his political rag, *The Scourge of Aristocracy*. In these writings, Federalists are portrayed as effeminate men who fawningly strive for British attachments to monarchy, making the signal of particular clothing fashions tantamount to an overattachment to pomp and pageantry much like drag's camp aesthetic.[5] A political cartoon of the 1798 fight in Congress between Matthew Lyon and Federalist Roger Griswold portrays the two in various states of disarray, flinging tongs and a phallus-like walking stick into one another (see Fig. 3.1). The wry smiles of most of the audience suggest the pleasure some received from such a spectacle. Historian Joanne Freeman notes that much of the complications around clothing—and their affiliation with either

---

[5] Joseph Dennie, one of the most prominent Federalist writers, exemplifies this effeminate attachment to the pomp and circumstance of Monarchy in the early Republic. See Sandra Tomc's chapter on him in *Industry & the Creative Mind: The Eccentric Writer in American Literature and Entertainment, 1790–1860* (2012), especially her reading of his letters to his mom, where he writes: "Had it not been for the *selfish* patriotism of that hoary traitor, Adams, and the bellowing of Molineux . . . I might now, perhaps, in a Literary Diplomatic, or lucrative Situation been in the service of my rightful King and instead of shivering in the bleakness of the United States, felt the genial sunshine of a Court" (59).

110 FEELING SINGULAR

aristocratic or common aesthetics—"were the natural result of the politics of self-presentation" (48).

Scholars have long developed theories about eighteenth-century flamboyance and its connection to masculinity, exploring the expressive side of masculine presentation and the showiness that historian Kate Haulman calls "acceptable means of garnering attention" (164–165). One might define masculinity as the making legible and acceptable one's appeal for attention. George E. Haggerty argues that eighteenth-century efforts to "codify gender difference and marginalize excessive behaviors" stabilized the question around who and what could be considered part of public discourse (172). Masculinity in the early U.S. context encodes within itself a desire to be recognized—an aspiration for fame and cultural longevity—and in that manner brings forward questions regarding acceptable publicness. To be masculine is to have an authorized and legible influence beyond the domestic and private, wielding the unspoken permit that shapes the imagined public. Delving into the aesthetics of gender performance, I argue that masculinity orients one toward publicness to manufacture posthumous legacies. Focusing on Timothy Dexter (1747–1806), who had been marked as someone whose "ruling passion appeared to be POPULARITY," as the writer of his pamphlet-form obituary maintains, I propose that his masculine performances slide into modes of self-indulgent narcissism that constitute the repressed and submerged motivations of Federalist Party politics. Dexter offers a unique study into the gendered dynamics of seeking attention: "he rather chose to render his name 'infamously famous, than not famous at all'" (6). I read masculinity as a showy mode of gendered accoutrement that aims to coalesce and control attention. What is made visible when we read masculinity as the effort to grab the public by the horns, as it were, and thereby assemble an audience for attention?

The word *cocky* comes to mind, with its lexical relation to roosters and its banished second cousin the horned cuckold. Male-centered claims to public attention often get euphemized by adjectives, such as "masculine intrepidity" and "masculine impudence"—two phrases gleaned from Joseph Dennie's Federalist *Port Folio* that highlight the conceptual overlap of courage and arrogance.[6] As such, this chapter excavates a paramount figure

---

[6] See *Port Folio* 2.52, p. 413 and 2.36, p. 234. In her analysis of the figure of the lounger, Laura Rigal in *The American Manufactory* describes Dennie's *Port Folio* as "faux-aristocratic and bric-à-brac—a cabinet of curiosities rather than a Linnaean museum" (119). This idea of aspiring toward aristocratic ease and leisure parallels Dexter's own sense of basking in ease and monied comforts. Furthermore,

FEDERALISM IN DRAG   111

in American cockiness through examining the life and writings of "Lord" Timothy Dexter and the economic fantasies that he deployed to make his eccentricities appear anodyne. Dexter offers something far more insidious, however, when one considers the depths he plumbed to secure his name to posterity. I begin by showing how Dexter's wish to produce physical relics of himself—on paper, wood, and stone—mimics other more well-known political celebrities. He produced wooden statues of himself and other culturally significant individuals to market his particular mode of patriotism and wealth building. Dexter's strangest performance, encapsulated in print as *A Pickle for the Knowing Ones*, presents his life's work in a freely distributed quasi-pamphlet that shares the aesthetics of Americanism on a stage of "home-spun" reality. I then turn from Dexter's own disheveled self into how he drew upon speculation practices to produce his own wealth in ways that place him within-though-askance to Federalist models of the economy. This led to tensions within his own family, as his daughter's marriage to iconoclast and rabble-rouser Abraham Bishop falls apart even as Dexter's capitalist aspirations come to fruition. I conclude by reflecting on the apocryphal story of his performing his own funeral to observe how others, particularly his family, would mourn his loss.

3.1. Timothy Dexter's Homespun Antics

The misapplication of psychoanalysis to understand the past is one of the delicious pleasures of metaphor.[7] In this mode, the past lies dormant, awaiting to emerge into meaning and significance as the scholar sleuths out a story, assembling materials—providentially repressed—that require specialists to tease out their implications. Always on the lookout for some new object in the archive that, once read, would function like a key that unlocks a new understanding, literary scholars seem most drawn to this model. We

Rigal's summary of how others have viewed the editor—"as degenerate, derivative, transitional, Romantic, gentlemanly, genteel, an ideologue, a flaneur, and a fop" (128)—usefully epitomizes the disregard Americans offer for the arts and literary commentary.

[7] Mike Goode in *Sentimental Masculinity and the Rise of History, 1790–1890* makes the case that New Historicist critics have not attended to the enabling metaphors of psychoanalysis that structure their critical project: "While certain psychoanalytic critics may object that language *is* desire, my point is simply that the New Historicist critics' desires, and the operations of their feelings more generally, never seemed to matter very much to them when it came to understanding and assessing the historicity of their own critical project" (2).

112 FEELING SINGULAR

are interested in the singular and the exceptional, the remarkable and the unique, in ways that demand a great deal of meaning and significance from potentially unmeaning and insignificant material. Literary historian Susan Scott Parrish makes this point, arguing that "these backward glances" foster a "mood of psychoanalytically-inspired critique" that insists on a type of teleological certainty—basically, that the precondition of the present is always the result of the past, and we can somehow better understand our present through unlocking the nascent mystery embedded in all forgotten textual material (293). "Nothing," she counters, "can live in its proper inchoate contingency when it has the weight of hundreds of years of exceptional futurity pressing down upon its neck" (293). Although Parrish is critical of this mode, the metaphor of archival repression suggests the past has splayed out its symptoms in the form of textual ephemera that, having been preserved and archived, may now rest on the couch of analysis and speak forth their truths through scholars seated close by. This metaphor is particularly compelling as it provides language to explain why one gravitates toward certain cultural forms—the forms of the eccentric, the weird, strange, or unassimilable, as this chapter and the next attest. In turning to the strange case of "Lord" Timothy Dexter and his aspirations to be read as important within the emerging pantheon of early U.S. celebrity cultures, I illustrate the active repression of what Emerson in *Nature* calls his "mean egotism," pointing toward the very construction of personality as problematic within the political culture of the early United States. This story highlights the vexed relation between the rhetoric of public good within republicanism and the unrepressed desire for self-promotion and self-advancement that preconditions such efforts to construct commonality.

There is a convention in introducing lesser-known figures who will subsequently receive the attention of a close reading to offer a brief biography, with dates that plot the individual into linear time. But with the eccentricity of Dexter the theme, I would prefer to begin in medias res, as it were, in 1793, about three years after the U.S. Constitution enabled Dexter to amass a large fortune (through speculation, which embroiled him in a domestic dispute with his son-in-law, as mentioned earlier), when he stood atop a table on a small island in the Merrimack River and drunkenly celebrated his own public funding of a bridge. His particular inebriated toast for Newburyport's Merrimack Bridge gained the attention of regional newspapers, with the *Newburyport Herald* mockingly declaring the "*Amateurs* of taste were regaled with a beautiful oration in French, delivered in a masterly stile by the

Hon. TIMOTHY DEXTER, *Esq.*"[8] The association of Dexter with the French, in this specific moment, attempts to connect him to Jacobin energies, though his efforts to attach his name with honorifics and class-markers belie such association. This incoherent description challenges the comprehension of Dexter's performance. Although this account ironically calls Dexter's rambling mess "truly *Ciceronian*," this event prompted the newspaper to humorously parody Dexter, reprinting his various public declarations with phonetic spellings and without punctuation. [9]

Despite the ironic "truly *Ciceronian*" moniker, Dexter already had his unconventional self presented in print a year before in a New Hampshire newspaper: "In compliance with his request," the article begins, "and to oblige the ingenious gentleman, who is the author of the following lucubrations, they are inserted *verbatim et literatim*, as they came from his pen." [10] The text then asserts the sacrilegious declaration of being a free thinker: "the A bove is Rote at one A Clock at Night that this world is hell & men are Devils therefore wee free thinkers Cant think know mor of them then Devels only there is Diferrunt Sorts of Divels." Declaring all men devils, these "lucubrations" offer a sense of imagined immediacy—the midnight thoughts of a free thinker—and cast suspicion toward "all men" in a way that shows a struggling power dynamic. Yet the tone of this dispatch is vexed and curious, flaunting religious mores while also playfully appearing as an uneducated jokester.

By the moment that Dexter had stood atop a table on an island in the Merrimack River, he had already made himself somewhat infamous for drawing attention to himself through such newspaper antics. Importantly, Dexter wished to build this bridge because he assumed the population of the town would soon double, and if he had a stake on the bridge, he could increase his wealth through a toll. In this sense, the tolled bridge would not simply benefit the city of Newburyport but also encourage Dexter's own commerce, as his yard often displayed what newspapers called "exotic curiosities," like an "African lion" in 1795, that visitors would pay to see. Very explicitly, with Dexter, we see the figure of an individual who tethers private interest with public infrastructure, funding the building of roads and bridges that would enable his own economic development. Such dynamics are pointed out in several 1799 newspaper notices that thanked Dexter for his "SERVICES pro bono public," which included paving the road between the bridge and town,

---

[8] *Impartial Herald* (July 6, 1793): 3.

[9] *Impartial Herald* (July 6, 1793): 3.

[10] See "From a NEWBURYPORT PAPER," *Columbian Centinel* (Sept. 5, 1792): 102.

114 FEELING SINGULAR

leading travelers up to the fence of his property. Desiring to make travel to Newburyport easier, he imagines how the funding of this bridge will facilitate his own moneymaking schemes, with animal menageries and eventual statues drawing attention to his front yard as a spectacle.

A more substantial and normative petition of Dexter's and eight other "Petitioners" mark their interest in producing this "bridge across Merrimac River" as it would "greatly subserve the public interest and convenience, by affording a safe, prompt and agreeable conveyance to carriages, teams, and travelers at all seasons of the year, and at all times of tide, whereas great dangers are incurred and great delays often suffered by the present mode of passing in Boats." The transitive verb "subserve" obscures the way the bridge would promote not only the city of Newburyport but further the interests of the petitioners. Published in a 1791 Newburyport newspaper, and before his table moment, this petition appeals "*To the Honorable the Senate and the Honorable the House of Representatives of the Commonwealth of Massachusetts in General Court Assembled*" and seeks for legislative clearance to produce such infrastructure. Positioning himself as an arbiter of infrastructure, and marrying public and private investments, Dexter wishes to produce the means necessary to facilitate his own goods on the local and transatlantic markets. As I discuss in earlier chapters, this entangling of public and private concerns comes to mark the very production of the republic.

Word got around about Dexter's tabletop performance, and a concerted effort to discredit him as a disreputable subject ensued. A Boston paper referenced this supposed speech in French, explaining "the Orator confesses himself deficient in that language, and assumed it as a medium for conveying his ideas, merely because '*Frenchmen can so express them by gestures, as to act a play, and make themselves understood without speaking a word;*' we do not think that justice could have been done it, had we obtained a copy."[11] This notion of translatable "*gestures*" that convey Dexter's expressions highlights his desires to emerge into something iconic, something that leaves a memorable trace on cultural memory. The Boston newspaper continues: "For as the good lady said of Mr. *Whitfield's* sermon, 'You may print it, but alas! who can print the *tone?*' "[12] This notion that "tone" slips beyond the possibilities of textual representation—but instead remains within the realm of affect—signals the affective performance that Dexter embodies while attracting notice on his

[11] *Columbian Centinel* (July 13, 1793): 3.
[12] *Columbian Centinel* (July 13, 1793): 3.

FEDERALISM IN DRAG 115

island table. Dexter escapes representation in his mess, in his flamboyance of personality, and his speech can only be referenced as incoherent gestures. Just like the textual unevenness of his free-thinking newspaper articles, here we get a comment about the impossibility of translating "the *tone*" of Dexter into print.

What Dexter's gestures enable, however, is an embedding of patriotic ideology that comes to saturate his particular mode. This same account offered what is declared a "translation" of the speech, writing that it was to celebrate "the eighteenth year of our glorious independence" and how "*America* is an asylum for the afflicted, persecuted and tormented sons and daughters of *Europe*. Our progress toward the glorious point of perfection is unparalleled in the annals of mankind." Very explicitly, America becomes written as the fulfilment of the European Enlightenment, a space where the "joyful occasion" of independence can lean into the fantastical possibilities where "good nature, breeding, concord, benevolence, piety, understanding, wit, humour, punch, and wine, grace, bless, adorn, and crown us henceforth and forever: *Amen*." The ramshackle list of attributes, with the concluding use of "*Amen*," highlights the religious ramifications of Dexter's patriotic gesture. Here in this moment the messiness of Dexter gets reconfigured into a cleaned-up mode of nationalism, one where commerce comes to signify the fulfilment of social transformations. The language of "good nature, breeding, concord," among other terms, registers as a Federalist aspiration for a type of model citizenry, where he is set up as a pattern for others to follow, but Dexter's own incoherence suggests something less than serious—perhaps a failed seriousness that resembles camp. Dexter desires to become incorporated into the logics of a "joyful occasion" that celebrates the production of his personality into a stalwart figure of Federalist patriotism's drag-like aesthetics.

Dexter counterbalanced this portrayal of him drunkenly fumbling French through having published in *The Essex Journal & New-Hampshire Packet* a corrective that interprets his "gestures" as nothing more than the excesses of civic pride and celebration for the public good. He notes that his "speech in French" was cut short "on the account of the ill-breeding of a blue puppy, who impertinently endeavoured to upset my pulpit, or rather the table on which I stood."[13] Again, we see a potentially confusing and paradoxical episode. Historian Joanne Freeman notes that the use of words such as "*Coward*,

[13] *The Essex Journal & New-Hampshire Packet*, No. 473, July 10, 1793, p. 3.

116 FEELING SINGULAR

liar, rascal, scoundrel, and *puppy* all demanded an immediate challenge, for they struck at the core elements of manliness and gentility" (173). The use of "*puppy*" in this written and printed "speech in French," however, seems to be self-aware in its specification of a "blue puppy." The word "puppy" brings forward questions of honor that would conventionally lead to a duel, though may also perhaps refer to the chien-gris/weimeroner or the grand bleu de Grascogne, which were a type of dog that General Lafayette famously gifted to George Washington in 1785.[14] Either way, he is questioning a form of patriotism, and it turns the toast that celebrates "these United and happy States" as the beneficiaries of European Enlightenment, making "unparalleled in the annals of mankind" the people's "progress toward the glorious point of perfection . . . unparalleled in the annals of mankind." Dexter very clearly appeals to the aesthetics of nationalism and, in doing so, seeks to bring notice to himself.

The slippage between "pulpit" and "table" combines the praise for commerce and trade infrastructure that Dexter desires. As Dexter stands on a table, drunkenly propounding his economic value to Newburyport, and praising the United States for its supposedly Enlightenment-driven economic system, he appears as a queer cheerleader of patriotic capitalism. Indeed, we might imagine him as an evangelical capitalist, self-promoting his own contributions to build infrastructure by centering himself as the agent, and then applauding the very system that would sustain him.

Within the logics of capitalism and Dexter's emphatic speculation, anything can be turned into a commodity.[15] In the most infamous of Dexter's speculations, he supposedly sent warming pans to the Caribbean, which were then used as ladles for the processing of sugar into molasses, thus facilitating enslaved labor economies.[16] Stephen Mihm reminds that in the early republic "capitalism was little more than a confidence game," ensuring that "even the most far-fetched speculations could get off the ground" (11).

---

[14] Special thanks to Lauren B. Hewes and Nan Wolverton for their insights on this connection.

[15] Joyce Appleby critiques how other historians have written about capitalism in *Capitalism and a New Social Order: The Republican Vision of the 1790s,* writing: "Capitalism figured in historical texts then as an entity—an organic object—like an oak whose form was determined from the planting of the first acorn. Rather than imagine different groups of people in the eighteenth century responding selectively to the possibilities afforded by the market, scholars wrote about capitalism as an external force bending men and nations to its needs" (45). She connects landholders and farmers as developing a "liberated . . . imagination" where "old assumptions undermined, radical theories about individual freedom acquired plausibility" (46).

[16] This account is usually tied to exemplifying Dexter's eccentricity, but in doing so it misses the way certain modes of eccentricity get deployed to justify exploitative labor relations.

FEDERALISM IN DRAG   117

The presumed virtues of white republicanism enabled this mode of self-advancement through the confidence game of colonial speculation. Dexter, through his self-indulgent newspaper announcements, "appears, at first sight, a very trivial thing, and easily understood," to draw upon Marx's language of the commodity in *Capital: A Critique of Political Economy* (82). But when considering how he is seeking to draw interest to himself—raise his own personal profile through chance speculations and textually marking himself as different and unusual—we might conceive of his efforts to attract attention and construct public interest to be less innocuous, indeed quite malignant. Dexter seeks to transform his personality into a commodity, and then to market that epiphenomenon to gain more cultural significance. As such, the table Dexter stands on to give his interrupted declaration parallels Marx's own understanding of an actual table transformed into a commodity, when he writes: "It not only stands with its feet on the ground, but, in relation to all other commodities, it stands on its head, and evolves out of its wooden brain grotesque ideas, far more wonderful than 'table-turning' ever was" (82). Standing atop his table, Dexter places his body and his personality as commodities that raise his speculative wealth, transforming his self into a structure that would sustain his name into futurity.

Other wooden brains grew in the yard of Dexter's mansion, in the forms of wooden statues that stood as sentinels around his fantasy of being included in the myth-making production of the early national United States. These statues are interesting not as individual works of art but in what they constellate as a fantasy of cultural celebrity (see Fig. 3.2). Specifically, there's a profound incoherence to the mixture of figures, from King George to George Washington, and from Louis XVI to Napoleon Bonaparte, that suggests an impulse to cover all bases, as it were—all possible iconographic resonances of political celebrity circa 1800. This celebration of a figure on an elevated position—one that allows a sense of perspective that can foresee the future, constructs the government as being a thing above the people, raised up on pedestals for the adoration of those below—is a queering of Federalist fantasies of U.S. nationalism that seeks to render a public through adoration of the aesthetics of state power. Dexter's imagined sense of political greatness and patriotic panache led him to put forward political antics that dovetailed with the new formations of speculation and celebrity culture of the Federalist United States. Though his performances have vanished, like his memory,

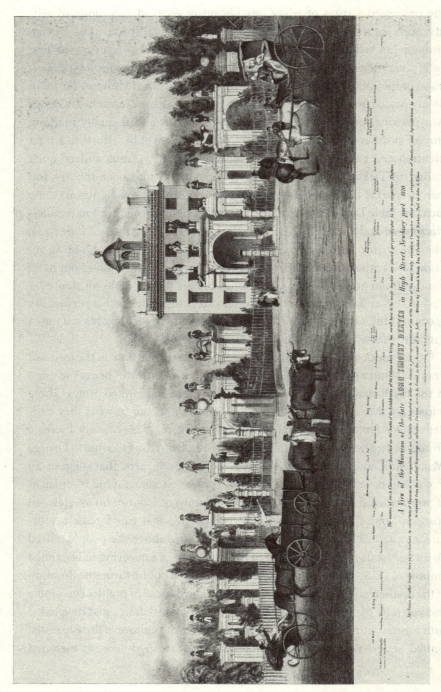

Figure 3.2 Lithograph of Timothy Dexter's house and yard statues by John Henry Bufford. Courtesy of the American Antiquarian Society.

their study occasions an opportunity to frame the construction of eccentric celebrity in the early United States.[17]

3.2. Eccentric Pickles

Dexter had built a persona for himself through his own unusual uses of print and self-centered advertising.[18] For instance, he had a picture of himself reproduced and then promoted its sale through dozens of advertisements throughout New England, noting: "THIS day published, and for sale at the Bookstore of Thomas and Whipple, sign Johnston's Head, Market Square, A full length Portrait of this Eccentric Character, with his *Dog*, engraved from Life by *James Aikin*".[19] Although Dexter himself dressed up in person and called himself a "Lord," he performatively dressed himself down—in "homespun dress"—in his curious textual legacy entitled *A Pickle for the Knowing Ones: or Plain Truths in a Homespun Dress* (1802) (see Fig. 3.3). Using no punctuation and disregarding the consolidating norms of English spelling, the book complicates his quasi-aristocratic social persona. Writing "TO mankind at Large," Dexter opens his strange text by referencing statues he placed in the front of his home of the first three presidents of the United States: "the time is Com at Last the grat day of Regoising [rejoicing] what is that whye I will tell you thous [those] three kings is Rased Rased you meane shoued know Rased on the first Royel Arch in the world olmost Not quite but very hiw up upon so thay are good mark to be scene so the womans Lik to see the frount and all peopel Loves to see them" (3) (see Fig. 3.4). Dexter's challenging prose attempts to model New England speech patterns, making intelligibility occur only through reading the syllables aloud. This curious use of print also emphasizes Dexter's particularity—how even his speech patterns refuse to be abstracted out of the form of print. Indeed, the lack

---

[17] One could say that Dexter is chasing the *It* factor that Joseph Roach explores in the book by the same name, though importantly the parameters of such celebrity continually frustrate his aspirations.

[18] The most recent extended focus on Dexter has been from the early twentieth-century novelist John P. Marquand, who began his career with a book about the myth of Dexter entitled *Lord Timothy Dexter* (1925). Where Marquand emphasizes Dexter's innocuous eccentricities, an anonymous biography in a typewritten manuscript at the Phillips Library renders Dexter less ideally, comparing him to Franklin and rendering them both unfavorable: "In spite of Franklin's genius, and brains, and self education; and the lack of all education, and all brains, in Dexter, there is, in many ways, a great resemblance between Dexter and Franklin, for Franklin was a peculiar man, a peculiar looking man, and Franklin's life was a cesspool kind of life" (3).

[19] See *Newburyport Herald* (Jan. 31, 1806): 4.

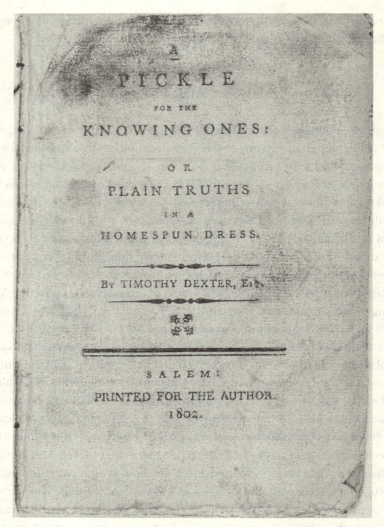

Figure 3.3 Title page of "Lord" Timothy Dexter's *A Pickle for the Knowing Ones*, printed for him in 1802. Courtesy of the American Antiquarian Society.

of punctuation shows Dexter's insistence on the aurality of reading print, exemplifying what Carolyn Eastman describes as the way "print and oratory were thoroughly interdependent and mutually constitutive" (5).[20]

---

[20] Carolyn Eastman in *A Nation of Speechifiers* explains: "Print and oral media helped lay Americans think of themselves as members of a unified body before nationalism had cohered and could be buttressed by institutions" (4).

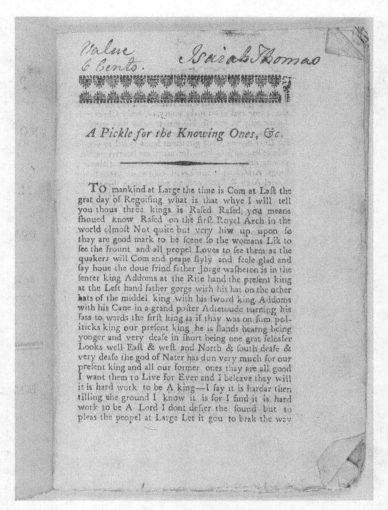

Figure 3.4 First page of "Lord" Timothy Dexter's *A Pickle for the Knowing Ones*. Courtesy of the American Antiquarian Society.

The individuals around what Dexter called his "Royel Arch" are very specific. George Washington, John Adams, and Thomas Jefferson in the center, with Adams's hat off in a sign of deference and Jefferson holding a paper that, in a sort of hodgepodge political reference, included the word 'Constitution' prominently, suggesting the Virginian as the author of that document while implicitly misremembering—or perhaps repressing—the Declaration's more equalizing function (see Fig. 3.5). Camp performance is on full display in

122 FEELING SINGULAR

Figure 3.5 The "Royel Arch" with John Adams, George Washington, and Thomas Jefferson. Courtesy of the American Antiquarian Society.

an anecdote the lawyer Samuel Knapp provides regarding the construction of the Jefferson statue.[21] Dexter, Knapp explains, confronts the artist, Mr. Babson, while the latter paints the Jefferson statue, insisting that the piece of paper the statue holds should be the Constitution. The artist "commenced his labor by taking the precaution to tie a rope around his body to prevent

---

[21] Knapp was a younger contemporary of Dexter, born in 1783.

FEDERALISM IN DRAG   123

accidents on the scanty staging, and made it fast to some part of the arch. He measured out his letter, 'The Declaration of Independence,' and . . . as soon as the painter had reached Dec, Dexter called out to him, 'That is not the way to spell Constitution'" (22). Directing the artist to transpose the "Constitution" as the "Declaration," Babson replies: "'You want,' returned the painter, 'the Declaration of Independence.' 'I want the Constitution, and the Constitution I will have'" (22). In this curious anecdote, Dexter does not conflate the two documents so much as exclude the one in praise of the other. The penchant to read the Declaration as a democratic and revolutionary text makes Dexter desire to submerge associations with it, prioritizing "the Constitution" for its work to stabilize economic markets from which he (unlike John Fitch) could amass wealth. Where the narrator of *The Blind African Slave* conflates the two documents as an act to claim Black belonging, here Dexter obscures the origin of the one to exploit his claims to the other.

Dexter resorts to violence to ensure that his prioritization of the Constitution above the Declaration is maintained.[22] This violence is marked by Knapp as a merely humorous anecdote, but Dexter's bullheaded, single-mindedness teaches readers about the excesses of masculine eccentricity when it becomes enabled through market speculation. Knapp continues:

the Declaration of Independence was a matter too deep in the recesses of ancient history for his lordship's memory; still, with the pertinacity of an honest mind, Mr. Babson would not erase his letters, for he knew what the artist intended. Dexter raved; the painter remonstrated most distinctly, when Dexter went into the house, brought out a large pistol and discharged it at his *man of letters* before the latter had a chance to escape. The ball entered the house and the marks of its passage were long afterwards seen there. The enraged lord

[22] Paul Downes, in a review essay of two books on early national literature and culture, writes: "Stripped to their bare rhetorical essentials, these documents have generated a familiar series of ideological oppositions: where the Declaration stands for liberty, natural rights, and the revolutionary rejection of authority, the Constitution connotes order, legal codification, and institutional security. The Declaration, with its opening temporal reference, invokes the immediacy of the revolutionary present (it was, and always will be 'live'); the Constitution, with its commitment to 'posterity' and to what 'shall be' ('in order to form a more perfect Union'), seems to sacrifice the charisma of the present in the name of a deferral that has everything to do with the 'establish[ment]'" (83). Downes notes that this insistence on toggling between these two disparate positions—one in favor of radical rupture, the other proposing staid and constitutional procedure—foregrounds many of the critical approaches of this period. What I find important to note, however, is how Dexter similarly enacts this type of bifurcation between the accompanying ideologies that have been read to inhere to these different texts.

124 FEELING SINGULAR

was no shot, and was fortunate in hitting the side of a house instead of the object of his wrath. The letters remain to this day, '*The Constitution*.' (23)

Although presented as the eccentric behavior of an egomaniac, the event is quite explicitly a violent enforcing and monumentalizing of a particular way to read history. Dexter forces the artist to create a monument of Jefferson that inscribes him into the role of writing the Constitution, reclaiming Jefferson in a campy effort at compromise. Indeed, the assortment of individuals—from William Pitt and King George to John Adams and Louis XVI, the guillotined king—signifies an incoherent menagerie of political significance, attaching to everyone in an effort to appease all parties (see Fig. 3.6).

In a later artistic rendering of the scene, it appears that Dexter uses language to draw upon a very ritualized presentation of political power, not the forms of mess that a revolution would produce. A 1795 pamphlet that declares it was published in what it pretends is the coherency of the "UNITED STATES," explains that "[i]mmediately after the declaration of independence, and before the articles of confederation were compleated, the thirteen States, altho they were united in their declaration of independence, yet they were *each* entirely, absolutely, and unlimitedly sovereign; possessing, *separately* all the rights of empire, of jurisdiction, and domain, acknowledged by the law of nations, to be attached to compleat sovereignty" (5). The configuration of the disparate political powers allowed the states autonomy and shut down the possibility of unison. In this manner, Dexter operates as a type of Federalist, one who seeks the iconography of centralized power even as he places himself amid those potential actors. Calling Washington, Adams, and Jefferson "kings," Dexter positions himself next to them. Invoking the pomp of monarchy, he refuses to settle into the margins of the early republic but insists that his Newburyport neighbors admire him as the center of government. The connection to monarchical aspirations seems a flagrant avowal of what others said about monarchy-loving Federalists.

A Pickle for the Knowing Ones, which Dexter paid to be published and distributed for free, signals his desire to produce a lasting legacy, and his refusal to reproduce the norms of writing illustrates his desire to demarcate himself as unusual. The aurality of the object, where its textual and linguistic cues insist on not reading but instead speaking, shows how Dexter wished to intervene in the print strategies that would otherwise stabilize the construction of an individual into a position of cultural significance. Class aspirations emerge front and center with Dexter's appeal to greatness, an

Figure 3.6 Close-up of the political celebrity statues surrounding Timothy Dexter's yard. Courtesy of the American Antiquarian Society.

126 FEELING SINGULAR

appeal that troubled the elite and established persons in New England. For instance, Salem minister William Bentley notes in a 1792 diary entry: "Saw upon my return the celebrated monied man of Newbury Port. He accosted me without knowing me at the public House, Lynn" (1.395). This reference to being "accosted" without a proper introduction signifies Bentley's sense of difference from Dexter, of whom he notes earlier that "by speculation had amassed a large sum of money & not content with his own sphere, first purchased the house of Nath. Tracy & there awkwardly exhibited his pranks, then put himself in a ridiculous situation in the meeting-house" (1.391). This focus on "sphere" and Dexter's class climbing returns through other entries in Bentley's diary, when he notes "[t]his man has secured many thousand pounds by speculations in the funds & paper money" (1.395).

Through his new money, Dexter sought to ingratiate himself with the elite and so-called worthy individuals. Doing so seemed to have an effect on Bentley, who wrote about a decade after their first "accosted" introduction: "Timothy Dexter of Newbury Port was with me this day. This singular man has presented his 'Pickle to the knowing ones' to the Governour & made a distribution of his farago farraginum [sic] among the first Characters. It is impossible not to call him a lunatic sui quo ad hoc. His intemperance does not appear to have been the original cause of his follies, as they appear in his whole character, & in his whole life" (2.435). Calling *A Pickle for the Knowing Ones* a "farago farraginum"—or a hodgepodge mixture of incoherence—Bentley offers insight on how those more established figures perceived Dexter and eventually accepted his society. The negative formulation of "[i]t is impossible not to call him a lunatic sui quo ad hoc" implies that Dexter was considered insane, though the last sentence implies that that insanity was not acquired so much as constitutive of his person. But this anecdote also shows how the elite began to accommodate this "lunatic," humoring him through accepting his bizarre writings.

Considered insane by his contemporaries, Dexter still managed to attract the notice and attention of the established families and personalities of New England, perhaps from his sudden and unexpected rise to wealth. One might imagine, however, that Dexter's difference helped facilitate that notice. Dexter's text illustrates the curious ways an individual claims significance in the early republic, producing statues in something he calls a "tempel of Reason" [sic] where he also positions likenesses of himself (4).[23] Knapp

---

[23] Unfortunately for cultural memory, most of Dexter's statues of "grat [sic] men" were destroyed in an 1815 hurricane that hit Massachusetts. Knapp notes that "[t]he rest of the columns stood the

FEDERALISM IN DRAG   127

notes: "Dexter had put himself among the great he delighted to honor, and labeled the column, 'I am the greatest man in the EAST;' and I believe once it was extended to the North, West and South, and his fame as a philosopher made an addendum. What a satire on monumental glory!" (Knapp 21). Dexter emphasizes his singular, exceptional self to justify his inclusion in the emerging pantheon of early republican greats.

Those who have written about Dexter's own personal writings tend to index his style as one of democratic eclecticism, but his self-presentation seems to border on a campy imitation of the aristocracy. Susan Sontag in her "Notes on Camp" suggests the overlap between aspirations to aristocracy and camp, writing: "Aristocracy is a position vis-à-vis culture . . . and the history of Camp taste is part of the history of snob taste" (200). Dexter seems to appeal to a common denominator that, as he writes, is "greater in views of men and things than College-learnt men." This misses the way the text attempts to striate the social sphere with various levels and hierarchies, however, especially when considering how the book performs a puzzle—a pickle—that only the select "knowing ones" can decipher. The pamphlet seeks to perform specialized logics of inclusion that come to refuse certain modes of belonging that require training: instead of "College-learnt men," Dexter seeks to attract not so much a reading audience than an in-the-know audience. For instance, in the opening of the 1802 version, he announces "TO mankind at Large" that "thous three kings is Rased Rased . . . on the first Royel Arch in the world" (3). Here he seeks to assert the centrality of his vision for a center of the world, making a form of monarchical centrality. He wants a firm, stable mode of identification, one that enshrines the first three U.S. presidents as "kings" that reign over the symbolics of the economic field, wanting something to be really grand and exquisite that can connect himself to a larger concept of the nation. He is serving Federalist *realness*, in the sense that he articulates all the fears of Republican anxieties of Federalist love of monarchy in an exaggerated manner. And he offers his fantasy in the language of his Massachusetts particularity.

Through the course of the 1790s, after continually raising money through financial speculation, Dexter situates himself among the emerging pantheon of elites. In *A Pickle for the Knowing Ones*, he takes upon himself the epithet "Lord" in this manner (see Fig. 3.7):

---

sunshine and storms until 'the great September gale,' which happened in 1815, when most of them were thrown down in that tornado" (26–27). The only known surviving fragments are in the Museum of Old Newbury of Newburyport, Massachusetts. The Smithsonian Museum has reconstructed the William Pitt statue and has loaned it out to the Museum of Old Newbury.

128 FEELING SINGULAR

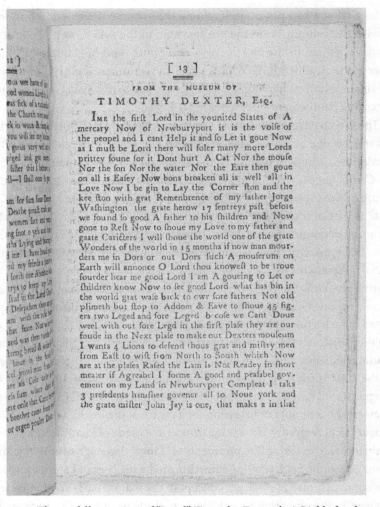

Figure 3.7 The middle portion of "Lord" Timothy Dexter's *A Pickle for the Knowing Ones*, when he describes the various statues in his front yard. Courtesy of the American Antiquarian Society.

IME the first Lord in the younited States of A mercury Now of Newburyport it is the voice of the peopel and I cant Help it and so Let it goue Now as I must be Lord there will foler many more Lords prittey soune for it Dont hurt A Cat Nor the mouse Nor the son Nor the water Nor the Eare then goue on all is Easey. (13)

FEDERALISM IN DRAG 129

A few important aspects come front and center here. The spelling of "America" as "A mercary" renders the word closer to "mercenary" in a way that positions the United States as a mercantile operation. For Dexter, the United States is a business, one that produces itself within the idea of market economics, though that reality must be dressed in "homespun" for people to swallow such a pickle. The markets that constitute the United States experienced difficulty in transporting goods, leading to the Constitution and later coalescing into the War of 1812 as the United States emerged into formidable state power on the global stage. In this way, "A mercary" also signifies Mercury, the messenger God, as connections are made in various manners that trouble the formulations of power. Additionally, the spelling "younited" renders aurally stable the second-person pronoun. Declaring himself the "first Lord," Dexter also inputs the "you" in "united" to recalibrate a mode of belonging that focuses on self-expression and self-advancement.

Additionally, through his odd book, Dexter attempts to traffic in a type of democratic form—with the "voice of the peopel" substantiating his claim to the epithet "Lord"—but obviously in doing so he demarcates himself as different, setting himself outside the people to assert his representativeness. Having been a leather dresser and now "the celebrated monied man of Newbury Port," he comes to facilitate a certain Munchausen imaginary that configures an individual who climbs up to cultural significance through his own disorder. How very American, to configure oneself as worthy of attention based on accidental speculation that has produced wealth, and then appointing oneself a political moniker to safeguard that name into perpetuity, perhaps troubling Jefferson's notion of a "natural aristocracy" that he elaborated in one of his post-1812 makeup letters to John Adams.

3.3. Federalist Fantasies and the Phantasmatic Self

Following historians David Hackett Fischer, Stanley Elkins, and Eric McKitrick, we might think of 1790s Federalism as an elite social formation that sought to enshrine hierarchical relations to stabilize the role of trade in furthering the implicit nationalizing project begun with the Constitution. Early Federalism, as I argue, became the means to articulate the structure of nationalism, imagining an aesthetics of state power in ways that would help produce a docile citizenry shaped around valorized and normalized market

130 FEELING SINGULAR

speculation.[24] Later in the 1790s, then, those persons occupying positions of authority within the Federal apparatus were accused of being aspiring (or actual) aristocrats, offering a sense of performed seriousness. Sontag makes the point that camp, as an aesthetic, has its origins in the eighteenth century. "In naïve, or pure, Camp," she writes, "the essential element is seriousness, a seriousness that fails" (196). A seriousness that intentionally flounders in its unraveling certainly defines Dexter's efforts to produce himself as a significant individual. Thinking of Federalism in terms of camp highlights the aspiration to a seriousness that fails.

As with the description of John Adams in the epigraph, the critique of Federalist power often coalesced around questions of gender, like when an anonymous writer (paid by Jefferson) described Adams as "that hideous hermaphroditical character, which has neither the force and firmness of a man, nor the gentleness and sensibility of a woman" (Callender 57). Returning to the opening anecdote of Jefferson's complicated admiration for Adams's rhetorical and flamboyant wig throwing, we might see here a type of disgust at the penchant for wig throwing. The alliteration "hideous hermaphroditical" offers a hissing sound that levels Adams down to the status of a monstrous gender, one that goes both ways, or is otherwise indeterminate. The inadequacies and excesses of gender inform the critique of Federalism, as those participating in buttressing Federalism are read as attached to the excesses of presentation. David Waldsreicher observes that "partisan causes had been equated with everything, including dress, manners, and religion" due to "the Republican antiaristocratic politics of style and the Federalist repression of 'Jacobinism'" (203). The politics of federalist belonging centralized on one's garb and hat, denoting a black cockade as a particularly Federalist fantasy, whereas the emerging Democrat-Republicans sported French-inspired colors to signify their distaste for the exclusionary practices of electoral votes and capitalist accumulation as tethered to restrictive property rights. The physical display of clothing attempted to paint solidarities and make in-group recognitions that coalesced around and validated white, male, propertied identities.

---

[24] The Yazoo Act of 1795, an illegal selling of real estate in the South (specifically from Western Georgia to the Mississippi) that moneyed Federalists speculated on, is a key moment that illustrates the burgeoning speculation culture enrapturing the early United States. For more on this, see forthcoming work by Franklin Sammons in his book manuscript "Yazoo's Settlement: Law, Finance, and the Political Economy of Dispossession."

The erection of a new government, in the post-ratified Constitution, sought to facilitate economic relations more fully, in ways that the Articles of Confederation had kept decentralized. But along these lines, the Constitution enabled the erection of corporate entities that streamlined the production and copyright of laboring devices that would then dominate the nineteenth century and expand enslaved labor, such as the cotton gin. A central power centralizes and materializes—at least ideologically—the means by which individuals attach to larger cultural formations. Dexter sought to capitalize on these newly available trade infrastructures. Yet as his biographer notes: "His acquisitions became so ample that money was no longer an object of his pursuit. He now fixed his heart on popularity; and, it is said, he made large sacrifices to it; giving large donations to riligious [sic] societies, and being very charitable to the poor. Whether the following instances of Lord Dexter's generosity, were sacrifices to fame, the reader will judge" (Plummer, "Something New," 9). In this manner, Dexter sought to utilize the forming government as a mechanism to write himself into the political and cultural landscape.

As referenced in Chapter 1, historians have narrated the transition from the Articles of Confederation to the Constitution as one of failed "weakness" to one of a robust checks-and-balances approach that facilitated the inception of state power into a consolidating formation. In the late 1780s, as the Articles of Confederation countered efforts to streamline the economies of the one-time colonies, a political coupe called the Constitutional Convention convened and proposed what is now known as the U.S. Constitution, which attempted to collect the states through a federal infrastructure that would lessen intra-state competition. The efforts to stabilize that contestable legitimacy, through what David Waldstreicher calls "perpetual fetes," set in motion the desire to attach to the emerging nation-state, following what Laura Rigal calls "a spectacular conjunction of fellow feeling with productive work" (25). The emergence of Federalism coincided with an aesthetics of hierarchy that affirmed differentiation. If there is productive work, there is also unproductive meandering, wasteful trash, the detritus that markets itself as productivity but eddies instead into the morass of consumption. The meaning of trash and waste, highlighted through the aspirations that seek to make detritus significant, structures how I think about the way one individual manufactured his own problematic greatness into a modicum of configured identity.

132   FEELING SINGULAR

The nascent capitalist impulse to tether the one-time colonies through the union of trade produced the waste of failure. The effort made visible a new stage of cultural belonging, one that envisioned markets for the products of cultural significance, and that positioned trade as the onus and agenda of belonging. In addition to these, they also unleashed avenues of self-promotion that individuals like Dexter took advantage of, orchestrating for themselves a fantasy of self-construction. The aspirational construction of state legitimacy in the United States is tethered to the elevation of such figures. Since its formation, the United States has made a business in self-promotion, a multitiered corporation that prioritizes economic advancement of the singular (through the language of democracy and virtue) and the fantasy of market independence, offering for some the figment of freedom through buying and selling oneself as a marketing strategy.

3.4. Anxiety of Legacy and the Production of Legitimacy

The question of how to secure a name and likeness into perpetuity dogged many of the Founding generation. The Atlantic world's homespun arts and presentation of celebrity facilitated a fawning interest in the celebrated likenesses of Benjamin Franklin, sporting a beaver hat or wielding lightning from the clouds, opening the way for individuals to feel in some manner attached to such a figure.[25] Just as newly emergent cultures of celebrity fostered interest in the visual likeness of certain individuals, the political leaders also sought to inculcate images that would stabilize themselves into historical perpetuity, to thereby secure the future of the republic. J. Hector St. John de Crèvecoeur sought to enshrine the imagined "New American" into text before he learned that the new government wished to produce a marble bust of General Washington, and while in France facilitated Thomas Jefferson's connection to such matters. Jefferson became a major driver to accomplish such busts of Revolutionary-famous individuals, expressing a desire to carve certain persons into the formation of cultural longevity. After Franklin and Jefferson convinced the State of Virginia to pay for as well as cover the life insurance of Jean Antoine Houdon, Washington coyly

---

[25] Edmund Morgan in his biography of Benjamin Franklin argues that "Franklin himself figured" prominently in the calculated risk France took to support the Americans: "Public opinion did not operate directly on the French government through any institution. But as Franklin had reminded the British government so often and so ineffectually, all governments depend ultimately on opinion" (260).

writes "though the cause is not of my seeking, I feel the most agreeable and grateful sensations" (qtd. McRae 8).[26] This need of Washington's to ensure he is not perceived as "seeking" the occasion to have his likeness carved into marble requires his own rhetorical distancing. Yet after Houdon portrayed him in neoclassical garb, Washington insisted on updating his clothing to be contemporary, illustrating his own anxiety about how his likeness would garner contemporaneous and future attention. Similarly, the portrayal of Benjamin Franklin as a type of homespun hero, toggled between neo-classical likenesses and more devil-may-care portrayals. The likenesses of Washington and Franklin that circulated within Atlantic-world celebrity economies attempted to fashion certain virtuous ideals surrounding loyalty and industry, novelty and genius, that framed others' entrances into the same field of imaginary excellence.[27]

The tradition of sitting for a portrait—and its resonances with efforts to enable a future that remembers one's likeness—was drawn upon by many in this turn-of-the-century moment of economic shifts and newly repositioned agency and mobility. Contrary to these grand images of selfhood, the mode of traveling artists painting portraits of the not famous but yet moneyed, like Erastus Salisbury Field, configured a type of fantasy around visual likenesses, available beyond the marble. The work of what is today called "folk art" offered a new economy of attention and celebrity. The ability to have produced a likeness of oneself ensured a new relation to the idea of social continuity and publicness. It meant you could be visually inserted into another mind's eye without being bodily present,

---

[26] Epistolary conversations regarding this proposed sculpture were at the earliest in 1784, which significantly predates the Constitution and remained under the Articles of Confederation. The fantasy of imagining Washington as a centralizing and unifying figure seems embedded in the motivation leading to secure the most sought-after artist, while the first "finished" date of the sculpture—1788—coincides with the Constitutional debates, even though the sculpture wasn't finished until 1791 or 1792, and not delivered until Washington's last year in office (1796). Jefferson writes to the Virginia delegates in 1785: "I would not have done this myself, nor asked you to do it did I not see that it would be better for Congress to put this business into his hands, than into those of any other person living, for these reasons: 1. he is without rivalship the first statuary of this age; as a proof of which he receives orders from every other country for things intended to be capital: 2. he will have seen General Washington, have taken his measure in every part, and of course whatever he does of him will have the merit of being original, from which other workmen can only furnish copies" (qtd. in *Houdon in America: A Collection of Documents in the Jefferson Papers in the Library of Congress* [Baltimore: Johns Hopkins P, 1930], 14). The Virginia Assembly waited until 1853 to authorize the recasting of the sculpture for other casts. (See *George Washington: Sculpture by Jean Antoine Houdon; a brief history of the most famous sculpture created of America's immortal patriot* [Providence: 1931], 23).

[27] There is a repressed narcissism that's involved in this desire to create likenesses. Jefferson himself had sat for Houdon in 1789, already positioning himself within an emerging tradition of emblazoning one's subjective self for others' gazes into perpetuity.

134 FEELING SINGULAR

having one's influence present in one's bodily absence.[28] With new accessibility to presenting the physical likeness of an ordinary individual, a shift in the significance of such matters became pronounced. If more individuals could have their likeness fashioned for future posterity, then the significance of such iconography demands renewed consideration. Within these changing circumstances of visualization, Timothy Dexter used his newfound wealth to circulate his likeness in the print economies of attention.[29]

We catch a glimpse of the physical likeness of Dexter in an 1805 woodcut made by the artist James Akin, who is more famously remembered for the "A Philosophic Cock" engraving of Thomas Jefferson and Sally Hemings.[30] In that latter image, a boastful Jefferson-as-cock flaunts his breast and plumes his feathers, with wattles hanging from his chin like male human testicles, offering penis imagery that comes to overshadow the hen figure of a symbol of an enslaved woman. The gender presentation of masculine dominance threatens menacingly, allegorizing Jefferson's sexual appetite through the lexicon of racialized animals. In the less malevolent image, we see Dexter bedecked in anachronistic fashion, a throwback to a bygone age (see Fig. 3.8). But counterpoised to that backward glance, the text "I am the first in the East, the first in the West, and the greatest Philosopher in the Western World" floats in the air, suggesting the effort at newness, an insertion of a coherent self onto the page in anachronistic garb. Below the figuration of Dexter and his hairless dog flourishes a quotation from *Hamlet*: "What a piece of work is Man! how noble in reason! how infinite in faculties, in form & moving,

---

[28] Consider the history of icons and iconography. The visual importance of circulating likenesses helped create the enduring celebrity around George Washington and Benjamin Franklin. In the emerging economies of the newly formed republic, visual likenesses of others played a significant role in stabilizing affection for power and influence. Visual likenesses create a lasting sense of influence.

[29] The titular character in Charles Brockden Brown's *Wieland* becomes obsessed with Cicero and "purchased a bust of Cicero" from what the artist claims were copied "from an antique dug up with his own hands in the environs of Modena" (23). The narrator explains that the "Italian adventurer" had "erroneously imagined that he could find employment for his skill, and sale for his sculptures in America" (23). This subtle judgement of "erroneously imagined" emphasizes the lack of artistry and Euro-centric cultural productions in North America.

[30] In Federalist Joseph Dennie's magazine *Port Folio*, there appeared between the years 1802 to 1803 a series of bawdy, racist poems regarding Jefferson and Hemings: "You call her slave—and pray were slaves / Made only for the galley? / Try for yourselves, ye witless knaves— / Take each to bed your Sally" (see Basker 571). The object of the critique seems to be at multiple levels, as the title "A Song Supposed to Have Been Written by the Sage of Monticello" transforms the then sitting president into more than a charlatan for exploiting economic needs and sexual desires. For a compelling reading of this print, see chapter 1 of Justine Murison's *Faith in Exposure*, titled "Infidelity," which she reads as "the insistent coupling of disordered private morality with deism" (23).

Figure 3.8 "The Most noble Lord Timothy Dexter," engraving by James Akin (1806). Courtesy of the American Antiquarian Society.

how express & admirable!"[31] Here Dexter stands as the new man, straddling time on the page, plodding toward a static and uncertain future where he can be imagined as a self-made wealth producer through the accidental and

---

[31] In the original context of the play, these words are spoken after Hamlet has recognized that his supposed friends and confidants are trying to discover if he is mad. In this repurposed

136 FEELING SINGULAR

arbitrary work of financial speculation. The figure's proportions invite a parallel with a balloon, as the clothing seems tied up and the midsection appears engorged, the personification of a type of speculative inflation, a fraud dressed up for the town.

Masculine cockiness and its ineptitudes are on full display. Dexter, here, is companion to a dog, and they both trod along together into the page's blankness. Masculinity is always fraught by its own dependence, which dependence it seeks to disavow and forsake, to pretend the singularly defined *masculine* subject is and has always been independent. Yet masculinity also exposes a body for examination and observation, with Dexter here on the page offered as something to look *at* in all his eccentricity. "The history of the benevolent is beneficial to society," Jonathan Plummer writes in his biography of Dexter, "by serving as a pattern or stimulus to good and charitable deeds" (3). Plummer, the focus of *Feeling Singular*'s next chapter, positions Dexter as a benevolent "Lord," bequeathing his patronage on those structurally beneath him. Reading Dexter very much like a Franklin figure, Plummer describes him "rising from nothing, to a fortune so splendid" (7), and "among the motely group of his qualities" would have to be added "his numerous acts of liberality, both public and private" (6). These "numerous acts of liberality," though, were always positioned within the track of Dexter's own self-advancement. All efforts at constructing futures rely on the manifestation of an ego that wishes to project itself into the built environment. Masculinity operates through wielding the power of the anecdote to solidify its own influence and power. That is how power operates to consolidate itself—through the circulating anecdote that wins applause or aspersion. Franklin's silence and Washington's forbearance overshadow their mutual obsession with controlling how they are perceived (and indeed were their strategies to manage such control).

As a rhetorical case in point, we might reflect on Washington's own performance of losing his eyesight—offering a carefully staged presentation of physical decline to circumvent the Continental military commanders' overturning of civil government. There are a few iconic moments of U.S. state power deflecting its own contested authority. In this moment, Washington rubs off the dust from his spectacles as Revolutionary War soldiers quietly

---

context—framing an image of Dexter as he walks into a decrepit sense of history—the words come to focus on reframing the bodily integrity of "Man" as a figure that constitutes a new history. Dexter's own narrative of a mishap into wealth turns his life into a trope for imagining paths to new wealth, waltzing from the straps of his worn leather bootstraps.

FEDERALISM IN DRAG   137

entertain multiple competing petitions at Newburgh, New York, when Washington concluded "Gentlemen, you will permit me to put on my spectacles, for I have not only grown gray but almost blind in the service of my country."[32] This casual cleaning comes to signify a supposedly watershed moment of bequeathing power, showing weakness to deflect (and thereby later obtain) power. The performative show of weakness to deescalate tensions transforms the militarized figure of Washington into one for civic adoration, who then is celebrated for this display of political savvy.

In *Performance in America*, David Román explains that archives, when they manifest as official, "are understood as the repositories of a national culture," functioning as "the site where the story of the nation can be retrieved and retold" (137). The desire to produce objects that could last for future posterity—and Jefferson and his administration's resistance to produce larger national apparatuses like universities and archives—makes Dexter's public aspirations that much more absurd.[33] Following Román's observation about the construction of national mythologies, Dexter comes to manifest a type of intensely personal attachment to the figures of nascent power that positions him in proximity to their potency. What Dexter provides is an intense manifestation of desired-for influence, one that manufactures the symbols and aesthetics of political significance. What we see in Dexter's political iconography, then, is an effort to be *made* into something official, a performative space of patriotic expression that produces and propels the new American republic as it transitions into something beyond Federalist expansion.

Dexter showcases an individual who resists ideals of unselfish public good and instead promotes himself, having two monuments made of himself and situated in his "tempel of Reason." He ignores the classed dynamics that would render him a nonentity, positioning himself on the same plane, as he describes in *A Pickle for the Knowing Ones*, with "father Jorge washeton [. . .] in the senter[,] king Addoms [. . .] at the Rite hand[,] and the present king at the Left hand" (7). In addition to attempting to rewrite history, Dexter inserts himself as an iconic figure among his statues of Atlantic World cultural shapers. This strange insistence on an anachronistic history illustrates

[32] Military historian Richard Kohn describes the scene: "Unaffectedly, the tall general murmured that he had grown gray in the service of his country, and now found himself going blind. The assemblage was stunned. . . . The tension, the imposing physical presence of the commander in chief, the speech, and finally an act that emotionally embodied the Army's whole experience, combined all at once and shattered the officers' equanimity. Spontaneously they recoiled. Some openly wept" (210).

[33] Jefferson's work in safeguarding the Library of Congress after the War of 1812 might be exception that proves the rule.

138 FEELING SINGULAR

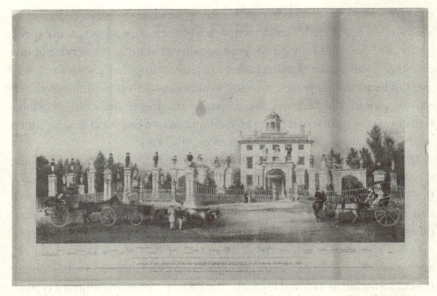

Figure 3.9 Large panoramic view of Timothy Dexter's house and yard. Lithograph by Benjamin Thayer (Boston: B.W. Thayer, 1841–1853). Courtesy of the American Antiquarian Society.

Dexter's desire to produce himself within the emerging iconography of the new republic. His projection of himself onto the center of the early national cultural stage comes to highlight his positionality as outside such possibilities. A lithographic representation of Dexter's house shows these curious wooden statues standing atop pillars in his front yard (see Fig. 3.9). The image depicts visitors and travelers stopping and pointing at the house, signaling their curiosity (see Fig. 3.10a–b). One might wonder if these gawking spectators are the "knowing ones" to which Dexter offers his pickle, who in pointing direct our gaze to the extravagant house; or perhaps they became "knowing" through querying the disavowing Plummer for the secrets kept safe from the normative conventions of print, as I explore in Chapter 4.

3.5. Dexter's Farraginous Domestic Scene

Dexter not only attempts to produce his yard as the symbolic center of the new republic but also endeavors to position himself as the proper and ideal

Figure 3.10a–b Close-ups of visitors pointing at the house and yard of Timothy Dexter. Courtesy of the American Antiquarian Society.

140 FEELING SINGULAR

citizen within such a world, contrary to all signs otherwise. After building his yard museum of statues, he began to publish more gibberish in newspapers, attracting notice and attention while making a name for himself through his eccentricities. In one New England newspaper, he claimed: "I AM greater in views of men and things, than College-learnt men, because they get into the habit of being waited upon, and use is second nature."[34] Asserting a superior position based on his experience, he offers a warning: "take care of your daughters, and young widows . . . for men that knows the earning of money," making himself sexually available through his amassing of wealth. "I ask the pardon of mankind for telling the truth," he concludes before including his name below his text: "For truth is not to be told at all times." Signaling a nontransparency through print—where sometimes the "truth" cannot "be told"—Dexter fashions a public interest in himself to then encourage readers to follow him, and then places himself as a particular threat to women.

Throughout Dexter's eccentric endeavors, he sought to make himself into a type of cultural commodity, beginning at least with his table-turned-pulpit and concluding with his bizarre yard antics. He offers not just himself, however, but a relation to expression and presentation, a flamboyance that uproots traditional stability through putting such optics of traditionalism on loud display. Albeit a flash in the pan, but a flash that reverberates into its own narcissistic gesture. He is very clearly self-promoting and through doing so laying bare the economic system of private wealth—as opposed to collectivism—that defines the American system. Private accumulation leads to an amassing of wealth under the pretext of building something for another. But unlike a conventional Federalist, who would deflect the commonness that a figure of the rabble embraces, Dexter wishes to insert his achieved significance into the sacrosanct halls of staid Federalist stability.

What does it mean to commodify oneself? In the cultures of personality, commodifying of the self signifies the desire to be heard and received by others, and to receive remuneration through that. Dexter seems to be empowered by this effort to make himself significant. In Lauren Berlant's *The Queen of America Goes to Washington City*, they note that "the fantasy of the American Dream" offers "[a] popular form of political optimism" that "fuses private fortune with that of the nation: it promises that if you invest your energies in work and family-making, the nation will secure the broader

---

[34] See "TO MANKIND AT LARGE," *Columbian Centinel* (Aug. 25, 1792): 190.

FEDERALISM IN DRAG   141

social and economic conditions in which your labor can gain value and your life can be lived with dignity" (4). Although Berlant is discussing a more post-Reagan discourse around citizenship, their theorization offers a way to see into the dynamics at play with Dexter's meandering saunter into (temporary) cultural significance.[35] He very explicitly draws out his own private property and personal speculative investment to construct infrastructure around his own selfhood.

The relationship between industry, consumption, and economic advancement was one of the more complicated issues that dogged Federalists in this period. Fisher Ames decried the commerce-obsessed Americans who were "governed by their passions" and thereby failed to arrive at the vestiges of true virtue that safeguard a republic ("American Literature" 27). These dynamics play out on a personal stage with Dexter surrounding his relationship to his son-in-law, Abraham Bishop, who he calls out in his Salem 1802 publication of *Pickle*, writing:

> T. DEXTER says four things—Wants good judgment to live in the world, in *giving* and *lending, trusting* and *borrowing*. For I begin to see I have already given my wife, that *was*, and my son Samuel L. Dexter, and Bishop, more than ten thousand dollars, in two years, and neither of them thank me. Now to all men that owes me, be so kind to themselves and me, as to pay me in a very short time, or else call and pay squire Bradbury's son and lawyer in *Newburyport*, without further trouble and cost. (19)

Asking for all the men who owe him to pay him back, he specifically notes the lack of thanks he has received from those whose family relations would presume more intimacy. What's particularly interesting is that he makes public his private and intimate life's failures: his wife "that *was*," his "son Samuel L. Dexter," and his son-in law "Bishop" have all transgressed, from his perspective, the gratitude he feels they owe him. Dexter's inflated sense of self-worth, and his preposterous advice to others, makes his strange public notice all about his lessons learned. He declares "Wants good judgment to live in the world" and specifies that judgment around monetary relationships of giving,

---

[35] Berlant continues in their theorization of the impoverished discourse around U.S. citizenship, by noting: "It is a story that addresses the fear of being stuck or reduced to a type, a redemptive story pinning its hope on class mobility. Yet this promise is voiced in the language of unconflicted personhood: to be American, in this view, would be to inhabit a secure space liberated from identities and structures that seem to constrain what a person can do in history" (4).

142   FEELING SINGULAR

lending, trusting, and borrowing. He configures himself as a repository of financial wisdom, and he clarifies that these guidelines inform his own intimate kinship relations.

Abraham Bishop's marriage to Nancy Dexter was short lived though it coincided with his rise to prominence as a vocal anti-Federalist. Beginning with his pamphlet protest of exploitative speculation practices that sought to transform Indigenous territories into parcels of U.S. nation-states, Bishop propelled invective against would-be speculators like his father-in-law in ways that suggest his own personal unraveling. In *Georgia Speculation Unveiled* (1797), he calls out the "usurped preemption" (10) and "frauds" (11) that were perpetrated against "the powerful, opulent and enlightened nations of the Creeks, Chactaws [sic] and Chickasaws" (35). Making the personal political, Bishop concludes his pamphlet with a long meditation on the east coast's business and commerce scramble for Indigenous territory. Known popularly as the Yazoo land scandal, where the State of Georgia sold land occupied by Indigenous nations and tribes (and also claimed by the Spanish Crown), the rising elite made a great deal of money off this affair.[36] Eventually this case went up to the Supreme Court, but Bishop draws upon this occurrence in order to think through the personal investments that defraud others, waxing evocative with repetitions and allusions:

> Long enough have friends stabbed friends, neighbours betrayed neighbours—and the wealth of centuries been wasted by the delusions of a moment.—Truth, honesty and commercial credit have suffered wounds deep enough: and all the friends of society feel grateful to the legislature, which arrested in its progress the destructive pestilence. Formerly the enemies of man frequented the public roads—put pistols to the breasts of unsuspecting travelers, and robbed them of the valuables they had about them; but the sufferers could return to their houses and lands, and by industry repair the loss.—We live to see robbery in a more refined stile. (38)

The repetitions at the beginning and the garrulous syntax, with multiple dependent clauses, set up the puncturing, staccato phrase at the conclusion: "We live to see robbery in a more refined stile." Contrasting highway robbery with speculative investments that steal from Indigenous peoples,

---

[36] Paul B. Moyer notes these efforts at speculation were also driven by "ordinary farmers searching for land on which to establish their (and their heirs') independence" (11).

FEDERALISM IN DRAG 143

defraud the public, and expand the coffers of private men in power, Bishop lambasts what he sees as the unbridled manner with which people create personal wealth.

> Men who never added an iota to the wealth or morals of the world, and whose single moment was never devoted to making one being wiser or happier throughout the universe—riding in their chariots—plotting the ruin of born and unborn millions—aiming with feathers to cut throats, and on parchments to seal destruction,—these are the robbers of modern days.—They bring desolation among our farmers—they spread distress in towns—they scorn the paltry plunder of pocket-books, and watches— they aim at houses and lands—strike at the foundation of many generations,—and would destroy families, root and branch. Long enough have fraud, falsehood and swindling stalked our streets:—often enough have our farmers left their fields and wrecked the industry of painful and honest years upon the mountains of Virginia:—often enough have our jails and dockets witnessed the ruined hopes of the dupes of Newtown and Stockbridge speculations.—These last are not imputable to the Georgia sellers,—unless by their superior address, and the wider ruin they have caused, they may claim the honor of ingurgitating these lesser robberies. (38–39)

Turning the instruments of writing into technologies of death—"aiming with feathers to cut throats, and on parchments to seal destruction"—Bishop declaims the type of wealth that enabled Dexter's rise, making him an important target of such invectives. Returning to these longer clauses that are framed by dashes, Bishop very aggressively calls out the manner with which certain individuals create wealth through destroying the lives and livelihoods of others.

Perhaps speaking directly about his one-time father-in-law Timothy Dexter in his *Connecticut Republicanism: An Oration on the Extent and Power of Political Delusion* (1800), Bishop exclaims: "The agents of delusion are the great, the wise, rich and mighty men of the world" (8). Dexter aspired to attain the status of the "mighty" and went about doing so through his opening himself to ridicule. The celebrity of Dexter extended beyond his local seaboard town, with an 1801 Norwich, Connecticut, newspaper quoting a Washington, D.C., paper that described "TIMOTHY DEXTER" as a man "who has many years excited much attention from his numerous blunders

144 FEELING SINGULAR

and unaccountable movements."[37] Called "a very illiterate person" with "high notions of grandeur and parade," the article provides a series of anecdotes that conveys the solipsistic desires of Dexter, noting that one day he knocked on his own door and asked "Does Timothy Dexter, *Esquire* live here" only to respond, when asked by his wife why he would do such a thing, that he "wanted to see *how it would sound* hereafter." Using his wife as a soundboard for his own fantasy of cultural significance, he desires a feedback loop that renders his acclaim hearable to himself. Bishop noted this type of fantastical feedback loop that structures the manufacture of imagined greatness:

> The great, wise and rich men well understand the art of inflaming the public mind, and generally present at the outset, *the delusive bubble of national glory*, a thing in which nine tenths of society have no kind of interest; but which, well managed, turns into crowns and diamonds in the hands of the blowers. Courtiers tell slaves, that liberty is in danger, or that infidels abound and the church is in hazard, or of plots at home, or invasion and insults abroad—Courtier's waiters echo the alarm. (17)

The reference to "courtiers" seems particularly poised to critique Dexter, as he by now had claimed for himself a "poet laureate" by the name of Jonathan Plummer. But what's also important to think through is this formulation of "*the delusive bubble of national glory*" as a type of shorthand for patriotism. We might think of this phrase "*delusive bubble of national glory*" as pointing toward the madness that inhabits Dexter—a madness that performs federalism as drag, turning Dexter into its strange, clownish performer on the burgeoning stage of nationalism.

3.6. Memorializing Mess

There is a risk embedded in studying unserious material. Why waste our precious time with the things of insignificant detritus? Are we the dupes of the self-important who fantasize about their own ability to publicize their supposed achievements, littered on the pages of newspapers or enshrined in

---

[37] *Norwich Packet* (Nov. 10, 1801): 2. This article also circulated in newspapers in Amherst, New Hampshire, and Walpole, New Hampshire, and in them they mention the article originally circulated in the *Washington Federalist*.

FEDERALISM IN DRAG   145

the wooden monuments of mediocrity? Or is there something to be gleaned and understood through the focus on the trash heaps of Federalist fantasy? Part of my argument here is that yes, studying what one might call trashiness offers a way into examining the cultural production of significance and meaning, and the concomitant aspirations that ground the desire to make a lasting, durable impression on the world.

Dexter's perhaps most infamous moment of trying to see how he would be remembered occurred when he faked his death to witness his own funeral. We get a notice of this in a letter written by Horace Holley to his fiancé Mary Austin, which simultaneously describes the odd statues that decorated Dexter's premises. After describing the house, Holley mentions Dexter "immediately accosted us in a sort of soliloquy, and in his own strange manner, putting his finger to his forehead," and said: "*Nature, Nature, I worship Nature; Reason, Reason is my God. The old man has not been well these few days—lost a little strength—memory affected—headwork gone—have done a great deal of head-work in my day—never mind—how do you like it—will show you much more yet—&c. &c.*" (qtd. Lee 361). From this recorded gibberish, Holley then explains the scene of Dexter's planned funeral:

> He showed us his tomb in the garden, not such as is commonly found, but a neat white building with a cheerful aspect, the room with windows above the earth like a parlour, where he has his coffin ready made, and painted, like his house, white, with green edges. This coffin he has had for several years, and once caused himself to be put into it, and carried, as to his grave, in a formal procession, in order to know how he should feel when near to being called out in earnest, or, if you please, *how he should feel when he was dead*. (qtd. Lee 361)

This story of Dexter's faux funeral circulated in the nineteenth century as a marker of his eccentricity, especially by writers of local histories. Yet the level at which Dexter manufactures his tomb shows the profound depth of egomania that motivates his campy efforts at Federalist iconography.

In an 1848 newspaper review of Samuel Knapp's book on Timothy Dexter, the author confesses that the book's stories about Dexter might seem "unworthy the serious temper of the times, and deem them better worthy of a place among things lost on earth."[38] Wondering if Dexter is better left in the

---

[38] *Newburyport Morning Herald* (March 16, 1848): 2.

146 FEELING SINGULAR

past, the author judges the past as less serious than the current moment. Here Dexter's textual material is remarked as being considered unremarkable, trash that does not fit within the too "serious" present moment. Indeed, the brief article notes that "in the midst of the burning light of the nineteenth century, with all its reforms, its too often pretended sobriety, its coldness, weakness, recklessness and nonsense, we often look back with some regret, to the rude manners, and more homely perhaps more honest demeanor of our fathers." Continuing, the article develops this comparison between seemingly disparate time periods:

> They had their occasional ebullitions and extravagancies, but we doubt whether they were any the worse men, citizens or christians for all this. Their peculiarities stood out sometimes, in pretty broad relief. *Now*, we are all alike, and we fear, all alike rather stupid in our uniformity. And we doubt very much whether sobriety has gained any thing by substituting for their occasional excesses, (the safety valve of the body natural, and body politic) our present very serious and sincere, perhaps, but mischievous, delusive, mind-perverting, heart-polluting and soul-destroying sophistries of Fourierism, non-resistance, anti-sabbath conventions, *et id genus omne*.

The past was more open, more capacious to difference than the present actively disallows, this author implies, making the thinking *with* that past particularly insightful in how it shapes the dissatisfaction with the present's repressive uniformity.

This fantasy of weirdness and oddity as a thing of the past, which gets ironed out in the uniformity of the present, informs Dexter's own desire to fashion himself for the future. Dexter's effort to drag himself into future remembrance, when thought alongside Sontag's reading of camp, elucidates his "attempt to do something extraordinary" as part of his aesthetic of failure (197). We might see the desire to make wooden trash into marble as part of the campy effort to fashion a coherent self. So along with the failed seriousness of Dexter, then, is the repressed aesthetics of camp that foreground early American politics, from George Washington's earnest washing of his spectacles to John Adams screaming and ripping his wig from his dusted head. Dexter is not necessarily unique so much as he is symptomatic of a cultural working through that triangulates federalist patriotism, campiness, and the politics of the desire to produce a lasting legacy.

FEDERALISM IN DRAG   147

I wish not to mourn the failure of Dexter's yard museum, which he imagined as a testament to some mode of future glory, but rather I want to think about the impulse to indiscriminately preserve as both a survivalist cultural strategy and a sign of culture's own undoing. What gets marked as useful to be preserved and what gets imagined as the material of detritus? Perhaps the very term *culture* embeds within it the sense of cyclical agricultural work, that harvests and crops must die off once their ability to offer sustenance ends. I am influenced by Caroline Steedman's evocative description that the historian's "craft is to conjure a social system from a nutmeg grater" (18), and so I try to imagine the arbitrary and unformed processes that tether certain individuals to positions of power and legitimacy and others to aspire, however failingly, to such positions. In looking toward the recesses of cultural memory, where Dexter's wooden fantasy of greatness festers and decays, one might consider the cultural work done through designating him as an "eccentric," and how that label would actually belie how forgetting, neglecting, and relegating certain cultural materials then *craft* a conception of a cultural field. What type of a society might produce a Timothy Dexter, and how does his production within the social mimic a series of social drives and norms that coalesce around such a figure of profound narcissistic drive?

Desperate to write himself into the cultural imaginary of his moment, Timothy Dexter drew upon the iconography of the early republic to position himself into its futurity. "As the archaeology of our thought easily shows," Michel Foucault concludes in his study of the construction of the human as a subject of study, "man is an invention of recent date. And one perhaps nearing its end" (*The Order* 387). If only that were the case, as it seems now we have simply aggrandized the tools to proliferate oneself, exasperating the conditions that produce the singularities that continue to demand and contain attention. That end of man appears nowhere in sight, as the technologies of self-representation proliferate and morph into new mediated categories of attention. Just as Dexter succeeded from being, in Foucault's terms, "erased, like a face drawn in sand at the edge of the sea," the apparatus of his historical continuity relies on the interest his likeness and figuration pose within textual archives. Dexter, in this manner, merely used the technologies and cultural imaginaries at hand to levy himself into future remembrance. His life and writings provide a phantasm of imagined greatness that has much to say about a particularly American dogged insistence on feeling significant.

Henry David Thoreau's posthumous diatribe against the amassing of wealth begins with a brief mention of Dexter's wooden statues. In "Life

148 FEELING SINGULAR

Without Principle," Thoreau runs across two men: one a sweaty laborer pushing a large stone and the other a frivolous man "who keeps many servants, and spends much money foolishly, while he adds nothing to the common stock" (485). Signaling a mode of effeminate labor that degrades the "honest, manly toil" that "Congress exists to protect," Thoreau laments seeing this stone deposited next to "a whimsical structure intended to adorn this Lord Timothy Dexter's premises" (485). Here the figure of Lord Timothy—his name transformed into an adjectival phrase—is deployed to downgrade the supposedly virtuous work. Thoreau begins this essay with a lament of hearing a lyceum lecturer who "described things not in or near to his heart, but toward his extremities and superficies" (484). It is important to think of how this rendering of space operates in Thoreau, where he positions intimacy within the realm of the heart and the "extremities and superficies" as that which is away from the heart, in the dirty nether regions of the body. Wanting an intimate and feeling subject, he then turns to Dexter as a symbol of all that is fraught with human personality, within the messy "extremities and superficies" of capital accumulation. Dexter stands in as a figure of frivolous showiness, unnecessary and wasteful, especially in relation to the work of "manly toil." The stone dragged by the man and his horses similarly *drags* Dexter into the fore, showing him to be a wasteful man who does not live up to the supposed promises of virtuous labor. Always one to lambast the pleasures of others, Thoreau states soon after referencing Dexter that "[t]he ways by which you may get money almost without exception lead downward." Dexter's own amassing of wealth was often portrayed contemporaneously as a fortuitous accident, with him sending bed-warming pans to the Caribbean, which ended up being repurposed to process sugar into molasses and thus creating the leather-dresser-turned-wannabe-aristocrat into a man of wealth. But when we think of his performing a type of speculative drag, dressed up in the accoutrements of eighteenth-century nouveau riche, we might see him performing for us fantasies of the self-aggrandized American market.

4

Perambulations in Print

Norms and Normativity in the Itinerant Republic

> If some sinners called the Lord Jesus Beelzebub, an honest old bachelor, may expect sometimes, to be called an hermaphrodite.
>
> —Jonathan Plummer[1]

> Marriage is a goal which every man, for his own happiness and honor and the good of society, cannot reach too soon.
>
> —Timothy Pickering[2]

The previous chapter follows the absurd life of "Lord" Timothy Dexter and his bizarre antics, noting how he developed a queer patronage relationship with the similarly derided and outcast Jonathan Plummer, whom he named his poet laureate in his campy production of Federalist fantasy. The following pages focus on the last remaining copy of Jonathan Plummer's life narrative—in addition to several of his broadsides—to illuminate how a person's desire to be *read* as normal can lead to a series of non-normative social relations, such as his queer patronage relationship with Dexter. Such patronage relations embed hierarchies that invite the queering that *Feeling Singular* has thus far plumbed. But if this book has mostly focused on *queer* to describe askance attachments to norms and power, this chapter combines those investments with the sexual connotations of the term. The epigraphs here outline such a formulation of sexual norms: Plummer, an unmarried bachelor, complains about being "called an hermaphrodite" in a New England region where, as Timothy Pickering suggests, marriage is essential to happiness. But that sense of heterosexual marriage as the goal for personal

---

[1] Jonathan Plummer, "A Vastly Remarkable Conversion" (Newburyport, 1818). Broadside.
[2] Quoted in Erica Burleigh, *Intimacy and Family in Early American Writing* (New York: Palgrave, 2014), 57.

Feeling Singular. Ben Bascom, Oxford University Press. © Oxford University Press 2024.
DOI: 10.1093/9780197687536.003.0005

150 FEELING SINGULAR

happiness is historically situated, informing how the construction of norms requires a great deal of power and effort, time and its passage, to come into what then appears stable.[3]

Plummer, in his itinerancy and ramblings, presents an alternative to the presumed stability of heterosexual coupledom. As I will show, he inscribes that instability on and around the material texts he produced. In *When Novels Were Books*, Jordan Alexander Stein reminds us that "what's on the page should not discourage us from reading the page as well, for the page it-self is not only a context for the history of novels; it is—and has historically been—*the* context for reading them" (20). Offering a materialist account of "the rise of the novel," Stein invites a capacious reading of books as material objects that reframes how scholars might think about the location of ideology. Throughout *Feeling Singular*, I have attended to very unique material texts to think ideologically about the early United States, from a manuscript written by an angry workaday mechanic to a hastily published and rare book by an anti-racist farmer seeking to levy a public complaint, and from printed scribblings by an eccentric proto-capitalist and wannabe demagogue to now the last (known) remaining copy of a printed text that was hawked next to broadsides, thimbles, and fish. Rather than arriving at the forms of republican significance that he aspired toward, however, Plummer's failure to circulate his life narrative beyond himself tells us a great deal about thwarted desires for public notice.

Plummer's efforts to counter rumor, evangelize, and narrate himself as a significant persona in the early republic all come to work against his best efforts, exposing his suspect relation to his era's norms. Although Plummer achieved short-lived local notoriety through the patronage of the eccentric "Lord" Timothy Dexter, in the end he failed to secure his name within the republic's traditions of life writings. In his life narrative, Plummer proceeds to narrate how his dreams and the hearing of divine voices set him apart from the masses, but those dreams also offer nascent moments of homosexual identification, showing Plummer cathect to bodies that render his desires queer.

---

[3] In *The Trouble with Normal: Sex, Politics, and the Ethics of Queer Life* (Cambridge: Harvard UP, 1999), Michael Warner reminds: "Even desires now thought to be natural and normative, such as equal romantic love, only came into being relatively late in human history; they depend just as much on politics and cultural change as do the stigmatized ones" (11). See also Warner's "Irving's Posterity," which offers a history of modern heterosexual attachment over and against patriarchal modes of inheritance (further referenced and developed in this book's Chapter 5). Jane Ward's *The Tragedy of Heterosexuality* (2020) does similarly important work at historicizing the formation of the heterosexual couple and tracks the amount of effort expended to make certain its relation to normative power dynamics.

PERAMBULATIONS IN PRINT   151

Rather than affirm a sense of printed narratives reproducing his textual self into futurity, Plummer instead configures a self so profoundly singular and queer that he cannot emerge into generality, turning his felt singularity into archival oddity and weirdness. Plummer illuminates a singularity so queer that his very presentation of masculinity gets coded as a problem, leading him to write "Another Looking-Glass for a Persecuted Saint: or Jonathan Plummer No Hermaphrodite" (1818) a year before his death.

4.1. Textual Insertions of the Queer Self

One may wonder how differently Jonathan Plummer (1761–1819) would have represented himself were psychoanalysis available for the itinerant peddler, poet, and preacher to interpret his own recorded dreams and their relationship to his life as a celibate bachelor. Freud's reading of dreams as a closed circuit that "may be assigned to a specific place in the psychic activities of the waking state" (137) renders the dreams of Plummer—which he recorded in his broadsides and sprawling life narrative—less in the realm of spiritual messages (as he would proclaim) and more a working through of his interpersonal frustrations with desire. With a career spanning Revolutionary War solider to New Hampshire schoolteacher, his subsequent invitation to perform as the eccentric "Lord" Timothy Dexter's poet laureate provided him with the means to expand his literary endeavors to a larger New England audience, though doing so earned him higher levels of infamy that followed his travels from Newburyport to Salem to Boston and back again. When Dexter died in 1806, Plummer moved in with his widowed and unmarried cousins, Eunice, Hannah, and Elizabeth Alexander, and furthered his preaching endeavors by including long sermons to accompany his broadside announcements about local tragedies.[4] Never marrying himself, his writings sketch out the figure of a cantankerous man who lambasts the lives and pleasures of others, perhaps decrying the indulgences he had tried to

---

[4] There is evidence that Plummer began his broadside broadcasting of local tragedies from a deeply personal place of mourning the way his brother's drowning death was spectacularized in the local broadside ballad circulation, such as "Verses, composed on the death of eight young men . . . of Newbury" (1790), which referenced two of Plummer's brothers dying. The American Antiquarian Society notes that this broadside was probably printed by John Mycall, who would print many of Plummer's future broadsides. It would be conceivable to think of this event as the origin story of Plummer's own religious affection and sense of divine providence when it comes to storms and boat accidents.

152   FEELING SINGULAR

deny himself. Yet even in those declamations against sin, Plummer betokens a knowingness that troubles the very moral superiority he claims, showing how his attempts to arbitrate norms are really about courting attention.

As an example of such insertions of self, I turn to an 1806 broadside about a political scandal, murder, and subsequent trial in Boston, where Plummer interrupts his narration of the events to include a story about why he drinks alcohol.[5] For other broadside peddlers and ballad writers at the time, such a rhetorical move would seem unusual, where the conventions of a public broadside require a more impersonal reporting of events. For Plummer, however, the opportunity to express himself before an audience incites him to more garrulous and intimate disclosures. After providing salacious details about the death of Charles Austin, who was killed by a Federalist lawyer named Thomas Selfridge, Plummer pushes himself onto the page, as it were, writing: "The ways of God are so unspeakable, and his judgments so much past finding out. . . . To shew the truth of this, a little of my own experience will perhaps be very proper."[6] The subsequent text is placed in smaller typeface, with extra spacing between preceding and succeeding paragraphs, emphasizing the sense of an insertion of himself onto the page of a public notice about a regional political tragedy (see Fig. 4.1):

A few years since, when I was studying divinity with a view to preach, I found considerable opposition; and when I began to speak in public, as an ambassador of Jesus I found very few willing to hear me, or to receive me in that capacity. . . . A false story, first told by some evil minded person, was circulated. The substance of the story was to this purpose, viz. "Plummer drinks a pint of rum a day, mixed with cider, and then he can speak." This was very unpleasant, especially on account of my being so heavy hearted and infirm, that I deemed almost half a pint of spirits in a day absolutely necessary; but he that holds me up and bears me through, was with me; and I had the following information in a dream, if I mistake not, viz. "You must adorn your profession, by leading a sober, righteous, and holy life."

This is one of many moments where Plummer exposes himself in public, confessing and admitting private details before a reading audience. But this

---

[5] For more on the particulars of this case, see Jack Tager, "Politics, Honor, and Self-Defense in Post-Revolutionary Boston: The 1806 Manslaughter Trial of Thomas Selfridge," *Historical Journal of Massachusetts* 37.2 (Fall 2009): 85–104.

[6] Jonathan Plummer, "Death of Mr. Charles Austin," 1806. Broadside.

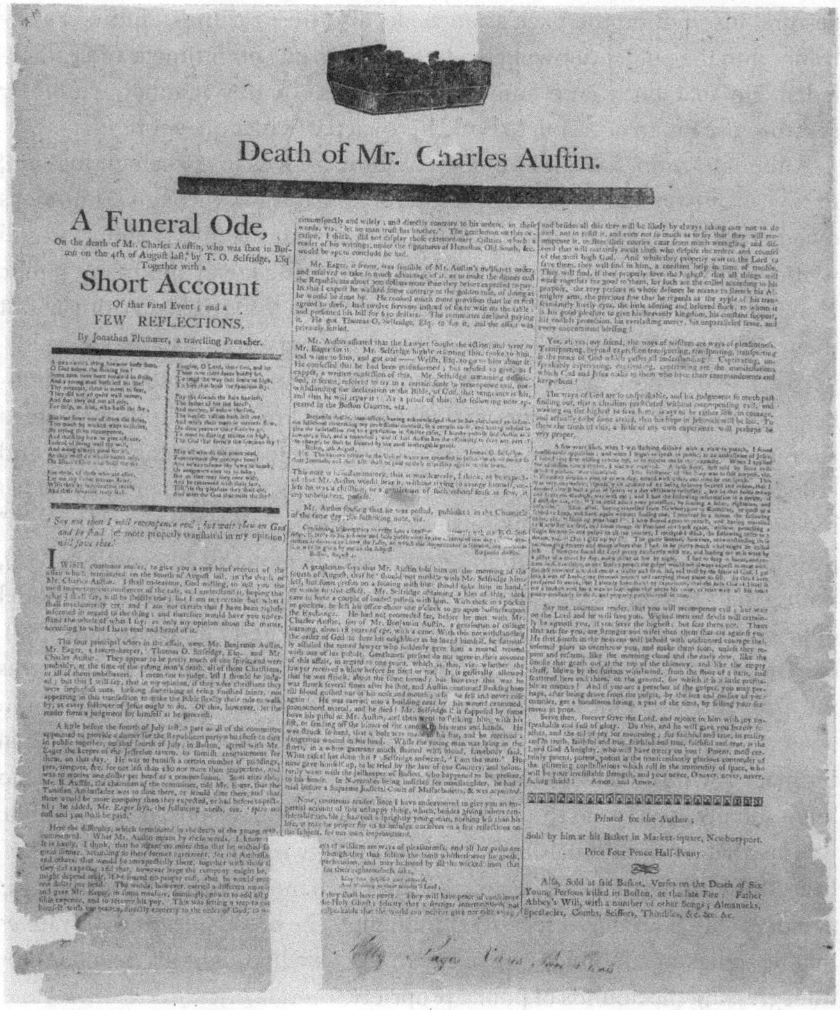
Death of Mr. Charles Auftin.

A Funeral Ode,

On the death of Mr. Charles Auftin, who was fhot in Bofton on the 4th of Auguft laft, by T. O. Selfridge, Efq Together with a

Short Account

Of that Fatal Event; and a

FEW REFLECTIONS.

By Jonathan Plummer, a travelling Preacher.

Printed for the Author;

Sold by him at his Basket in Market-square, Newburyport.

Price Four Pence Half-Penny.

Figure 4.1 Broadside by Jonathan Plummer about a political scandal and murder. "Death of Charles Austin: A funeral ode, on the death of Mr. Charles Austin, who was shot in Boston on the 4th of August last, by T.O. Selfridge, Esq.: Together with a short account of that fatal event, and a few reflections" (Newburyport, MA: 1806). Courtesy of the American Antiquarian Society.

154 FEELING SINGULAR

gesture, inserted on the page as an aside, also theatricalizes Plummer's entrance into the public, allowing readers a view inside his intimate and rumor-laden life that both entertains and intrigues. In this manner, Plummer self-discloses as an occasion to build his own particular queer brand.

Although rumors about Plummer abound, such as his penchant for rum, they are only made accessible to literary historians through Plummer's own efforts to disabuse public readers, to tamp out the fires that his life and writings enflamed. Curiously, then, we have evidence of the many public complaints against the itinerant peddler and poet *through* his writing about them. Where scholarship has emphasized the era's print as a mode of impersonal expression, facilitating the construction of the disinterested republican as rendered through a figure like Benjamin Franklin, Plummer instead attempts to use such forms of written discourse to project his desires and individual particularities into a reading public. Michael Warner in *Letters of the Republic* argues that Franklin succeeded at "the elimination of the self" through his particular use of an anonymous persona in his writings (87), noting that "Franklin's famous ambition of perfection is formed on the model of print, on the submersion of the personal in a general reproduction" (89). Christopher Looby specifies that Franklin, "in the act of utterance which was the assertion of his individuality, embarked on a course of self-alienation in language" (115). This model of print expression—that it abstracts personal intimacy and individual particularity—works the opposite for Plummer, who intentionally inserts and re-presents himself in all the various forms of public writing that he undertakes in ways that disallow his ability to hide himself. Indeed, Plummer queers the abstracting mechanisms of print through his personal (often rendered secretive) thoughts. The broadsides and narratives that he writes to announce public calamities also highlight his penchant for transgressing the bounds of public propriety.[7]

What makes Plummer of particular interest is that he wrote a book that he desired to circulate within the public (see Fig. 4.2). The so-called Founding Fathers of the United States declined to write themselves personally into the textual fabric of the new nation, with figures like George Washington, John Adams, and Thomas Jefferson spurning the idea of producing memoirs for

---

[7] Many contemporaneous peddlers were known for selling risqué literature in their wares. See, for instance, Marcus A. McCorison's work on obscenity, where he describes a Pennsylvania itinerant peddler being charged with selling salacious material, causing "the populace of Lancaster [to] turn[.. .] out and forc[ing] the miscreant to burn his stock of books in the public square" (185). This type of animosity came to Plummer, too, though it arrived because he would perform street preaching.

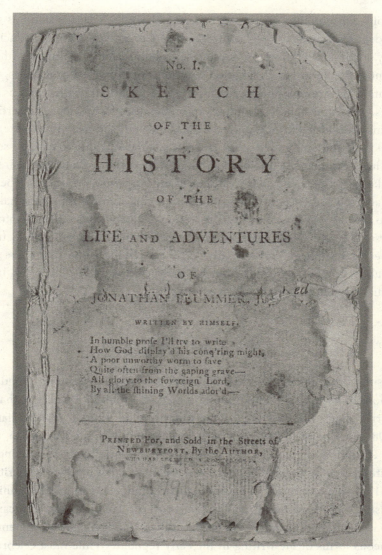

Figure 4.2 Cover page of the extremely rare first installment of Jonathan Plummer's *Sketch of the History of the Life and Adventures of Jonathan Plummer* (1796). Courtesy of the Phillips Library.

156 FEELING SINGULAR

public consumption, preferring instead to have their legacy stand as self-evident testaments to their contributions.[8] Contrary to this public taciturnity, Jonathan Plummer produced a sprawling account of himself within a printed life narrative, in addition to dozens of preserved broadsides, that contain his sermons, poems, and thoughts about local tragedies, such as mill fires, boat explosions, and contagious outbreaks, all with curious insertions of his dreams, personal experiences, and uncouth confessions, like the textual protrusion of himself at the death of Charles Austin. Projecting a sense of the messy manufacture of early national life writing, Plummer desires to make his private life public, to articulate and perform his *singular self* before an adoring audience. In this manner, Plummer enmeshes his personal life into the public forms of written expression to entangle his audience into his personality and his sense of self. The sense of self that Plummer manufactures relies on the relations he built with Dexter and the individual customers who would purchase his ballads from his basket, becoming legible as an individual through such patronage relationships.

4.2. Queer Peddling

Despite being an inconsequential peddler, Plummer harbored grandiose visions of his own self-importance. In fact, he wrote a life narrative that he carried about with him to sell along with his other wares. Daniel Williams's 1998 essay—one of two relatively recent pieces of scholarship to take up Plummer—focuses on the peddler–poet's effort "to make a living by writing, thus becoming one of the early republic's first professional writers" (151). Williams continues, explaining that Plummer "maintained a unique sense of self-importance" and "refused to accept his own insignificance" (153). Plummer's narrative, however, differs markedly from contemporaneous forms of life writing in the early republic. While most celebrated

---

[8] It is important to remind that even the first section of Benjamin Franklin's four-part *Autobiography* began as an intimate letter to his illegitimate son. The latter two sections, far less personal, were written with the intention of being eventually printed as part of his life writing. This is all to say that Franklin—the paragon of self-writing in this period—was far less intentionally self-expressive than most cultural representations of him allow. Additionally, Jefferson, in the *Memoirs* that he undertook in 1821, notes that he "begin[s] to make some memoranda, and state some recollections of dates and facts concerning myself, for my own more ready reference, and for the information of my family" (1). At one point, after spending the majority of his text outlining his political work, Jefferson notes: "I am already tired of talking about myself," without delving very deeply beyond reciting nationally significant dates and events (41).

autobiographical figures were asked to write their memoirs to provide lessons to their fellow countrymen—or peddling authors like Mason Locke Weems accrued their income through riffing on such lives—Plummer writes his from an entirely different motivation, stemming from mercenary reasons and the desire for self-advancement. Indeed, no one appears to clamor for Plummer's decidedly strange life story, and he writes his narrative in part to demonstrate his very exclusion from the normal and typical early republican narrative. Plummer, through his narrative, sought to position himself as singular within the republic, rejecting the idea that life narratives are produced *after* an individual has already left an impact on the world and that one type of life should be the model for all others. Instead, he repeats throughout his life narrative words he heard in a dream: "*Your noble fame shall reach the sky, / Your gloriousvoice* [sic] *be heard on high*," which he attaches to himself as divine validation to go forward and produce his life into printed book form. Plummer seeks, then, to write a narrative that will *make* him important, altering the conventional approach to such matters by seeking to insert himself into the cultural memory of his moment. By writing the "history of my life" that he "penned, but not always in quite a faithful and true way," and peddling it to an uninterested public, Plummer uses one of the major forms of republican significance (life writing) to express his desire for public attention, even admitting that he blends history with fiction to make his life more attractive. Yet considering Federalist Timothy Dwight's complaints of "shiftless, diseased, or vicious" peddlers in New England towns (194)—in other words, the position of peddlers as social outsiders who infect proper society with their wandering ills—Plummer's decision to embrace the life-narrative form signals his desire to appropriate the conventions and genres of the social norms that exclude him.

Before Plummer died in 1819, he expected that he would be long remembered. He outlines this desire in his final will and testament, stating that his "executor shall have six hundred copies of the Occurrences of my life printed from the manuscript which I may leave at my disease and have the same bound in boards, out of the proceeds of my estate, and the same to give or cause to be given away, not exceeding one copy in a family" (qtd. in Currier 438). Through hoping to distribute copies of his life narrative to families, Plummer manifests his desire to linger within the form of the republican family. He had grown estranged from members of his own: "Should my Father, or any, or either of my brothers have the hypocrisy to follow me in mourning," he specifies in a 1793 broadside publication of his will, "I desire

158　FEELING SINGULAR

my Executor to endeavour to prevent their so doing."[9] Continuing, Plummer explains: "As the usage which I have received from my Father and Brothers, has given me tortures which no tongue can express: I do not mean that they shall be much the better for any property which I may happen to leave in the World." Distributing texts about this family rupture into the reading public of Newburyport and surrounding communities, Plummer signals his sense of a public sphere that encompasses his domestic and intimate life.[10]

Although marriage and family life were normatively ensconced in the private sphere and away from ostensible public attention, the domestic sphere was central to how public personalities became rendered visible and validated for early national Americans. When a man refused to marry, he risked having his masculinity questioned as inadequate and insufficient.[11] Where a figure like Mason Locke Weems (1759–1825) could earn his living and support a family by peddling books throughout the Southern and Mid-Atlantic states, selling creative and didactic narratives of the period's "Great Men," Plummer remained local and insignificant, entangled into his inept desires for renown. In a letter to Mathew Carey, Weems shares his vision for making money out of the cultural myths accruing around the Founders, contending that the "greatest grief of my life is to see so clearly as I do the fairest chance that heart coud [sic] desire to make wealth & do great good, and yet this chance never improved as it ought to be" (Weems, *Weems*, 3.204).[12] Where Weems feels he can see a clear course for "wealth" and "great good" through his immense book sales on "great men," Plummer inserts himself into his own writings in such a way that he complicates his goals for attention and recognition.

---

[9] Jonathan Plummer, "To the Inhabitants of Newburyport" (Newburyport, 1793). Broadside.

[10] Amy Kaplan reads the production of "separate spheres" ideology in nineteenth-century domestic fiction in contradistinction to the foreign/domestic dichotomy, arguing that criticism of this model has perpetuated such ideologies through assuming "that nationalism and foreign policy lay outside the concern and participation of women" (583). In the case of Plummer, it is a man who refuses to observe this domestic ideology, expressing unconcern about maintaining differentiation between concerns private and public.

[11] Howard P. Chudacoff in *The Age of the Bachelor: Creating an American Subculture* (1999) lists the colonial laws, "penalties and restrictions" placed against single men to "suggest that to a considerable extent a single adult male in the American colonies actually gained his freedom, rather than lost it, when he married" (27). John Gilbert McCurdy in *Citizen Bachelors: Manhood and the Creation of the United States* (2009) follows on what he calls Benjamin Franklin's "consistently antibachelor" ideas to illustrate the emergence of the bachelor as a significant cultural identity, one who both accrued social power while inspiring other forms of social control and surveillance (107).

[12] Weems had developed his particular market of homegrown books on national heroes, as François Furstenberg notes, after failing to sell more expensive European books: "Earlier in the [1790s], Weems had earned and then lost a small fortune selling large, multivolume works of European origin. . . . Toward the end of the decade, however, he began selling smaller, cheaper books, many by domestic authors. He realized he could earn more money by selling a larger volume of cheap books than a smaller number of expensive ones" (105–106).

Figure 4.3 Image of the last surviving copy of Jonathan Plummer's life narrative. *Sketch of the History of the Life and Adventures of Jonathan Plummer* (1796). Courtesy of the Phillips Library.

Not only did Plummer never marry and establish a family—two hallmarks of republican belonging in the new nation—but his life narrative failed to be the family-focused and circulated cultural artifact he wished it to be, with his executor giving Plummer's money to the peddler's estranged family instead of using it to print the manuscript into book form.[13] Plummer presented his printed life in three yearly installments, from 1796 to 1798, and then peddled them with little success throughout Massachusetts and New Hampshire. What we are left with today is just a remnant of Plummer's 1797 printing,

---

[13] On Plummer's will, see John J. Currier, *The History of Newburyport, Mass. 1764–1909*. Plummer wished that "the whole edition of this work [be given away] within four years after my decease" (438). At his death, his estate was appraised at $1,573.14. It was a common practice for wills to be broken if subjects were considered mentally "distracted," as New Englanders called it. My use of "distracted" was usefully clarified through Cornelia Dayton's work-in-progress manuscript, "Frames of Distraction: Self and Sanity in Pre-Asylum New England." While eighteenth-century descriptions of what today might be called mental illness utilized the term "distracted," that term simultaneously has the sense of being divided internally in such a way that manifests through social orientation, as the third *Oxford English Dictionary* definition explains: "Mentally drawn to different objects; perplexed or confused by conflicting interests; torn or disordered by dissension or the like."

160 FEELING SINGULAR

the only extant copy missing several pieces, from the concluding pages of the first section and various pages throughout (see Fig. 4.3). As a cultural object not considered valuable enough to be preserved in its contemporaneous moment, Plummer's *Sketch of the History of the Life and Adventures of Jonathan Plummer, jun. (Written by Himself.)* wears the precarity of its uneven preservation. The single material copy, preserved as a curiosity at the Phillips Library in Massachusetts, indexes the contemporaneous insignificance he experienced. In a period when the papers of men presumed culturally significant and valuable were being collated and preserved, Plummer's absence from such an archive signals the norms and protocols that make certain lives legible to historical and cultural consciousness. Despite these challenges to the printed circulation of the text, the nearly two hundred extant pages tell us much about the dynamics of belonging and attachment in the early republic, especially for those individuals who did not fit neatly within the period's stable domestic formations yet still had access to the means of self-representation and left behind writings, however piecemeal their preservation.

In writing his life narrative, Plummer places himself in company with the "great men" of the early republic. Other life-narrative writers began their work with a familial and domestic purpose: Benjamin Franklin began what eventually became consolidated into his *Autobiography* as a letter to his son and Benjamin Rush wrote his book solely for his family; Plummer, however, turns to writing his life narrative without such an occasion, having never achieved the heteronormative success that would enshrine him within a family. Even though Rush and Franklin had families to tether the occasion of their narrative productions, Plummer approaches the writing of his life to connect himself to such ideals and *asks* for other families to be the site of his reception.[14] Where most life narratives outline the reason for the printing at the beginning, with a conventional gesture toward some patron or friend who requested the narrative, Plummer arrives halfway through his preserved text before explaining the outside influence that brought him to write.[15]

---

[14] Franklin, of course, famously begins his narrative for his son and then, after disowning him for loyalist sympathies, shaped the narrative around its proposed social value to a larger public. Rush opens his autobiography by asserting the text is only to be read within his family, though it is later published and circulated.

[15] Revolutionary War veteran and Pennsylvania Federalist Alexander Graydon expresses in his 1811 narrative a desire to avoid undue attention. Graydon acknowledges that "dealers in self-biography, ever sedulous to ward off the imputation of egotism, seldom fail to find apologies for their undertakings," whereas Plummer asserts his own authorship and never indexes the same anxiety

PERAMBULATIONS IN PRINT 161

He explains: "Mr. Bishop Norton, having read some of my publications, concluded that a history of my life, might possibly be serviceable to the world, and one day communicated to me, his opinion on the subject" (137). Similarly gesturing at an individual in some position of authority and influence asking for his life narrative, Plummer explains that he then had a dream wherein he heard: "Your noble fame, shall reach the sky!!! / Your glorious voice, be heard on high!!" (138). Within Plummer's logic, God asked for his name to be asserted and inserted within the supposedly inspired texts the peddler produced.

Plummer plans midway through his narrative to write his "history" in such a way that, he believes, will inevitably lead him to fame and fortune.[16] Writing that he "wished to have my history partly serious, thinking that it would sell the better for it" (138–139), Plummer attempts to sell himself on the early national cultural market, thinking of ways to increase the book's desirability. Wishing to produce a textual self that would be consumed by others, Plummer mixes a religious tone with the picaresque (best described, perhaps, as a marriage between Jonathan Edwards and Laurence Sterne). "Not finding the first two numbers saleable enough to suit me," he writes, "I resolved to suspend the remainder of my history" (139). This short-lived suspension ends when he has a dream that leads him to believe that he and his narrative are destined for renown, and that he must hurry and conclude its last installment. He never explains the specifics of his dream, but simply that he heard a voice assure him of his cultural longevity: "From this I concluded that my history would be to me a very fortunate affair, most certainly, at some part of my life, though I could not determine how many years would roll away before the thing would become popular" (139).[17] Wishing to become popular and successful on the early national book market—no easy thing

about self-representation (3). Even Stephen Burroughs begins his memoir by noting that someone else had told him "that a relation of my adventures would be highly gratifying at some convenient time" (1).

[16] In this way, Plummer seems to embody what Linda Kerber describes as the "[l]uxury, effeminacy and corruption" that the early republic sought to disavow (350).

[17] Plummer, juxtaposed to someone like Joseph Smith (1805–1844), offers the figuration of American religious enthusiasm but fails to emerge into any form of lasting cultural significance. Where Joseph Smith's followers wrote into Mormon scripture that "Joseph Smith, the Prophet and Seer of the Lord, has done more, save Jesus only, for the salvation of men in this world, than any other man that ever lived in it," Plummer instead fails to court a readership that would look to him as a model for religious attachment. For more on how Smith's eccentricities facilitated a queer religious affiliation, see Peter Coviello's *Make Yourself Gods: Mormons and the Unfinished Business of American Secularism*.

162   FEELING SINGULAR

considering the material limitations—Plummer finishes and prints his life narrative, selling it from his basket throughout Newburyport.[18]

With his own life narrative printed, Plummer tried to position himself for cultural achievement in the early republic, but falling short he notes in the last installment of his narrative that he "was deemed a lunatic by many" because of his "high opinion of dreams" (233). Dreams, for Plummer, both fed his desire for sharing his life with others and became part of the rationale that pushed him outside the normative parameters of republican citizenship. "By a dream I was now fully satisfied," he writes, wrapping up the last preserved installment of his narrative; "that it was best for me to publish the third number of my life" (232).[19] Throughout the narrative, Plummer describes how dreams provide motivation and impulse to pursue his sometimes strange and unconventional ways, dictating the things he eats and drinks and even where he travels and seeks employment. In this moment, near the end, he notes that a dream motivated him to bring his written life narrative into print, making him "resolved that not a foe on earth, should hinder my putting my history to the press, and that raging hell might lift its opposing voice in vain." Fantasizing a "raging hell" that beleaguers him, Plummer represents himself as embattled, if not entirely in his right senses. Confronting obstacles and opposition, he continues: "Two of my neighbours talked of purchasing my life; but nearly all the rest with whom I talked about the thing, laboured to discourage me" (232). But Plummer does not relent, continuing to proclaim and disseminate his significance despite the rejection he faces. "My spirits had now returned to such a degree," he explains, "that I began to talk freely & eloquently. This made me appear a little singular" (232). Refusing to be quiet about his own imagined importance and the value he ascribes to his life narrative, Plummer represents himself as standing out for all the wrong reasons, resorting to understatement—"appear a little singular"—to re-narrate how his particularities push him outside the very norms he seeks to occupy. Importantly, this use of "singular" differs from John Fitch's use when he calls himself "one of the most singular men perhaps that has been born this age," as analyzed in Chapter 1. Fitch's "singular" emphasizes his special uniqueness (something that he ascribes to himself), whereas Plummer's

---

[18] Most of Plummer's broadsides conclude with a note mentioning that the particular text is available for sale, in addition to other materials, inside Plummer's basket that would be located in the town's market.

[19] It is this third sequence in the life narrative that is missing in the preserved version held at the Phillips Library in Massachusetts. There are no known alternative copies.

PERAMBULATIONS IN PRINT 163

"singular" illustrates his desire to make society notice him, though that gesture eventually places him into positions of public exposure.

4.3. Dreams of Significance in the Early Republic

Plummer presents the figure of one too religiously inclined and out of sync with the forms of secular modernity inscribed in the project of early national life writing.[20] Despite his belief that his dreams are destining him for greatness and cultural significance, early in his narrative Plummer confesses that he "had no positive proof . . . that the dreams were from God" (66). The status of dreams, demarcating one within the realm of the imagination and not in material reality, remained suspect in the early republic (a throwback to the previous generation's distrust with enthusiasm), yet by the end of his narrative he seems convinced of their divine origin. Plummer constructs dreams as prophetic, using them as evidence that he could obtain the material success of a Weems.[21] Weems's popular *The Life of Benjamin Franklin* (1818) similarly portrays a complicated relationship to dreams as a site of social prophecy and market economics.[22] While a young boy in Boston, "going into a fresh part of the town," Ben, as Weems calls him, meets "a neat old woman" sitting next to a table of toys and one book. The old woman begins *"well my little man do you ever dream dreams?"* (29). Ben becomes startled by

[20] Rodger M. Payne in *The Self and the Sacred: Conversion Autobiography in Early American Protestantism* (1998) notes how evangelical writings about conversion rose in tandem with "the concept of the 'self' as the independent and autonomous seat of human sensation, intellect, and consciousness" (7). In this sense, religious writings incorporated the tropes of self-making found in nonreligious life narrative texts.

[21] Mechal Sobel in *Teach Me Dreams* argues that individuals turned to dreams for their revolutionary potential regarding self-determination. Where prior to the eighteenth century "people seemed to regard themselves as having porous boundaries and as part of a wider or 'we-self,'" in the "greater Revolutionary period," Sobel argues, "many people in America first came to accept that they had an inner self that controlled their emotions and actions and to believe that they themselves might alter this self" (3). Dreams became the format to delve into the representation of interior lives and selfhoods. Plummer's emphasis on dreams similarly highlights the emergence of a particular self, unconstrained by previous notions of collective subjectivity. That is to say, where previous examples of life narratives sought to enfold individuals into *genres* of living, Plummer implies that the self emerges unfettered from past projects. My thoughts on Plummer's shifting of life narrative genres is influenced by Lauren Berlant, who describes how genres operate through "an aesthetic structure of affective expectation," constellating a "form of aesthetic expectation with porous boundaries" (*The Female Complaint* 4).

[22] I focus on the 1818 edition, as opposed to the 1815 edition, as it's one of the first iterations of Weems's Franklin narrative that transforms the statesman's language into third person *and* invents fictional moments and scenes.

164 FEELING SINGULAR

"so strange a salutation" and replies that he does not believe his dreams mean anything of significance, that he "looked on 'em as a mere matter of indigestion" (30). Indexing an enlightenment perspective on dreams, Ben interprets them somatically, not, like Plummer, as evidence of divine communication. "*Well now,* replied the lady, laughing. *I, for my part, always takes* [sic] *great notice of dreams, they generally turn out so true*" (30). As an example of such a dream, the "old lady" remarks that she "dreamed last night, that a little man just like you, came along here and bought that old book of me" (30). "Well, Madam," Ben says, acknowledging the apparent sales pitch though also accommodating her eccentricities in his gesture of republican inclusion, "as your dreaming has generally, as you say, turned out true, it shall not be otherwise now: *there's your money*—so now as you have another reason for putting faith in dreams, you can dream again" (30). Yet the old woman continues to extrapolate on her dream: "I have not told you the whole of the dream yet.... But though my dream showed that the book was to be bought by a *little* man, it did not say he was always to be little. No; for I saw, in my dream, that he grew up to be a GREAT man" (30).

In this dream sequence, we might map Plummer into the position of the dreaming woman, whose eccentricities call for gracious accommodation from the public *insofar* as the sales pitch is not shown to trouble too many norms. "Ben" accommodates the woman's eccentricities and strange attachment to dreams in a quintessentially republican gesture of condescension and qualified validation. Where dreams are skeptically approached in Weems's story of Franklin, in Plummer the incessant iteration and repetition of dreams demonstrate his anxiety about proving his significance and appealing to the potential of dreaming to usher in his singularity. Indeed, Plummer's reception in the public sphere was decidedly unrepublican, often fraught with loud animosity against him. William Bentley records in his private journal a description of the Newburyport poet and preacher: "The poor man Plummer who lately exhibited on our Common on Sunday, was refused at Newburyport the liberty of field preaching. He was not exposed to the riotous insults of the populace as at Boston. We fear for the consequences of his return among us" (3.383). Plummer, here, is portrayed as a social ill, one whose presence disrupts the everyday life of early national Americans. Referencing a time in August 1808 when Plummer "was insulted on Boston Common" for street preaching, Bentley writes Plummer into the position of the outcast, emphasizing his contorted relation to normative republican citizens (3.380). Instead of being accommodated like the woman in Weems's representation of Franklin, who is somewhat condescendingly humored by the enlightened Ben, Plummer comes to signify the figure of the unruly dreamer, troubling the norms and protocols of proper social life in the early republic through excessive attachments to his own sense of imagined greatness.

Weems's production of a fictionalized Franklin, with anecdotes about dreams destining him to significance, did not go unremarked. Washington Irving's *Analectic Magazine* laments Weems's "editorial abuse," emphasizing how his career as "an author, a pedlar, [sic] and a preacher" may predispose him to extrapolate ("Article 1" 389). After noting Weems's particular desire to earn money, the reviewer writes: "Now as we take Mr. Weems to be one of those men, who mean no harm, we have a little piece of information for his own especial ear—namely, that, when he re-prints a memoir of a person, written by himself, the critics will not hold him guiltless, if he presumes to add or to omit any thing whatsoever" (390). Weems is a doubly problematic figure for his desire both to earn money and his tenacity to bend the truth. Weems had written to Thomas Jefferson for personal anecdotes about Franklin, asking for his "assistance in a little book on a Great man" that "may help to multiply the Virtues of Industry, Sobriety, Frugality, Honesty, Patriotism, Devotion to useful science &c for which Dr Franklin was so illustrious, & which you, better than most men, know to be the only true Gypsum of our young Republican Vine & all its future Interests, & Glories" (qtd. Skeel 1.130).[23] Thinking of narratives of "Great Men" as the fertilizer to grow "our young Republican Vine," the reproductive connotations of using such virile content suggests that stories about men will lead other men to consume their narrative plots and become like them. Weems thought necessary to embellish such stories for the good of building and sustaining the image of the paragons of republican belonging, seeking to provide an ideological foundation to the fledgling union even if that meant producing fantasies, embellishing and emblazoning Franklin with new, dreamt-up fictions.

Plummer similarly combines fact and fiction, but with the intention to propel *himself* forward into cultural significance, providing a unique model of republican belonging in contrast to Weems's conflicted production of Franklin, Washington, and others. Where Weems wove fiction from fact to

---

[23] Jefferson responded tersely with "I know but little," claiming that he experienced very little of the personal and intimate Franklin. Jefferson, as a conventional cordial turn, then invited Weems to visit Monticello next time he should be passing through the area on his bookselling business.

166 FEELING SINGULAR

produce "salutary effects" for "the prosperity of a young republic" (*Life of Franklin* 6), Plummer produces a ploddingly realistic, messy and "aukward" [sic] identity that Weems's cultural productions implicitly sought to eradicate (47); one way to see this is that Plummer portrays a self who remains unconverted to republican ideals, more attracted to religious enthusiasm than civic engagement. Weems's Franklin is set up as a republican model for normative belonging and self-development, whereas Plummer faces the lack of public interest in his life narrative with an insistence that marks his desire as troubling the normative confines of republicanism.[24] Trying to garner interest in his narrative, Plummer promotes himself directly, attempting to produce a cultural memory of himself through his own writing and self-promotion. Plummer's very gestures to gain notice become the sites of his rebuffed republican belonging. For instance, he notes that his "high opinion of dreams, confirmed people in their notions and shewed me, that I had still heavy obstacles to surmount" (233). But instead of feeling resigned to this cultural aspersion, he becomes "resolved . . . that they might call me fool, or madman, or what they pleased, if I could not discharge my duty, to my immortal Sovereign, without having these disgraceful epithets annexed to my name, and found myself such an hero that I often continued my discourse, on dreams, after people told me to my face, in plain words that I was crazy" (233). Setting himself up as a singular, unique figure with knowledge about dream interpretation that he believes will help others, Plummer refuses to quit his "discourse" despite how it marks him as "crazy." In this sense, Plummer insists on submitting himself to public exposure.

Even though Plummer's self-important dreams never materialized as the successes of Weems's Franklin, he continues to assert his sense of empowerment through them. "What I have told you courteous reader about dreams," he writes:

> will make you think me a little superstitious, and perhaps cause you to doubt my veracity. Three times have I thought of erasing it from my history, on this account, deeming it unwise to tell a large story, even when I am

---

[24] We might consider Michael Millner's revision of Michael Warner's argument about the relation between printedness and disinterestedness. Millner "break[s] down the too-easy alignment of the public sphere, secularism, and critical reason on one side and private ritual, religion, and uncritical belief on the other. While familiar, this dichotomy is, I suggest, not historically accurate and more an ideological formation than an actual one" (122–123). Plummer certainly shows how these two seemingly dichotomous modes were at play with his forays into printing his private life for the public.

PERAMBULATIONS IN PRINT   167

positive, in a belief of its authenticity; but be the consequences what they will, I will not scratch it out. To the eternal glory, of that transcendentally wise, potent, and benevolent being, who has designed thus highly to bless me, let it stand recorded. Let it ring wherever the name of Plummer is read or heard. (102–103)

Expressing a desire for an intimate relationship to an anonymous "courteous reader," Plummer configures himself as holding secrets that would not be received well to a larger public (even though, to him, that public needs his disclosure). Despite this, he continues to expose himself, waxing garrulous about his need to self-censor. Relying on the rhetoric of protestant evangelicalism to offer himself a sense of empowerment that he feels has been denied him, he insists on the truth of his dreams—their "authenticity"—to occupy a position of cultural significance. Plummer wishes to lend himself as a vessel to let "ring" the glory of God, with such "glory" reverberating "where the name of Plummer is read or heard." This self-effacing becomes convoluted to read, as he wishes to be recognized as a "worm" to carry his divine dreams into print. This becomes more pronounced when he declares: "O! Ladies, ah! Gentlemen, a greater than Adams hath been constantly with me: The unrivaled President, of the glittering worlds" (221). Explicitly comparing his deity to President John Adams—signaling a relationship to a power that supersedes national belonging—Plummer asserts his place in "the glittering worlds" of heaven as opposed to the material world of earth, despite that it is in this lower region that he wishes his narrative to circulate.

Plummer's dreams illustrate a disjunction between his self-perception and his cultural reception. Plummer proceeds to declare that this "greater than Adams" "deigned to snatch from death and hell, an infidel, a worm, an insect!" (221). Once again referring to himself as the lowliest of the low, Plummer continues to assert how this "greater than Adams" has helped him, though he does not attend to enumerate the particularities: "He has but alas! I cannot tell what he hath done for me! I cannot describe it. I cannot cannot [sic] utter it. I cannot write it. I cannot conceive it: No tongue sufficient" (221). The repetition of "cannot" emphasizes his sense of pleasure in his powerlessness to enunciate what God has done for him. Similarly, the emphasis on being unable to "utter" focuses around the unspeakable aspect of his feelings for this "greater than Adams." This emphasis on the inexpressible nature of a relationship that Plummer perceives between himself and the "unrivaled President, of the glittering worlds" suggests his intense—and

168   FEELING SINGULAR

unnameable—relationship with a figure who differentiates him within the early republic. Yet Plummer cannot give "tongue" to this relationship due to his lack of ability—in *cannot*s that emphasize his failure and gesture at an apparent inability to ever adequately make his dreams a reality.

4.4. The Messy Submissions of Jonathan Plummer

One aspect of republican masculinity that Plummer tries to attain but fails at is the art of deference, which he takes to excessive levels of submission. "PERHAPS courteous reader," Plummer begins one of his last recorded broadsides (1818), "you have seen a fellow named JONATHAN PLUMMER, travelling not long since in some of the tranquil streets of the United States, with some of his own works in print, and various other matters to sell."[25] Plummer assures readers they have probably seen him "in so humble a situation, making a figure so droll, and so much persecuted, despised, hated, slandered, and defamed with one gloomy, real, distressing, and uncommon infirmity in the bargain, viz. an offensive breath, occasioned by a catarrh of the nose."[26] In addition to his bad breath and unsightly nose, Plummer depicts himself as a figure frequently and harshly judged by society. Despite how Plummer portrays himself as being somewhat abject, it is through his ability to document such aspersions that allows him to survive in the cultural record.

Plummer's confession of his nasal ailments is part of his penchant to disclose personal foibles in such a manner that renders him visible as a suffering subject. The historical resonances of the term "catarrh" we might understand today to be seasonal allergies. Plummer represents himself with this sense of nasal recognition, something that marks him as odd, perhaps not dissimilar from Augustus Hoppin's humorous book *Hay Fever*, which similarly marked "Mr. A. Wiper Weeps" as recognizable through olfactory discomfort.[27] The images obviously exaggerate the condition of catarrh; yet

[25] Jonathan Plummer, "A Vastly Remarkable Conversion" (Newburyport, 1818). Broadside.

[26] Plummer's nasal catarrh, perhaps a mixture of seasonal allergies and persistent illness, remains an important trope throughout his writing, signaling a common way of recognizing him. Arguing that readers could potentially identify him for his supposedly well-known malady, Plummer asks others to see him *through* the points of departure that render him visibly non-normative. In other words, he marks as significant and exceptional his particular bodily maladies, claiming pathology as part of his identity.

[27] For a compelling reading of this comic, see the forthcoming *Lost Literacies: Experiments in the Nineteenth-Century U.S. Comic Strip* by Alex Beringer (The Ohio State University Press).

PERAMBULATIONS IN PRINT 169

through those exaggerations showcase a certain enlarged exposure to what might be considered the environment. The apparatus of smell, in Hoppin's image, has become engorged through a surfeit of stimulation and exposure to the environment. British physician John Bostock published an early nineteenth-century account of a "periodical affection of the eyes and chest" (subsequently called "Bostock's Catarrh" in the British Atlantic) that offered the first thoroughgoing account of what we today call allergies. Although the etymology of the word "allergies" comes from the Greek word *allos* for "other, different, strange" (in conjunction with a term that signifies "energy or reactivity"), the early studies of the embodied phenomenon implied "that all the cases are in the middle and upper classes of society, some indeed of high rank," with Bostock exposing his class pretensions in noting that he has "not heard of a single unequivocal case occurring among the poor" (440).[28] The connotations of a foreign object that invades the upper-class body turns Plummer's demarcation of his nose as enflamed by sneezing fits into a cite of class aspiration.

Imagining the nose as the conduit that marks a classed position of susceptibility, as historian Mark Jackson notes in his book-length study subtitled "The History of a Modern Malady," these early studies suggest that the catarrhal reaction is "putatively provoked by the aroma of certain flowers" (57). Kyla Schuller's reading of body porosity usefully illustrates the biopolitical investments of allergies. Schuller's study shows how "[b]iopower depends on the governmentality of the orifice" (132), and in Plummer his nasal orifice becomes too open to the environment, undiscerning of the pathogens that cause his nasal "catarrh." If the nose is the portal through which catarrh manifests—and sparked by fancy, garden-variety flowers—Plummer's curious belief that others will recognize him through his nasal catarrh seems oddly detailed.[29]

[28] John Bostock, "On the Catarrhus Aestivus or Summer Catarrh," *Medico-Chirurgical Transactions* 14 (1828). See also work by Clemens von Pirquet, who in 1906 came up with the term "allergy" to describe the reactive state.

[29] Gregg Mitman in *Breathing Space: How Allergies Shape Our Lives and Landscapes* (2008) argues that by the late nineteenth century "hay fever had become the pride of America's leisure class and the basis for a substantial tourist economy that catered to a culture of escape" (11). Later, Mitman implies that "civilization and progress spawned hay fever" (27). With Plummer, however, the class-based possibilities for describing his catarrh seem much more mired in depicting his bodily debility, and indeed his body seems to become enmeshed with his environment in such a manner that illustrates the type of panic about bodily degradation that Greta LaFleur accounts for in *The Natural History of Sexuality*.

170 FEELING SINGULAR

Plummer's imbalanced and unrepublican attachments become particularly pronounced as he discusses his time as a soldier in the Revolutionary War. He explains that "[h]ard usage from my father, the love of Daphne, the want of money, and a regard for my country, prompted me to go forward" to fight in the war, though the focus on motivating factors places him outside priorities of selflessness and striving for a common good (30).[30] "Just before the ship was ready for sea," he explains, "I was suddenly induced to believe, that certain death, or something very bad during that cruise, would be my lot unless I deserted the privateer. Thus was my mind altered more suddenly than the wind shifts, or the tide alters its course" (30). In this moment, Plummer portrays himself as an unstable individual, prone to plummet toward fatalistic actions. Plummer's unstable attachments highlight what historian Nicole Eustace has noted as the challenge to *feeling* like one belonged as a citizen in the early American republic. Eustace argues for a capacious sense of republican belonging, arguing "the *activity* of populating the nation was the surest way of being included in population as a *category* of national belonging" (31). But Plummer's problematic attachment to war enfolds into his refusal to leave behind the normative legacy of offspring, further placing him within marginal insignificance in early national culture. Instead of the continuity of feeling that republicanism sought to inculcate and manage, with individuals emerging into seeming self-made wholeness like the cultural imaginary of Franklin, Plummer's narrative sketches out the life of one who easily disavows appeals for his attention and attachment. Rather than a stability of feeling, then, Plummer messily interacts with the emerging republican ideologies around him.

Plummer uses the form of the life narrative to justify his unrepublican feelings and actions, and to turn his story of illness and debility into something of use. This is to say, through writing and narrating his strange experiences and whimsical feelings, he attempts to normalize his life. "It is possible that mere cowardice might produce a sudden change in the mind of a man like that which I have just recorded," he writes, attempting to delve into the motivations that brought him to leave the boat (34). He then turns to what he belatedly discovered about the fate of that very ship. Shortly after its departure, "a British frigate, in a pretty brisk breeze of wind, gave chace [sic]

---

[30] Christopher L. Tomlins in *Law, Labor, and Ideology in the Early American Republic* examines how self-interest shaped the emerging post-Revolutionary epoch of U.S. history, noting how this period saw a transformation from thinking of the common good to a belief that "[i]ndividual pursuit of self-interest was the only route to freedom and happiness" (309).

PERAMBULATIONS IN PRINT 171

to Capt. Tracy, . . . that she overset, and drowned him and all his crew! All met with a briny grave! All sunk low in the boisterous deep!" (34). Although Plummer confesses that he "was long ignorant enough to suppose that my own wisdom was the principle [sic] thing that saved me from the same fate" (34), he later ascribes his "miraculous escape" as the result of "wisdom and power incomparably and inconceivably greater than my own," thanking his "Almighty Father" for replacing "[t]he shame of cowardice" with "this un- speakable favor" (43). He turns his experience into a typology of recovered grace, where at one point he felt "spurred . . . on to a hapless fate" he next comes to praise the "guardian God . . . who is able to redeem the sons of men from the destroying power of death, from the annihilating influence of the darksome tomb" (43). Thus, Plummer narrates how his "instantly re- solved on" (30) desertion was inspired by a higher power than the emerging Revolutionary cause and his own sense of fear, thereby excusing himself from the problem that such desertion could play into valuations of patriotism in the late 1790s. He also deploys familial tropes of conflicted relations between fathers and sons to justify his move toward a questioned patriotism. Turning away from the secular cause of political independence to the personal and private facilitation of his relationship to spirituality, Plummer demonstrates his attachment to models of authority that supersede the emerging repub- lican government.[31] Refusing to submit himself to the norms and protocols of republican belonging, and disclosing his unstable affections for the cause of the Revolution, Plummer turns toward the dreamscape of his own imagined significance.

Despite Plummer's sense of being a significant individual, his writings betray how abjection—feeling the power differentials that his failure at norms exposes him to—is crucial for how he manufactures his sense of

---

[31] Stephen Carl Arch traces the emergence of the early national form of life writing "from the assumptions and conventions of other and earlier genres of self-life-writing—memoir, confession, history, personal relation, conversion narrative, and the novel among them" (6). While Arch provides a more political sense of the function and use of self-written narratives, Susan Clair Imbarrato finds that "the spiritual act of self-representation" in the earlier genres of life writing "culminate[d] in the secular art of self-construction" that early national life writers and memoirists produced (xiv). Both scholars emphasize "independence" as being a hallmark of the early national life narrative, with Imbarrato indexing this in the very title of her book: *Declarations of Independency in Eighteenth-Century American Autobiography*. Arch continues by defining autobiography "as *any narrative written or told by one person in which that person struggles to tell the story of how he or she came over time to be an independent, often original, agent*" (6; emphasis in original). Where Imbarrato and Arch emphasize and valorize emerging forms of independence, I would argue that Plummer shows a self that disavows these secular pursuits of independence to instead assert a dependence on religion's lon- gevity as a cultural form.

172   FEELING SINGULAR

identity. Plummer's pleasure in subjection complicates the rotating feelings of inadequacy and grandiosity that followed him wherever he wandered, informing his expressions of religious devotion and shaping the course of his life. In the last quarter of his recorded life narrative, covering June to October of 1797, such feelings of inferiority made Plummer defer to others during a series of fevers and illnesses—when "the hand of death was on me!" (194). Although he comes to "suspect[. . .] that my debility was providential, and that the result to me, would be advantageous" (181), the forty pages (constituting a quarter of the preserved printing) that record his progressively worsening fevers delve into representations of intense pain and suffering: "A most tremendous, and incessant cannonading was kept up by the victorious artillery of death!" he writes.[32] "A dreadful heaviness of head," he continues, "and peculiar weariness of mind, that I never before nor since experienced, told me metaphorically speaking in a voice of thunder, that I must in a few minutes surrender the fort!" (191). Referencing the metaphoricity of his own language, Plummer explains that he "resolved patiently to submit, to the allotments of providence" (192). This submission, despite the intensity of the represented sufferings, shows Plummer's dogged insistence on cowering to "my immortal general" (185). Orienting his self as subordinated to a power that "saved" and "bore [him] through many difficulties" (201), Plummer reifies a hierarchy within which he positions himself as subordinate.

In submitting to illness, Plummer hones his ability to interpret dreams, thereby feeling closer to—indeed, more intimate with—"my immortal protector" (189). Although these direct communications from "the voice of God" tell him such things as "Playing cards is an innocent diversion: and I advise you to get a pack!!!" (177) and "Camomile [sic] tea take!" (187), he momentarily doubts their divine veracity when a doctor attends him. Looking at this man as an authority figure, Plummer falters in his beliefs regarding his ability to interpret his dreams accurately. "My earthly physician understood his business," he writes:

> but alas he could not save me! He attempted to conceal his sentiments from me; but he could not do it. After examination, feeling my pulse &c., I could see the hedious [sic] traces of despair, triumphant in his face! An

---

[32] Maria Frawley's *Invalidism and Identity in Nineteenth-Century Britain* (2004) centers the figure of the invalid and their self-representation.

awfully ominous sigh instantly assaulted my troubled ears! This to me was much the same as saying: "Ah poor Plummer! all is over! your glass is run! I cannot save you! All the Physicians in the world cannot do it! You tell me that you have assurance in dreams, of assistance from above; but you are mistaken! They are empty nothings! They are barren sallas! [sic] They are nocturnal bubbles, totally destitute of meaning, sense or use!" (210)

This instance of doubt hinges on a synesthetic moment when seeing a facial expression registers as an aural "sigh"—where two distinct sensations are rendered "much the same." This conflation of disparate senses mimics Plummer's own strange intelligibly. Imagining being told through a sigh that his dreams are "nocturnal bubbles," Plummer simply retorts with his own certainty that "my dreams were supernatural" (211). To help Plummer's health improve, "Doctor Bond ordered" him to eat chicken, but Plummer "took time to consider it" because he had "nothing from heaven on the subject." Two weeks later, and after the physician had already obtained a chicken, Plummer hears in his dreams "The Cock is not dead yet!" which he reads as signifying he can proceed to eat the chicken. Securing himself in a hierarchy with the voice of God, Plummer hearkens to what he imagines as his dream connection to a higher power instead of submitting to the advice of an "earthly physician."

Scholars of disability studies render norms of ablebodiedness as the structure that makes visible the queered disabled body. Robert McRuer writes: "the system of compulsory able-bodiedness . . . in a sense produces disability" (2). Plummer's sprawling narrative manifests the compulsory designs of republican normativity, with nearly a quarter of it describing his bedridden state. Where other such histories, like those by Stephen Burroughs and Benjamin Franklin, focus on movement and mobility, Plummer's emphasizes his debilitation and immobility. Sari Altschuler has provocatively highlighted the absence of "very many impaired bodies in early national fiction," though within Plummer we see the figuration of textual debility, where the narrative (while ostensibly nonfictional) remains both fragmentary and centered on a body that has foreshortened mobility, and that suffers from debilitating allergies (246). Reading Plummer as a disability narrative—a story about the failure to perform a healthy body—illustrates how the norms of ablebodiedness coalesced around such outsider figures. That is to say, figures *like* Plummer became the limit case for designating who was ill or healthy, pathological or proper.

174 FEELING SINGULAR

While in the midst of his long illness, Plummer turns to the "unrivaled President, of the glittering worlds." Prior to this debilitating illness, Plummer had narrated temporary excursions into unbelief, explaining that during his severe 1797 fevers that Thomas Paine was "a much less obstinate infidel than I was!" (105).[33] Where other spiritual autobiographers, like Jonathan Edwards, narrate shifts and intensities of religious zeal, Plummer represents a specific mode of unbelief that transitions into religious fervor, one that removes all the struggle and ambiguity that remain in Edwards's.[34] Specifically, Plummer explains that he rejected religion after encountering a former preacher-turned-deist, explaining that he "visited a lay preacher of great abilities" who "had been long a great and zealous Christian: but he now informed me that he had wholly renounced Christianity!" (71). Troubled by this, Plummer determined to remain "a few minutes with him at this time" but subsequently received a letter that completely "changed me from a tolerable sort of christian, to a superlatively obstinate infidel" (73). Plummer explains that this shift occurred "less than a week from the time I first talked with my friend on this subject" (73). The power of this written letter, which Plummer never recites in his narrative nor summarizes, radically transforms his orientation toward religion, leading him to "no longer bend my knees in secret to the author of my existence! No more in plaintive strains acquainted him with my difficulties!" (74). Being suddenly transformed through the process of reading, Plummer represents himself refusing to submit to the claims of religious affiliation. Plummer's represented conversion into deism validates the qualms that contemporaneous ministers held regarding Paine's dissemination of cheap editions of his *Age of Reason*, which Plummer himself wrote at length about after his conversion.[35]

[33] Plummer references Paine in relation to another individual who similarly renounced Christianity and placed "all his affections on his earthly possessions!" This person, "a Dutchman whose name was Foot," Plummer explains, "was considerably like brother Paine and me. He had placed nearly, or quite all his affections on his earthly possessions!" (196), emphasizing the presumed worldliness and materialism of deists.

[34] In the 1765 publication of Edwards's life narrative, he is portrayed taking an assessment of his life and conversions: "Tho' it seems to me, that in some Respects I was a far better Christian," he notes, reflecting on his initial turn from sin, "for two or three Years after my first Conversion, than I am now; and lived in a more constant Delight and Pleasure: yet of late Years, I have had a more full and constant Sense of the absolute Sovereignty of GOD, and a delight in that Sovereignty; and have had more of a Sense of the Glory of CHRIST, as a Mediator, as revealed in the Gospel" (38). Contrary to this, Plummer represents his conversion as never slackening strength—neither getting better nor worse. Instead, Plummer flattens out the complexity of accounts of religious conversion.

[35] See Seth Cotlar's reading about the anxiety surrounding the public reception of Paine's *Rights of Man* and *Age of Reason* in *Tom Paine's America: The Rise and Fall of Transatlantic Radicalism in the Early Republic*, 42.

PERAMBULATIONS IN PRINT   175

With the practice of reading able to transform Plummer's religious affiliation (turning him into an "obstinate infidel"), he also portrays the process of writing his narrative as leading him to become the garrulous itinerant preacher that made him locally infamous. Plummer notes in a late broadside that after he began writing about his life he found that he "had been surpizingly [sic] favored indeed by some invisible friends or friend, and I began heartily to love the Lord God Almighty, with ardent affections." Plummer narrates his (re)conversion to Christianity as stemming from the process of writing out "the adventures I had gone through." While removed from apparent religious belonging, he explains that he found himself waiting for "an eternal period to my existence!" "Having secured a copy right of my history," he explains, he determined to enumerate all that he feels he lost out on by his short foray into infidelity. "Never did I expect to know or see the altogether lovely being who had born me up when surrounded by ten thousand difficulties!" he explains; "I did not expect that my life would be prolonged, by the particular kindness of God, nor—but I must forbear, must go forward with my history, courteous reader, without telling you a fiftieth part of what I lost by becoming an infidel!!!" (75). Plummer makes his matter of (re)conversion public, addressing the Enlightenment figure of the "courteous reader" even as he seeks to make his spiritual attachment legible.[36]

4.5. The Sexual Secrets of Jonathan Plummer

"I had been laughed at . . . and ridiculed by many of my comrades while a soldier," Plummer writes, "for my uncommon veneration for virtue in regard to the article of celibacy" (64). Enumerating more of the many reasons he

---

[36] Literary scholar Michael Cohen notes that Plummer's reconversion became quite visible in his writings, altering his subject matter and leading him to distance himself from his deceased patron, Timothy Dexter (who died in 1806). Cohen argues that after Plummer "underwent a religious conversion" that "his poems . . . adopted the language of providential utterance, using disasters and catastrophes . . . as evidence of the wondrous interventions of God into human affairs, and as an impetus to exhort his audiences to repent while they still had time" (20). Following Plummer's intense conversion, he begins to narrate the many illnesses and sicknesses—"Tortures inutterable" [sic] (206), he calls them—that provide him with scenes of "supernatural" dreams (225), further confirming his belief in a higher power. Noting that "[t]he direct communications which I had in dreams during the whole of this dreadful sickness, I should guess deserve a place in my history," he then worries that he will not live through his illness to write and print them (206). "If there are printing presses in Heaven," he notes, "I may perhaps then undertake to pen my history" (222). Imagining print as particularly poised to express spiritual conversion, Plummer wishes to have his narrative circulate throughout both space and time, even if it means accessing printing presses in heaven.

176 FEELING SINGULAR

deserted from the Revolutionary War, Plummer adds: "my oddity in this respect was no secret in my native place." Not keeping his refusal of sex a secret,
Plummer broadcasts his personal choices and relishes the "oddity" he makes
of himself. Plummer's insistence on declaring his particular orientation toward sex strikes his surrounding public as an annoyance.[37] In one of his last
broadsides, "A Looking-Glass for Lovers of Strong Drink & Another Looking-
Glass for a Persecuted Saint: or Jonathan Plummer No Hermaphrodite"
(1818), Plummer recounts men who took umbrage at his "celibacy,"
spreading rumors: "He's an hermaphrodite" (see Fig. 4.4).[38] Plummer quotes
from the men who held grudges against him: "He rails against pleasure that
he cant enjoy, begrudging those who can enjoy it, their happiness. You may
rest assured that it was not christianity that kept him from being forced to
marry, or pay for a bastard long ago." This passage suggests the implicit aspersion levied against Plummer, where his suspect embodiment becomes a
joke for others to speculate on his public declamations against sex. Seeking to
disabuse the public of these rumors, Plummer includes a medical summary
from a doctor who examined his body. Quoting from Dr. Israel Gale's report,
the broadside notes: "concerning Jonathan Plummer, the pedlar, and poet, . . .
this may certify, that I being a physician, having inspected the said Plummer,
and found him to be truly and properly, a man." Plummer's insistence on
sharing the doctor's examination immediately after repeating the gossip—
putting that language in print and even repeating the phrase "truly and properly, a man" in subsequent broadsides—illustrates his desire to avoid secrets
when it comes to his gender. He wishes to use print to assert the validity of his
personal sexual choices—that of abstinence—but in doing so subjects himself to the public's interest in uncovering secret motivations.

Plummer's desire to assure readers that he was "truly and properly a man"
stems from the implications of being an illegibly masculine male in the early
republic. Indeed, the stakes for being called a "hermaphrodite" in the early
republic, as historian and gender studies scholar Elizabeth Reis argues,
center on an imagined sense of deception: "The possibility of swindle and
deceit looms large in nineteenth-century discussions of hermaphroditism,"
she argues, noting that "themes of dishonesty and sexual promiscuity lurk in

---

[37] In calling Plummer's representation of his celibacy a type of sexuality, I follow Benjamin Kahan's
argument in *Celibacies: American Modernism & Sexual Life* (2013), who "understands celibacy pri-
marily as a coherent sexual identity rather than as a 'closeting' screen for another identity" (2).

[38] Jonathan Plummer, "A Looking-Glass for Lovers of Strong Drink & Another Looking-Glass for a
Persecuted Saint: or Jonathan Plummer No Hermaphrodite" (Newburyport, 1818). Broadside.

Figure 4.4 Jonathan Plummer's "A Looking-Glass for Lovers of Strong Drink: & Another Looking-Glass for a Persecuted Saint: or Jonathan Plummer no Hermaphrodite" (1818). Courtesy of the Collection of the Massachusetts Historical Society.

178 FEELING SINGULAR

what are otherwise dispassionate and clinical medical cases". (30). A desire to avoid the charge of dishonesty perhaps motivates Plummer to submit himself to medical practices to avoid inspiring suspicion regarding his promotion of celibacy. Yet in placing the findings in print, Plummer validates the way intimate secrets of his life have become part of public discourse. Using the broadside form to disabuse an apparently misinformed public, Plummer instead produces *more* discourse regarding his contested sex.[39] The cultural work of such sexual ambiguity might be further indexed through the representation of Mademoiselle le Chevalier d'Eon, who transitioned genders in France and then lived the rest of her life in England.[40] Destabilizing contemporaneous notions of gender identity, after her death in 1810 she was caricaturized in the Boston journal *Omnium Gatherum* a few months after a foppish likeness of Timothy Dexter circulated (see Fig. 4.5 and Fig. 4.6). Where d'Eon's relationship to gender expression in this image portrays a perfect balance of a dichotomized gender, Plummer's sexual ambiguity became a site indexing his supposed repression of secrets, withholding motivation for his declamations against sex.[41] In this sense, d'Eon emblematizes a

[39] Karen Weyler defines the broadside as "a medium, rather than a genre" (28) that "represented a quick, inexpensive means of communicating information to large numbers of people" (29). Plummer's use of the broadside medium suggests his interest in appealing to a "common denominator" that other forms of writing—such as his life narrative—would not allow (29).

[40] D'Eon wrote an autobiography, entitled *The Great Historical Epistle*, in 1785 that proclaims her conversion to Christianity while simultaneously documenting her transition to live her life as a woman. The editors to the collection of d'Eon's writings note: "D'Eon was thus born again *simultaneously* as a Christian and as a woman. Christianity helped d'Eon cross the gender barrier; it gave him [sic] the spiritual strength and mental courage to live as a woman among the same people who had known him as a man. It also gave him the inner conviction that what he was doing was no lie or trick—even if it obviously required a level of deceit—but rather constituted a moral regeneration. Far from being a sin, switching gender was a way to purify oneself and become closer to God" (Champagne et al. xxii). In important ways, this follows Scott Larson's incisive work on the Public Universal Friend. See "Indescribable Being: Theological Performances of Genderlessness in the Society of the Publick Universal Friend, 1776–1819," *Early American Studies* 12 (Fall 2014): 576–600.

[41] See Gary Kates, *Monsieur d'Eon Is a Woman: A Tale of Political Intrigue and Sexual Masquerade* for more on the background of this individual. Kates notes that d'Eon met with Benjamin Franklin when the statesman invited her to dinner: "Among the most notable rendezvous of this period was d'Eon's meeting with the other famous newcomer to the Paris social scene, Benjamin Franklin. In town to gather support for the American War of Independence, Franklin exploited an entirely different kind of popular image, the rustic philosopher. Armed with bifocals rather than a sword, without any wig or other accoutrements of male aristocracy in France, he played up to the great noblemen by donning a leather coat and fur hat. Thus Franklin and d'Eon were something alike, insofar as each in his [sic] own way mocked the stylized dress of the French establishment. And for at least one brief historical moment these two diplomats became an odd couple" (33). This dinner between the two individuals is referenced in the eighteenth-century novel *History of a French Louse; or the Spy of a New Species*, which follows a louse who embeds itself into d'Eon's garments and witnesses the conversation with Franklin. The novel critiques Franklin's morality and calls d'Eon "a woman whose manners were so absurd, so masculine, and unsuitable to her sex; always in motion, full of grimace, awkward in the habit, and impatient of the conversation of women" (14). The louse then

PERAMBULATIONS IN PRINT 179

Figure 4.5 Caricature portrait of Mademoiselle le Chevalier d'Eon in *Omnium Gatherum* 1.11 (September 1810). Courtesy of the American Antiquarian Society.

Figure 4.6 Caricature portrait of Timothy Dexter accompanying his biography in the *Omnium Gatherum* 1.8 (June 1810). Courtesy of the American Antiquarian Society.

PERAMBULATIONS IN PRINT   181

transparent gender legibility—where private matters are made public—that in Plummer becomes the representation of something hidden and in need of his printed clarifications.

Plummer had not always determined to live a life of celibacy. Much like his intense conversion to Protestant Christianity during his debilitating illnesses, Plummer has an encounter with one specific individual who inspired him to embrace celibacy. Plummer describes "an ugly, silly, hard drinking, bad tempered, ill-bred prostitute" who "wanted me . . . to take certain liberties with her, which I had never allowed myself to take with any female; & finding herself disappointed, began the next day, to treat me in the most domineering & abusive manner, . . . rendering my life by this means very unhappy" (93). Plummer portrays the woman as unfeminine to seem justified in refusing her sexual advances. In doing so, Plummer portrays a self that differs remarkably from other life writers like Benjamin Franklin and Stephen Burroughs, who both reference their sexual appetites as leading them to violence against women.[42] Contrary to that, Plummer represents himself as being pursued by women, falling into another "vicious connection with a certain woman" that causes him further frustration (167). For Plummer, women are the aggressors who challenge and threaten him, leading him to renounce all desires for marriage. After making this resolution, he writes that he "began to suspect that the happy augmentation of spirits which I found, was the natural consequence of celibracy [sic]" (167). In connecting his happiness to "celibracy," Plummer unthreads the normative logics in narratives and tracts of the early republic that would assert "THE BLISS OF MATRIMONY" over the "disconsolate . . . condition of the old Bachelor!" (Weems Hymen's 6).[43] Where one allows sex, the other hints at

---

explains that Franklin and d'Eon participated in "a little teté à teté" (20), leading the louse to imagine how sexual dalliance between "his excellency and the female chevalier would be curious; but I was cruelly disappointed" (21).

[42] We might also think here of Benjamin Franklin's confession/warning to his son in what became the first section of his autobiography. Franklin warns his son of the "Passion of Youth" that "hurried me frequently into Intrigues with low Women that fell in my Way, which were attended with some Expense & great Inconvenience, besides a continual Risk to my Health" (75). Yet this "Risk" becomes portrayed as an inconsequential "erratum" that Franklin, as the writer of his life, can correct. In writing out this supposed "errata," Franklin presumes that he can fix or repair all the wrong he has done, similar to how Burroughs's confession in his narrative attempts to absolve him of wrong by showing his performance of penitence.

[43] Weems's text outlines eight items that constitute the "BLISS OF MATRIMONY," which phrase is repeated in all eight section headings. In addition to being a site of imagined happiness, marriage and "romantic love," Karen Lystra notes, "was closely intertwined with a cultural commitment to individual differentiation from the group" (31). The importance of romantic love, Lystra continues, is that

182   FEELING SINGULAR

the problem of self-abuse and masturbation: the lonely status of the bachelor leads to a life of disconsolate and solitary dissipation. Plummer seemingly attempts to make celibacy normative, even misspelling the word with the extra "r" to draw its pronunciation closer to *celebrate* (see Fig. 4.7). He wishes to make his unusual and unconventional life less problematic to the domestic norms of the early republic.

Yet Plummer notes that even his resistance to legible sexuality cannot be freely expressed in republican print. After describing his turn to "celibracy," he then discusses "[s]everal communications in dreams on the subject [that] have since been received" (167). Importantly, he insists that his insights— his "communications in dreams"—would not be proper to put in print, that indeed they must remain secretively outside the public sphere of print and ensconced in private and interpersonal relationships and encounters. This reference to secrecy is strange for Plummer, as he otherwise appears so open to speak his mind and share his unusual dreams and experiences. "These either have something in them, or some discoveries were made in consequence of them, that renders them improper to be printed, till there is more sense, and less hypocrisy in the world," Plummer writes (167). Referencing an aspect of his dreams that cannot be printed, Plummer describes himself as having knowledge that he would like to share with others but that would be in tension with the norms and protocols of print publication, which norms make transgressive items of a secretive nature. Plummer then transitions: "That part of my subject which I am now on, is truely [sic] delicate. A very great number of ideas must remain unrecorded. These are of such amazing importance to the world, that I believe people who prize health at any thing near a proper rate, will do well to call on me in private and to pay me for a few observations, which it is my humble opinion, would be more serviceable to them than one or two, three or four, five, or six hundred millions of dollars would be!" (167–168).[44] Harboring a secret, Plummer believes he has knowledge that would both be improper to put into print and worth a great deal of money to sell person to person. Having just a moment before explained how he celebrates "celibracy," the secret he has may very well have something

---

it "was a ready-made incubator of the romantic self in nineteenth-century American life. In America, romantic love was an active agent, not only a passive index, of the crucial social change that brought modern—meaning romantic—selfhood to a large group of men and women" (31).

[44] It is possible that Plummer would be drawing upon discourses around spermatorrhea, or the contemporaneous medical concern with excessive, involuntary ejaculations, in his subtle intrigue concerning secrecy.

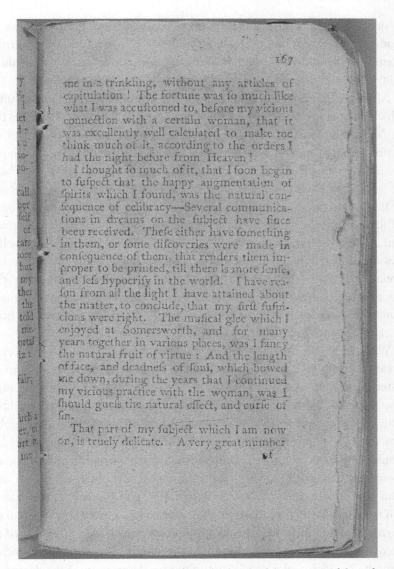

Figure 4.7 Page 167 of Jonathan Plummer's *Sketch of the History of the Life and Adventures of Jonathan Plummer* (1796), where "celibacy" is turned into "celibracy," mimicking the word "celebrate." Courtesy of the Phillips Library.

184 FEELING SINGULAR

to do with the anxieties and fears about masturbation. Plummer asks his readers to approach him individually and privately to know more, warning them that the knowledge he has to impart is too provocative for the durability of printing, but that it is worth "six hundred million of dollars."

Although Plummer considers himself laboring under "the same difficulties which laid before the prophets, historians &c, in days of yore," he writes that he "should be fond, of penning what hath been revealed to me about the matter was it prudent for me to do it" (169). Yet he worries that if he should record the secret that was revealed to him after his declaration of celibacy, he "should be likely to ruin or greatly injure the sale of my history" because of the "Wide mouthed, hypocritical, ignorant critics, [that] would unmercifully censure the whole book, on account of what a few pages contained, and loudly yawl against the vanquished author" (169). Portraying himself as embattled by a public that refuses to receive and appreciate the secrets and dreams he has to share (even if it means visiting him in private to learn what the celibate itinerant preacher has learned for himself), Plummer connects himself to a tradition of "prophets" and people from "days of yore" to build intrigue and interest around his information.[45]

While in his life he renounced sexual relations with women, in his retold dreams he implies a particular knowledge about sex that belies such an insistence on celibacy.[46] Plummer writes: "I dreamed, that a poor old man, displaying one of his members, which must not be named, and overwhelmed with grief, stood before me. He seemed to be awfully afraid, that the member was too big, or too little: too long, or two [sic] short.—What seemed to trouble him most, was, that he could not tell whether it had any, all, or none of them [sic] failings!" (200–201). Considering his encounter with the woman who accuses him of being a "hermaphrodite" and the subsequent rumor, this narrated dream may illustrate Plummer's anxiety at measuring up to the norms of masculinity. This dream seems deeply invested in an imagined inadequacy that Plummer seeks to undo through his broadsides that declare himself "No Hermaphrodite." Continuing his description of the dream, he

---

[45] For more on the relation between presumed prophets, dreams, and resistant publics in the early national period, see Susan Juster, *Doomsayers: Anglo-American Prophecy in the Age of Revolution* (2003).

[46] I am particularly interested in thinking here with Freud's sense of dreams as *"disguised fulfilments of repressed wishes"* (165). In this sense, we can wonder what hoped-for fantasy Plummer is projecting through articulating his dream, and also what type of intimate attachment he imagines through narrating this specific dream of assessing a man's penis. Specifically, Plummer's dream may gesture toward his desire to repress the public rumors about his contested manhood while also acting out his desire to be read as a normatively gendered subject.

writes: "I was ready to tell him, that the length, and girth of it, could certainly be taken, when the idea of what I was going to say, made me smile so heartily in my sleep, that I awoke without speaking" (200–201). Plummer's reference to waking up "without speaking" suggests many things, but I would like to focus on two: a repression from voluminously sharing his thoughts, as he is wont, and the use of his mouth for other purposes inhibiting from speaking. Similar to his refusal to share in print whatever he learned through his process of embracing "celibracy," he evokes silence and a smile upon waking up from the imagined experience of having another man's penis displayed for his view. The smile may be productively considered in relation to Plummer's orientation toward secrets, hinting at how he keeps parts of himself undisclosed to produce moments of secretive intimacy.

This dream opens up several queer possibilities when considering Plummer's refusal to stabilize his desire and pursue it through marriage and family building. In this moment, Plummer responds with laughter when asked about the fitness of a penis, thinking that its measurement "could certainly be taken."[47] But the passive voice "be taken" also may suggest that the penis itself, as an object, could "be taken" in a sexual sense. If we imagine Plummer suggesting he could take "it," he places himself in the position of sexual reception, rendering himself the bottom to the dream's top. With the dreamt penis exposed to Plummer's assessment, he imagines being asked to subject the appendage to protocols of measurement to assess its worth, value, and function, waking up just before endeavoring to do so. Similar to how the woman assessed his hidden penis—and he asserted he could "have convinced her quickly, in the street where she stood, that the Highest had made me well, and made me truly and properly a man"—he assesses the man's displayed penis in his dream. Following Freud's assertion that one is "justified in asserting that *a dream is the (disguised) fulfilment of a (repressed) wish*," we might wonder how this dream articulates a desire of which Plummer has refused himself ("An Autobiographical Study" 28). Affirming that he could take the measurement and *know* if the penis proved "too much" or "too little," Plummer suggests a hidden knowledge of sexual dynamics that in his writings he otherwise seems to actively deny.

Lauren Berlant's reading of Lacan and the phallus usefully orients the power dynamics in this dream sequence. "For Lacan," writes Berlant,

---

[47] Lennard J. Davis in *Enforcing Normalcy* notes that this period saw the rise of measurement as an arbiter of norms.

186 FEELING SINGULAR

"sexual difference is organized not around the penis and vagina, but the *gendering of anxiety*. Neither the male nor the female ever 'possesses' the phallus: it can only represent loss and desire" (*Desire/Love* 57). In this sense, the male identified subject with the exposed penis experiences the anxieties of inadequacy or excessiveness—"too big, or too little"—and gets gendered along terms of lack. Similarly, in this dynamic Plummer positions himself within the prerogatives of "the Law," operating as the figure who stabilizes and assesses the meaning of the penis, its potency or impotency, its adequacy or inadequacy.[48] Instead of being subjected to assessment— as he seems to feel when accused of being a "hermaphrodite"—this dream repositions himself as an arbiter of normativity, rather than a pathological subject. Returning from his failed family relationships—tired of the "[h]ard usage from my father"—in this dream Plummer works out his own sense of impotence, inability, and failure. Curiously, then, he makes public this personal and intimate working-out of such gendered power dynamics. As the un-anxious male in this dreamt encounter, Plummer asserts dominance, assessing a penis that becomes imaginatively exposed to him, and then spontaneously laughs for an undisclosed reason. Yet in telling the old man that the measuring of his penis "could certainly be taken," Plummer opens himself up as the assessor, fantasizing about positioning himself as being aware of desirable "girth" and "length" of the bodily appendage that "must not be named."[49]

Does Plummer's assessment that the penis's measurement could "be taken" suggest a latent desire to be penetrated by it? Is his interest in measuring the penis symptomatic of his failure to maintain a relationship to his father, indexing his wish for the recognition and attachment that he

---

[48] Berlant's model of desire follows Lacan, who "would call desire less a drive that is organized by objects and more a drive that moves beyond its objects, always operating with them and in excess to them, with aims both to preserve and destroy them" (19–20). Berlant's model of desire allows one to observe how Plummer's dream illustrates his complicated and unbounded desire for intimate belonging. Through representing himself as assessing the old man's penis, Plummer attempts to circumvent the Law of the Father, which would subject him to norms and protocols of belonging. Having consistently fallen short of such ideals, his laughter becomes a corrective to the inflation of masculine egos in his life.

[49] In thinking of queerness as the troubling of norms and protocols, I follow Judith Butler's "gender performativity" thesis, where repetition builds to a stasis of gender identities that forms their cultural expectations and generic conventions. Plummer's dream queers the stability and normativity that would otherwise ensure that a man could not express desire for another man's penis to "be taken." Butler notes that "[t]he heterosexualization of desire requires and institutes the production of discrete and asymmetrical oppositions between 'feminine' and 'masculine'" (*Gender Trouble* 24). With Plummer, we encounter the figure of sexual *and* gender ambiguity, with the implication of those "subversive matrices" played out in a dreamscape.

narrates being foiled from receiving again and again? As Berlant writes, desire "describes a state of attachment to something or someone, and the cloud of possibility that is generated by the gap between an object's specificity and the needs and promises projected onto it" (6). In Berlant's reading of desire, however, the desiring subject never fully knows what she wants; indeed, Berlant's model of desire suggests that it expands boundaries and continually gets reined in by the normative structures and conventional forms of propriety, confined within bounded, measurable expectations. In this sense, desire is desire because it aims to transgress the horizon of its fantasy object. Plummer fantasizes through this dream a moment that we can imagine as the figuration of a queer attachment, one that refuses the imperatives of republican marriage and reproduction, indexing what might be considered a homosexual encounter. Secreting these implicit desires into a dream—though in doing so presenting homosexual desire in plain view—Plummer interrupts his fantasy with his own giddy laughter, and then puts this queer scenario into print.

4.6. Straightening the Early Republic

Although the popular story of the American Revolution suggests a shift from patron- to merit-based economies, such cultural transformations are, of course, never fully realized. Historian Steven Watts in *The Republic Reborn: War and the Making of Liberal America, 1790–1820* (1987) charts "an interconnected shift toward liberal capitalism as the crucial fact of early national life" (xvii), which historian Joseph F. Kett further unpacks by considering the emergence of merit within that economy as a culturally determinant characteristic that "accounted for an individual's rise" within the republic's nascent capitalist market (15). Where the stories these historians tell focus on the emergence of (white male) individualism and the burgeoning of the U.S. political economy, there is an unexamined queer tale with Jonathan Plummer about how patronage lingered within the republic. Requiring the assistance of others—such as the eccentric "Lord" Timothy Dexter—Plummer illustrates the uneven power differentials that constituted the early republic even as he negotiates an attachment to a supposedly vanishing system of cultural value associated with patronage.

188 FEELING SINGULAR

Despite how Plummer's contemporaries called him "a droll fool,"[50] throughout his life and writings he latched on to the notion of self-improvement, an attribute growing into prominence in the new century as so-called self-made men like Franklin emerged as types within cultural imaginaries.[51] Indeed, Plummer seems quite invested in making himself appear normative, desiring to attract the notice of financially and socially established men to fund his declamations against sin. Plummer describes meeting Joseph McKeen, a minister and eventual president of Bowdoin College, with whom he wants to have a closer relationship. "The dazzling lustre of Mc'Keen's deportment by shewing me in some measure my own emptiness and how much I had yet to learn produced much diffidence in me," Plummer writes, referencing his apparent bashfulness and wish to be accepted by the "dazzling" man (68). Plummer continually portrays himself as lacking, as an unformed individual in need of being finished, attracted to the "lustre" of men like McKeen: "I consoled myself with hopes that I should in time most probably acquire a part of [McKeen's] accomplishments.—I often wished for more of his company and sometimes had it, but he and I could both see with half an eye that I was quite unqualified for a companion to him" (68–69). "I had hopes of enjoying more of Mc'Keens conversation," Plummer continues, "and hopes of falling in, in time in [sic] the United States, with some other Gentleman, or Lady nearly or quite equal to him," recognizing an inequality between himself and McKeen that signals social and intimate incompatibility (69). Plummer wants betterment and improvement, committing "to read the best books and to keep the best company that I could," but in the end he explains that he "was however immensely troubled with fears that I should never attain half the degree of perfection which I wished to possess" (69). Plummer hopes—repeating the word thrice—but concludes by announcing his unfitness for McKeen's "company."

Feeling unfit for the proper McKeen, Plummer finds company—and the fruition of his hopes for improvement—in "Lord" Timothy Dexter, who took the peddling poet under his wing, as it were, after Plummer praised his newly

---

[50] William Bentley calls Plummer "a droll fool" in his diary (2.205) and describes his broadsides as "ridiculous" (3.22).

[51] In his reading of reform literature in the early nineteenth century, Christopher Castiglia argues that the central theme in many such writings focuses on "how to discern real from feigned virtue, given that interior 'nature' rather than public actions has become the guarantor of trust" (158). This move from public performance to interior introspection highlights the stakes of Plummer's own desire to publicly declare his relation to the norms of republican masculinity. He articulates a desire to fit within a series of norms that he falls short of occupying.

PERAMBULATIONS IN PRINT   189

made fortune through investing in whalebone corsets: "I a suit of clothes must have, / to sing my joy in, and the best, Sir, / A suit of red; not black and grave" (171). Plummer would eventually attach his literary career to Dexter's, positioning himself as the vehicle for Dexter to manifest his greatness. Plummer initially obtained Dexter's approval and patronage through a 1793 broadside he wrote congratulating the one-time leather dresser with his newfound financial success: "When you sold your freedom suit, to raise money to put yourself into business," Plummer writes, "the action was heroic in the highest, and I doubt whether ever Dr. Franklin in his lowest estate, and in the strictest course of his economy, ever displayed superior firmness."[52] Favorably comparing Dexter to Franklin, Plummer then asks him to "furnish me your affectionate bard, with a suit equally good, to enable me to rejoice at your prosperity with increased gracefulness and gentility." Once Plummer was thusly dressed he began declaring himself the "poet lauret to his Lordship," seeking to promote Dexter even after his death, writing: "May he enjoy his life in peace, / And when he's dead his name not cease" (*Something New* 14).

A few years after Dexter's death, Plummer distanced himself from the "celebrated monied man of Newbury Port." In attaching his career to Dexter, Plummer had demonstrated his desire to be part of the center of early national cultural myth making, at least insofar as Dexter manufactured for himself his own center. In his broadside announcing Dexter's death, Plummer wonders if his patron is in hell: "Thus far, with joy can I survey the subject; but a tho't more important presses into my mind, and that is this, viz. where will my generous patron be in the mean time? Will he be in hell lifting up his eyes in torments and cursing his existence? or will he be in heaven joining with ten million times ten millions of angels, cherubims, seraphims & spirits of saints made perfect, enjoying the matchless grace of him, that was, and is, and is to be?"[53] Plummer switches from glorying in his strange position as a poet laureate of a self-appointed Lord to instead loudly and aggressively proclaim the divine

[52] Jonathan Plummer, "The Author's Congratulatory ADDRESS to Citizen Timothy Dexter, on his attaining an Independent FORTUNE" (Newburyport, 1793). Broadside.

[53] See "THE LAST WILL AND TESTAMENT OF HIS EXCELLENCY Sir TIMOTHY DEXTER, dec'd. TOGETHER WITH A SHORT SERMON. By JONATHAN PLUMMER, a Travelling Preacher; formerly Poet Laureat to his Lordship" (Newburyport, 1806). Broadside. This shift in broadside rhetoric after Dexter's death is more pronounced in other broadsides, which assert that deaths are the immediate result of sin. For instance, in "Dreadful sickness at Amesbury" (1814), Plummer notes that "It is likely perhaps that they were so much like the people of Sodom, that they were in a way of boasting of a part of their sins, glorying in their shame, and wishing to be highly applauded when they told of some of their hell defying, heaven daring crimes."

190 FEELING SINGULAR

judgments and retributions of an angry God, switching and renouncing patrons as he fashions his queer affiliations. In another broadside, Plummer reflects on the lives of "the people killed lately by the fevers," asserting:

> it is likely that many of them brought forth such fruit, that they are hewn down, and cast into the fire that many of them did not love God so well as they did money, cattle, land, houses, lying, cheating, fornication, drinking, defamation, the praise of wicked people &c. or some of these things. It is likely that many of them loved their lives better than they did their creator, and his commandments, and of course that their situation is now miserable, forlorn and inexpressibly unhappy. Woes everlasting woes, and endless horrors, will await the audacious rebels, who hate and despise, the lovliest [sic] of the lovely, and live and die in their sins![54]

In this manner, the queer, perambulating Plummer, leaving behind his privileged attachment to the "the first Lord in the younited States of A mercury," determines to turn into a voice that straightens out the early republic, returning the normalizing gaze of divine decrees that protest "sin" after shunning the weird and strange particularities of eccentric America.

Unlike Dexter, Plummer left neither progeny nor wooden monuments, but instead sought to produce a print legacy that would ensure the continuance of his name in the republic. As an unreproductive bachelor who, according to the written archive he left, was at least publicly uninterested in normative sex, Plummer explains he once found himself "[p]assing . . . near a woman that I expect is very fond of adultery" and "happened . . . to hear her utter words. . . . [T]hese I expect are the following ones, viz. 'He is an hermaphrodite.'" In putting this abbreviated accusation into print, Plummer publicizes and perpetuates the charge against him, highlighting his anxious desire to correct any potential gossip even as he tries to perform unconcern, writing: "I might have convinced her quickly, I believe, in the street where she stood, that the Highest had made me well, and made me truly and properly a man, but I did not stop to do it, and so little did I care what she said about me, that without even telling her, that she was an impudent lying woman, I went on my way."[55] Plummer attempts to make certain his contested manhood by

---

[54] See Jonathan Plummer, "Dreadful sickness at Amesbury, &c. and melancholy destruction by the blowing up of a Powder-Mil" (Newburyport, 1814). Broadside.

[55] Mechel Sobel in *Teach Me Dreams: The Search for Self in the Revolutionary Era* argues: "For the writers, presenting oneself for evaluation in a narrative was a form of 'public confessional,' a new

PERAMBULATIONS IN PRINT 191

policing the woman's sexuality, implying that she "is very fond of adultery." Just as Plummer is apparently called out as not fitting within a normative gendered embodiment, he casts aspersion through mobilizing the figure of a promiscuous woman. Where Dexter advertises his interest in sexual promiscuity, Plummer here and elsewhere emerges as a figure of moral reformation, seeking to normalize himself through pointing out the excesses of others while denying his own.

The way disavowal operates to shore up one's sense of norms is illustrative in a strange, anonymous typewritten manuscript that projects queer insight into Timothy Dexter's and Jonathan Plummer's lives. Written in the 1930s and deposited in the Phillips Library, this text describes the self-declared "Lord" as a "mushroom man, also uneducated, who . . . had a son who imitated the vice of Oscar Wilde, a very prevailing vice in Newburyport, at all periods of its history" (10). Focusing on the charge of illicit homosexuality, the anonymous writer of "A Concise Life of Lord Timothy Dexter" explains that Dexter's son roamed free from any penalty because he caught "his millionaire father in a worse sexual sin" (10). The unknown author, in this bitter and caustic biography, makes this curious assessment:

> Yet society stood for these monsters in Newburyport, for Newburyport went wild over following Oscar Wilde, and over following his example, and Newburyport always is an Oscar Wilde City, and always has been one, while the same crowd, and their descendants ridiculed and ostracised [sic] Dexter, whose beastly habits and immorality was at least natural, not unnatural. (10)

Reading Newburyport as a coded homosexual enclave, this representation of Dexter marks queerness in the guise of homosexual "monsters," thereby rendering Dexter as at least not *that* bad (even if his son caught him in an unmentionable sex act). If homosexuality is the barometer by which Dexter becomes normal, it's through an anachronistic timeline that marks the early national seaport as "following Oscar Wilde." Chronology is queered to stabilize the norms that would otherwise mark Dexter as innocuous.

What's striking about this homophobic formulation of Newburyport's faux history is the amateur historian's insistence that such acceptance of

disciplinary form, a new way to reframe the past, and at the same time a way to get income. It was a selling of the self, in both material and psychological terms" (13).

192　FEELING SINGULAR

homosexuality was rampant "at all periods of [Newburyport's] history" (10). Such a gesture collapses linear time into an abstract sense of widespread non-normative sexual practices that, through their wide dissemination, became regionally normative. This formulation breaks the norms and protocols of historicist understanding, inserting an anachronistic frame to make visible what should ostensibly be nonexistent: that is, marking a homosexual identity prior to its historical emergence. We might follow here Christopher Looby's argument that "sexuality is itself a fiction, an imaginary composite of many difference experiences, identifications, and performances" (843).[56] In this manner, reading a queer—or, homosexual—figuration of the past helps both defamiliarize that past while also redefining the terms and ideas that make it, and Plummer, approachable.

---

[56] Christopher Looby makes the important case for reading homosexuality as a form of aesthetics, describing sexuality itself as "essentially a literary phenomenon" (841). My thinking on queer temporalities and anachronism has been influenced by Jordan Alexander Stein's "American Literary History and Queer Temporalities," which invigorates questions of methodology by asking literary studies to rethink periodization (through *queering* periodization) and Valerie Rohy's *Anachronism and Its Others: Sexuality, Race, Temporality.*

5

The Queer Hermit

William "Amos" Wilson and the Antisocial Republic

> Democracy is Lovelace and the People are Clarisa. The artful villain
> will pursue the lovely girl to her ruin and death.
> —John Adams letter to William Cunningham

> Immediately then the thought came sweeping across me, What miserable friendlessness and loneliness are here revealed! His poverty is
> great; but his solitude, how horrible!
> —Herman Melville, "Bartleby, The Scrivener"

In an 1804 letter about "the awful spirit of democracy" then purportedly
seducing the U.S. citizenry from republican virtues, John Adams laments that
he is "no match for these times, nor for the actors who now tread the stage"
(18). Developing his social critique, he analogizes his cultural moment with
Samuel Richardson's famous eighteenth-century seduction novel *Clarissa*,
noting that troublingly democratic ideologies appear "handsome and well
made" but "[w]hen the people once admit his courtship, and permit him the
least familiarity, they soon find themselves in the condition of the poor girl"
(19). That condition, euphemistically called "abandoned," highlights the gendered logics of republicanism, where the submissive *people* are imagined secure through the patriarchal codes that keep them safe from the supposedly
seductive siren of liberal democracy.

In histories of liberalism, the self-autonomous individual, born in a state
of nature before becoming a public citizen, is always a male. "Citizens were
made, not born" (11), Helena Rosenblatt notes in her study of liberalism,
reminding readers that "the consent of the governed," in the American context, established governments to "secure the unalienable rights of men" (35).
The paradox of something "unalienable" that needs safeguarding—namely,

---

Feeling Singular. Ben Bascom, Oxford University Press. © Oxford University Press 2024.
DOI: 10.1093/9780197687536.003.0006

194 FEELING SINGULAR

requiring a government for protection—belies the gendered implications of the rights-bearing subject and *his* penchant for setting the frameworks of property, sociality, and consent. Without a government to stabilize society, this line of thinking goes, the parameters of proper relations would be troubled, leading to strife and alienation. Just as the Declaration of Independence sought to affirm that power derives "from the consent of the governed," not all subjects in the early United States were socialized to give consent or positioned as structural agents to be allowed to do more than demure.

The early national literary form that best encapsulated gendered questions of agency and desire was the seduction plot. The period's most popular seduction novels emphasize the trouble that female-gendered subjects encounter through transgressing (or being made to transgress) social norms and the structural forces that constrain them. Susanna Rowson's *Charlotte Temple* (1791) describes the "seduced" Charlotte feeling "herself a poor solitary being in the midst of surrounding multitudes" (69), and Hannah Webster Foster's *The Coquette* (1797) has the moralizing Lucy Sumner tell the soon-to-be-fallen Eliza Wharton to "Avoid solitude" (195). Solitude, in the realm of the aftereffects or threat of seduction, indexes a specifically gendered punishment. There is a repressed origin story here between the seduction plot and the hermit tale that this chapter traces, one that entangles them and suggests their structural dependency. One example of this doubling between seduction and hermit tropes can be found in the eighteenth-century Robinsonade *The Female American, or, The Adventures of Unca Eliza Winkfield* (1767), when the narrator finds herself on a deserted island with a hermit's manuscript notes in her hand.[1] The hermit-composed manuscript describes the conditions of the island to future wayfarers, informing whoever finds themselves stranded how to survive alone. "Though the hermit's manuscript assured me there were no inhabitants nor animals to hurt me," Unca considers, "yet the thought of wandering alone was terrifying" (60). What makes this idea "terrifying" is that solitude inscribes gendered violence. The "Female American" Unca is made to feel particularly at risk on the island, whereas the male hermit found it a refuge. As such, the lonely Unca, who reads the last writings of a solitary man, shows the disparate ways gender makes one *feel* alone when outside the normative confines of society.

---

[1] The 1800 Newburyport edition of the novel was printed for and sold by Angier March, who just two years before began printing Jonathan Plummer's life narrative, and the book offers a curious return to the issues Plummer raises regarding gender, sociality, and outsiders.

THE QUEER HERMIT 195

Most of the figures this book examines are enmeshed into the condition that Lauren Berlant has called "cruel optimism." They are not misfits because they did not *want* to be like everyone else in early republican U.S. culture; they are misfits *despite* their desire to work within the system that devalued them. But this chapter moves away from failed desire *for* social attachment and instead turns to those individuals who *disavow* normative social belonging. I thus focus on William "Amos" Wilson, known as the Pennsylvania Hermit, a man who, like Melville's Bartleby, preferred *not* to belong and instead ensconced himself away from such conventional social formations. Wilson, as I will show, chose to become "a recluse from the jars of a contending world" after the State of Pennsylvania convicted and executed his sister for infanticide (9). He lived in obscurity in Pennsylvania from the 1760s to the 1820s but gained posthumous celebrity for the circumstances that led him to "prefer solitude" when his story was published in a series of pamphlets. By becoming a hermit, Wilson initially determined to decathect from the social world that, in Sara Ahmed's terms, "constructs desire as a magnetic field" (*Queer* 85). But what I show is how his choice to remove himself ends up having political resonances in his textual afterlife. The hermit's removal from the public sphere, after all, is already a quintessentially republican gesture: he removes himself from ostensible public influence but in doing so asserts another form of influence, lamenting the presumably fallen public and seeking to influence that domain through a posthumous text. In this sense, he remains attached to social formations *through* his disavowal of them. That circuitous dynamic, I will argue, offers a way into considering the gendered formations of what constitutes republicanism in the early republic, especially through unearthing the context that led to Wilson's solitude.

The hermit narrative becomes symptomatic of a repressed transgression at the heart of a liberalizing republic, making social ostracism the punishment for a gendered crime: in the particularities of this case, a mother's infanticide. The hermit tale encapsulates the narrative fulfillment of the cultural production of the seduction plot, where the shame of a sexual crime leads to abjection and seclusion.[2] One's solitary life is rendered visible as a result of seduction, unrequited love, or some other romantic misdeed. In this manner, solitary

---

[2] Marxist psychoanalytic theory from Herbert Marcuse allows one to consider a formulation of repression that engages with the cultural connection between seduction and hermit narratives, showing how the hermit becomes the symptom of a tormented libidinal drive that seeks shelter outside of the republican norms that have been broken. The surplus repression, in Marcuse's formulation, could be said to guard society against seduction but then extends to the pathologizing of the hermit's solitude.

196 FEELING SINGULAR

lives become the result of a troubling of sex—generally, a making public of sex when sex should otherwise be curtained within the private. The hermit reorients the public around a visible privacy that his solitary life outlines. Leaving behind a manuscript for someone else to discover, the hermit signals an attenuated attachment to a public *because* of a transgressive intimate life. Bruce Burgett notes that "the liberal nation-state emerges out of . . . republican government with political paranoia and subjectifying institutions" (68). Burgett centers sexual and gender differences as key to constituting republicanism, arguing for how the legibility of sexual desire, and the opportunities to express contested attachments, signal such formations: republican ideology would repress the expression of self-interested attachments, whereas a liberal model makes such attachments paramount. As a figure who wishes to emerge unscathed from such institutions, the hermit catalyzes the tensions that would otherwise push liberal belonging outside the purview of social attachment.

To outline what follows, I will begin by telling the story of William Wilson's sister, Elizabeth, showing how narratives about her crime transformed in the print public sphere from that of a woman wrongly executed to a conventional anti-seduction diatribe. These later printings in the 1820s altered the names of the accused (Harriot) and the hermit (Amos) in an odd gesture of anonymity. From there, I will then turn to William/"Amos" himself, to show how his celebrity as a hermit ultimately superseded Elizabeth's story. What I call the suppression of Elizabeth occurs partly because hermit tropes in the early nineteenth-century United States offered a particularly masculinist way to represent the relation between the public and private spheres, and the aspirations to make one significant. I then connect the hermit's desire for asocial belonging with queer studies' work in considering the politics of withdrawing oneself from society, particularly drawing upon the relation between solitude and the rise of state institutions. All of this sets up a conclusion that thinks more about the stakes of the production of solitude within institutional settings, and the legacies of state power in the U.S. Republic.

5.1. The Commonplace of Solitude

On the morning of January 3, 1786, the civil authorities of Chester County, Pennsylvania, executed Elizabeth Wilson by hanging, closing a trial that had received short newspaper notices before her death and unleashing a host of

THE QUEER HERMIT   197

disparate attention afterward.[3] Charged with the murder of her six-week-old twin infants, Elizabeth offered no account for why her children were found dead in the woods until her brother, William Wilson—who had initially held back his involvement with the case because she already "had three children in an unlawful way"—visited and encouraged her to confess to whatever she knew about the deaths of the infants (*A Faithful Narrative* 5).[4] The unmarried Elizabeth told her brother that a sheriff in Sussex County, New Jersey, had seduced and abandoned her, murdering the infants after she appealed to him for protection.[5] Reassured by her story, William convinced the state authorities in Philadelphia to delay the execution twice to do his own detective work, but his second attempt to return a stay of execution proved inadequate as a torrential downpour raised the nearby river Schuylkill to an impassable depth, making him just twenty-three minutes late to stop the execution. "When he came with the respite in his hand," one eighteenth-century account states, "and saw his sister irrecoverably gone, beheld her motionless, and sunk in death . . . who can paint the mournful scene? . . . Let imagination if she can!" (*A Faithful* 16–17).[6] The experience is said to have shaken William to his core, some accounts noting that he soon followed his sister in death. That death, however, turned out to be more symbolic than literal, as subsequent accounts describe him wandering into the westward regions of Pennsylvania and living out the remainder of his life as a hermit.

We learn about these details of Elizabeth Wilson's life from her 1786 printed confession, *A Faithful Narrative of Elizabeth Wilson* (subsequently reprinted in 1807), which was "Drawn up at the request of a friend unconnected with

---

[3] The short news announcement before Elizabeth's execution about "a woman . . . committed to Chester gaol, on suspicion of murdering her two sucking infant twins" circulated throughout January 1785 on the second or third pages of newspapers in Philadelphia; Baltimore; New Haven; Alexandria, Virginia; Salem, Massachusetts; Norwich, Connecticut; and Windsor, Vermont. Beginning in Rhode Island's *The Providence Gazette*, the narrative of her life—entitled *A Faithful Narrative of Elizabeth Wilson*—circulated from multiple newspapers in New York, Connecticut, Massachusetts, Vermont, and South Carolina from April to May of 1786. One newspaper used the entirety of the first and last page to reprint it. See *The Plymouth Journal, and The Massachusetts Advertiser* 2 (May 23, 1786): 1, 4.
[4] This detail about William's hesitation to come to the aid of his sister is found in Charles Biddle's autobiography, who as the vice-president to Benjamin Franklin issued the initial warrant for the execution. See Biddle, *Autobiography of Charles Biddle*, 199. For citational purposes, I am using the 1807 version of the confession narrative as it suggests the longevity of this tale and the printers' desires to circulate it (setting up for the subsequent 1822 narratives of "The Sweets of Solitude" and "The Victim of Seduction," which improvised and extrapolated on the events narrated).
[5] Throughout, and for clarity's sake, I use "Elizabeth" to refer to the sister and "Wilson" to refer to the brother. Additionally, I refer to "William" in this section to refer to the man who became a hermit.
[6] Information about the stays of execution that William Wilson obtained can be found in *Minutes of the Supreme Executive Council of Pennsylvania* 14 (Harrisburg, 1853), 586. The reasons behind Wilson's inability to return to Chester in time center around weather-related problems, with either rivers being made impassable or roads washed out.

198 FEELING SINGULAR

her" (3; see Fig. 5.1). The fantasy of a text written by one "unconnected" suggests the seemingly disinterested nature of the printing, one that is done for an imagined public good. But, of course, the text also seeks to justify the actions of the state in executing her, including the caveat: "Thus ended the life of Elizabeth Wilson, in the 27th year of her age; innocent, we believe, of the crime for which she suffered, but guilty in concealing, or rather attempting to conceal, a crime of so horrid a nature, which she was privy to" (17). The text struggles to find a way to depict her, explaining that "before she was turned off" her sincerity was again called into question, but then "in a moment was turned off" (16). This repetition of the euphemism "turned off" signals the struggle the text has with depicting Elizabeth. Indeed, the text describes Elizabeth dichotomously, noting at one moment that "her behaviour was such . . . as gave reasons to conclude she was [either] innocent of the murder of which she was charged, or was an insensible, hardened creature, and did not expect to die for this crime" (4).[7] The picture that emerges of Elizabeth is one that emphasizes her loneliness and despair, with the text asserting that "[s]he said the dungeon was the happiest place she ever was in, in her life" (6). As a way to access Elizabeth's interiority, this narrative includes manuscript pages that she left behind in the jail that articulate her desire to see her brother before she dies. A single asterisk draws the reader to the note at the bottom of the page, cordoning the passage away from the main body of the text while also implying its significance:

> O could I but see my own brother! to speak just a few words to him, to ease my broken heart, that is so distressed. Oh how hard a thing it is that I cannot see him! Was he in my place and I in his, I would go to him, if it was on my hands and knees; but he will not come to me, to speak one word to me, before I depart this life. (5)

This manuscript fragment lets readers inside the otherwise opaque (described as "insensible, hardened") Elizabeth Wilson, telling us what she is thinking and feeling so that readers can feel a sense of closeness with her. This fantasy of proximity further develops as Elizabeth even goes on to imagine

---

[7] In one historical contextualization of the case, Meredith Peterson Tufts writes: "it was precisely the historically amorphous, indeterminate nature of Elizabeth Wilson's identity that enabled different authors to shape her story to their own purposes and allowed her to become variously an example of redemption through faith; an emblem of motherhood in the new republic; and a seduced and abandoned innocent servicing as a moral lesson for succeeding generations" (153).

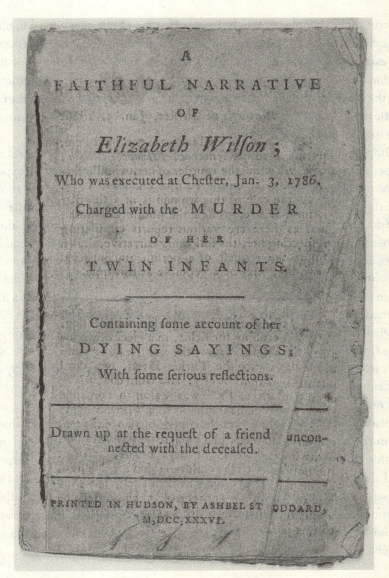

Figure 5.1 One of several republications of *A Faithful Narrative of Elizabeth Wilson*. Printed in Hudson, New York, by Ashbel Stoddard, 1786. Courtesy of the American Antiquarian Society.

200 FEELING SINGULAR

her brother in her place: "Was he in my place and I in his, I would go to him," Elizabeth writes, collapsing her identity with his, as if their life stories could be exchanged, in a sentimental gesture that promotes sympathetic identification between brother and sister, on one hand, and speaker and audience, on the other. Eventually reduced to *types* as the seduced woman and the hermitic man, the passage indexes the impulse to make sense of tragedy through the tug and pull of stock conventions.

Improbable as the idea of changing places seems, William Wilson did experience a type of isolation that parallels Elizabeth's gendered experience of social ostracism—and like her he left behind a manuscript record for future recovery. Let us turn, then, to a cave in rural Pennsylvania just outside Harrisburg, where Elizabeth Wilson's brother chose to live alone. Subsequently dubbed the "Pennsylvania Hermit," William Wilson is said to have deposited inside his stone home a record explaining why he chose a life of solitude before dying in 1821.[8] The first printed account of this story comes from an obituary in the October *Harrisburg Intelligencer*, which notes a man named "Mr. — Wilson" had "Died, lately, at his lonely hovel among the hills" ("Died"). This man, "who for many years endeavored to be a solitary recluse from the society of men," was newsworthy for the unique circumstances that led to his solitary life. Readers are told: "His retirement was principally occasioned by the melancholy manner of the death of his sister, by which his reason was also partially affected. She had been condemned to die near Philadelphia, for a crime committed in the hope of concealing her shame from the world, and the day of execution was appointed." Wilson emerges in this and other print publications as the recipient of his sister's unspecified shame, living his life alone as a testament to the broken social and domestic codes that prescribe particular virtues to women. The tale of this hermit thus highlights the gendered production of shame, where a narrative about a mother accused of infanticide becomes cloaked in euphemism and recentered on a brother's seclusion.[9]

---

[8] Although William and Elizabeth are recorded as real historical persons, in the subsequent narratives about them ("The Victim of Seduction" and "The Sweets of Solitude") their names are changed to Amos and Harriot. I have not found any evidence for why this was done, though there is something to be said about the possibly incestuous relationship between William and Elizabeth and the renaming of Elizabeth as Harriot as a gesture to the seduction novel *The Power of Sympathy*, whose protagonist is also named Harriot and nearly marries her half-brother Thomas.

[9] The possibilities of incest tropes are subtle but not absent in the story. For more on the destabilizing force of incest as a narrative trope, see Brian Connolly's *Domestic Intimacies: Incest and the Liberal Subject in Nineteenth-Century America* (2014).

THE QUEER HERMIT 201

Soon after the hermit's death, a pamphlet hurriedly assembled, stitched together with thread and containing a Boston imprint, expanded upon the story contained in the obituary (see Fig. 5.2a–b). This pamphlet, entitled "The Sweets of Solitude, or Directions to Mankind How They May Be Happy in a 'Miserable World!'" purports to offer the authentic final words of the hermit, the written testament to his life and the sad story that brought him to prefer seclusion. The framing device that introduces Wilson's text concludes with the manuscript's provenance, explaining that: "In October last, this extraordinary and singular character expired in his hut, unattended by a single friend to close his eyes!" (10).[10] Presented as a "singular character" whose life merits print publication, the narrator continues:

> his exit must have been very sudden, as he was left the evening before in tolerable health by the writer; in a corner of his cave was found a bunch of manuscripts, among which . . . the contents of the following pages is an exact copy, and which he requested particularly might be published, and in conformity to which, we here present it to the public:

Concluding with a colon, the introductory frame presents the ensuing text as the final words of the solitary man. Paralleling Elizabeth's own fleeting thoughts written down on pages pining for her brother, the hermit's words build from the accused's gesture of putting forward one final, brief desire. The "bunch of manuscripts" are transformed into the material and textual object held in the hands of readers curious about the hermit's rationale for living apart from society. The transition from a collection of manuscripts into a printed artifact materializes Wilson's desire to present his message to a public. Wilson offers his double absence (dead and a hermit) from the public as insistence to secure his works for future readership, experiencing what Thomas Dumm calls "*the pathos of disappearance*" (34). Eric Slauter notes how early national hermit narratives "are of course by nature audience-oriented, directed toward a reading public (increasingly made up of solitary readers) curious and anxious about privacy" (220). This insistence on a future

---

[10] This reference to dying while "unattended by a single friend" may be productively compared with the ending of Hannah Webster Foster's *The Coquette* (1797), which notes that Eliza Wharton, the victim to the seductive wiles of a man, was "Far from every friend; / And exhibited an example / Of calm resignation." In this sense, the hermit becomes the figural position of the fallen women, whose death is narrated by others as the logical conclusion to seduction.

Figure 5.2a–b Title page of "The Sweets of Solitude," published for John Wilkey in 1822, and the accompanying image of "Amos" Wilson as a hermit living in a cave. Courtesy of the American Antiquarian Society.

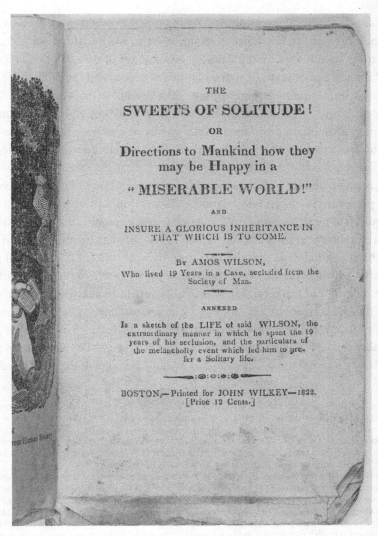

Figure 5.2a–b Continued.

voice—on a message surviving the passing of one's life—provides an ironic return of social attachment embedded into the very gesture of rejecting it.

Despite the irony of such hermit narratives—composed in seclusion for public consumption—a deeper irony emerges in Wilson's thirty pages of printed text. While the introductory frame briefly references Elizabeth Wilson's death, the majority of the text is essentially a commonplace book: a collection of famous eighteenth-century aphorisms that cover topics as broad

204 FEELING SINGULAR

as solitude, desire, and worldliness, strung together as if they were the words of the deceased hermit. That is to say, even in his imagined solitude, the hermit is surrounded by the writings and sayings of dozens of eighteenth-century and earlier texts, from translations of Seneca and the Bible to Johann Georg Zimmermann among others. "The Sweets of Solitude," then, is a very odd kind of fiction—the conglomerated words of eighteenth-century public philosophers positioned as the words of a private hermit. The text quotes from these without explicit attribution or acknowledgment, offering them instead as the original writings of the recently deceased hermit, whose words, then, are not his own, but rather the assemblage of disparate voices and perspectives placed into relation.[11] As a commonplace book (albeit one disguised as a life narrative), Wilson's text acts, in Meredith McGill's words, as "a storehouse of texts through which experience can be managed and understood" (361).[12] The hermit's narrative, then, abstracts his individual personality through the incorporation of disparate public figures and voices. Like all commonplace books, Wilson's "is anti-individualistic insofar as it highlights the means by which subjects, understood to be plural and iterable, are produced" (361).[13] These capacities of Wilson's text—to abstract his personality through the incorporation of canonical texts—demonstrates a particularly gendered mode of producing a public persona in the early republic.

[11] In fact, the only aphorism that the text places in quotation marks is from Benjamin Franklin, who is similarly never named. The text only describes the words as "a maxim, the truth of which, many unthinking youth has, too late, been forced to acknowledge" (22). The incorporation of an unattributed Franklin quote may very well be the ultimate gesture to illustrate that personality's fixture in the early republic. Franklin has become, by the printing of Wilson's text, so prevalent that his ostensible words require quotes though do not necessitate direct references.

[12] McGill argues that "Commonplace books are a mode of cultural transmission that allows for the deracination and reframing of cultural authority" (361). With Wilson, partly because the book does not announce itself as a commonplace book, we see less a reworking of cultural authority than a reaffirming of the particularly republican ways of organizing public life through the appeal to a type of cultural canon. That canon remains unmarked within Wilson as a way to substantiate it as such. The entire text is filled with Seneca and Seneca-esque aphorisms ("Not to amuse ourselves with hopes or fears, but to rest satisfied with our present circumstances, is alone the way to contentment" [12] and "Never pronounce any man happy who depends upon fortune for his happiness" [14], are just a few) to suggest that Wilson laments the early republic's fall from the ideals of republican belonging, but through leaving them as unmarked quotations the text reaffirms their ideology.

[13] In this manner, Wilson very interestingly coincides with Foucault's argument about how the "author function" emerges through "a system of ownership for texts" that establishes "strict rules concerning author's rights, author-publisher relations, rights of reproduction, and related matters . . . at the end of the eighteenth and the beginning of the nineteenth century" ("What" 108). Foucault argues that to think of the author, in modern discourse, one must ask: "What are the modes of existence of this discourse? Where has it been used, how can it circulate, and who can appropriate it for himself? What are the places in it where there is room for possible subjects? Who can assume these various subject formations?" (120). In this manner, Wilson-as-author through the arrangement of others' words produces the *effect* of a singular self, but that effect is always counteracted by the republican truisms that ground his rhetoric.

Similar to how Benjamin Franklin, a generation before, earned notoriety by appropriating others' aphorisms and suppressing his individual personality, often through the production of a female voice, such as Silence Dogood, Celia Single, and Martha Careful, the hermit here draws upon the wisdom of others—but also abstracts the specificities of Elizabeth's own life—to claim a final testament for his farewell to the public sphere.

5.2. Solitude's Seductions

Hermits invite intrigue, summoning fascination for others to discover the particular rationale behind their privacy. In the early nineteenth century, the figure of the hermit produced a series of questions about the social and intimate ruptures that must have occurred for individuals to live beyond the normative attachments that would otherwise tether them to society. Through examining dozens of hermit narratives that circulated in the early United States, the question as to *why* one would live such a life emerges as a pronounced motif. Such narratives are generally set up through a frame tale that describes an encounter between a traveler and the secluded hermit, followed by a series of questions that unfold the story as to why such a solitary life was pursued.[14] The singular, lonely individual who lives beyond the realm of social propriety inspires a questioning audience to locate what set forth the individual on this journey to live alone. Hermits are thus depicted in these frame narratives as glitches and abnormalities in need of explanation. As such, the hermit narrative illuminates a series of social norms that assume intimacy with others as a basic human trait, demarcating as deviant the impulse to live alone, outside social norms.

Henry David Thoreau, well-known for his decision to leave Concord for the relative solitude of Walden Pond in the 1840s, suggested in *Walden* that most readers would probably assume that "To be alone was something unpleasant" (92). Thoreau, however, contends that "To be in company, even with the best, is soon wearisome and dissipating. I love to be alone. . . . We are for the most part more lonely when we go abroad among men than when

---

[14] There are many examples of hermit narratives that utilize this trope of discovery, with varying print forms from books to pamphlets to broadsides. Some of these include *The Hermit of Virginia* (1807), *The Benevolent Old Man of the Rock* (1810), "A Wonderful Discovery of a Hermit. Who Lived Upwards of 200 Years" (1816), *Life and Adventures of Robert Voorhis, the Hermit of Massachusetts* (1829), and *Narrative of the Extraordinary Life of John C. Shafford—The Dutch Hermit* (1840).

206 FEELING SINGULAR

we stay in our chambers" (94–95). Though, of course, Thoreau declares that he is "naturally no hermit" and obscures the gendered labor that enabled his time at Walden Pond. Instead, he wishes to make his solitary life public to reorient the conventions of his society, and he uses his time mourning his brother's death as an occasion to philosophize. Similar to Wilson's composite of eighteenth-century aphorisms, *Walden* endeavors to manufacture a new mode of reading that affects the reader, explaining that such reading "requires a training such as the athletes underwent, the steady intention almost of the whole life to this object" (72).

Wilson's "The Sweets of Solitude" similarly positions itself as a subversion of normative social conventions. Specifically, the hermit's preference for solitude over society is a queer gesture, one that shows him taking upon himself the figural position Elizabeth occupied as she awaited her death. I am thinking of *queer* as a mode of critique that refuses the social *as constituted* and actively imagines an otherwise. Wilson's text hinges on an impulse that Lee Edelman has called antisocial self-shattering—an idea which valorizes the negativity that refuses collective identification. The hermit, by embracing the outsider position, offers a queer response to the dominant heteronormative society that privileges social continuity and domestic reproduction, consummated through marriage and domesticity (and buttressed by the state that metes out death to those, like Elizabeth Wilson, who transgress their boundaries). In *No Future*, Edelman encourages the embrace of the figural queer position to destabilize the social forms that legislate heteronormative futures.[15] But what does it mean to refuse "reproductive futurity," embracing the figural position of the outsider as a hermit, at the start of the early U.S. republic? Considering the popularity of such hermit tales, and their inevitable buttressing of social reproduction, it seems important to think about what this figure galvanizes.

The figure of the hermit in early national narratives offers readers an opportunity to reflect on social attachments. The imperative to discover *why* a hermit is a hermit—uncovering the interpersonal factors that led to his removal from society—often dominates the frame tale of such encounters. The narratives themselves, furthermore, often expose some form of domestic trauma (such as seduction and failed intimate attachments) as the instigating

---

[15] Indeed, Edelman would have queer theory resist all forms of identitarian politics for the way they end up reifying liberal models of (straight) subjectivity. Instead of placing new seats on the table of the liberal republic, Edelman would prefer to destroy the signifying system that makes inclusion desirable.

factor in the hermit's decision to live in seclusion. For instance, in Frederick Farnsworth's 1818 hermit narrative *The Man of the Mountain*, the narrator comes upon a hermit's dwelling while on a hunting trip in Pennsylvania's Alleghenies. The narrator, upon introducing himself to the hermit, ventures: "[p]erhaps ingratitude, or the loss of wealth and friends, has given you a disgust of the world" (6). The hermit, who identifies himself as William Warland from Massachusetts, says to the narrator: "You are young, and perhaps my story may be of use to you; you have taken an interest in my fate, which does not appear to be prompted by unworthy motives, and to you will I confide my griefs and my wrongs" (7). Once gaining the hermit's trust, the narrator elaborates the unfolding conversation: "The old man raised his head, and grasping my hand with energy, exclaimed in tones which thrilled to my very soul, and made the blood to curdle round my heart—'*Young man, BEWARE OF SEDUCTION*'" (7). What follows is a story of Warland's daughter being seduced, dying in childbirth, and Warland's determination to live beyond the realm of such influence for his now orphaned granddaughter. After reciting his history, the hermit reminds: "You have heard my story—if it has interested you, wonder not that I commenced by cautioning you to '*beware of seduction!*'" (20).

Leonard Tennenhouse notes that American seduction narratives evince a "longing for a reconstructed family with a father at its head" (45).[16] The patriarchal function of the seduction narrative elucidates the desire for reifying masculinist power and privilege. Seduction plots generally inscribe men into positions of public and private agency. The hermit narrative, surprisingly, does a similar thing, yet we can see how the tropes of the hermit and the fallen woman occupy two opposite modes of imagined social belonging in the early United States. Where the fallen woman registers a desire to police the domestic sphere, the hermit signifies a specifically masculine privilege to detach from domestic formations, seemingly escaping the presumed constraints of normative family relations. In the end, seduction narratives reaffirm the heteronormative family's reproductive potential, whereas the hermit narrative initially troubles such futurities, foreclosing the social

---

[16] Leonard Tennenhouse has examined the popularity in America of Samuel Richardson's *Pamela* (1740) and other seduction narratives, in the early republic, writing that the "American seduction novel . . . produced a break in the heroine's lineage so that readers could then consider how one might remain English" (193). Writing that the seduction narrative shows an American attachment to the seemingly more conservative English ways, Tennenhouse shows the inseparability of English and American cultural forms in the years following the Revolution. See "The Americanization of *Clarissa*," *The Yale Journal of Criticism* 11.1 (1998): 177–196.

208   FEELING SINGULAR

forms that ensure domestic continuity. This subtle difference between the cultural work of these two narrative types—one reaffirming social control and the other imagining social mutability—comes to the foreground in the early iterations of William Wilson's narrative. Wilson's supposed last words are first presented to the public by a man named John Wilkey in 1821 and 1822, who produced a contemporaneous pamphlet on Elizabeth Wilson, titled "The Victim of Seduction," with one printing portraying a voluptuous woman kneeling and pleading on the page and the other offering the stark image of a black coffin (see Fig. 5.3a–b). That pamphlet focuses on Elizabeth's fall—assuming her guilt—and then uses her as an example to reaffirm a separate-spheres ideology, with the narrator instructing the female reader to view "the gradation of evils attendant on a departure from that dignified modesty which renders you respected and loved by the good and worthy of the other sex" (11). The text emphasizes the gendered implications of sexual transgression, as the conclusion turns to "depict woman in her state of depravity" (12):

> View the scenes of dissipation, and the closing resort upon earth of those misguided females, who, too credulous, lost all that rendered them dear to society, by not hearkening to the suggestions of the inward monitor . . . see what was once beautiful, now sunk into a state of the lowest human degradation! Behold at last her final exit; an ignominious death on the gallows closes the painful scene! (12)

The pamphlet ends with the silence of a woodcut figuring a woman's form hanging from a scaffold (see Fig. 5.4). The directive to view "the painful scene" parallels the original *A Faithful Narrative*'s impulse to invite readers to learn from the case, with repetitive imperatives—"May others reflect" (17), "May they consider," and "May they seriously reflect" (18). The texts ask readers to *imagine* for the narrative to affectively shape the reading experience.

This story of Elizabeth and William Wilson—a seduced sister and a reclusive brother—went through many other changes as different versions of the story were published in the 1830s and 1840s. By the late 1830s, the complicated details of Elizabeth's death—those that suggest she may have indeed been actively subverting the gendered expectations of her confession—were nearly entirely scrubbed from the texts that discussed it. These new publications of the story, printed in Philadelphia, New York, and Boston, abbreviated "The Victim of Seduction" and expanded upon "The Sweets

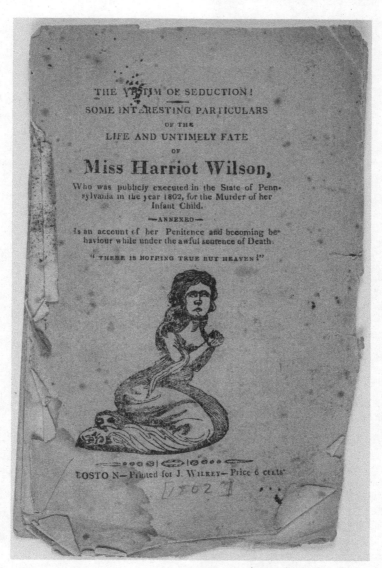

Figure 5.3a–b The two variant title pages of "The Victim of Seduction," similarly printed for John Wilkey and contemporaneous with his narrative about the hermit called "The Sweets of Solitude." Courtesy of the American Antiquarian Society.

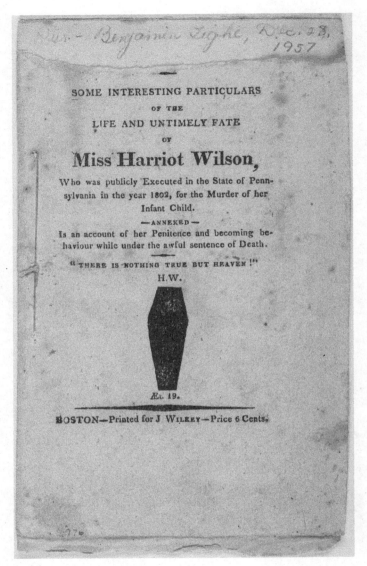

Figure 5.3a–b Continued.

of Solitude," focusing specifically on William "Amos" Wilson's subsequent life as a hermit. This text, entitled *The Pennsylvania Hermit*, consolidates itself around the fantasy of the brother's asocial afterlife, following the generic conventions of the period's reform literature (see Fig. 5.5). By excising Elizabeth from the story, *The Pennsylvania Hermit* subordinates the tale of

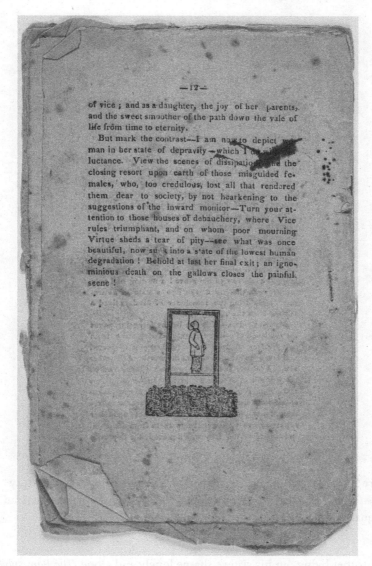

Figure 5.4 Final page of "The Victim of Seduction." Courtesy of the American Antiquarian Society.

seduction and execution to focus on a life concluded in solitude. The suppression of Elizabeth's story suggests the ways the public/private divide was both gendered and policed in the early nineteenth century, but it also reasserts gendered norms in another way, erasing the queerness that inheres to the tale

212 FEELING SINGULAR

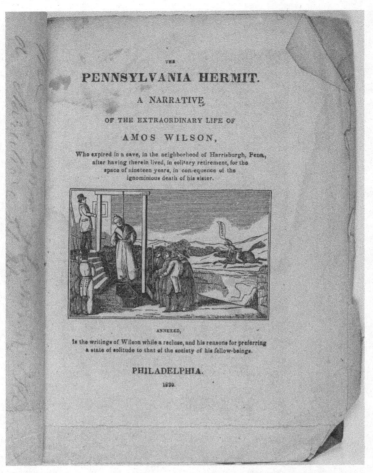

Figure 5.5 Title page of the final version of William "Amos" Wilson's story as *The Pennsylvania Hermit* (Philadelphia: 1839). Courtesy of the American Antiquarian Society.

of a brother living out his sister's shame lonely and alone. *The Pennsylvania Hermit* thus obscures its own backstory. Elizabeth's death is the repressed motivating factor that set into motion the hermit's eventual seclusion and the subsequent manuscript that documents his life. But the printed story turns away from an account of a mother remembered as being wrongly executed for the death of her children, to one that assumes her guilt but blames her actions on a man's seduction, and then finally transforms all of that into a briefly mentioned framing device for a hermit's tale, making Elizabeth a secondary character at her own execution.

Although these shifts in the Wilsons' story document a fairly conventional didactic trajectory (using salacious events for a moral warning), there is another way to read this dynamic, one that engages with what queer studies has called the antisocial thesis. Heather Love, in a 2015 issue of *differences* organized around moving queer theory beyond the anti-normative stance represented by someone like Lee Edelman, argues that "[q]ueer studies . . . remains invested in the idea of an impossible—because absolute—withdrawal from the social" (89). Drawing upon a queer imaginary indebted to the anti-normative work of the 1990s and early 2000s, Love configures a mode of queer inquiry that builds from social deviance studies. In the early national United States, the fallen woman and the hermit occupy two modes of deviance, but in the print history of Wilson's story they become enmeshed with each other. In the concluding section, I will linger with this figure of the impossible antisocial gesture as the aspirational horizon of queer resistance.[17] After arriving late to Elizabeth's execution, William Wilson felt there was nothing left to do but pursue that aspirational "withdrawal from the social." In this case, then, Wilson's life as a hermit invites us to see how his turning away from the social world as presently constituted provides insight on the politics of profound disappointment—of failing to work within the confines of the burgeoning early republic that required a piece of state-sanctioned paper to stop an execution. As Rei Terada argues, "the desire to discover alternative forms of experience is a queer desire, one that can inspire both self-development and longing for a new self that is no longer queer" (116). Wilson's dissatisfaction with the received world—and his transformation into a hermit—may begin as a queer rejection but that rejection comes to obscure the story of Elizabeth. Through bringing all of these histories and narratives together, we are able to imagine the gendered constructions that constitute dominant narrative tropes in the early republic. The Wilsons offer a way to narrate the fissures and the disconnections that govern how scholars talk about this period, and they illustrate how an attention to the overlapping

---

[17] Heather Love, in the same article, defines queer studies as a field of inquiry with an "emphasis on marginality, nonconformity, and miscellaneous forms of difference," arguing that queer studies today remains implicitly indebted to post–World War II deviance studies (75). The figure of the deviant, for Love, resists the normative protocols of social belonging that queerness continually destabilizes.

214 FEELING SINGULAR

tropes of seduction and solitude offers a queer way to interrogate the gendered public and private spheres of the early United States.

5.3. Executed Feelings

Although the 1786 narrative comes after Elizabeth's trial, the text places her before another moral tribunal that endeavors to prove her innocence on the basis of gendered expectations. Pennsylvania's legal codes at the time made it such that if an unmarried woman birthed a stillborn—or if the infant died soon after birth—the woman could be convicted of infanticide if she had not made clothing during the pregnancy.[18] Most important in the logic of Elizabeth's unfolding story, then, is *how* she narrates her side of the story and the way that narrative reflects upon her as a feeling subject. The news story that circulated locally explains that Elizabeth "acknowledged having placed the children by the road side, in order that any person passing that way, and who had humanity enough, might take them up" ("Philadelphia" 2), but in her confession a year later she claims that her lover, after demanding that she kill her children, murdered them in front of her. In the first account, Elizabeth's implicit appeal to a passerby's "humanity" contradicts the later story she tells of an already married lover attempting to escape the social stigma of his children's bastardy. The multiple stories might have something to do with the traumatic event in and of itself, causing a rupture in the effort to frame the events in a linear manner.

"What renders the catastrophe of this unhappy Woman truly shocking," one printed advertisement for the 1786 pamphlet of Elizabeth's confession states, "is, that between her condemnation and execution such striking proofs of her innocence appeared, as induced the president of the state to send a respite to delay the sentence" ("Just" 4).[19] That evidence, which her brother William used to convince the Supreme Executive Council of Pennsylvania

[18] Pennsylvania's legal codes did not change until after the Constitution. G. S. Rowe writes: "Like their counterparts in neighboring states and in England, Pennsylvania juries often acquitted females of infanticide and worked diligently to gain pardons for the few convicted. In Pennsylvania as elsewhere juries commonly accepted a single piece of 'ready clothes' or a single item prepared for the child by the mother as evidence of the absence of evil intent in order to vote not guilty. Only after Pennsylvania law was revised in 1786 and 1790 to define lesser penalties for concealment of a child's death did veniremen on occasion choose to convict women and see them sentenced to prison" (360).

[19] This advertisement circulated through many of the newspapers that published the full narrative. See also *Independent Journal* 242 (March 25, 1786): 3.

THE QUEER HERMIT 215

initially to delay the execution, suggested that an unnamed sheriff in Sussex County, New Jersey, had been a lover to Elizabeth and, when she told him about the twin children they had conceived, "persuaded her to take a walk with him, saying he intended to put the children out to nurse; that when they got into the woods, he took them from her and laying them on the ground, the inhuman monster put his feet on their breasts, and crushed them to death" (Biddle 199). Where the story initially read as a case of a woman seeking to hide her sexual misdeeds, the unfolding narration turned the event into a story about the seduction of an "innocent and unsuspecting young lady" (*Life* 7) and her lover's "inhuman" attempt to escape bastardy laws.

In her reading of gender and the public sphere in early America, Elizabeth Maddock Dillon similarly notes the curious ways in which Elizabeth Wilson seemingly narrated her own seduction as a way to insulate her from charges, explaining that the narrative "indicates that doubts remain as to Wilson's account, as does anxiety on Wilson's part as to whether she has established herself as credible" (218). Those doubts, however, seem entirely absolved from the private and public discourses about the case, from Charles Biddle's personal diary (who presided over the state-sanctioned writ of execution) to the pamphlets and newspapers that circulated after her death. Daniel E. Williams argues that the eighteenth-century account of Elizabeth Wilson was "structured to achieve the greatest effects on readers by carefully controlling the devices of disclosure and progression" (*Pillars* 49). This is to say, there is something to the unfolding nature of the narrative—the way readers already know she is dead from the title, yet somehow remain affectively oriented by the disclosure of the brother's delay to return the stay of execution.[20] In this sense, the narrative works through controlling disclosure, producing its own sense of privacy unveiled as the various, layered components of the story slowly unfold.

The 1786 execution in the county of Chester, Pennsylvania, occurred one year after the bodies of Elizabeth Wilson's twins were found dead in the woods. The first accounts of the infants' death gruesomely reference a dog sniffing and dragging out the head of a decapitated child and mention that the woman "charged with the murder" was "seen sucking the children near

---

[20] Lloyd Pratt's reading of the disparate temporalities of early America—showing the uneven emergence of timeliness—bears useful point of reference here. See *Archives of American Time: Literature and Modernity in the Nineteenth Century.* There's something to the way time is erotized, too, in the sense that disclosure becomes delayed and attenuated for the pleasurable experience of shock and wonder for the reader.

216 FEELING SINGULAR

the spot but a little time before the bodies were discovered."[21] These details are used to dehumanize the accused similar to how Wilkey's "The Victim of Seduction" invites readers to "View the scenes of dissipation" where "misguided females" have "lost all that rendered them dear to society" (12). Articulating the norm that Elizabeth falls out of ends up reaffirming the very norms that she transgressed. The salacious details are presented to uphold a sense of propriety that has been broken, warning readers that should they be similarly "misguided" that their lives would be transformed into a piecemeal morality play for consumption. But what is most significant to Elizabeth's account is that where she initially is portrayed as outside the norms of the gendered republic, she is just as quickly transformed into a victim to those norms.

Just as the initial circulating narratives affirm Elizabeth's innocence, the printed iterations emphasize William's inadequate efforts to return the stay of execution that would have saved her. These later accounts describe William setting out to save his sister the same day the Schuylkill flooded. "When he came with the respite in his hand," the eighteenth-century narrative states, "and saw his sister irrecoverably gone . . . who can paint the mournful scene? . . . Let imagination if she can!" (*A Faithful* 12). The appeal to "Let imagination if she can!" conscripts readers to model an implied feeling of sympathy about the untimely death of the sister at the brother's delay. Teresa Brennan calls *affect* the "things that one feels" and *feeling* the "things that one feels with" (23). In this sense, feelings are affects temporalized into language, and the rhetorical question posed here asks readers to construct the feeling that one *should* feel in such a circumstance, calibrating and manufacturing the affects that make the circumstances of the Wilsons' trials particularly traumatic. This aporetic trope—referencing emotions and feelings that cannot be represented textually but instead experienced bodily—highlights how feelings lose their immediacy and directness when filtered into the intelligibility of language. Yet in this example, the text attempts to carve out the figurative possibility of feeling that one cannot linguistically represent, gesturing toward something so horrifying that only "*imagination*" can approach it. The particularly overwhelming feelings associated with traumatic events—such as William's discovery of his dead sister—demonstrates what Cathy Caruth calls "[t]he peculiar temporality of trauma," wherein a traumatic event has

---

[21] The first reports of this double murder were published throughout the states, though generally on the last page of the publication as an advertisement of a piece of curious news. See *The Pennsylvania Journal* (January 5, 1785).

THE QUEER HERMIT   217

implications that transgress normative and linear conceptions of temporality, disrupting the mechanisms of representation (*Unclaimed* 143).[22] But part of the trauma of this story, I argue, becomes acted out within the subsequent hermit narrative, which abstracts the story of the sister to focus on the account of masculine resignation in the face of a troubled public sphere.

It seems, from the printed accounts of Elizabeth's confession circulating that spring in New York, Connecticut, Massachusetts, Vermont, and South Carolina newspapers and pamphlets, that the public imagination refused to consider her guilty after the execution. In this manner, her death at the hand of the state seems to produce her life into a narrative of mistake, though one that absolves the state from wrongdoing. Ezekiel Russell renewed interest in the case in his fledging *American Bloody Register* through a broadside elegy on her death, which extrapolated from the 1786 *A Faithful Narrative*.[23] Focusing on Elizabeth's presumed innocence, the poem exclaims: "Bloody Wretch! infernal Fiend! / From Satan you were sent; / DESHONG! could you such malice find? / So hellish schemes invent? / Such cruelty sure ne'er was known / in our *America*." The "kind POETESS" then references the *Register*, suggesting that "all may see when in't they look, / And from such Crimes deter." The idea that reading about crimes will deter them moralizes on the death of Elizabeth to assert value and meaning in the case. But it also ensures that the public continue to read Elizabeth solely in terms of her victimization.

One of the few certainties about this unusual case is that the initial reports about the execution focused on the affecting nature of a woman supposedly wrongly accused. The story, in all of its iterations, brought forward modes of

[22] Cathy Caruth's work on trauma's belated temporalities—how it is marked as trauma through its late arrival to the subject's consciousness—informs the relation between the failure to represent a scene and its lingering material trace. In her introduction to *Trauma: Explorations in Memory*, Caruth notes "trauma is not a simple or single experience of events but that events, insofar as they are traumatic, assume their force precisely in their temporal delay" (9).

[23] Elizabeth's confessional narrative portrays a more intimate representation of an accused's inner life than was conventional in *The American Bloody Register*, which in 1784 published the dying confessions of Richard Barrick, John Sullivan, and Alexander White, who all merely outlined their crimes without representing their psychic interiorities. Published intermittently from 1784 to 1790, *The American Bloody Register* promised a "judicious Collection of all the most remarkable Trials for Murder, Treason, Rape, Sodomy, High-way Robbery, Piracy, Housebreaking, Perjury, Forgery, and other Crimes and Misdemeanors" (Russell 4), and the majority of its issues focused on merely conveying the barest details and facts with a rare humanizing touch. As Stephen John Hartnett notes, these crime publications appropriated the "violence committed by both rogues and the state as the raw material for a nascent culture industry that would henceforth blanket large markets with consumable terrors, pleasurable violations, and the easy thrill of watching others suffer in the name of law and order" (124). Considering this emergence of salacious print culture, the confession of Elizabeth Wilson appeals to a desire for a public to know about the internal life of the accused, and the gendered dynamics of seduction enable her story to frame such interiority.

218 FEELING SINGULAR

feeling that, in mobilizing them, normalized the social formations that assured no mother could *really* have murdered her own children. The narratives after the execution endeavor to produce a sympathetic Elizabeth, victim to the "Hard-hearted Wretch," as a popular elegy and broadside described her lover, "a Monster sure / Disgrace to human eye" ("Elegy"). After the execution, little to nothing was done to locate and charge the murdering lover, however, who escapes under the false name of "Joseph Deshong." (Indeed, the only individual who seemed to exert any actual effort to prove her innocence—her brother, William—shunned public life and became a hermit.) Even Biddle, the vice-president of the council that issued Elizabeth's first execution date "on Wednesday the seventh day of December" 1785 (*Minutes* 586), wrote in his privately printed autobiography:

> For my own part, I firmly believed her innocent, for to me it appeared highly improbable that a mother, after suckling her children for six weeks, could murder them. The next day when Council met, and we heard of the execution, it gave uneasiness to many of the members, all of whom were against her being executed, at least until her brother had had full time to make his inquiries, and I am sure, if he had not been successful, there was a large majority would have been for pardoning her. (201)

The "uneasiness" that Biddle explains he and other Council members felt attempts to retroactively absolve him from guilt in facilitating the execution. This, of course, is poor memory on the part of Biddle (or, indeed, an intense form of denial), as he signed the "death warrant, ordering her execution on Tuesday the 3d day of January, 1786" (*A Faithful Narrative* 4). He even imagines Elizabeth "suckling her children for six weeks" as evidence that she in no way could be guilty. What I wish to highlight here is that Biddle had the power to stop any further execution dates but did not, and then later (mis) remembers himself as doubting that he could ever have actually *believed* Elizabeth guilty. Differentiating himself from the familial responsibilities placed on William, Biddle turns his feelings of unease into his way of feeling right about the case—that, all along, he knew no mother could really have killed her children. Thus, despite presiding over the council's decision to grant Chester the right to execute Elizabeth (with Benjamin Franklin gone for the day, on occasion of painful gout), Biddle remembers and narrates his feelings in such a way as to absolve himself of the guilt of executing the very person that print and cultural memory strove to remember as innocent.

THE QUEER HERMIT 219

These feelings of unease demonstrate the way power orients bodies around hierarchies and social formations, illuminating the role of sentimentality to critique a state power that prosecuted a supposedly innocent woman and yet failed to pursue the individual described as a rake. What's being confessed in this seduction plot and hermit narrative, then, is a state power that leverages feelings to absolve itself from wrongdoing, deploying an affecting tale of a seduction that leads to a hermitic life as a way to absolve its own sins.[24] While Biddle narrates how he came to feel appropriately—that he *felt* the unfortunateness of Elizabeth's death, however belatedly—his change of heart regarding the capability of a mother to kill her children renders his "uneasiness" as the delayed feeling that corrects the problem of having executed a woman "innocent . . . of the crime for which she suffered, but guilty to concealing, or rather attempting to conceal, a crime of so horrid a nature, which she was privy to" (*A Faithful Narrative* 17). If Elizabeth's late confession makes her the justified subject of an execution, then Biddle's change of feeling—his expressed unease that, after all, no *real* mother could kill her children—highlights the affective and subjective demarcations that inhere to narrative itself. Even the belated "The Victim of Seduction" narrative includes a supposed letter from the accused, writing to her brother: "I never thought, in the former part of my life, that it was possible for me to be so weaned from earth" (9). The metaphor of being "weaned" will figure prominently in how the soon-to-be hermit self-narrates his own refusal of sociality, but here it emphasizes the gendered forms of dependence that separate Elizabeth from her world.

Where moments in the initial written confession show a complicated side to Elizabeth—leaving open the possibility that she killed her infants—the subsequent stories flatten and uncomplicate the question of Elizabeth's agency, turning her story into an account of seduction that removes the possibilities for her to have desire (even murderous desire) and seek its fulfillment. This is to say, the nineteenth-century narratives that focalize around the hermit *assume* seduction as the only viable cause to explain why a mother would abandon her children. As in "The Sweets of Solitude," Elizabeth is

---

[24] Playing with what Michel Foucault writes in *The History of Sexuality*—that "the confession became one of the West's most highly valued techniques for producing truth. We have since become a singularly confessing society. . . . Western man has become a confessing animal" (59)—we might think of the ways state power deploys affecting tales that produce emotional responses as a means to confess and vouchsafe attachment to the narratives that buttress the nation-state.

220 FEELING SINGULAR

remembered as acting "with the hopes of concealing her shame, . . . in an unreflecting moment, committed a crime, which by the laws of our land is punishable with death!" (6).

For William Wilson, the execution of his sister sparks an event that sets in motion his eventual solitude. In Alain Badiou's theorization, events *are* events only through hindsight, produced as such when "following the event's consequences, not in glorifying its occurrence" (211). As such, the memorialization of the series of events that impact William's life shifts the focus of the story from a woman's supposed confession and declaration of innocence to a man's determined aloofness, his separation from a society that he feels has wronged him (though it more pronouncedly wronged Elizabeth). The nineteenth-century texts that narrate Elizabeth as a victim to seduction simultaneously begin narrating and focusing on the hermitic life of her brother. These shifts in the representation of the story across the span of a few decades document a fairly conventional pedagogical transformation of a salacious news story into a sanitized moral allegory. The messy, incoherent lives of real people—abstracted into printed narratives and thereby absolved from the consuming dustbin of history even as (state) powers determined their dénouement—are expectedly impossible to narrate fully from the partial records that survive. Instead, we are left with the end product of both historical absence and archival surplus. The tale turns from an account of a mother potentially killing her children, to one that assures such a thing could never have happened, and then finally transforms into the hermit's tale. These shifts suggest a unique connection between two ostensibly discrete narrative trajectories, one focusing on the policing of female sexuality and the other on the curious life of a man who refuses social intercourse. But where the seduction narrative reifies social control and expectation, the hermit narrative troubles the presumed certainty of social control and mediation that the seduction narrative fosters; the former seeks to contain subversion under the powers of heteropatriarchy, whereas the latter instances the (male) privilege of examining and critiquing the social powers and pressures that make solitude political. In the next section, I will look more into the institutionalization of this divide between the hermit and the seduction narrative through looking at the cultural work of solitude in the early republic.

THE QUEER HERMIT 221

5.4. The Institutionalization of Solitude

Scholars and historians have offered compelling accounts of the intricate practices that facilitated the emergence of penal institutions in the early United States by focusing on the rise of solitary confinement. Louis P. Masur tracks how the new penitentiary institution "punished with solitude those who previously might have been hanged," specifically locating a shift from "depravity" to "social influences" that created the circumstances of crime in the first place (5). This new understanding that environmental conditions produced crime helped set up a series of tactical incursions into individuals thus accused to determine their proximity to what was considered the path to criminality, which led to the emergence of institutions that sought to control a body's environment through solitary confinement. Discussing the Eastern State Penitentiary, Jodi Schorb describes that "prisoners were kept in total isolation the first days of arrival—no Bible, no labor—an immersion meant to awaken them to their guilt and prepare them for the new routine that awaited them" (120). Schorb discusses how the rise of the penitentiary produced the figure of the reading prisoner, offering such figuration as a site of reformation. Reading and its solitary practices offered a juncture to extract the individual from the circumstances that supposedly led to criminality. The solitary figure—the singular individual—became the site of reformation.

Anti-federalist writer and politician James Wilson asserts the use of solitude for punishment in the republican nation. Speaking before a Philadelphia university audience in 1790, Wilson asserted that "[i]t is not an uncommon opinion, and, in this instance, *our opinions must be vouched by our feelings*, that the most exquisite punishment, which human nature could suffer, would be, in total solitude, to languish out a lengthened life" (248; emphasis added). Declaring that feelings assert the truth or accuracy of opinion, Wilson's Bentham-like notion coincides with the emerging practice of reform-oriented prison practices. The emphasis that "our opinions must be vouched by our feelings" conveys the self-affirming relationship between feeling and certainty, with Wilson's sense that social estrangements and ostracism are the severest of punishments.[25]

---

[25] Biddle asserts that he was certain (despite having signed the execution order) of Elizabeth Wilson's innocence because he *felt* no mother could kill their children. In thinking about the gendered components to the United States' production of solitary confinement, we might turn to Charles Dickens's visit to Philadelphia's "solitary prison" in the 1830s, where he observes that such

222 FEELING SINGULAR

Solitary confinement, as a republican Enlightenment project, has always been about sequestering an individual from others for them to be disciplined by their presumably fractured inner soul.[26] Benjamin Rush's contemporaneous effort to discourage the "punishment of murder by death" centered on the processes and institutions of isolation. Colin Dayan explains that the rise of solitary confinement in prisons, which placed generally white criminal bodies far from public sight, marks the moment when "the state decided to punish criminals psychically without executing them" (70). As Dayan notes, Rush had resented execution for the way it shortchanged the work of Christian repentance because "[t]he unknowability of punishment's limits, as well as the loss of personal liberty, would, by increasing 'terror,' cure 'diseases of the mind'" (68). As all social transgressions, for Rush, were products of poor biology and bad environment, the process of limiting a body's receptiveness to the outside world seemed to be the ideal cure for moral maladies. The state, for Rush, could usefully intervene into the lives of such unruly bodies, transforming them into proper subjects by containing their circulations in the broader world. Where Rush imagines the supposed benevolence—or at least benignity—of a state power that can "convert men into republican machines" for "them to perform their parts properly, in the great machine of the government of the state," the actual mechanisms of such power were far from innocuous (14–15). If Rush seeks to imagine solitude—indeed, solitary confinement—as a necessary step in the emergence of liberal

punishments affect the men and women differently, noting that all the women he met "were very sad, and might have moved the sternest visitor to tears, but not to that kind of sorrow which the contemplation of the men awakens" (126). Distinguishing between men and women prisoners, Dickens suggests that the women "had grown quite beautiful" in "the silence and solitude of their lives" (126), whereas all the men appear haggard and slovenly, failing to elicit the type of transformative sympathy he gains from the women. One man in particular, "looking as wan and unearthly as if he had been summoned from the grave" (124), creeps to and fro like an "animal" (125), filling Dickens with disgust. The changes the solitary prison make on men and women are more forcefully brought forward when Dickens states: "The faces of the women . . . [are] humanize[d] and refine[d by the prison]. Whether this be because of their better nature, which is elicited in solitude, or because of their being gentler creatures, of greater patience and longer suffering, I do not know; but so it is" (130). Importantly, the prison and its solitary practices becomes a site for the gender binary to be solidified and reaffirmed.

[26] Caleb Smith's reading of the emergence of prison reform in the early nineteenth century argues that "the cellular soul—self-binding and self-correcting" became the dominant "centerpiece of the great model penitentiaries of the Pennsylvania and Auburn systems, and it shaped the terms according to which many in the world at large imagined the great institution of modern punishment" (97). See *The Prison and the American Imagination* (New Haven: Yale UP, 2009).

THE QUEER HERMIT   223

independence, then we might look more closely into the relation between solitude, punishment, and the feelings they constellate together.

Rush imagines a state power that replicates the intimate relations of the family structure, creating paternal relations that circumscribe a subject's relation to the government. This model of state power replaces the image of a benign state power cultivating its citizens to instead fantasize about the material production of an absolute state power, a power that controls all the variables constituting individual subjects. This dynamic is particularly pronounced in his treatment for his son, John, whom he hospitalized and subjected to his newly created Tranquilizer Chair when the son appeared "insane" after killing his friend Benjamin Taylor in a duel on October 1, 1807. Before that tragedy, John's father and mother wrote to him prior to setting sail to Calcutta to begin his seafaring career:

> Be sober and vigilant. Remember at all times that while you are seeing the world, the world will see you.—Recollect further, that you are always under the eye of the Supreme Being. . . . Whenever you are tempted to do an improper thing, fancy that you see your father, and mother kneeling before you, and imploring you with tears in their eyes to refrain from yielding to the temptations, and assuring you at the same time that your yielding to it will be the means of hurrying them to a premature grave. (777)

Fixating onto their son's mind the image of his appealing parents, the letter seeks indirectly to influence John through producing within his imagination the force of familial obligation. The appeal to "fancy" constructs in the mind's eye the figure of prostrate parenthood, imploring their son to bring up their image should he be "tempted to do an improper thing" that would lead to "a premature grave." In this sense, the letter seeks to turn whatever bad or salacious thing John may do into an act done in front of his parents, producing a form of disciplinary control and internalized surveillance that warns the son that *his* actions can indirectly kill his parents.[27]

In tandem with Rush's interest in the psychologically medicinal benefits of solitude, he includes in "On the Different Species of Phobia" (1798) a

---

[27] Rush's interest in practicing a total state power modeled over the heteronormative family structure is further pronounced in his representation of his life as a youth, when he explains his fascination with his uncle's discipline who ran a boarding school: "His government over his boys was strict but never severe nor arbitrary. It was always by known laws which were plain, and often promulgated" (29). This desire to actively construct his children's lives echoes the earlier reference to "republican machines" that he imagines the new government fostering.

224   FEELING SINGULAR

discussion of "The SOLO PHOBIA; by which I mean the dread of solitude. This distemper is peculiar to persons of vacant minds, and guilty consciences. Such people cannot bear to be alone, especially if the horror of sickness is added to the pain of attempting to *think*, or to the terror of *thinking*" (222). Rush proposes a periodic removal from public and social intercourse to be a proper and contributing republican citizen. Similar to how Eric Slauter notes that "[d]iscussions of solitude and retirement in the revolutionary period represented fantasy narratives of self-liberation from the public sphere" (219), Rush examines the medical efficacy of being alone, criticizing those with "guilty consciences" who cannot handle solitude. For Rush, solitude is the very ground that enables the social machine to run smoothly, but only if there is a structure of restraint to modulate the guilty subject's solitude.

Where the republican Rush ascribes value to solitude as a healthy option for all minds (and that its absence marks an unhealthy one), Sylvester Graham—noted moral and health reformer during the 1830s—pathologized all forms of solitude for their relation to the "solitary vice" of masturbation.[28] Lecturing on the "secret and solitary vice" (96) throughout the 1830s, Graham asserts that sexualized books should not be read, especially when alone, because "[l]ascivious thoughts and imaginations will excite and stimulate the genital organs, cause an increased quantity of blood to flow into them, and augment their secretions and peculiar sensibilities; and, on the other hand, an excited state of the genital organs, either from the stimulations of semen, or from diseased action in the system, will throw its influence upon the brain, and force lascivious thoughts and imaginations upon the mind" (43). Providing several anecdotes of young men who "no sooner [were] left alone" (210) than they would return to their "secret solitude" (98), Graham desires a type of public solitude, one that remains legible to the normative structures of moral reform. As opposed to the figure of the solitary reader becoming transformed, with Graham we see such activity as a site of sexual deviancy.[29]

---

[28] One biographical detail important to consider is that Sylvester Graham (1794–1851) was the seventeenth child born to John Graham (1722–1796). Three years after his birth, his mother was institutionalized and a local farmer raised Sylvester. With this in mind, it is perhaps ironically important to note, Graham died at the age of fifty-seven, perhaps failing to live out his own regimented health form. See Stephen Nissenbaum, *Sex, Diet, and Debility in Jacksonian America: Sylvester Graham and Health Reform* (Westport, CT: Greenwood P, 1980).

[29] The complexity of this reform literature similarly produced gendered ramifications. When Graham turned to discuss the "solitary vice" and women, massive crowds of men would come to protest and threaten mob actions. For more on this, see April R. Haynes in *Riotous Flesh: Women, Physiology, and the Solitary Vice in Nineteenth-Century America* (2015).

The disciplines of solitude—and the panic over what it means to *choose* solitary lives—became part of the social apparatus that formulated sex as a function defined within the private. Solitude and solitariness bring forward questions regarding what later would be understood as sexuality. In "Jane Austen and the Masturbating Girl," Eve Kosofsky Sedgwick notes that "The identity of the masturbator was only one of the sexual identities subsumed, erased, or overridden in this triumph of the heterosexist homo/hetero calculus. . . . It is of more than chronological import if the (lost) identity of the masturbator was the proto-form of modern sexual identity itself" (826). Solitude as a mode of sexuality—as an orientation toward foreclosure of connection—positions the hermit's choice to live alone as part of an ongoing negotiation of the modern formations of sexual identity. The interconnection between the seduction plot and the hermit narrative gets at the heart of the sexualization of solitude.

5.5. Happy/Queer

Just as solitude became institutionalized, the figure of the unattached individual—the hermit or the bachelor—emerged as a recalcitrant critique of the institution of the heteronormative family. The queer bachelor can be found throughout the early national literary archive, most famously in Washington Irving's instantly successful *A History of New York* (1809), which is framed by the tale of a husband and wife who come into possession of a manuscript by one of their tenants. Described as a disheveled "stranger" with a beard "of some four and twenty hours growth," Diedrich Knickerbocker is a bit asocial himself, refusing to be integrated into the household, despite the best efforts of the wife and her friends (373). This "very worthy good sort of an old gentleman, though a little queer in his ways," ends up disrupting the lives of Seth Handaside and his family, particularly his wife who is "taken with his looks" when one day Knickerbocker wanders away from the domestic space, leaving behind his strange and rambling history of New York (373). Wandering away from the domestic space where, Seth laments, he had been treated as family, Knickerbocker signals the dis-attached male subject who uncouples himself from any social arrangement from which he no longer wishes to belong. This gesture certainly recalls in some ways Benjamin Franklin's removal from the obligations of his indentures, which indicates the emergence of a liberal self unencumbered by the trappings of paternal and familial obligations. Yet unlike

226 FEELING SINGULAR

the late Franklin, Diedrich Knickerbocker and William "Amos" Wilson keep on resisting the logics of familial reproduction enshrined within heterosexuality. Shirking their "obligatory investment in the social," as Lee Edelman writes about figural queers, Wilson and Knickerbocker refuse the received and expected modes of social belonging (45).

Male figures that wander away from social formations show up regularly in Washington Irving's work. Michael Warner explains that "Irving's ambivalence about bachelorhood says much about the transitional period between patriarchy and modern heterosexuality" ("Irving's Posterity" 776). Consider, for instance, Rip Van Winkle's rejection of his normative relations to his wife, preferring companionship with his dog and, really, any stranger that comes his way. Rip wanders into the woods and takes part in an unusual woodland ritual of mutual staring as mysteriously dressed men take part in the "most melancholy party of pleasure." Rip is confronted with a queer temporality that mixes the past with the present, emerging on the other side of consciousness after visiting the flagon over and over again, "[o]ne taste provoke[ing] another." Rip resists being organized into the flow of time or the coming of the future, figuring instead an anachronistic introduction of the past to highlight, for readers, that regardless of change most things remain the same. In his assessment of the disparate temporalities of the early republic, Lloyd Pratt notes that "Rip remains the same over the course of the story" (30). Yet this designation of Rip's continuity separates him as a figure from the particular context of an altered (though contiguous) revolutionary America. Rip emerges from the woods a changed man, with his solitary sleep of twenty years reforming his identity in its detachment from normatively legible relations with his wife. Erving Goffman's mid-twentieth-century assessment that "in an important sense there is only one complete unblushing male in America: a young, married, white, urban, northern, heterosexual Protestant father" (128) might productively frame the way figures like Rip Van Winkle, Diedrich Knickerbocker, and "Amos" Wilson disrupt the normative endgoals of social formation, becoming figures of curiosity in their removal from domestic attachment.

The queerness of loners, the way they disrupt social formations, is key to how queerness and solitude operate in William "Amos" Wilson's supposed manuscript. The title page to the introductory frame tale explains that the hermit "expired in a cave, in the neighborhood of Harrisburgh [sic], Pennsylvania, after having therein lived, in solitary retirement, for nineteen years, in consequence of the ignominious death of his sister" (1). Calling the sister's death "ignominious," the story positions William's solitary life as a logical response to the shame of family association with a woman accused not only of infanticide but guilty of subverting the public's gendered expectations regarding female sexuality. The social stigma that drives his seclusion from society renders him as a queer object of public interest, and the very manuscript he is said to leave behind has its own tangential relation to print, described as manuscript within a printed text and trumpeted within the emerging evangelical print public sphere as "Instructions to Mankind How They May Be Happy in a Miserable World" (24). Indeed, in "The Sweets of Solitude," "Amos" asks a very simple question: how is it that "a great portion of mankind" can pursue "True happiness" (22) and yet that happiness always remains ephemeral? For "Amos," physical sensation and material acquisition—"the excesses of wine or of women . . . [or] the largest prodigalities of fortune"—cannot offer happiness; instead, one must "set aside his money, his fortunes, his dignity and examine himself naked" (32). Doing so, "Amos" asserts, would be to have the dream of the "second Scipio," who in a vision saw "the whole earth . . . [and] could scarcely discern that speck of dirt, the Roman Empire" (38–39). "Amos" values extracting oneself from social belonging to better see its constraints.

Wilson's "instructions" revolve around cultivating a self that is unencumbered with the trappings of the world, desiring a "naked" and exposed selfhood free from outside influence. This fantasy of an unfettered (white) (male) self certainly resonates with emerging discourses on masculinity in antebellum America, such as the portrayal of manhood in the *Crockett Almanacks*, which represented such men as the solitary harbingers and supposed white saviors of civilization in unincorporated frontier regions. Yet if Davy Crockett and his *Almanacks* (1835–1856) index a rough-and-tumble masculinity, Wilson's hermitic life suggests a resistance to such a mode of adventurous exposure (see Fig. 5.6). Where Crockett stands in as a cultural icon of masculine aggression, Wilson refuses to conform to such a model, bending and folding his life into a cave where he "can rest securely in resignation" (39).

If Elizabeth's confession narrative makes public her private life in ways that end up reaffirming the period's gendered conventions, reconstructing female innocence and negating the possibility of criminality, then the hermit's turn toward solitude—to making his public life private—shifts those dynamics. One's desires for happiness must have free circulation beyond the constraints of social structure, Wilson theorizes in "The Sweets of Solitude," imagining

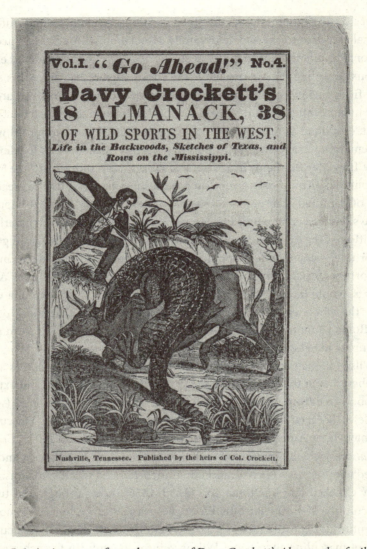

Figure 5.6 Action scene from the cover of *Davy Crockett's Almanack, of wild sports in the West, life in the backwoods, sketches of Texas, and rows on the Mississippi*, which popularized a rough-and-tumble masculinity (Nashville, TN: 1837). Courtesy of the American Antiquarian Society.

a world free from the constraints of society. Returning to Wilson's quotation of Bolingbroke, the hermit offers a way to "become weaned from the world" (24). His writings, then, become the rationale for how to be "weaned," as he repeats throughout his writings, to be identified outside of its powers (24). In this imagined configuration, the world figures as a maternal formation from which Wilson wishes to extract his singular self. The metaphor of a nursing hermit emphasizes how he has grown tired of the particular orientation that places him in subordinate relations to the world, but it also implies the repressed centrality of Elizabeth Wilson's execution to his story, who, after all, is remembered to have nursed her infants only moments before their death.

This desire to be "weaned from the world," we must remind ourselves, arose within William when he "was doomed to experience one of the severest trials of this life," as he repeatedly describes at the close of his "Sweets of Solitude," "when doomed to witness the melancholy fate of an affectionate and only sister, the companion of my youth, torn from the bosom of her fond parents, and for many months confined within the thick walls of a gloomy prison, and from thence conveyed (at the very moment a pardon was obtained for her) to the gallows there to suffer like one of the greatest monsters of human depravity, an ignominious death!" (46). The repetition of the word "doomed" signals the social judgment levied against women who move beyond social conventions. It is at this point—after witnessing "her lifeless corpse suspended in the air, surrounded by a throng of unpitying spectators!" (46–47)—that William decided to wean himself from the world. The metaphor of weaning, with its maternal associations, suggests an intimate connection between brother and sister, but it simultaneously queers the gendered expectations of a brother living outside the social expectations of his life to assert the queer feelings of happiness when his society would assume he would feel nothing but unhappiness.

Figments of happiness and unhappiness open and close William "Amos" Wilson's narrative. He is described as "the most unhappy of human beings" (6), and even comments on such a configuration at the conclusion, writing: "my situation has no doubt been pronounced unhappy and miserable by many of my fellow beings" (35). With unhappiness the presumed mental state, the hermit seems to feel obligated to resist a dominant discourse on happiness—one that equates "worldly pleasures" with happiness—to suggest an alternative paradigm. Following Sara Ahmed's work in *The Promise of Happiness* (2010), we might consider how Wilson's writings queer dominant notions of happiness. In the context of writing

230 FEELING SINGULAR

about representations of colonial subjects assimilating into British culture, Ahmed shows how deployments of happiness as the end-goal are rife with national and imperial implications. Because, as Ahmed explains, migrants in England are asked to remove the "family or tradition" (137) that would be potential barriers to "[t]he civilizing mission . . . redescribed as a happiness mission" (125), "happiness," as an object of pursuit, produces the very conditions that inculcate unhappiness. If, as Ahmed writes, "happiness is imagined as what allows subjects to embrace futurity, to leave the past behind them" (137), then Wilson rejects what he considers a problematic happiness—one that produces unlivable consequences for himself. Instead, Wilson redefines the terms of happiness his culture sets before him. Society, for Wilson, produces the need for antisocial behavior, arguing that "[t]he contending passions of man render the acquirement of true happiness in a state of society abortive" (32). If the social produces the very desires that become in their pursuit the source of unrequited longing for connection, then Wilson would have his posthumous readers rely on their own internal life and personal resources to ensure that happiness. Indeed, in his conclusion, he asserts: "I solemnly declare that I have enjoyed more real happiness in retirement, than what all the riches and superfluities of this world could afford me" (35). But when considering that his supposed happiness is founded on the abstraction of his sister's death, then that happiness appears even more a masculine projection that asserts final control over one's public perception, an ability that was always already attenuated for Elizabeth Wilson.

The way a story of a woman becomes eclipsed by the account of a man is, of course, quite conventional within heteropatriarchy. In a lesser known contemporaneous story, the dynamics of female abstraction become more pronounced. An 1804 Hudson, New York, newspaper article about a woman known popularly as the "Hermitess of North-Salem," explains: "We often hear of men from various motives, preferring a life of solitude in some gloomy cavern of the earth; but to find one of the fair sex immured in a cave, wholly secluded from human society, is a rare phenomenon" ("The Hermitess" 316). Focusing on a woman named Sarah Bishop who "discovered an unusual antipathy to men"—feeling "[d]isgusted with them, and consequently with the world"—the narrative betrays a fascination for why a woman would spend "her best years, self excluded from all human society." Not much is known about Bishop, though the nineteenth-century author Samuel Griswold Goodrich remarks about her in his history for "children and youth" and his

THE QUEER HERMIT   231

later *Recollections* (1856). In the former, Bishop is portrayed as a victim of the Revolutionary War, raised on Long Island before the British burned down her parent's home, and euphemistically notes that "she was cruelly treated by a British officer" (39). In his end-of-life *Recollections*, Goodrich recalls Bishop again, explaining that "[u]pon her early history she was invariably silent; indeed, she spoke of her affairs with great reluctance. She neither seemed to have sympathy for others, nor to ask it in return" (293). The turn to disaffection, and a refusal to feel in a normative sense, seeks to explain the gendered violence of seduction and its production of unfeeling.[30]

The 1804 news account of Bishop offers an interesting moment of identity construction, asserting that when "human events . . . deviate from [their] wonted course" and produce "characters altogether new and unexampled" that such events ought "to be perpetuated." This attention to deviating from norms registers what Heather Love has called the hallmark of queer studies' work to attend to the production of "norms and deviance" for how they shape social lives (*Underdogs* 136). The passage about Bishop suggests that deviance from the normal or ordinary—the "wonted course"—can be foundational to new identities. Sarah Bishop's life offers a model of something "to be perpetuated" in its difference from the presumed norms of masculine solitude and highlights the queer impulse that departs from normative narrative tracks. The queer novelty of "a young lady of considerable beauty, a competent share of mental endowments, and education," then, choosing "to forsake the society of man" becomes a model for feeling toward a new, singular subject.

---

[30] For a compelling critique of the racial and sexual politics of unfeeling, see Xine Yao's *Disaffected: The Cultural Politics of Unfeeling in Nineteenth-Century America* (2021).

Coda

Masculinity's Monumental Hair Problem

A few weeks after Donald J. Trump encouraged his followers to overthrow the U.S. government on January 6, 2021, he issued the "Executive Order on Building the National Garden of American Heroes." First referenced during a July 4th campaign rally at Mount Rushmore, the grandiose project aspired to create a space "where the legends of America's past will be remembered." The initial proclamation of 31 statues ballooned to 244, with 192 male presenting figures such as William F. Buckley, Herman Melville, and Elvis Presley holding court with one another. Unsurprisingly, the now aborted venture had no material plans in place but instead was grounded in the affectual terms that imagined a space where visitors could fantasize "the awesome splendor of our country's timeless exceptionalism" with the purpose to "renew their vision of greatness" when gazing at hundreds of statues. This desire to create a lasting legacy that would inculcate a patriotic nationalism seems the logical end result for when feeling singular has become the norm, proliferating copies of its own monuments to singular selfhood as a way to draw attention to itself *for* itself. The abstract language of "timeless exceptionalism" envisions the United States as a manufactory of significance, mushrooming individuals onto pedestals for public adoration. Indeed, Trump's twenty-first-century excesses dovetail with the eighteenth-century gaudiness of "Lord" Timothy Dexter, who fashioned contemporaneous celebrities into wooden statues in his front lawn to similarly entice attention.

One may propose, then, that the United States has an obsession with its masculinity. Or rather, the political formulation that constitutes the governing apparatus synecdochally referred to as the 'United States' attracts (dare I say produces) a psychosocial investment in the parameters of exceptional individuality, such that nearly everyone wants to be a celebrity, almost everybody wants to feel famous. Permit the hyperbole, as this popular way of thinking about the public lives of American individuals—who aspire to their own imagined City-on-a-Hill-ness—encourages exceptional

Feeling Singular. Ben Bascom, Oxford University Press. © Oxford University Press 2024.
DOI: 10.1093/9780197687536.003.0007

CODA   233

amounts of disavowal.[1] This book has tracked American individuals' desire to feel singular—to be special and representative—and the failure to arrive at such status. That desire to emerge into something like representativeness produced a series of grandiose affects that verge into the excessive and the eccentric, the motley and the muddled. Historically, the cultural formation of the United States has been narrated as citizens who deflect individual significance (or at least perform this deflection) in favor of a cohesive republic, yet this cohesion is an illusion that relies on codified gender roles, deracinated whiteness, and access to capital in an upwardly mobile economy, just to briefly gesture to three major vectors of structural power. When citizens emerge who don't conform to these early republican narratives, their stories are narrated as regressive ruptures.[2] One way to read this book is that even at the moment of fantasizing about independence, a series of lives fell under the spell of their own inevitable insignificance, only to be recovered posthumously when times changed and a different set of values made them interesting.[3]

As established earlier, the iconography of obsessive masculinities—of singular selves who desire to stand in for the messy and rambunctious whole and be in some manner representative—has been a force propelling this book's trajectory. In the previous five chapters, *Feeling Singular* has explored the lives and narratives of men who desired social attachment and recognition, imagining themselves as singular and important within the world of the early republic. Sometimes indignantly and other times doggedly, these individuals—John Fitch, Boyrereau Brinch/Jeffrey Brace,

[1] The deep, embedded centrality of that disavowal may easily be indexed by Abram C. Van Engen in *City on a Hill: A History of American Exceptionalism* (2020), who notes that "origin stories are present-day definitions cast back onto history" (3). Finding that the trope of a "City on a Hill" was only popularized in the twentieth century and then folded back into narratives about the Puritans to construct the idea of a founding idea or value, Van Engen's work implies a type of obsession with self-narrating as a form of grandiosity that structures narratives that buttress American exceptionalism.

[2] Elizabeth Maddock Dillon explains that "liberalism produces individual bodies in newly codified terms (those of gender as well as race) at the moment when the coherence of the social body as a whole (the organicist metaphor) no longer obtains" (133). Focusing on the rupture of the public sphere, and the shifting terms that mark one's ability to be included in that imaginative space, I am interested in how differently positioned bodies unevenly approached the imagined collective. Along these lines, in *The Traumatic Colonel: The Founding Fathers, Slavery, and the Phantasmatic Aaron Burr*, Michael J. Drexler and Ed White argue that early U.S. republican appeals to "authenticity and sincerity" actually work to hide the motivations of power and selfishness (53).

[3] Sianne Ngai's work on "interesting" as a complicated aesthetic category informs my register of the word "remarkable" here, especially with how she defines this category "as a subjective, feeling-based evaluation" (112). The belated interestingness of the figures I examine suggests something about the sense of the world that constituted these figures but also reflects what Ngai describes as "ascribing value to that which seems to differ, in a yet-to-be-conceptualized way, from a general expectation or norm whose exact concept may itself be missing at the moment of judgment" (112).

234   CODA

Timothy Dexter, Jonathan Plummer, and William "Amos" Wilson—pursued the cultural forms of belonging they felt they had access to, only to be spurned and cast aside, unable to obtain their desired forms of attachment. Although they insist on the singularity of their voice, contesting the emerging norms that would frustrate them, they became entangled within the republican ideals that both attracted and repelled their desires.[4] In putting themselves forth in manuscript and print, and seeking to create a series of republican attachments to the ideals of industry and liberty, public service and virtuous domestic stability, their lives and narratives instead come to illuminate the underside to those values. These men wrote—or had another transcribe—their life narratives in an attempt to assemble a readership that would be changed through reading. Fitch not only wants his readers to believe that *he*, as a singular individual, invented the steamboat but also worries that his manuscript has the capacity to delegitimize the new government; Brace affirms that the reading of his narrative will turn enslavers into abolitionists, securing for other Africans in America the promises of liberty and independence that his narrative asserts the Constitution safeguards; Dexter envisions finding himself surrounded by the trappings of the Federalist elite but, through doing so, becomes a laughingstock; Plummer presumes his life narrative will model for readers ways to interpret their own dreams and thus come to subject themselves not to the earthly government but "The unrivaled President, of the glittering worlds" (221); and William "Amos" Wilson believes his solution to his sister's execution was to "wean" himself from the world and occupy the structural position of the abandoned woman. Each narrative calls forth an imagined readership: but through doing so, each narrative fails spectacularly in its great hopes. To various degrees, these men sought to advance themselves on cultural stages that refused them, whether national, regional, or transatlantic, and the gaps between their aspirations and their foreshortened realities illuminate the limits of desire for individual change in this period.

Although this book examines the writings of anti-Franklinian figures who were unable to utilize the public powers of print the way the lionized figure could, Franklin still stands as a grand absent signifier for this book,

---

[4] Michael Schudson's *The Good Citizen: A History of American Civic Life* (1998) explains that "[t]he institutions that today people focus on in thinking about what makes a vibrant democratic public were for the founding generation either a secondary concern (the press) or positively discouraged (parties and, for some, voluntary associations)" (87).

one who occupies the subject of standardization that highlights the difference and (in)significance of all others. Franklin's overwhelming exemplarity might be indexed simply by the prominence his *Autobiography* plays in the literary history of the period.[5] To both writers in the early nineteenth century and scholars today, Franklin provides a frontispiece that orients how we think about the ideologies and uses of life writing. His book, which is now consolidated into one material object, began as a collection of manuscript papers with four distinct occasions of writing that spanned two decades.[6] The various pieces of his manuscripts circulated disparately after his death and were thought lost for a time, and what is now considered the *Autobiography* was first printed in English from a French translation. Douglas Anderson compares these manuscripts with the dissevered snake image the inventor popularized in the 1750s, describing "[t]he life story that he left behind at his death in April 1790 [as] yet another segmented snake, but one that he went to some trouble to avoid assembling from head to tail in an unbroken narrative stream" (4). Escaping this history, the book as a published material object becomes remembered and consumed as a singular text, printed as a single cultural object with the sutures of its material past only textually rendered. There is something inhuman about Franklin's afterlife, living on within a culture that manufactures him into something larger than life, one that abstracts the messiness of composition into the orderliness of printed prose, contrasting the mess of manuscript to the cleaned-up and bound book.[7] Franklin's Mona Lisa smile on the hundred-dollar bill completes the circle of association, from mess to cultural symbol. This process from disheveled manuscript to cultural icon illuminates an entire system of cultural significance that orients a set of power relations that the figures in *Feeling Singular* desired to attract. The production of Franklin into one who supersedes the human—so great and pronounced that he deserves the countless, proliferating, and durable.

---

[5] The centrality of Franklin in thinking about early national life narratives may be briefly indexed in the title of Stephen Carl Arch's *After Franklin: The Emergence of Autobiography in Post-Revolutionary America* (2001), which argues that the fluidity of self-making began "to replace the fixed and average public self" by the end of the eighteenth century (13).

[6] For a more thorough history of the production of Franklin's book, see James N. Green and Peter Stallybrass, *Benjamin Franklin: Writer and Printer* (2006).

[7] It is not uncommon to encounter books that continue to describe Franklin as "one of the most accomplished men of his time as well as one of the most fascinating figures in American history" (Huang xv) or that affirm how "[h]is virtue is predicated on his absorption into generality" (Warner, *Letters*, 77). Franklin has emerged into a figure that reinforces an exceptionalist narrative, though in the end he could very well be described as simply a singular individual.

236 CODA

nods to his name—signals a major component of early national myth-making. But there is something about an undead Franklin lingering in the cultural and ideological fabric of the United States that this book seeks to reexamine through interrogating the writings of other individuals who felt such possibilities of grandeur were available to them but who fell short of having their textual selves preserved and consumed for such a hoped-for futurity. This book does not examine *why* Franklin became a touchstone, then, but takes as the assumption (and, really, the observation) that he did, after all, evolve into a larger-than-life cultural reference that constellated certain norms for success in a capitalist and heteropatriarchal society. Against that background, I put the lives of less popular figures who slid into the corners of insignificance or disrepute; their contrary positions offer a way into seeing the nature of republican celebrity.

Franklin's emergence into a figure who stabilized the republic's norms belies his own embodied messes and memorable mistakes. He was, of course, never the fantastical figure of liberal independence but instead managed and curated an identity that sought alliances and forged connections, an oppor-tunist who aligned with a new emerging consensus even as he attempted to instruct his own illegitimate son away from the trappings of failure. If Franklin, as a cultural type, comes to personify a series of conventions and ideals against which the figures of this inquiry were measured against, then focusing on them reshapes how we understand belonging in the early republic. Franklin encapsulates the rags-to-riches story of white mascu-line self-determination so sacrosanct to the myth of American mascu-line exceptionalism. This narrative trope has become so thoroughly woven into the fabric of U.S. cultural politics that it is even automatic to associate Franklin as its very exemplar, a paragon, if transitional personage whose emergence as a celebrated public persona also tells the story of the birth of the U.S. republic as an independent nation. This book explicitly marks how mas-culine gender norms buttress that myth, readily evident when considering how Franklin's emergence into what scholars consider his independence in Philadelphia partly occurs because a sea captain believed the indenture-breaking fugitive "had got a naughty Girl with Child, whose Friends would compel me to marry her, and therefore I could not appear or come away pub-licly" (23). Those details about Franklin's masculine privileges are expunged from the early national editions of his autobiography, as are his references to "venery" and other sexual appetites (83). Where Franklin had an entire so-cial and political apparatus that cleaned up his mess, the figures I look at had little to no institutionalized saviors. In this sense, the figures I examine in this book did not have access to the editorial apparatus that would clean up and make proper their cultural reception.[8]

Enter Ben Franklin stage right, busily running around Philadelphia with new-to-him bread under each arm and in his mouth, writing to his son that he "thought I made as I certainly did a most awkward ridiculous Appearance" (25). The repeating "I" and the image of a mouthful Benjamin chomping on bread may seem humorous, but there's a more insidious implication embedded within this self-narration. Indeed, it is a dangerous image *because* it plays with humor, personalizing this figure *as* relatable when in his backward glance and his profound Atlantic World notoriety he needed *something* to make himself seem relatable. The ability to control how one is perceived is the promise of these forms of excessive masculinity that this book has explored. In another widely disseminated anecdote that provided the façade of virtuous and visible labor, he notes: "I sometimes brought home the Paper I purchas'd at the Stores, thro' the Streets on a Wheelbarrow" (66). Signaling that he attempted to make himself *appear* industrious to others, Franklin's fake-it-until-you-make-it persona resonates with the fantasy of a self-made individual. At least that is how he would like himself to be remembered. This anecdote foregrounds much of the imagined mythos that attempts to structure the meaning of the United States, jumping from singular (narrated) event into iconic touchstone of supposed American bootstrap individualism.

The myth of the singular soul who pulls himself (it's always "himself") up from his bootstraps owes part of its cultural origins not just to Franklin's presentation of "being esteem'd an industrious thriving young Man" but also to Rudolf Erich Raspe's *The Surprising Adventures of Baron Munchausen*, who pulls himself and his horse out of water by his own hair. This picaresque novel combines a Don Quixote flair with extravagant tall tales and outright lies. Returning the bootstrap metaphor to the original context of Raspe's Munchausen, we might see how what has been called Munchausen syndrome offers an important context around the aspirations to extricate oneself from circumstances that cause floundering. This figment of success operates

---

[8] In thinking about archives and messiness, I am indebted to Martin F. Manalansan's work on how "mess, clutter, and muddled entanglements are the 'stuff' of queerness, historical memory, aberrant desires, and the archive" (94). Manalansan reads non-normative relationalities and spaces as "the 'stuff' of queerness," noting that "mess is a way into a queering of the archive that involves not a cleaning up but rather a spoiling and cluttering of the neat normative configurations and patterns that seek to calcify lives and experiences" (99). In this manner, I aim to highlight the way the figures I examine exceed the norms and protocols of archives.

238 CODA

as an unreachable fantasy, a superpower that promises to uplift, though un-like the Baron and his horse, never fully extracting the subject from the sur-face of their entanglement. If the origin story of "pulling oneself up by their bootstraps" emerges from a facetious story about pulling oneself out of water from one's hair, then we might think more about the ideological origin of American masculine singularity. Trapped by the fantasies of remarkableness, the great and the good, the powerful and the capable, U.S. Americans' desire for uniqueness and significance demands remediation lest, like the Baron, they pull all their hair out. Continuing and concluding on hair, there is a notion that when the American comedian Jimmy Fallon tussled the hair of Donald Trump on *The Tonight Show* in the middle of September 2016—hot on the campaign trail—that he humanized the political candidate in a way that made the gilded-toilet-using businessman in some manner relatable, that even *he* has hair that can be made into a mess. But much like Benjamin Franklin's confession of erratum, the hair tussle attempts to obscure the re-publican figure's prominent attachment to sexism and racism, blocking from momentary view a particular political trajectory through the aesthetics of masculine mess.

Works Cited

Abbott, Elizabeth. *A History of Celibacy*. New York: Scribner, 2000.

Adam, John. "Thoughts on Government." *Classics of American Political and Constitutional Thought: Origins through the Civil War*. Eds. Scott J. Hammond and Kevin R. Hardwick. Indianapolis: Hackett, 2007. 291–296.

Adams, Henry. *History of the United States of America during the Second Administration of Thomas Jefferson*. Vol. 1. New York, 1890.

Adams, John Quincy. "An Oration upon the Importance and Necessity of Public Faith, to a Well-Being of a Community," July 18, 1787, *Diary of John Quincy Adams*. Eds. David Grayson Allen et al. Cambridge: Harvard UP, 1981.

Adorno, Theodore. *The Culture Industry: Selected Essays on Mass Culture*. Ed. J. M. Bernstein. Taylor & Francis, 2005.

Ahmed, Sara. *The Promise of Happiness*. Durham: Duke UP, 2010.

Ahmed, Sara. *Queer Phenomenology: Orientations, Objects, Others*. Durham: Duke UP, 2006.

Altschuler, Sari. "'Ain't One Limb Enough?' Historicizing Disability in the American Novel." *American Literature* 86.2 (2014): 245–274.

Anderson, Douglas. *The Unfinished Life of Benjamin Franklin*. Baltimore: Johns Hopkins UP, 2012.

"An Appeal to the People and the Representatives." *The Washington National Monument*. Washington City, 1871.

Appleby, Joyce. *Capitalism and a New Social Order: The Republican Vision of the 1790s*. New York: NYU P, 1984.

Appleby, Joyce. *Inheriting the Revolution*. Cambridge: Harvard UP, 2000.

Appleby, Joyce. *Relentless Revolution: A History of Capitalism*. New York: Norton, 2010.

Aptheker, Herbert. *Early Years of the Republic and The Constitution, 1783–1793*. New York: International Publishers, 1976.

Arch, Stephen Carl. *After Franklin: The Emergence of Autobiography in Post-Revolutionary America*. Hanover, NH: UP of New England, 2001.

Armstrong, Tim. *The Logic of Slavery: Debt, Technology, and Pain in American Literature*. New York: Cambridge UP, 2012.

"Article 1." *The Analectic Magazine* 9 (May 1817): 351–395.

Badiou, Alain. *Being and Event*. Trans. Oliver Feltham. New York: Continuum, 2005.

Bailyn, Bernard. *The Ideological Origins of the American Revolution*. 1967. Cambridge: Harvard UP, 1992.

Ballou, Hosea. *A Sermon Designed to Notice, in a Religious Manner, The Deth of the Rev. George Richards*. Portsmouth, NH: Whidden, 1814.

Barnes, Joseph. *Remarks on Mr. John Fitch's Reply*. Philadelphia: Joseph James, 1788.

Basker, James G., ed. *Amazing Grace: An Anthology of Poems about Slavery, 1660–1810*. New Haven: Yale UP, 2002.

Bell, Richard. *We Shall Be No More: Suicide and Self-Government in the Newly United States*. Cambridge: Harvard UP, 2012.

240 WORKS CITED

Bellesiles, Michael A. *Revolutionary Outlaws: Ethan Allen and the Struggle for Independence on the Early American Frontier*. Charlottesville: UP of Virginia, 1993.

Ben-Atar, Doron S. *Trade Secrets: Intellectual Piracy and the Origins of American Industrial Power*. New Haven: Yale UP, 2002.

Benjamin, Walter. *Illuminations*. Ed. Hannah Arendt. Trans. Harry Zohn. New York: Schocken Books, 1986.

Bentley, William. *Diary of William Bentley*. 4 Vols. Gloucester, MA: 1962.

Berlant, Lauren. *Cruel Optimism*. Durham: Duke UP, 2011.

Berlant, Lauren. *Desire/Love*. New York: Punctum Books, 2012.

Berlant, Lauren. *The Female Complaint: The Unfinished Business of Sentimentality in American Culture*. Durham: Duke UP, 2008.

Biddle, Charles. *Autobiography of Charles Biddle, Vice-President of the Supreme Executive Council of Pennsylvania*. 1756–1821. (privately printed) Philadelphia: E. Claxton and Company, 1883.

Bishop, Abraham. *Connecticut Republicanism: An Oration on the Extent and Power of Political Delusion*. Philadelphia: 1800.

Bishop, Abraham. *Georgia Speculation Unveiled*. Hartford: 1797.

Bostock, John. "On the Catarrhus Aestivus or Summer Catarrh." *Medico-Chirurgical Transactions* 14 (1828): 437–446.

Bradburn, Douglas. *Citizenship Revolution: Politics and the Creation of the American Union, 1774–1804*. Charlottesville: U of Virginia P, 2009.

Branson, Susan. *These Fiery Frenchified Dames: Women and Political Culture in Early National Philadelphia*. Philadelphia: U of Pennsylvania P, 2001.

Brennan, Teresa. *The Transmission of Affect*. Ithaca: Cornell UP, 2014.

Brooks, Joanna. "The Unfortunates: What the Life Spans of Early Black Books Tell Us About Book History." *Early African American Print Culture*. Philadelphia: U of Pennsylvania P, 2012. 40–52.

Brooks, Peter. *Reading for Plot: Design and Intention in Narrative*: New York: Alfred A. Knopf, 1984.

Brown, Charles Brockden. *Wieland; or, The Transformation*. Eds. Philip Barnard and Stephen Shapiro. Indianapolis: Hackett, 2009.

Bruce, Dickson D. *The Origins of African American Literature, 1680–1865*. Charlottesville: U of Virginia P, 2001.

Burgett, Bruce. *Sentimental Bodies: Sex, Gender, and Citizenship in the Early Republic*. Princeton: Princeton UP, 1998.

Burleigh, Erica. *Intimacy and Family in Early American Writing*. New York: Palgrave, 2014.

Burroughs, Stephen. *Memoirs of the Notorious Stephen Burroughs of New Hampshire*. New York: Dial P, 1924.

Butler, Judith. *The Force of Non-Violence*. New York: Verso, 2020.

Butler, Judith. *Gender Trouble*. New York: Routledge, 1990.

Butler, Judith. *Undoing Gender*. New York: Routledge, 2004.

Cahill, Edward. *Liberty of the Imagination: Aesthetic Theory, Literary Form, and Politics in the Early United States*. Philadelphia: U of Pennsylvania P, 2012.

Callender, James. *The Prospect Before Us*. V. 2 pt. 2. Richmond: 1800–1801.

Capers, Corey. "Black Voices, White Print: Racial Practice, Print Publicity, and Order in the Early American Republic." *Early African American Print Culture*. Eds. Lara Langer Cohen and Jordan Alexander Stein. Philadelphia: U of Pennsylvania P, 2012.

Caric, Ric N. "To the Convivial Grave and Back: John Fitch as a Case Study in Cultural Failure, 1785–1792." *The Pennsylvania Magazine of History and Biography* 126.4 (Oct. 2002): 537–589.

WORKS CITED 241

Caruth, Cathy. *Trauma: Explorations in Memory*. Baltimore: Johns Hopkins UP, 1995.

Caruth, Cathy. *Unclaimed Experience: Trauma, Narrative, and History*. Baltimore: Johns Hopkins UP, 1997.

Casper, Scott E. *Constructing American Lives: Biography and Culture in Nineteenth-Century America*. Chapel Hill: U of North Carolina P, 1999.

Castiglia, Christopher. *Interior States: Institutional Consciousness and the Inner Life of Democracy in the Antebellum United States*. Durham: Duke UP, 2008.

Cavitch, Max. *American Elegy: The Poetry of Mourning from the Puritans to Whitman*. Minneapolis: U of Minnesota P, 2006.

Champagne, Roland A., Nina Ekstein, and Gary Kates. "Introduction." *The Maiden of Tonnerre: The Vicissitudes of the Chevalier and the Chevalier d'Eon*. Trans. Roland A. Champagne, Nina Ekstein, and Gary Kates. Baltimore: Johns Hopkins UP, 2001.

Cheng, Anne. *The Melancholy of Race: Psychoanalysis, Assimilation, and Hidden Grief*. New York: Oxford UP, 2001.

Chinn, Sarah. *Spectacular Men: Race, Gender, and Nation on the Early American Stage*. New York: Oxford UP, 2017.

Chudacoff, Howard P. *The Age of the Bachelor: Creating an American Subculture*. Princeton: Princeton UP, 1999.

Cobb, Michael. *Single: Arguments for the Uncoupled*. New York: NYU P, 2012.

Cohen, Daniel A. *Pillars of Salt, Monuments of Grace: New England Crime Literature and the Origins of American Popular Culture, 1674–1860*. Boston: U of Massachusetts P, 2006.

Cohen, Lara. *The Fabrication of American Literature: Fraudulence and Antebellum Print Culture*. Philadelphia: U of Pennsylvania P, 2012.

Cohen, Michael. "Peddlars, Poems, and Local Culture: The Case of Jonathan Plummer, a 'Balladmonger' in Nineteenth-Century New England." *ESQ: A Journal of the American Renaissance* 54.1–4 (2008): 9–32.

Collection of the Penal Laws of the Commonwealth of Pennsylvania. Philadelphia: Rudd and Bartram, 1810.

"Communication: The Hermitess of North-Salem." *Weekly Visitor, or Ladies' Miscellany* 2.14 (Sept. 29 1804): 410–411.

"A Concise Life of Lord Timothy Dexter." Lord Timothy Dexter Papers, Acc 2009.014. Phillips Library, Peabody Essex Museum, Rowley, MA. 1935.

Cooper, Davina. *Feeling Like a State: Desire, Denial and the Recasting of Authority*. Durham: Duke UP, 2019.

Cotlar, Seth. *Tom Paine's America: The Rise and Fall of Transatlantic Radicalism in the Early Republic*. Charlottesville: U of Virginia P, 2011.

Couch, Daniel Diez. *American Fragments: The Political Aesthetic of Unfinished Forms in the Early Republic*. Philadelphia: U of Pennsylvania P, 2022.

Couser, G. Thomas. *Altered Egos: Authority in American Autobiography*. Oxford UP, 1989.

Coviello, Peter. *Intimacy in America: Dreams of Affiliation in American Literature*. Minneapolis: U of Minnesota P, 2005.

Coviello, Peter. *Make Yourself Gods: Mormons and the Unfinished Business of American Secularism*. U of Chicago P, 2019.

Crevecoeur, J. Hector St. John. *Letters from an American Farmer*. 1782. New York: 1904.

Crevecoeur, J. Hector St. John. *Sketches of Eighteenth-Century America*. Eds. Henri Louis Bourdin, Ralph Henry Gabriel, and Stanley Thomas Williams. New Haven: Yale UP, 1925.

242   WORKS CITED

Crocker, Henry. *History of the Baptists in Vermont.* Bellows Falls, VT: 1913.

Cultures of United States Imperialism. Eds. Amy Kaplan and Donald Pease. Durham: Duke UP, 1994.

Currier, John J. *The History of Newburyport, Mass. 1764–1909.* Newburyport, MA: 1909.

Dain, Bruce R. *A Hideous Monster of the Mind: American Race Theory in the Early Republic.* Cambridge: Harvard UP, 2003.

Davis, Lennard J. *Enforcing Normalcy: Disability, Deafness, and the Body.* New York: Verso, 1995.

De Beauvoir, Simone. *The Ethics of Ambiguity.* 1948. Trans. Bernard Frechtman. 1976.

Deleuze, Gilles, and Félix Guattari. *A Thousand Platteaus: Capitalism and Schizophrenia.* Trans. Brian Massumi. Minneapolis: U of Minnesota P, 1987.

DeLombard, Jeannine. *Slavery on Trial: Law, Abolitionism, and Print Culture.* Chapel Hill: U of North Carolina P, 2007.

Demos, John. *The Heathen School: A Story of Hope and Betrayal in the Age of the Early Republic.* New York: Knopf, 2014.

Dennie, Joseph. *Port Folio* 2.52, 2.36 (1805).

Dexter, Timothy. *A Pickle for the Knowing Ones: or, Plain Truths in a Homespun Dress.* Salem, MA: 1802.

Dickens, Charles. *American Notes for General Circulation.* 1842. Ed. Patricia Ingham. New York: Penguin, 2001.

DiCuirci, Lindsay. "Found among the Papers: Fictions of Textual Discovery in Early America," *Early American Literature* 56.3 (2021): 809–843.

Dillon, Elizabeth Maddock. *The Gender of Freedom: Fictions of Liberalism and the Literary Public Sphere.* Stanford: Stanford UP, 2004.

Ditz, Toby L. "Contending Masculinities in Early America." *New Men: Manliness in Early America.* Ed. Thomas A. Foster, Mary Beth Norton, and Toby L. Ditz. New York: NYU P, 2011.

Dolan, Frederick M. *Allegories of America: Narratives, Metaphysics, Politics.* Ithaca: Cornell UP, 1994.

Douglass, Frederick. *Narrative of the Life of Frederick Douglass, an American Slave, Written by Himself.* 1845. Ed. William L. Andrews and William S. McFeely. New York: W. W. Norton & Company, 1997.

Downes, Paul. "Eighty-Nine Divided by Seventy-Six." *American Literary History* 23.1 (Spring 2011): 83–101.

Dumm, Thomas. *Loneliness as a Way of Life.* Cambridge: Harvard UP, 2010.

Durrett, Rueben T. *John Filson, the First Historian of Kentucky.* Louisville: Filson Club, 1884.

DuVal, Kathleen. *Independence Lost: Lives on the Edge of the American Revolution.* New York: Random House, 2015.

Dwight, Edwin Welles. *Memoirs of Henry Obookiah.* New Haven: Converse for Whiting, 1819.

Dwight, Timothy. *Travels; in New-England and New-York.* New Haven: 1821.

Eastman, Carolyn. *A Nation of Speechifiers: Making an American Public after the Revolution.* Chicago: U of Chicago P, 2009.

Eastman, Francis Smith. *A History of Vermont, from Its First Settlement to the Present Time.* Brattleboro, VT: Holbrook and Fessenden, 1828.

Edelman, Lee. *No Future: Queer Theory and the Death Drive.* Durham: Duke UP, 2004.

WORKS CITED 243

Edwards, Jonathan. *The Life and Character of the Late Reverend Mr. Jonathan Edwards, President of the College of New-Jersey. Together with a Number of His Sermons on Various Important Subjects*. Boston: 1765.

"Elegy, &c. Fair Daughter of America." Ed. Ezekiel Russell. Boston: Russell, 1786.

Ells, Benjamin Franklin. "Biographical Sketch of Lord Timothy Dexter." *The Western Miscellany* 1.5 (November 1848): 137–139, 179–182, 221–224, 286–291, 294–296, 320–323.

Equiano, Olaudah. *The Interesting Narrative of the Life of Olaudah Equiano, or Gustavus Vassa, the African. Written by Himself. Vol. 1 and 2*. London: 1789.

Eustace, Nicole. *1812: War and the Passions of Patriotism*. Philadelphia: U of Pennsylvania P, 2012.

Ezell, Margaret J. M. "Looking Glass Histories." *Journal of British Studies* 43.3 (July 2004): 317–338.

Faherty, Duncan. *Remodeling the Nation: The Architecture of American Identity, 1776–1858*. Lebanon: U of New Hampshire P, 2007.

A Faithful Narrative of Elizabeth Wilson. Philadelphia: 1786.

Faragher, John Mack. *Daniel Boone: The Life and Legend of an American Pioneer*. New York: Hold, 1992.

Farnsworth, Frederick. *The Man of the Mountain*. Boston: 1818.

Fehrenbacher, Don E. *The Dred Scott Case: Its Significance in American Law and Politics*. New York: Oxford UP, 1978.

Finseth, Ian. "Irony and Modernity in the Early Slave Narrative: Bonds of Duty, Contracts of Meaning." *Early American Literature* 48.1 (2013): 29–60.

"First Steamboat on the Delaware." *The Western Monthly Magazine and Literary Journal* 3.20 (Aug. 1834): 447.

Fitch, John. *The Autobiography of John Fitch*. Ed. Frank D. Prager. Philadelphia: The American Philosophical Society, 1976.

Forten, James. "The Making and Meaning of James Forten's *Letters from A Man of Colour*." Ed. Julie Winch. *William and Mary Quarterly* 64.1 (2007): 1–6.

Foster, Frances Smith. Introduction. *"Minnie's Sacrifice," "Sowing and Reaping," "Trial and Triumph": Three Rediscovered Novels by Frances E. W. Harper*. Ed. Frances Smith Foster. Boston: Beacon, 1994. xi–xxxvii.

Foster, Hannah Webster. *The Coquette*. Ed. Carla Mulford. New York: Penguin Books, 1996.

Foucault, Michel. *The Order of Things: An Archaeology of the Human Sciences*. New York: Vintage Books, 1970.

Foucault, Michel. *"Society Must Be Defended": Lectures at the Collège de France, 1975–1976*. Trans. David Macey. New York: Picador, 2003.

Foucault, Michel. "What Is an Author?" *The Foucault Reader*. Ed. Paul Rabinow. New York: Pantheon, 1984. 101–120.

Franklin, Benjamin. *The Autobiography of Benjamin Franklin and Other Writings*. Ed. Kenneth Silverman. New York: Penguin, 2003.

Frawley, Maria. *Invalidism and Identity in Nineteenth-Century Britain*. Chicago: U of Chicago P, 2004.

Freeman, Joanne. *Affairs of Honor: National Politics in the New Republic*. New Haven: Yale UP, 2002.

Freud, Sigmund. "An Autobiographical Study." Ed. Peter Gay. New York: Norton, 1995. 3–41.

244 WORKS CITED

Freud, Sigmund. "On Dreams." *The Freud Reader*. Ed. Peter Gay. New York: Norton, 1995. 142–72.

Furstenberg, François. *In the Name of the Father: Washington's Legacy, Slavery, and the Making of a Nation*. New York: Penguin, 2006.

Gardiner, Judith Kegan. "Introduction." *Masculinity Studies and Feminist Theory*. Ed. Judith Kegan Gardiner. New York: Columbia UP, 2002.

Garrett, Matthew. *Episodic Poetics: Politics and Literary Form after the Constitution*. New York: Oxford UP, 2014.

George Washington: Sculpture by Jean Antoine Houdon; a brief history of the most famous sculpture created of America's immortal patriot. Providence: The Gorham Company, 1931.

Gilmore, Ruth Wilson. "Race and Globalization." *Geographies of Global Change*. Eds. P. J. Taylor, R. L. Johnstone, and M. J. Watts. Oxford: Blackwell, 2002.

Ginzburg, Carlo. *The Cheese and the Worms: The Cosmos of a Sixteenth-Century Miller*. Baltimore: Johns Hopkins UP, 1980.

Godbeer, Richard. *The Overflowing of Friendship: Love Between Men and the Creation of the American Republic*. Baltimore: Johns Hopkins UP, 2009.

Goddu, Teresa A. *Gothic America: Narrative, History, and Nation*. New York: Columbia UP, 1997.

Goffman, Erving. *Stigma: Notes on the Management of Spoiled Identity*. New York: Simon & Schuster, 1963.

Goode, Mike. *Sentimental Masculinity and the Rise of History, 1790–1890*. Cambridge: Cambridge UP, 2009.

Goodrich, Samuel Griswold. *The First Book of History: for Children and Youth*. Boston: 1850.

Goodrich, Samuel Griswold. *Recollections of a Lifetime, or Men and Things I Have Seen*. New York: 1856.

Gould, Eliga H. "The Laws of War and Peace: Legitimating Slavery in the Age of the American Revolution." *State and Citizen: British America and the Early United States*. Eds. Peter Thompson and Peter S. Onuf. Charlottesville: U of Virginia P, 2013. 52–76.

Green, James N., and Peter Stallybrass. *Benjamin Franklin: Writer and Printer*. New Castle, DE: Oak Knoll, 2006.

Gustafson, Sandra M. *Imagining Deliberative Democracy in the Early Republic*. Chicago: U of Chicago P, 2011.

Guyette, Elise A. *Discovering Black Vermont: African American Farmers in Hinesburgh, 1790–1890*. Burlington: U of Vermont P, 2010.

Hager, Christopher. *Word by Word: Emancipation and the Act of Writing*. Cambridge: Harvard UP, 2013.

Haggerty, George E. *Men in Love: Masculinity and Sexuality in the Eighteenth Century*. New York: Columbia UP, 1999.

Halberstam, Jack. *Female Masculinity*. Durham: Duke UP, 1998.

Halberstam, Jack. *The Queer Art of Failure*. Durham: Duke UP, 2011.

Harris, Cheryl I. "Whiteness as Property." *Harvard Law Review* 106.8 (June 1993): 1709–1791.

Harris, Sharon M. *Executing Race: Early American Women's Narratives of Race, Society, and the Law*. Columbus: Ohio State UP, 2005.

Hartman, Saidiya. *Lose Your Mother: A Journey Along the Atlantic Slave Route*. New York: Farrar, Straus and Giroux, 2008.

WORKS CITED 245

Hartman, Saidiya. *Scenes of Subjection: Terror, Slavery, and Self-Making in Nineteenth-Century America*. New York: Oxford UP, 1997.

Hartnett, Stephen John. *Executing Democracy: Capital Punishment and the Making of America, 1683–1807*. Vol. 1. East Lansing: Michigan State UP, 2010.

Haulman, Kate. *The Politics of Fashion in Eighteenth-Century America*. Chapel Hill: North Carolina UP, 2011.

Haynes, April R. *Riotous Flesh: Women, Physiology, and the Solitary Vice in Nineteenth-Century America*. Chicago: U of Chicago P, 2015.

The Hermit of Virginia. Printed in Wilbraham, MA. 1807.

"The Hermitess of North-Salem." *The Balance and Columbian Repository* 3.40 (Oct. 2, 1804): 316–317.

Holland, Sharon Patricia. *The Erotic Life of Racism*. Durham: Duke UP, 2012.

Howell, William Huntting. *Against Self-Reliance: The Arts of Dependence in the Early United States*. Philadelphia: U of Pennsylvania P, 2015.

Huang, Nian-Sheng. *Benjamin Franklin in American Thought and Culture, 1790–1990*. American Philosophical Society, 1994.

Hyde, Carrie. *Civic Longing: The Speculative Origins of U.S. Citizenship*. Cambridge: Harvard UP, 2018.

Imbarrato, Susan Clair. *Declarations of Independency in Eighteenth-Century American Autobiography*. Knoxville: U of Tennessee P, 1998.

Irving, Washington. *A History of New York*. 1809. New York: Library of America, 1983. 363–730.

Jackson, Mark. *Allergy: The History of a Modern Malady*. Chicago: U of Chicago P, 2006.

Jackson, Zakiyyah Iman. *Becoming Human: Matter and Meaning in an Antiblack World*. New York: NYU P, 2020.

Jacobs, Harriet. *Incidents in the Life of a Slave Girl*. 1861. Ed. Nell Irvin Painter. New York: Penguin, 2000.

Jefferson, Thomas. *Memoir, Correspondence, and Miscellanies*. Ed. Thomas Jefferson Randolph. Charlottesville, VA: 1829.

Jefferson, Thomas. *Notes on the State of Virginia*. 1787. *The Selected Writings of Thomas Jefferson*. Ed. Wayne Franklin. New York: W. W. Norton & Company, 2010.

"Just Published." *Middlesex Gazette* 1.24 (April 17, 1786): 4.

Juster, Susan. *Doomsayers: Anglo-American Prophecy in the Age of Revolution*. Philadelphia: U of Pennsylvania P, 2002.

Kahan, Benjamin. *Celibacies: American Modernism & Sexual Life*. Durham: Duke UP, 2013.

Kann, Mark E. *A Republic of Men: The American Founders, Gendered Language, and Patriarchal Politics*. New York: NYU P, 1998.

Kaplan, Amy. "Manifest Domesticity." *American Literature* 70.3 (Sept. 1998): 581–606.

Kaplan, Catherine O'Donnell. *Men of Letters in the Early Republic: Cultivating Forums of Citizenship*. Charlottesville: U of North Carolina P, 2008.

Kates, Gary. *Monsieur d'Eon Is a Woman: A Tale of Political Intrigue and Sexual Masquerade*. Baltimore: Johns Hopkins UP, 2001.

Kenslea, Timothy. *The Sedgwicks in Love: Courtship, Engagement, and Marriage in the Early Republic*. Boston: Northeastern UP, 2006.

Kerber, Linda K. "The Paradox of Women's Citizenship in the Early Republic: The Case of *Martin vs. Massachusetts*, 1805." *American Historical Review* 97 (April 1992): 349–378.

246   WORKS CITED

Kett, Joseph F. *Merit: The History of a Founding Ideal from the American Revolution to the Twenty-First Century*. Ithaca: Cornell UP, 2013.

Kippola, Karl. *Acts of Manhood: The Performance of Masculinity on the American Stage, 1828–1865*. New York: Palgrave, 2012.

Kittredge, George Lyman. *The Old Farmer and His Almanack*. Cambridge: Harvard UP, 1920.

Klein, Martin. "Understanding the Slave Experience in West Africa." *Biography and the Black Atlantic*. Eds. Lisa A. Lindsay and John Wood Sweet. Philadelphia: U of Pennsylvania P, 2014. 48–65.

Knapp, Samuel L. *Life of Lord Timothy Dexter*. Boston: 1858.

Knighton, Andrew Lyndon. *Idle Threats: Men and the Limits of Productivity in Nineteenth Century America*. New York: NYU P, 2012.

Kohn, Richard. "The Inside History of the Newburgh Conspiracy: America and the Coup d'Etat." *The William and Mary Quarterly* 27.2 (Apr. 1970): 187–220.

LaFleur, Greta. *The Natural History of Sexuality*. Baltimore: Johns Hopkins UP, 2018.

LaFleur, Greta. "'What's in a Name?': They/Them." *Journal of the Early Republic* 43.1 (Spring 2023): 109–119.

Lane, Christopher. "The Psychoanalysis of Race: An Introduction." *The Psychoanalysis of Race*. Ed. Christopher Lane. New York: Columbia UP, 1998. 1–37.

Larson, Edward. J. *The Return of George Washington, 1783–1789*. New York: William Morrow, 2015.

Larson, Scott. "Indescribable Being: Theological Performances of Genderlessness in the Society of the Publick Universal Friend, 1776–1819." *Early American Studies* 12 (Fall 2014): 576–600.

Laws of the Commonwealth of Pennsylvania, from the Fourteenth Day of October, One Thousand Seven Hundred, to the Twentieth Day of March, One Thousand Eight Hundred and Ten. Vol. 2. Philadelphia: John Bioren, 1810.

Lee, Rebecca Smith. "A Contemporary View of Lord Timothy Dexter Comes to Light in Kentucky." *The Filson Club History Quarterly* 35.4 (Oct. 1961): 357–366.

Lewis, R. W. B. *The American Adam: Innocence, Tragedy, and Tradition in the Nineteenth Century*. Chicago: U of Chicago P, 1955.

Livingston, Jennie. *Paris is Burning*. Off White Productions, 1990.

Looby, Christopher. "The Literariness of Sexuality: Or, How to Do the (Literary) History of (American) Sexuality." *American Literary History* 25.4 (2013): 841–854.

Looby, Christopher. *Voicing America: Language, Literary Form, and the Origins of the United States*. Chicago: U of Chicago P, 1996.

Loughran, Trish. *The Republic in Print: Print Culture in the Age of U.S. Nation Building, 1770–1870*. New York: Columbia UP, 2007.

Love, Heather. "Doing Being Deviant: Deviance Studies, Description, and the Queer Ordinary." *differences* 26.1 (2015): 74–95.

Löwy, Michael. "Against the Grain." *Walter Benjamin and the Demands of History*. Ed. Michael P. Steinberg. Ithaca: Cornell UP, 1996.

Luciano, Dana. *Arranging Grief: Sacred Time and the Body in Nineteenth-Century America*. New York: NYU P, 2007.

Lystra, Karen. *Searching the Heart: Women, Men, and Romantic Love in Nineteenth-Century America*. New York: Oxford UP, 1989.

Madison, James. *Selections from the Private Correspondence of James Madison, from 1813 to 1836*. Washington: 1859.

WORKS CITED   247

Manalansan, Martin F. "The 'Stuff' of Archives: Mess, Migration, and Queer Lives." *Radical History Review* 120 (2014): 94–107.

Mann, Herman. *The Female Review, or Memoirs of an American Young Lady.* Dedham: Printed by Nathaniel and Benjamin Heaton. 1797.

Marcuse, Herbert. *Eros and Civilization: A Philosophical Inquiry into Freud.* Boston: Beacon P, 1966.

Marx, Karl. *Capital: A Critique of Political Economy.* 1867. Ed. Friedrich Engels. Vol. 1. New York: Cosimo Classics, 2007.

Masur, Louis. "'Age of the First Person Singular': The Vocabulary of the Self in New England, 1780–1850," *Journal of American Studies* 25.2 (Aug. 1991): 189–211.

Masur, Louis. *Rites of Execution: Capital Punishment and the Transformation of American Culture, 1776–1865.* New York: Oxford UP, 1989.

Matthiessen, F. O. *American Renaissance: Art and Expression in the Age of Emerson and Whitman.* New York: Oxford UP, 1941.

McCorison, Marcus A. "Printers and the Law: The Trials of Publishing Obscene Libel in Early America." *The Papers of the Bibliographical Society of America* 104.2 (June 2010): 181–217.

McCurdy, John Gilbert. *Citizen Bachelors: Manhood and the Creation of the United States.* Ithaca: Cornell UP, 2009.

McEwan, Barbara. *Thomas Jefferson: Farmer.* Jefferson, NC: McFarland & Co., 1991.

McGill, Meredith. "Common Places: Poetry, Illocality, and Temporal Dislocation in Thoreau's *A Week on the Concord and Merrimack Rivers.*" *American Literary History* 19.2 (Summer 2007): 357–374.

McRae, Sherwin. *Washington: His Person as Represented by the Artists.* Richmond, VA: R.F. Walker, 1873.

McRuer, Robert. *Crip Theory: Cultural Signs of Queerness and Disability.* New York: NYU P, 2006.

Mihm, Stephen. *Nation of Counterfeiters: Capitalists, Con Men, and the Making of the United States.* Cambridge: Harvard UP, 2007.

Miller, Perry. *Errand into the Wilderness.* Cambridge: Harvard UP, 1956.

Millner, Michael. *Fever Reading: Affect and Reading Badly in the Early American Public Sphere.* Hanover: U of New Hampshire P, 2012.

Mills, Charles. *The Racial Contract.* Ithaca: Cornell UP, 1997.

Minutes of the Supreme Executive Council of Pennsylvania, from Its Organization to the Termination of the Revolution. Published by the State. Vol. XIV. Harrisburg: Printed by Theo. Penn & Co., 1853.

Mitman, Gregg. *Breathing Space: How Allergies Shape Our Lives and Landscapes.* New Haven: Yale UP, 2008.

Morgan, Edmund Sears. *Benjamin Franklin.* New Haven: Yale UP, 2002.

Morris, Charles E. III, ed. *Queering Public Discourse: Sexualities in American Historical Discourse.* Columbia: U of South Carolina P, 2007.

Moyer, Paul B. *Wild Yankees: The Struggle for Independence Along Pennsylvania's Revolutionary Frontier.* Ithaca: Cornell UP, 2015.

Muñoz, José Esteban. *Cruising Utopia: The Then and There of Queer Futurity.* New York: NYU P, 2009.

Murison, Justine. *Faith in Exposure: Privacy and Secularism in the Nineteenth-Century United States.* Philadelphia: U Pennsylvania P, 2022.

Nancy, Jean-Luc. *Being Singular Plural.* Trans. Anne O'Byrne. Stanford: Stanford UP, 2000.

248   WORKS CITED

Nash, Gary B., and Jean R. Soderlund. *Freedom by Degrees: Emancipation in Pennsylvania and Its Aftermath*. New York: Oxford UP, 1991.

"Negro Slavery: An Apostrophe." *New-York Weekly Museum* 11.52 (17 Aug. 1799): 2.

Nelson, Dana. *National Manhood: Capitalist Citizenship and the Imagined Fraternity of White Men*. Durham: Duke UP, 1998.

Newman, Richard S. *Freedom's Prophet: Bishop Richard Allen, the AME Church, and the Black Founding Fathers*. New York: NYU P, 2008.

Newman, Richard S. *The Transformation of American Abolitionism: Fighting Slavery in the Early Republic*. Chapel Hill: U of North Carolina P, 2002.

Ngai, Sianne. *Our Aesthetic Categories: Zany, Cute, Interesting*. Cambridge: Harvard UP, 2012.

Nietzsche, Friedrich. *Untimely Meditations*. Ed. Daniel Breazeale. Cambridge: Cambridge UP, 1997.

Nissenbaum, Stephen. *Sex, Diet, and Debility in Jacksonian America: Sylvester Graham and Health Reform*. Westport, CT: Greenwood P, 1980.

Nyong'O, Tavia. *The Amalgamation Waltz: Race, Performance, and the Ruses of Memory*. Minneapolis: U of Minnesota P, 2009.

Otter, Samuel. *Philadelphia Stories: America's Literature of Race and Freedom*. New York: Oxford UP, 2010.

Paine, Thomas. *The Rights of Man*. 1791. London: 1795.

Palmer, Elihu. "Extract from an Oration, Delivered at Federal Point . . ." *Political Miscellany* (1793): 22–26.

Parish, Susan Scott. "Rummaging/In and Out of Holds." *American Literary History* 22.2 (Summer 2010): 289–301.

Parkinson, Robert G. *Thirteen Clocks: How Race United the Colonies and Made the Declaration of Independence*. Chapel Hill: U of North Carolina P, 2021.

Payne, Rodger M. *The Self and the Sacred: Conversion and Autobiography in Early American Protestantism*. Knoxville: U of Tennessee P, 1998.

The Pennsylvania Hermit. Philadelphia: 1840.

"Philadelphia, Jan. 5." *Providence Gazette* 12.1099 (January 22, 1785): 2.

Plumer, William. "Lord Timothy Dexter: Account of his Life Taken from the Diary of Governor William Plumer of New Hampshire." *Journal of American History* 18.1 (1824): 51–53.

Plummer, Jonathan. *Sketch of the History of the Life and Adventures of Jonathan Plummer*. Newburyport, MA: June 1795.

Plummer, Jonathan. "Something New, or Memoirs of that Truly Eccentric Character, the Late Timothy Dexter, Esq." Montpelier, VT: Parks P, 1808.

Pope, Alexander. *An Essay on Criticism*. London: Printed for W. Lewis in Russel-Street, 1711.

Pratt, Lloyd. *Archives of American Time: Literature and Modernity in the Nineteenth Century*. Philadelphia: U of Pennsylvania P, 2010.

Prentiss, Benjamin Franklin. *The Blind African Slave, Or Memoirs of Boyrereau Brinch, Nicknamed Jeffrey Brace*. Ed. Kari J. Winter. Madison: U of Wisconsin P, 2004.

Price, Richard. *Observations on the Importance of the American Revolution*. London: 1785.

Ramage, James A., and Andrea S. Watkins. *Kentucky Rising: Democracy, Slavery, and Culture form the Early Republic to the Civil War*. Lexington: UP of Kentucky, 2011.

Raspe, Rudolf Erich. *The Surprising Adventures of Baron Munchausen*. 1785.

WORKS CITED   249

Reis, Elizabeth. *Bodies in Doubt: An American History of Intersex*. Baltimore: Johns Hopkins UP, 2009.

Richards, George. *Mr. Richards's Oration on Independence*. July 4, 1795. Portsmouth, NH: 1795.

Richards, George. *Repent! Repent! or Likewise Perish!* Philadelphia: Lydia R. Bailey, 1812.

Rifkin, Mark. *When Did the Indians Become Straight?: Kinship, The History of Sexuality, and Native Sovereignty*. New York: Oxford UP, 2010.

Rigal, Laura. *The American Manufactory: Art, Labor, and the World of Things in the Early Republic*. Princeton: Princeton UP, 1998.

Roach, Joseph. *It*. Ann Arbor: U of Michigan P, 2007.

Rohy, Valerie. *Anachronism and Its Others: Sexuality, Race, Temporality*. New York: SUNY UP, 2009.

Rollins, Alden M. *Vermont Warnings Out, Vol. 1: Northern Vermont*. Rockland, ME: Picton P, 1995.

Román, David. *Performance in America: Contemporary U.S. Culture and the Performing Arts*. Durham: Duke UP, 2005.

Rosenblatt, Helena. *The Lost History of Liberalism: From Ancient Rome to the Twenty-First Century*. Princeton: Princeton UP, 2020.

Rothberg, Michael. *Multidirectional Memory: Remembering the Holocaust in the Age of Decolonization*. Stanford: Stanford UP, 2009.

Rowe, G. S. "Women's Crime and Criminal Administration in Pennsylvania, 1765–1790." *Pennsylvania Magazine of History and Biography* 109 (1985): 335–368.

Rowson, Susanna. *Charlotte Temple*. 1791.

Rumsey, James. *A Short Treatise on the Application of Steam*. Philadelphia: Joseph James, 1788.

Rush, Benjamin. *An Account of the Sugar Maple-Tree, of the United States*. Philadelphia: Printed by R. Aitken & Son, 1792.

Rush, Benjamin. *Essays, Literary, Moral & Philosophical*. Philadelphia: Thomas & Samuel F. Bradford, 1798.

Rush, Benjamin. *Letters of Benjamin Rush*. Vol. 2. Ed. Lyman Henry Butterfield. Princeton: Princeton UP, 1951.

Rush, Benjamin. "Observations intended to favour a supposition that the Black Color (as it is called) of the Negroes is derived from the LEPROSY." *Transactions of the American Philosophical Society*. Vol. 4. Philadelphia: American Philosophical Society, 1799.

Rush, Benjamin. "On Slave-Keeping." *The Selected Writings of Benjamin Rush*. Ed. Dagobert D. Runes. New York: Philosophical Library, 1947.

Russell, Ezekiel. *The American Bloody Register*. Boston: 1784.

Sachs, Honor. *Home Rule: Households, Manhood, and National Expansion on the Eighteenth-Century Kentucky Frontier*. New Haven: Yale UP, 2015.

Saillant, John. "The Black Body Erotic and the Republic Body Politic, 1790–1820." *Sentimental Men: Masculinity and the Politics of Affect in American Culture*. Eds. Mary Chapman and Glenn Hendler. Berkeley: U of California P, 1999. 89–111.

Saillant, John. *Black Puritan, Black Republican: The Life and Thought of Lemuel Haynes, 1753–1833*. New York: Oxford UP, 2002.

Sale, Maggie Montesinos. *The Slumbering Volcano: American Slave Ship Revolts and the Production of Rebellious Masculinity*. Durham: Duke UP, 1997.

Sandage, Scott. *Born Losers: A History of Failure in America*. Cambridge: Harvard UP, 2005.

250 WORKS CITED

Saxton, Alexander. *The Rise and Fall of the White Republic: Class Politics and Mass Culture in Nineteenth Century America*. 1990. New York: Verso, 2003.

Schlereth, Eric. "A Tale of Two Deists: John Fitch, Elihu Palmer, and the Boundary of Tolerable Religious Expression in Early National Philadelphia." *The Pennsylvania Magazine of History and Biography* 132.2 (January 2008): 5–31.

Schocket, Andrew M. *Fighting Over the Founders: How We Remember the American Revolution*. New York: NYU P, 2015.

Schorb, Jodi. *Reading Prisoners: Literature, Literacy, and the Transformation of American Punishment*. New Brunswick: Rutgers UP, 2014.

Schudson, Michael. *The Good Citizen: A History of American Civic Life*. New York: The Free P, 1998.

Schuller, Kyla. *The Biopolitics of Feeling: Race, Sex, and Science in the Nineteenth Century*. Durham: Duke UP, 2017.

Sedgwick, Eve Kosofsky. *Between Men: English Literature and Male Homosocial Desire*. New York: Columbia UP, 1985.

Sedgwick, Eve Kosofsky. *Epistemology of the Closet*. Berkeley: U of California P, 1990.

Sedgwick, Eve Kosofsky. "Jane Austin and the Masturbating Girl." *Critical Inquiry* 17.4 (Summer 1991): 818–837.

Sedgwick, Eve Kosofsky. *Touching Feeling*. Durham: Duke UP, 2003.

Shain, Barry Alan. *The Myth of American Individualism: The Protestant Origins of American Political Thought*. Princeton: Princeton UP, 1994.

Sidbury, James. *Becoming African in America: Race and Nation in the Early Black Atlantic*. New York: Oxford UP, 2007.

Slauter, Eric. *The State as a Work of Art: The Cultural Origins of the Constitution*. Chicago: U of Chicago P, 2009.

Smith, Caleb. *The Oracle and the Curse: A Poetics of Justice from the Revolution to the Civil War*. Cambridge: Harvard UP, 2013.

Smith, Caleb. *The Prison and the American Imagination*. New Haven: Yale UP, 2009.

Smith, Venture. *A Narrative of the Life and Adventures of Venture, a Native of Africa: But Resident above Sixty Years in the United States of America*. New London: C. Holt, 1798.

Sobel, Mechel. *Teach Me Dreams: The Search for Self in the Revolutionary Era*. Princeton: Princeton UP, 2000.

Sontag, Susan. "Notes on 'Camp.'" 1964. *Against Interpretation*. New York: Picador, 1966.

Sprague, William Buell. *Annals of the American Pulpit*. Vol. 3. New York: 1859.

Steedman, Caroline. *Dust: The Archive and Cultural History*. New Brunswick: Rutgers UP, 2002.

Stein, Jordan Alexander. "American Literary History and Queer Temporalities." *American Literary History* 25.4 (Winter 2013): 855–869.

Substance of the Report Delivered by the Court of Directors of the Sierra Leone Company. London: James Phillips, 1794.

Swart, Koenraad W. "'Individualism' in the Mid-Nineteenth Century." *Journal of the History of Ideas* 23.1 (Jan.–Mar. 1962): 77–90.

Tager, Jack. "Politics, Honor, and Self-Defense in Post-Revolutionary Boston: The 1806 Manslaughter Trial of Thomas Selfridge." *Historical Journal of Massachusetts* 37.2 (Fall 2009): 85–104.

Takaki, Ronald. *Iron Cages: Race and Culture in 19th-Century America*. New York: Knopf, 1978.

WORKS CITED   251

Tamarkin, Elisa. *Anglophilia: Deference, Devotion, and Antebellum America*. Chicago: U of Chicago P, 2008.

Taylor, Alan. "From Fathers to Friends of the People: Political Personas in the Early Republic." *New Perspectives on the Early Republic: Essays form the Journal of the Early Republic, 1981–1991*. Eds. Michael A. Morrison and Ralph D. Gray. Chicago: U of Illinois P, 1994. 149–163.

Taylor, Alan. *William Cooper's Town: Power and Persuasion on the Frontier of the Early American Republic*. New York: Alfred A. Knopf, 1996.

Tennenhouse, Leonard. *The Importance of Feeling English: American Literature and the British Diaspora, 1750–1850*. Princeton: Princeton UP, 2007.

Terada, Rei. *Looking Away: Phenomenality and Dissatisfaction, Kant to Adorno*. Cambridge: Harvard UP, 2009.

Thoreau, Henry David. "Life Without Principle." *Atlantic Monthly* 12.72 (October 1863): 484–495.

Thoreau, Henry David. *Walden*. 1854. Ed. William Rossi. New York: Norton, 2008.

Thornton, William. *Papers of William Thornton*. Vol. 1. Ed. C. M. Harris. Charlottesville: U of Virginia P, 1995.

Titular, Tim. "The Tortoise—No. III." *The Eye: by Obadiah Optic* 1.8. Ed. John W. Scott Philadelphia: 1808. 89–91.

Tomc, Sandra. *Industry and the Creative Mind: The Eccentric Writer in American Literature and Entertainment, 1790–1860*. Ann Arbor: U of Michigan P, 2012.

Tomek, Beverly C. *Colonization and Its Discontents: Emancipation, Emigration, and Antislavery in Antebellum Pennsylvania*. New York: NYU P, 2011.

Tomlins, Christopher L. *Law, Labor, and Ideology in the Early American Republic*. Cambridge: Cambridge UP, 1993.

Traub, Valerie. "The New Unhistoricism in Queer Studies." *PMLA* 128.1 (2013): 21–39.

Traub, Valerie. *Thinking Sex with the Early Moderns*. Philadelphia: U of Pennsylvania P, 2016.

Tufts, Meredith Peterson. "A Matter of Context: Elizabeth Wilson Revisited." *Pennsylvania Magazine of History and Biography* 131.2 (April 2007): 149–176.

Turkle, Sherry. *Alone Together: Why We Expect More from Technology and Less from Each Other*. New York: Basic Books, 2012.

Twain, Mark, and Charles Dudley Warner. *The Gilded Age*. London, 1883.

Urban, Greg. *Metaphysical Community: The Interplay of the Senses and the Intellect*. Austin: U of Texas P, 1996.

Van Engren, Abram C. *City on a Hill: A History of American Exceptionalism*. New Haven: Yale UP, 2020.

The Victim of Seduction! Boston: J. Wilkey, 1802.

Viswanathan, Gauri. *Outside the Fold: Conversion, Modernity, and Belief*. Princeton: Princeton UP, 1998.

Waldstreicher, David. *In the Midst of Perpetual Fetes: The Making of American Nationalism, 1776–1820*. Chapel Hill: U of North Carolina P, 1997.

Walkiewicz, Kathryn. *Reading Territory: Indigenous and Black Freedom, Removal, and the Nineteenth-Century State*. Chapel Hill: U of North Carolina P, 2023.

Walton, John. *John Filson of Kentucke*. Lexington: U of Kentucky P, 1956.

Ward, Jane. *The Tragedy of Heterosexuality*. New York: NYU P, 2020.

Warner, Michael. "Irving's Posterity." *ELH* 67.3 (Fall 2000): 773–799.

252 WORKS CITED

Warner, Michael. *The Letters of the Republic: Publication and the Public Sphere in Eighteenth-Century America*. Cambridge: Harvard UP, 1990.

Warner, Michael. *The Trouble with Normal: Sex, Politics, and the Ethics of Queer Life*. Cambridge: Harvard UP, 1999.

Washington, George. "From George Washington to the States, 8 June 1783." *founders.archives.org*.

Watson, John F. *Annals of Philadelphia and Pennsylvania*. Vol. 2. Philadelphia: 1844.

Watts, Steven. *The Republic Reborn: War and the Making of Liberal America, 1790–1820*. Baltimore: Johns Hopkins UP, 1987.

Webster, Noah. *A Collection of Essays and Fugitive Writings*. Boston: 1790.

Weems, Mason Locke. *Hymen's Recruiting-Serjeant*. Philadelphia: 1800.

Weems, Mason Locke. *The Life of Benjamin Franklin*. Philadelphia: 1818.

Weems, Mason Locke. Mason Locke Weems, *His Works and Ways in Three Volumes*. Ed. Emily Ellsworth Ford Skeel. New York: 1929.

Weems, Mason Locke. *The Philanthropist; or Political Peace-maker between All Honest Men or Both Parties*. Philadelphia: 1809.

Weems, Mason Locke. *The True Patriot: or, An Oration, on the Beauties and Beatitudes of a Republic; and the Abominations and Desolations of Despotism. With an Affectionate Persuasive to the American People, to FEAR GOD, and to Honor Their Rulers*. Philadelphia: 1802.

Westcott, Thompson. *Life of John Fitch: The Inventor of the Steamboat*. Philadelphia: 1857.

Weyler, Karen. *Empowering Words: Outsiders and Authorship in Early America*. Athens: U of Georgia P, 2013.

White, Ed. *The Backcountry and the City: Colonization and Conflict in Early America*. Minneapolis: U of Minnesota P, 2005.

Whitfield, Harvey Amani. *Blacks on the Border: The Black Refugees in British North America, 1815–1860*. Burlington: U of Vermont P, 2006.

Whitfield, Harvey Amani. *The Problem of Slavery in Early Vermont*. Montpelier: Vermont History Society, 2014.

Whittlesey, Charles. *Western Literary Journal and Monthly Review* 1.4 (Feb. 1845): 193–202.

Wiegman, Robyn. "Unmaking: Men and Masculinity in Feminist Theory." *Masculinity Studies & Feminist Theory: New Directions*. Ed. Judith Kegan Gardiner. New York: Columbia UP, 2002. 31–59.

Wiegman, Robyn, and Elizabeth A. Wilson. "Introduction: Antinormativity's Queer Conventions." *differences* 26.1 (2015): 1–25.

Wilde, Oscar. *The Artist as Critic: Critical Writings of Oscar Wilde*. Chicago: U of Chicago P, 1982.

Williams, Daniel E. *Pillars of Salt: An Anthology of Early American Criminal Narratives*. Madison: Madison House, 1993.

Williams, Daniel E. "Reckoned to Be Almost a Natural Fool: Textual Self-Construction in the Writings of Jonathan Plummer—No Hermaphrodite." *Early American Literature* 33.2 (1998): 149–172.

Wills, Garry. *Cincinnatus: George Washington and the Enlightenment*. New York: Doubleday & Company, 1984.

Wilson, Amos. "The Sweets of Solitude." Boston: 1822.

Wilson, Ivy. *Specters of Democracy: Blackness and the Aesthetics of Politics in the Antebellum U.S.* New York: Oxford UP, 2011.

WORKS CITED 253

Winkfield, Unca Eliza. *The Female American, or, The Adventures of Unca Eliza Winkfield*. 1767. Ed. Michelle Burnham. Peterborough: Broadview, 2001.

Winter, Kari J. "Introduction" to *The Blind African Slave, Or Memoirs of Boyrereau Brinch, Nicknamed Jeffrey Brace*. Ed. Kari J. Winter. Madison: U of Wisconsin P, 2004.

Winter, Kari J. "The Strange Career of Benjamin Franklin Prentiss, Antislavery Lawyer." *Vermont History* 79.2 (Summer/Fall 2011): 121–140.

Wood, Gordon. *Empire of Liberty: A History of the Early Republic, 1789–1815*. New York: Oxford UP, 2009.

Yao, Xine. *Disaffected: The Cultural Politics of Unfeeling in Nineteenth-Century America*. Durham: Duke UP, 2021.

Index

For the benefit of digital users, indexed terms that span two pages (e.g., 52–53) may, on occasion, appear on only one of those pages.

Figures are indicated by *f* following the page number

able-bodiedness, 173–74
Adams, Henry, 107–10
Adams, John, 193
  in Dexter's "Royel Arch," 121–23, 122*f*, 124
  memoir writing declined by, 36–37, 154–56
  Plummer's evocation of, 167–68
  wig throwing by, 107–8, 130
Adorno, Theodor, 11–12
African identity, 90. *See also* Blackness; race and racism
Ahmed, Sara, 195, 225
Akin, James, 134–36, 135*f*
Allen, Ethan, 48–49
Allen, Richard, 77n.15
allergies, 168–69
Altschuler, Sari, 173
American Antiquarian Society, 151n.4
American Bloody Register, 217
American Colonization Society, 73n.8
American exceptionalism, 4n.5, 30–33, 232, 233n.1, 236–37
Ames, Fisher, 141
Anachronism
  Brace and, 72, 85–87
  Dexter and, 22, 134–36, 137–38, 191–92
Anderson, Douglas, 234–36
anti-slavery movement
  Blind African Slave and, 94–95, 103–4
  Christianity and, 98–100
  expatriation of emancipated slaves and, 82–85
  See also slavery
antisocial thesis, 5n.8, 206, 213–14, 229–30

Appleby, Joyce, 35–36, 116n.15
Aptheker, Herbert, 51n.31
Arch, Stephen Carl, 35–36, 48, 52–53, 171n.31, 235n.5
archives
  Dexter and, 147
  founding mythos in, 17–18, 137
  messiness in, 237n.8
  Plummer and, 150–51, 159–60
aristocracy and camp aesthetics, 127, 129, 130
Articles of Confederation, 50–51, 51n.31, 131
aurality and oratory, 119–20, 124–26
Austin, Charles, 152, 153*f*, 154–56
autobiography. *See* life narratives; *specific individuals*

bachelors and bachelorhood, 15–16, 158n.11, 159–60, 170, 175, 190–91, 225–26
Badiou, Alain, 220
Bailyn, Bernard, 51–52
Barrick, Richard, 217n.23
Beauvoir, Simone de, 14n.23
belonging. *See* republican significance and belonging
Ben-Atar, Doron S., 50n.30
Bentley, William, 124–26, 164–65, 188n.50
Berlant, Lauren, 1, 10n.16, 140–41, 163n.21, 185–87, 195
Biddle, Charles, 197n.4, 215, 217–19, 221–22n.25
biography. *See* life narratives
Bishop, Abraham, 107, 110–11, 141, 142–44
Bishop, Sarah, 230–31
Blackness, 75–76, 77–78. *See also* race and racism; whiteness

256 INDEX

Blind African Slave, The (Brace), 72
   anti-slavery discourse of, 94–95, 103–4
   authenticity of, 80–81
   composition of, 73–74, 80
   as hybrid collaborative text, 80–81, 88–90
   masculinity and, 70–71
   material characteristics of, 19, 81, 82*f*, 83*f*, 89*f*, 105, 106*f*
   republican belonging in, 72–74, 85–90, 93–95
blindness, 88–90
bodies
   liberalism's orientation of, 233n.2
   masculinity and, 14–16
   memorials and, 27
   race and, 70, 74–78, 94–95
   state power's orientation of, 4n.5, 11–12, 219, 222–23
Boone, Daniel, 48–49, 55–58, 62–63
Bostock, John, 168–69
Brace, Jeffrey, 5, 70–71, 233–34
   citizenship and, 72–73, 75–76, 80–81, 82–85, 86–87, 105–6
   conversion to Christianity, 88–92, 95–98
   domestic sphere and domestic reproduction, 70–71, 75–76, 77–78, 82–85, 90–92, 98
   queerness and, 17–18, 72, 93–95, 104–6
   settlement and maple farming in Vermont, 72, 78–79, 90
   ·transportation to Americas, 71–72
   warned out of town, 19, 87–88, 98, 104–5
   See also *Blind African Slave, The* (Brace)
Branson, Susan, 107–8
Brennan, Teresa, 216–17
Brinch, Boyrereau. *See* Brace, Jeffrey
Broadsides
   "Another Looking-Glass for a Persecuted Saint: or Jonathan Plummer No Hermaphrodite," 150–51, 175–81, 177*f*
   defined, 178n.39
   Plummer's insertion of self in, 152–56, 153*f*, 157–58, 178n.39
   Plummer's patronage relationship with Dexter and, 188–90
   Wilson execution and, 217–18

Brooks, Joanna, 84n.18
Brooks, Peter, 67
Brown, Charles Brockden, 134n.29
Bruce, Dickson D., 80–81
Bufford, John Henry, 118*f*
Burgett, Bruce, 52n.34, 195–96
Burroughs, Stephen, 160–61n.15, 173, 181–82
Butler, Judith, 18–19, 186n.49

Cahill, Edward, 50–51
camp and camp reading practices, 22, 107–8, 115, 121–23, 124, 127, 146, 149–50
Caric, Ricn., 43–44
Caruth, Cathy, 216–17
Casper, Scott E., 49n.26
Castiglia, Christopher, 69, 188n.51
catarrh (nasal condition), 168–69
celebrity, 111–12, 117–19, 132–34, 143–44, 195, 196, 232–33, 234–36. *See also* cultural influence
celibacy, 175. *See also* sexuality
chattel slavery. *See* slavery
Chevalier d'Eon, Mademoiselle le, 176–81, 179*f*
Christianity
   anti-slavery discourse and, 98–103
   Brace and, 90–92, 95–98
   heathen's supplication in, 96–97
   republican belonging vs., 96–98
   See also religion and religious enthusiasm
Chudacoff, Howard P., 158n.11
citizenship, 69
   Berlant on, 141n.35
   Brace and, 72–73, 75–76, 80–81, 82–85, 86–87, 105–6
   domestic reproduction and, 75n.13, 86–87
   Plummer and, 162–63
   See also republican significance and belonging
class difference, 50n.29
   absence of, in "early republic" discourse, 52n.33
   allergies and, 168–69
   Dexter's *Pickle*, 124–27, 137–38

INDEX 257

Federalism and, 131
Jefferson on, 75n.11
See also market capitalism; wealth and
speculation
clothing and fashion, 130, 134–36
Cobb, Michael, 105–6
Cohen, Michael, 175n.36
common good
private interest presented as, 113–14, 116
self-interest vs., 170n.30
settler colonial expansion as, 55–58,
111–12
state power performing, 69
whiteness and, 70
commonplace books, 203–5
confession narratives, 219n.24
Constitution of the United States (1787):
in *Blind African Slave,* 85–87, 121–23
Dexter and, 112–13
in Dexter's "Royel Arch," 121–24
ideology of Declaration of
Independence vs., 123n.22
synecdoche in, 23
trade and transportation of goods and, 131
transportation of goods and, 129–30,
Washington and, 68–69
conversion narratives
Brace and, 88–92, 96–98
Chevalier d'Eon and, 178n.40
Edwards and, 174n.34
gender switching and, 178n.40
life narrative form and, 171n.31
Plummer and, 174–75, 181–82
self-making tropes in, 163n.20
Cooper, Davina, 5n.8
Cope, Thomas P., 25
Corey, Dorian, 25
Couch, Daniel Diez, 2n.3
Couser, G. Thomas, 48n.25
Crockett, Davy, 227, 228f
Crockett Almanacks, 227, 228f
cultural influence
American insistence on, 20–21, 147
hermits and, 195
individualism and, 2
print strategies for, 124–26
self-commodification and, 116–17, 129
self-effacement and, 70–71

through life writing, 8–9, 10–11, 156–
57, 233–36,
through markets, 132
See also celebrity; legacies, desire for;
republican significance and belonging

Dayan, Colin, 222–23
Dayton, Cornelia, 159n.13
Declaration of Independence
in *Blind African Slave,* 85–87, 121–23
consent of the governed in, 193–94
in Dexter's "Royel Arch," 121–24
in *Dred Scott* decision, 85–86n.19
ideology of Constitution vs., 123n.22
racial subjectivity of, 68–69
deists and deism, 1–2, 134n.30, 174
Deleuze, Gilles, 48–49, 68
Democratic-Republican Party, 33n.10,
77n.15, 107–8, 130
Demos, John, 97–98
Dennie, Joseph, 109n.5, 110–11, 134n.30
desire, 52n.35
Berlant on, 186–87
Brace and, 94–95, 103n.33
Brooks on narrative and, 67
Fitch's expressions of, 19, 48, 67
Plummer and, 151–52
role of 9–10
See also legacies, desire for; sexuality
deviance studies, 6, 12–13, 213–14, 231
Dexter, Nancy, 142
Dexter, Samuel L., 141–42
Dexter, Timothy, 5, 110–11, 233–34
antics of, 112–20
camp reading practices, 22, 107–8, 115,
121–23, 124, 127, 146, 149–50
commodification of self by, 116–17,
131–32, 140–41
death of, faked, 145
Fitch compared to, 121–23
Franklin compared to, 119n.18
legacy and likenesses of, 133–36, 135f,
137–38, 146–48, 176–81, 180f
market speculation and wealth, 124–29,
131, 135–36n.31, 140–42, 143–44
*A Pickle for the Knowing Ones: or Plain
Truths in a Homespun Dress,* 119–20,
120f, 121f, 124–27, 128f, 137–38, 141

258 INDEX

Dexter, Timothy (*cont.*)
  Plummer's relationship with, 136, 144, 149–52, 154–56, 175n.36, 188–91
  queerness and, 117–19, 149–50, 191
  Thoreau on, 147–48
  Trump compared to, 232
  wooden statuary of, 117–24, 118*f*, 125*f*, 126–27n.23, 137–38, 138*f*, 139*f*, 147–48
Dickens, Charles, 221–22n.25
Dillon, Elizabeth Maddock, 9–10, 11n.18, 51–52, 93–94, 215, 233n.2
disability narratives, 173–74
distraction, 159n.13
Ditz, Toby, 13n.21
Dolan, Frederick M., 22n.30
domestic sphere and domestic reproduction
  Brace and, 70–71, 75–76, 77–78, 82–85, 90–92, 98
  Filson and, 60
  Fitch and, 15–16
  hermit narratives and, 206–8, 225–26
  life narratives and, 160–61
  Plummer and, 15–16, 157–58, 185
  republican belonging and, 170
  seduction narratives and, 207–8
Doolen, Andy, 53–54
Douglass, Frederick, 93
Downes, Paul, 123n.22
drag, 107–8
  Dexter's performance of, 147–48
  Federalist emotiveness as, 108–10
  Trump's harassment of Giuliani and, 108n.4
Drag Race, 107–8
dreams, 163, 172–73, 175n.36, 182–87
Dred Scott v. Sandford (1857), 85–86n.19
Drexler, Michael J., 14n.24, 233n.2
Dublin, Susannah, 92–93, 98
Dumm, Thomas, 201–3
Durrett, Rueben T., 60, 61*f*, 63
DuVal, Kathleen, 51n.31
Dwight, Timothy, 97n.27, 156–57

Eastern State Penitentiary, 221
Eastman, Carolyn, 119–20
eccentricity, 20, 23–24, 111–13, 123–24, 136, 147, 232–33. *See also* singularity

Edelman, Lee, 206, 213–14, 225–26
Edwards, Jonathan, 161–62, 174
Elkins, Stanley, 129–30
Ellis, Joseph, 17
English cultural forms, 207n.16, 229–30
Enlightenment
  capitalist self-making and, 75–76, 115
  courteous reader figure, 175
  race and, 69–70n.4
  settler colonialism and, 58–59
  slavery and, 71–72
  solitary confinement and, 222–23
Equiano, Olaudah, 9n.14, 90–92, 96–97
Eustace, Nicole, 75n.13, 170
evangelicalism, 163n.20, 167, 226–27
Executive Order on Building the National Garden of American Heroes, 232
expatriation of emancipated slaves, 73n.8, 77–78n.16, 82–85, 85–86n.19
Ezell, Margaret J. M., 18n.29

Fabian, Ann, 17–18
failure, 11–12, 13n.20
  archival materials and, 17–18, 19–20
  Articles of Confederation as, 51n.31
  collective identity in, 103
  Dexter's aesthetic of, 146
  to feel singular, 232–34
  Fitch and, 1–2, 12–13, 15–16, 33–34, 43–44
  imagined opportunity and, 70–71
  memorials and, 26–28
  norms critiqued through, 6–7
  Plummer and, 171–72
  solitude/withdrawal from the social and, 16n.26, 213–14
Faithful Narrative of Elizabeth Wilson, A, 197–200, 199*f*, 208, 214–15, 217, 219
Fallon, Jimmy, 237–38
Farnsworth, Frederick
  The Man of the Mountain, 206–7
Federalism
  abstract resolutions to conflicts of, 51–52
  camp reading of, 129–30
  Dexter's queering of, 117–19, 124, 127, 140, 144, 145
  making of trash and waste and, 131–32

pageantry of, as drag, 108–10, 109f, 115, 144, 147–48
power fantasies of, 117–19, 129–30
wealth and, 141
feelings and affect, 2
Bishop and, 230–31
Brace and, 75–78
Dexter and, 147–48
Elizabeth Wilson and, 198–200, 214, 216–18, 219
Fitch and, 34–35, 62, 66
messiness of, 20
nationalism as, 108n.3, 131, 232
Plummer and, 170–73
public role of, 9–10
solitary confinement and, 221
Trump's National Garden of American Heroes and, 232
Wilson execution and, 216–20
See also singularity
The Female American, or, The Adventures of Unca Eliza Winkfield (1767), 194–95
femininity
fallen women and, 194, 201n.10, 208–14
hermit narratives and, 230–31
masculinity and, 13n.20
Pennsylvania legal codes and, 214
seduction narratives and, 207–8, 217–18, 220, 227–29
solitary confinement and, 221–22n.25
Field, Erastus Salisbury, 133–34
Filson, John
The Discovery, Settlement and Present State of Kentucke, 55–60, 56f, 57f, 63–64
poem on desire for death, 60
self-portrait, 60, 61f
Fischer, David Hackett, 129–30
Fitch, John, 5, 233–34
biographical sketch, 28–30, 46n.23
burial spot of, 25–26, 26f
desire and, 19, 48, 67
Dexter compared to, 121–23
disinterment and reburial, 46n.22
as failure, 1–2, 12–13, 15–16, 33–34, 43–44
manuscript books of, 30f, 31f, 39–44, 40f, 41f
masculinity and, 28–35, 43–44, 45–46, 49–50

poem on steamboat failure, 27–28, 65–66
queerness and, 3–4, 60
singularity of, 1–2, 30–33, 39n.16, 44–45, 52–53, 162–63
steamboat technology and, 28–30, 33–34, 35–36, 54
folk art, 133–34
Forten, James, 9n.14, 77n.15
Foster, Hannah Webster, 194
Foster, Thomas, 13n.21
Foucault, Michel, 77–78n.16, 147, 204n.13, 219n.24
Founding Fathers, 6–7, 11–12, 14n.24, 17, 72–73, 154–56. See also *specific individuals*
Franklin, Benjamin, 10–11
antibachelor thought of, 158n.11
autobiographical writing of, 39–42, 156n.8, 160–61, 173, 181–82
Chevalier d'Eon and, 178–81n.41
Dexter compared to, 119n.18
epitaph of, 45–46
female voices of, 203–5
French aid to Americans and, 132n.25
likenesses and legacy, 132–33, 136
as model republican and Founding Father, 6–7, 10–11, 12–13, 13n.21, 14–15, 18–20, 234–37
print culture and, 154
in "The Sweets of Solitude," 204n.11
Weems's embellishment of, 163–65
Freeman, Joanne, 108–10, 115–16
French aid to Americans, 132n.25
Freud, Sigmund, 151–52, 184n.46, 185
Furstenberg, François, 158n.12

Gardiner, Judith Kegan, 12n.19
Garrett, Matthew, 39–42
gender
Berlant on production of, 10n.16
Chevalier d'Eon and, 176–81
Federalist power and, 130
as genre, 108n.2
Plummer and, 184n.46, 185–86, 190–91
public legibility of, 176–81
public personas and, 203–5
reform literature and, 224n.29
republican logic of, 193, 195–96

260　INDEX

gender (*cont.*)
　seduction narratives and, 194, 213–14,
　　219, 227–29
　shame and, 200, 208–13
　solitary confinement and, 221–22n.25
　solitude and, 194, 213–14
　Wilson trial and, 214, 215–16
　See also femininity; masculinity;
　　queerness; sexuality
Gilmore, Ruth Wilson, 70
Giuliani, Rudy, 108n.4
Goddu, Teresa, 53n.36
Goffman, Erving, 226
Goldsmith, Oliver
　*History of the Earth and Animated
　　Nature*, 69–70n.4
Goode, Mike, 111n.7
Goodrich, Samuel Griswold, 230–31
Goram, Jery, 92–93, 98
Graham, John, 224n.28
Graham, Sylvester, 224
Graydon, Alexander, 8–9, 160–61n.15
Griswold, Roger, 108–10
Guattari, Félix, 48–49, 68
Guyette, Elise A., 96n.25

Haggerty, George E., 110
hair and wigs, 107–10, 130, 146, 178–
　81n.41, 237–38
Halberstam, Jack, 7–8n.12, 12n.19, 14–
　15, 33–34
happiness, 225
Harrod, James, 55–58
Hartman, Saidiya, 90n.22
Hartnett, Stephen John, 217n.23
Haulman, Kate, 110
Haynes, Lemuel, 90–92
heathen's supplication, 90–92, 96–97
Hemings, Sally, 134n.30, 134–36
Henry, Patrick, 51n.31
hermaphroditism, 17–18, 37n.15, 130,
　175–81, 185–86, 190–91
hermit narratives
　attachment to social formations and,
　　195–96, 206–7
　discovery trope of, 205
　femininity and, 230–31
　gendered production of shame in, 200,
　　201n.10

　seduction/solitude tropes of, 194,
　　195–96, 207–8, 213–14, 220, 225
　state power and, 196, 219–20
heteronormativity and heteropatriarchy,
　15n.25, 186n.49, 206–8, 220, 223n.27,
　225–26. *See also* domestic sphere and
　domestic reproduction; sexuality
Hewes, Lauren B., 116n.14
Holland, Sharon, 103n.33
Holley, Horace, 145
homosexuality, 150–51, 186–87, 191–92
　See also sexuality
Hoppin, Augustus, 168–69
Houdon, Jean Antoine, 132–33
Howell, William Huntting, 2n.3, 44–45
Hoxie, Frederick, 53–54
Humphreys, David, 49n.27

Imbarrato, Susan Clair, 17–18, 171n.31
Imlay, Gilbert, 58–59
incest and incest tropes, 200nn.8–9
Indigenous peoples and territories, 55–58,
　75n.12, 98–100, 103, 142–43
individualism, 2
　common good vs., 170n.30
　as cultural value, 49n.28
　Fitch's insistence on, 49–50
　Franklin and, 237–38
　liberalism and, 193–94
　marriage and, 181–82n.43
　masculinity and, 14n.23
　republican belonging vs., 11n.18, 34–35,
　　44–45, 51–53
　republican market ideology and, 53n.36
　singularity and, 21–22
　in "The Sweets of Solitude," 203–5
inheritance, 2, 12n.19, 50n.29, 150n.3
intellectual property rights and patents,
　50–51, 52–53
Irving, Washington, 165, 225–26
isolation, 95–96, 105–6, 200, 221, 222–23.
　See also republican significance and
　belonging; solitary confinement
　practices; solitude

Jackson, Mark, 169
Jackson, Zakiyyah Iman, 69–70n.4
Jacobs, Harriet, 93
James, Abel, 10–11

January 6 insurrection (2021), 232
Jefferson, Thomas, 16–17, 72–73, 107–8
 Adams's wig throwing and, 130
 anxiety of legacy and, 132–33,
  133nn.26–27, 137
 Dennie's poetry on, 134n.30
 in Dexter's "Royel Arch," 121–23,
  122f, 124
 expatriation of emancipated slaves to
  Africa, 73n.8, 77–78n.16
 likenesses and legacy, 134n.28,
  137, 154–56
 Memoirs of, 36–37, 75n.11, 156n.8
 Notes on the State of Virginia, 136
 "Philosophic Cock" engraving
  of, 134–36
 racialization of republican belonging
  and, 77–79, 97–98
 Weems and, 165
Jones, Absalom, 77n.15

Kahan, Benjamin, 176n.37
Kaplan, Amy, 4n.5, 158n.10
Kates, Gary, 178–81n.41
Kentucky
 Boone narratives and, 55–59, 62–63
 Brace on, 90–92
Kerber, Linda, 161n.16
Kett, Joseph F., 187
Klein, Martin, 80
Knapp, Samuel, 121–23, 126–27, 145–46
Knighton, Andrew Lyndon, 15–16
Know-Nothings, 26–27n.4
Kohn, Richard, 137n.32

Lacan, Jacques, 185–86
LaFleur, Greta, 23n.31, 169n.29
Lane, Christopher, 86–87
Larson, Edward J., 64n.43
legacies, desire for
 Dexter and, 124–26, 129, 132, 146–48
 individualism and, 2
 Plummer and, 157–58
 portraiture and, 133–34
 republican reproduction and, 11–12
 Trump's National Garden of American
  Heroes and, 232
Lehman, George: "Tomb of Washington," 29f
Lewis, R. W. B.: *The American Adam*, 30–33

liberalism
 coherence of, 4–5
 as critical lens, 2, 52n.34
 masculinity and, 193–94
 queer theory vs., 206n.15
 republicanism and, 11n.18, 195–96
 solitary confinement and, 222–23
Library Company of Philadelphia, 30f, 31f,
  32f, 38f, 38–39, 40f, 41f, 42–43
life narratives
 Brace and, 72
 broadsides compared to, 178n.39
 commodification of self in, 116–17,
  131–32, 140–41, 161–62, 190–91n.55
 cultural influence through, 8–9, 10–11,
  156–57, 233–36
 emergence and characteristics of, 171n.31
 Franklin and, 234–37
 messiness of, 154–56
 Plummer and, 2–4, 3f, 150–51, 154–57,
  155f, 160–61, 163n.21
 secularism vs. religion in, 163–64, 171n.31
 self-promotion and self-justification
  through, 165–67, 170–71, 181–82
literacy, 75–76
loneliness, 16n.26, 105–6. *See also* solitude
Looby, Christopher, 154, 191–92
Loughran, Trish, 13n.22
Love, Heather, 213–14, 231
Lyon, James, 108–10
Lyon, Matthew, 108–10
Lystra, Karen, 181–82n.43

Madison, James, 78–79, 85–86n.19
Manalansan, Martin F., 237n.8
Mann, Herman, 10n.17
maple sugar production, 78–79
March, Angier, 194n.1
Marcuse, Herbert, 195n.2
market capitalism, 44n.20, 75–76
 Articles of Confederation and, 131
 Brace's self-assertion through, 75–
  76, 93–94
 Dexter and, 116–17, 121–23, 132
 dreams and, 163–64
 early republic emergence of, 187
 heteronormativity and, 15n.25
 in historical texts, 116n.15
 masculinity and, 15–16

262 INDEX

market capitalism (*cont.*)
  publicly performed disinterest in, 9–10
  self-construction in, 129–32
Marquand, John P., 119n.18
marriage, 149–50, 150n.3, 158–60, 170,
    181–82, 185, 186–87. *See also* domestic
    sphere and domestic reproduction
Marx, Karl, 116–17
masculinity, 3–4, 110
  Brace's *Blind African Slave* and, 70–71, 92
  definitions, 12–15, 13n.21, 14n.23
  desire for recognition and, 14–15,
    110–11, 232–34
  Dexter and, 136
  fantasies of greatness and, 31n.8, 237
  Federal pageantry and, 108–10
  Fitch and, 28–35, 43–44, 45–46, 49–50
  Founding Fathers and, 6–7
  Franklin and, 236–37
  hermit narratives and, 196, 207–8,
    216–17, 220, 227–30
  in histories of liberalism, 193–94
  marriage and, 158
  Plummer and, 184–85, 186n.48,
    188n.51, 190–91
  queering of, 12
  racialized particularity within, 69
  resistance to slavery and, 93
  settler colonialism and, 62
  solitude and, 225–26
  textual self-assertion motivated by, 13–
    14, 16–17
  See also republican significance and
    belonging
masturbation, 181–84, 224–25
Masur, Louis P., 221
material textuality, 10–11, 19–20
  Brace's *Blind African Slave* and, 19
  Dexter's *Pickle* and, 119–20
  Filson's *Discovery, Settlement and
    Present State of Kentucke*, 56f, 57f,
    61f, 63
  Fitch's manuscripts, 30f, 31f, 32f, 38f,
    40f, 65f
  Franklin's *Autobiography* and, 234–36
  Plummer's *Sketch* and, 155f, 159f, 159–60
  "The Sweets of Solitude" and, 201–3
McCurdy, John Gilbert, 158n.11
McGill, Meredith, 203–5

McKeen, Joseph, 188
McKitrick, Eric, 129–30
McRuer, Robert, 173
Melville, Herman, 193
*Memoirs of Henry Obookiah, a Native of
    Owhyee* (1819), 97–98
memory and memorials. *See* legacies;
    monuments and memorials
Merrimack Bridge, 112–14
mess and messiness
  of affect, 20
  emergence of Federalism and, 131–32
  Franklin vs., 234–37
  logics of inclusion vs., 4–5
  memorializing, 144
  Plummer and, 154–56, 165–66, 168
  queerness and, 237n.8
  Whitman and, 13–15
microhistory, 6
Mihm, Stephen, 44n.20, 116–17
Millner, Michael, 166n.24
Mitman, Gregg, 169n.29
monarchy, 109n.5, 124, 127
monopoly, 50n.30
monuments and memorials
  Dexter and, 117–24, 118f, 125f, 126–
    27n.23, 137–38, 138f, 139f, 147–48
  dialectic of failure in, 26–28
  to feeling singular, 232
  Filson's poem as, 60
  Fitch and, 45–46
  of mess, 144
Morgan, Edmund, 132n.25
Morgensen, Scott, 75n.12
Muñoz, José Esteban, 17–18, 104–5
Museum of Old Newbury, 126–27n.23
mushroom gentlemen, 2, 191, 232
Mycall, John, 151n.4

Nancy, Jean-Luc, 23–24
nationalism
  belonging and, 108n.3
  Dexter and, 115–16, 117–19, 144
  early Federalism and, 129–30
  life narratives and, 49n.26
  See also patriotism; republican
    significance and belonging
natural disasters, slavery as cause of, 100–3
natural rights, 71–72, 123n.22

Nelson, Dana, 15–16
Newburyport, Massachusetts, 112–14
New Historicism, 111n.7
Newman, Richard S., 82–85
Newman, Simon, 52n.33
Ngai, Sianne, 233n.3
Norton, Mary Beth, 13n.21

oratory and aurality, 119–20, 124–26

Paine, Thomas, 174
Parkinson, Robert G., 70n.5
Parrish, Susan Scott, 111–12
patents and intellectual property rights, 50–51, 52–53
patriarchy. *See* heteronormativity and heteropatriarchy; masculinity
patriotism
    Bishop on, 144
    campiness and, 146
    Plummer and, 170–71
    See also nationalism
patronage relations, 149–50, 154–56, 187–91
Payne, Rodger M., 163n.20
Pease, Donald E., 4n.5
penises, 184–87
penitentiaries and prisons, 221–23
Pennsylvania Hermit, The, 208–13, 212f, 226–27
Pennsylvania legal codes, 214
Perdue, Theda, 53–54
periodization, queering of, 192n.56
personal merit, 49–50
Pickering, Timothy, 149
Pickle for the Knowing Ones: or Plain Truths in a Homespun Dress (Dexter), 119–20, 120f, 121f, 124–27, 128f, 137–38, 141
Plummer, Jonathan, 5, 149, 233–34
    allergies and illness, 168–74
    "Another Looking-Glass for a Persecuted Saint: or Jonathan Plummer No Hermaphrodite," 150–51, 175–81, 177f
    bachelorhood and sexuality of, 159–60, 170, 175, 190–91
    commodification of self by, 161–62
    conversion narratives and, 174–75, 181–82

death of brothers, 151n.4
deference and submissions, excesses of, 12–13, 168
Dexter's relationship with, 136, 144, 149–52, 154–56, 175n.36, 188–91
dreams of significance, 163
patronage relationships and, 187–91
public reception of, 164–65, 167–68, 188
queer peddling and, 156
Revolutionary War service and desertion, 170–71, 175–76
Sketch of the History of the Life and Adventures of Jonathan Plummer, 3f, 155f, 159f, 159–60, 183f
straightening the early republic, 187
textual insertions of queer self, 151
will of, 159n.13
Pocock, J. G. A., 51–52
Pope, Alexander, 21
portraiture, 133–34, 134n.28, 137
Prager, Frank D., 35–36, 42n.17
Pratt, Lloyd, 215n.20, 226
Prentiss, Franklin, 80–81, 87–90, 103–4
Price, Richard, 50n.29
print culture
    conversion narratives and, 175n.36
    Dexter's aurality and, 124–26
    early African American authorship in, 84n.18
    Plummer's insertion of self in, 154
    private/public dichotomy in, 8–9, 166n.24
privacy and private sphere, 8–9
    Brace and, 95–96
    desire for recognition and, 9–10, 16–17
    Dexter and, 140–42
    Fitch and, 34–35
    gender legibility of, 176–81
    hermit narratives and, 195–96, 201–5, 213–14, 225, 227–29
    masculine transgression of, 12–13
    Plummer and, 152–56, 157–58, 166n.24, 182–84
    republicanism's dismantling of, 9–10, 114
    republican vs. liberal, 11n.18
    seduction narratives and, 207–14, 215
    See also public sphere

264 INDEX

property rights
  Brace and, 92–93, 94–95
  Fitch and, 50–51, 52–53
Protestant evangelicalism, 163n.20,
  167, 226–27
psychoanalysis, 111–12, 151–52, 195n.2
public infrastructure, 113–14, 116
public interest, 49–50
public sphere, 52n.35, 166n.24
  African Americans incorporated in,
    77–78
  Black citizens in, 90–92
  Brace and, 98
  Christian imagining of, 98–100
  domestic life in, 157–58
  gender legibility in, 176–81, 208–13
  hermits and, 195
  life narratives and, 8–9
  masculinity and, 9–10, 12–17, 110
  private desires in, 12–13
  republican performance in, 9–10, 73–74
  republican production of, 9–10, 49–50,
    111–12, 204n.12
  seduction/solitude tropes and, 213–14
  See also privacy and private sphere
Putnam, Israel, 48–49, 49n.27

queerness, 5, 6
  ablebodiedness and, 173
  antisocial thesis and, 5n.8, 206, 213–
    14, 229–30
  Brace and, 17–18, 72, 93–95, 104–6
  Dexter and, 117–19, 149–50, 191
  Fitch and, 3–4, 60
  gender performativity thesis and,
    186n.49
  happiness and, 229–31
  hermits and withdrawal from the social,
    60, 196, 206, 213–14, 225–31
  messiness and, 237n.8
  Plummer and, 3–4, 150–51, 154, 185,
    186n.49, 190, 191–92
  reading past through, 191–92
  republican significance and, 17–24
  Wilson and, 17–18

race and racism
  bodies and, 70, 74–78, 94–95
  Christian belonging and, 96–98

  definitions, 68, 70, 70n.7
  republican belonging and, 72–73, 73n.8,
    77–78, 94–95, 98–103, 105–6
  state power and, 69–71
  See also Blackness; whiteness
Ramage, James A., 58–59
Raspe, Rudolf Erich
  The Surprising Adventures of Baron
    Munchausen, 237–38
reform literature, 208–13, 221, 224n.29
Reis, Elizabeth, 176–81
religion and religious enthusiasm
  Brace and, 90–92
  life narratives and, 163n.20
  Plummer and, 161–62, 163–64, 167–68,
    170–71, 173, 174–75, 190–91
republicanism
  as critical lens, 52n.34
  cultural canon of, 204n.12, 204n.13
  gendered logic of, 193, 195–96
  liberalism and, 11n.18, 195–96
  production of publicness in, 9–10, 49–
    50, 111–12, 204n.12
  racialized futurity of, 74–75
  state power and, 10n.17
republican significance and belonging, 10–11
  Blind African Slave's articulation of,
    72–74, 85–90, 93–95
  Brace's claims to, 76–78, 104–5
  capitalism and, 44n.20
  coherence of, 4–5, 10n.17
  Elizabeth Wilson and, 215–16
  failure and, 11–13, 17–18
  Franklin and, 10–11
  life writing and, 38–39, 156–57
  loneliness and, 105–6
  marriage and, 149–50, 150n.3, 159–60, 170
  masculinity vs., 34n.13
  Plummer and, 156–57, 165–66, 170–71
  queerness and, 17–24
  selflessness and, 8–9, 20–21, 51–53, 55–
    58, 232–34,
  singularity and self-assertion vs., 2, 5, 6,
    10–11, 44–45
  Weems's narration of, 165–66
  whiteness and racial limits of, 72–73,
    73n.8, 77–78, 98–103
  Wilson and, 204n.12
  See also masculinity

INDEX 265

reputation and prestige. *See* cultural influence
Revolutionary War, 70–71, 72
 Black belonging and, 90–92
 Plummer's service in, 170
Richards, George, 98–104, 101*f*
Richardson, Samuel
 Pamela, 193, 207–8
Richmond, Virginia theater fire (1811), 98–103
Rifkin, Mark, 75n.12
Rigal, Laura, 35–36, 110–11n.6, 131
Roach, Joseph, 119n.17
Román, David, 137
Rosenblatt, Helena, 193–94
Rowe, G. S., 214n.18
Rowson, Susanna
 Charlotte Temple, 194
RuPaul's *Drag Race*, 107–8
Rush, Benjamin, 8–9, 77–78, 160–61, 222–24
Rush, John, 223
Russell, Ezekiel, 217

Sachs, Honor, 55n.38
Saillant, John, 75–76, 90–92
St. John de Crevecoeur, Hector, 79n.17, 132–33
Sampson, Deborah, 10n.17
Sandage, Scott, 17–18, 43–44
Schorb, Jodi, 221
Schudson, Michael, 234n.4
Schuller, Kyla, 169
Sedgwick, Eve Kosofsky, 21–22, 225
seduction narratives
 domestic reproduction and, 207–8
 Elizabeth Wilson's confession and, 214–15, 217n.23, 219–20
 hermit narratives and, 194, 195–96, 201n.10, 206–14, 220, 225
 sexualization of solitude and, 225
 state power and, 196, 219–20
self-improvement narratives, 10–11, 188, 236–38
selflessness
 Fitch and, 49–50
 Franklin as model of, 154
 hermits and, 195
 in life narratives, 8–9, 160–61
 Plummer's excessiveness in, 168

as public performance, 20–21
race and capacity for, 70n.6
republican belonging and, 8–9, 20–21, 51–53, 55–58, 232–34,
self-justification vs., 170–71
Washington as model of, 9–10, 16–17, 68–69, 132–33
Selfridge, Thomas, 152, 153*f*
sentimentalization. *See* feelings and affect
separate sphere ideology, 158n.10. *See also* domestic sphere and domestic reproduction; public sphere
settler colonialism
 Brace and, 97–98, 100n.32
 domestic reproduction and, 75n.12
 expatriation of emancipated slaves and, 73n.8
 Filson's *Discovery, Settlement and Present State of Kentucke* and, 58–59
 Fitch's steamboat and, 53–54, 64
 republican self-effacement and, 62
sexuality
 as fiction, 191–92
 Franklin and, 181–82
 Plummer and, 175, 190–92,
 republican logics of, 195–96
 solitude and, 195–96, 220, 224–25
 See also femininity; gender; homosexuality; masculinity; seduction narratives
Shain, Barry Alan, 49–50
Sidbury, James, 90
singularity, 233–34
 Brace and, 93–94
 definitions, 21–22
 eccentricity emergent from, 20, 21
 Fitch and, 1–2, 30–33, 39n.16, 44–45, 52–53, 162–63
 Plummer and, 3–4, 150–51, 154–57, 162–63, 164–65
 racial difference and, 9n.14, 70n.6
 Sarah Bishop and, 231
 scholarly focus on, 111–12
 synecdochal telescoping of, 23–24
 Wilson and, 201, 204n.13, 227–29
Sketch of the History of the Life and Adventures of Jonathan Plummer (Plummer), 3*f*, 155*f*, 159*f*, 159–60, 183*f*

266 INDEX

Slauter, Eric, 201–3, 223–24
slavery
  Black belonging and, 77–78
  Christian conversion narratives and,
    90–92, 97–98
  gendered resistance to, 93
  legal end to transatlantic trade in, 82–85
  as national sin, 8–9, 76–77, 98–103
  as republican corruption, 8–9
  sugar trade and production, 72, 92–93
  Washington and, 68–69
  See also anti-slavery movement
Slotkin, Richard, 55–58, 64
Smith, Billy, 52n.33
Smith, Caleb, 98–100, 222n.26
Smith, Henry Nash, 64
Smith, Joseph, 161n.16
Sobel, Mechal, 163n.21, 190–91n.55
social deviance studies, 213–14, 231
socioeconomic status. *See* class difference
solitary confinement practices, 221–23
solitude
  as gendered punishment, 194, 195–96
  hermit narratives and, 194, 195–96,
    207–8, 213–14, 220, 225
  institutionalization of, 221
  Lewis on masculine figure of, 30–33
  queer happiness in, 229–30
  as queer interrogation of public/private
    spheres, 213–14
  Thoreau of, 205–6
  Wilson and, 195, 208–13
  See also hermit narratives
Sontag, Susan, 22, 127
speculation culture, 130n.24
state power, 69
  anti-slavery movement and, 82–85
  execution of Elizabeth Wilson and,
    197–98, 219
  Federalist fantasies of, 117–19, 129–30
  gendered logic of, 193–94
  queerness and, 17–18
  racism and, 77–78n.16
  republican significance and, 10–11
  Rush on family structure of, 223
  seduction/hermit narratives and,
    196, 219–20
  self-promotion and, 132

transnational turn and, 4n.5
  Washington's performance of weakness
    and, 136–37
states rights, 50–51, 50n.30
steamboat technology, 28–30, 33–34,
  35–36, 54, 64, 67
Steedman, Caroline, 147
Stein, Jordan Alexander, 150, 192n.56
Sterne, Laurence, 47n.24, 161–62
sugar trade, 72, 78–79,
Sullivan, John, 217n.23
Swart, Koenraad W., 49–50, 49n.28
"The Sweets of Solitude, or Directions
  to Mankind How They May Be
  Happy in a 'Miserable World!'"
  201–5, 202f, 206. *See also* Wilson,
  William "Amos"

Takaki, Ronald, 53–54
Tamarkin, Elisa, 108n.3
Taney, Roger, 85–86n.19
Taylor, Alan, 79
Tennenhouse, Leonard, 207–8
Terada, Rei, 17–18, 60, 213–14
Thoreau, Henry David, 147–48, 205–6
Thornton, William, 27
Todd, Levi, 55–58
Tomc, Sandra, 109n.5
Tomlins, Christopher L., 170n.30
transnational turn, 4–5
transportation of goods, 9–10, 129–30
trash and waste. *See* mess and messiness
Traub, Valerie, 19–20
trauma and traumatic events, temporality
  of, 216–17, 217n.22
Trump, Donald, 108n.4, 232, 237–38
Tufts, Meredith Peterson, 198n.7
Turkle, Sherry, 16–17
Twain, Mark, 27n.5

United States Constitution. *See*
  Constitution of the United States
United States empire, 34–35, 53. *See also*
  settler colonialism
Urban, Greg, 8n.13

Van Engen, Abram C., 233n.1
Velour, Sasha, 107–8

INDEX 267

Vermont
    anti-slavery activism in, 73–
        74n.9, 82–85
    Black settlers in, 80, 96n.25
    Brace's settlement in, 70–71, 72, 73–74, 90
    maple sugar production and, 78–79
Vermont Colonization Society, 82–85
"Victim of Seduction, The" (Wilkey),
        207–13, 209f, 211f, 215–16, 219
Virginia theater fire (1811), 98–103
virtue, 53–54, 69
    in production of legacy, 132–33
    republican performance of, 73–74
Viswanathan, Gauri, 97–98

Waldsreicher, David, 130, 131
Walkiewicz, Kathryn, 58n.39
Ward, Jane, 150n.3
Warner, Charles Dudley, 27n.5
Warner, Michael, 44–45, 93–94, 150n.3,
        154, 166n.24, 226
Washington, George, 68–69
    in Dexter's "Royel Arch," 121–23,
        122f, 124
    as Founding Father, 6–7
    likenesses and legacy, 132–33, 133n.26,
        134n.28, 136–37, 146
    memoir writing declined by, 36–
        37, 154–56
    as model of selflessness, 9–10, 16–17,
        68–69, 132–33
    monuments and memorials of, 26–28
    steamboat technology and, 64
Washington Monument, 26–27
Watkins, Andrea S., 58–59
Watts, Steven, 187
wealth and speculation
    Bishop on, 142–44
    citizenship and, 140–41
    Dexter and, 124–29, 131, 135–36n.31,
        140–42, 143–44
    Fitch's steamboat failure and, 33–34
    masculinity and, 15–16
    settler colonial expansion in Kentucky
        and, 55–58
    Thoreau on, 147–48
    Weems on, 158
    See also market capitalism

Weber, Max, 98–100
Webster, Noah, 48–49
Weems, Mason Locke, 156–57, 158
    The Life of Benjamin Franklin, 163–65
    on marriage, 181–82n.43
    The True Patriot: or, An Oration, on the
        Beauties and Beatitudes of a Republic,
        74–75
Weyler, Karen, 17–18, 178n.39
Wheatley, Phillis, 9n.14, 90–92, 96–97
White, Alexander, 217n.23
White, Ed, 14n.24, 54n.37, 233n.2
white male masculinity. See masculinity
whiteness
    citizenship and, 72–73
    common good constructed in, 70
    domestic reproduction and, 75n.12
    republican belonging and, 72–73, 73n.8,
        77–78, 98–103
    See also Blackness; race and racism
Whitman, Walt, 13–14
Wiegman, Robyn, 13n.20
wigs and hair, 107–10, 130, 146, 178–
        81n.41, 237–38
Wilde, Oscar, 1, 191
Wilkey, John, 207–8, 215–16
Williams, Daniel E., 156–57, 215
Wilson, Elizabeth, 196
    brother's story obscuring, 213–14, 216–
        17, 220, 227–30,
    execution of, 196–97, 208–13, 215–
        16, 218
    A Faithful Narrative of Elizabeth Wilson,
        197–200, 199f, 208, 214–15, 217, 219
    name change in narratives of, 200n.8
    in "The Sweets of Solitude," 203–
        5, 219–20
    in "The Victim of Seduction," 207–13,
        209f, 211f, 215–16, 219
Wilson, Ivy, 86–87
Wilson, James, 221
Wilson, William "Amos," 5, 195–
        96, 233–34
    execution of sister, 196–97, 198–200,
        213–14, 216–17, 220
    name change in narratives of, 200n.8
    in The Pennsylvania Hermit, 208–13,
        212f, 226–27

268 INDEX

Wilson, William "Amos" (*cont.*)
  sister's position taken up by, 206,
    208–13, 233–34
  sister's story obscured by, 213–14,
    216–17, 220, 227–30
  in "The Sweets of Solitude," 203–5,
    219–20, 226–29
  Thoreau compared to, 205–6

  withdrawal to solitude, 200–3, 213–14,
    220, 225–31
Winter, Kari J., 80–81
Wolverton, Nan, 116n.14
Wood, Gordon, 20–21, 51–52, 52n.33

Yazoo Act (1795) and Yazoo land scandal,
  130n.24, 142